BORDERLANDS SAINTS

LATINIDAD

Transnational Cultures in the United States

This series publishes books that deepen and expand our knowledge and understanding of the various Latina/o populations in the United States in the context of their transnational relationships with cultures of the broader Americas. The focus is on the history and analysis of Latino cultural systems and practices in national and transnational spheres of influence from the nineteenth century to the present. The series is open to scholarship in political science, economics, anthropology, linguistics, history, cinema and television, literary and cultural studies, and popular culture and encourages interdisciplinary approaches, methods, and theories. The series grew out of discussions with faculty at the School of Transborder Studies at Arizona State University, where an interdisciplinary emphasis is being placed on transborder and transnational dynamics.

Matthew Garcia, Series Editor, School of Historical, Philosophical, and

Religious Studies; and Director of Comparative Border Studies

Rodolfo F. Acuña, *In the Trenches of Academe: The Making of Chicana/o Studies*

Adriana Cruz-Manjarrez, *Zapotecs on the Move: Cultural, Social, and Political Processes in Transnational Perspective*

Marivel T. Danielson, *Homecoming Queers: Desire and Difference in Chicana Latina Cultural Production*

Rudy P. Guevarra Jr., *Becoming Mexipino: Multiethnic Identities and Communities in San Diego*

Lisa Jarvinen, *The Rise of Spanish-Language Filmmaking: Out from Hollywood's Shadow, 1929–1939*

Regina M. Marchi, *Day of the Dead in the USA: The Migration and Transformation of a Cultural Phenomenon*

Desirée A. Martín, *Borderlands Saints: Secular Sanctity in Chicano/a and Mexican Culture*

Marci R. McMahon, *Domestic Negotiations: Gender, Nation, and Self-Fashioning in US Mexicana and Chicana Literature and Art*

A. Gabriel Melendez, *Hidden Chicano Cinema: Film Dramas in the Borderlands*

Priscilla Peña Ovalle, *Dance and the Hollywood Latina: Race, Sex, and Stardom*

Luis F. B. Plascencia, *Disenchanting Citizenship: Mexican Migrants and the Boundaries of Belonging*

Maya Socolovsky, *Troubling Nationhood in US Latina Literature: Explorations of Place and Belonging*

BORDERLANDS SAINTS

Secular Sanctity in Chicano/a and Mexican Culture

DESIRÉE A. MARTÍN

RUTGERS UNIVERSITY PRESS

New Brunswick, New Jersey and London

Library of Congress Cataloging-in-Publication Data
Martín, Desirée A., 1972–
Borderlands saints : secular sanctity in Chicano/a and Mexican culture / Desirée A.
Martín, Rutgers University Press.
pages cm. — (Latinidad: Transnational Cultures in the United States)
Includes bibliographical references and index.
ISBN 978–0–8135–6234–6 (hardcover : alk. paper) — ISBN 978–0–8135–6233–9
(pbk. : alk. paper) — ISBN 978–0–8135–6235–3 (e-book)
1. American literature—Mexican American authors—History and criticism. 2.
Mexican American literature (Spanish)—History and criticism. 3. Mexican-American
Border Region—Civilization. 4. Mexican literature—History and criticism. 5.
Secularism in literature. 6. Holy, The, in literature. 7. Heroes in literature. I. Title.
PQ7070.5.M37 2013
810.9'868—dc23   2013000429

A British Cataloging-in-Publication record for this book is available from the British
Library.

Visit our website: http://rutgerspress.rutgers.edu

Manufactured in the United States of America

Para Santiago y Mateo: mi luz, mi esperanza

CONTENTS

ACKNOWLEDGMENTS

This book has been many years in the making. Over that time I have incurred many debts to family, friends, teachers, mentors, students, and colleagues. These relationships are formative, and I am humbled by the generosity that so many people have shown me. Before I acknowledge these debts, however, I want to express gratitude for the privilege of research and writing itself. While the process of writing this book has often been frustrating, it has also, quite unexpectedly, been a companion and a refuge for me through some very hard times. Looking back, I can say that writing this book has reinvigorated me for the work ahead even as it has taught me to embrace my time with loved ones, especially my children, all the more.

I thank Walter Mignolo, Carolyn Porter, and Antonio Viego for guiding me through different stages of my academic journey. Special thanks go to Alberto Moreiras, Gabriela Nouzeilles, and Janice Radway, who saw the earliest incarnations of this project at Duke University and inspired me to embrace the borderlands condition in every sense. At UC Davis, I have been fortunate to work alongside brilliant and indomitable colleagues. I am especially grateful for the intellectual, professional, and moral support provided me by Emilio Bejel, Nathan Brown, Miroslava Chávez-García, Seeta Chaganti, Chen-Nee Chuah, Frances Dolan, Margaret Ferguson, Kathleen Frederickson, Elizabeth Freeman, Bishnupriya Ghosh, Danielle Heard, Hsuan Hsu, Mark Jerng, Michael Lazzara, David Lloyd, Christopher Loar, Colin Milburn, Elizabeth Miller, Ana Peluffo, Riché Richardson, Matthew Stratton, Julie Sze, Cecilia Tsu, Louis Warren, Claire Waters, and Michael Ziser. I must single out Scott Simmon for his support and friendship; he has been the best chair I could have hoped for during my tenure year. Lastly, I have learned much from the students I have taught and mentored at UC Davis, especially Sharada Balachandran-Orihuela, Emily Davidson, Isabel Porras, and Kaitlin Walker. I look forward to seeing their careers develop.

I am deeply grateful to Leslie Mitchner and everyone at Rutgers University Press for their expert stewardship of my project, and to Pippa Letsky for her excellent editorial work. Special thanks go to the anonymous readers of my manuscript and tenure file for their incisive and helpful comments. Many other friends throughout the academy have been important interlocutors and have provided much needed support. Thanks to Aimee Bahng, Rafael Díaz, Ricardo Domínguez, Kirsten Silva Gruesz, Laura G. Gutiérrez, Simon Hay, Javier Krauel,

Jorge Marturano, Claudia Milian, Gabriela Nuñez, Catherine Ramírez, José David Saldívar, Alanna Thain, Christian Thorne, Virginia Tuma, and Maarten Van Delden for their inspirational friendship. Most of all, I thank *mis hermanas del alma* Amy Sara Carroll and Tabea Linhard, who have always been ready to listen and share their love with me through good times and bad. Finally, I am so blessed to be friends with Robert McKee Irwin (*gracias por todo, querido*) and Valeria La Saponara (*grazie, bellissima*).

My family and oldest friends deserve special mention. Thank you to the Dobbins family: Maureen, Terry, and especially Greg, for the love and support they showed me over the years. Steve Otroshkin, thank you for always making me laugh when I need it most. To Jean Rebholz, *hermana de otra madre*, I hope that you know what you mean to me. Thank you for always being there. Nothing would have been possible without *mi familia*. I owe everything to the Coke family, especially Chris, Bill, Mike, and Apple; to *toda la familia* Clamont; to my brother, Eddie, my sister-in-law, Sylvia, my niece, Amelia, and my nephew, Elías; and most of all, to my late parents Frederick and María Elena Martín. *Siempre están en mi corazón.* My greatest blessing is my children, Santiago and Mateo. So much of this book was written while holding one of them inside or out there, in the world. *Les dedico este libro por toda la luz y esperanza que me traen.*

BORDERLANDS SAINTS

INTRODUCTION
The Secular Sanctity of Borderlands Saints

To SEEK FAVOR FROM *La Santísima Muerte* (Saint Death), folk saint and guardian of the dispossessed, devotees prepare candles and recite a novena, which may be repeated up to three times until the petition is answered. The novena consists of a prayer or invocation called a *soneto* (sonnet) followed by a short, fervent prayer or refrain called a *jaculatoria*, both of which are to be repeated daily for nine days. In addition, each of the nine days features a differ-ent prayer to recite after the sonnet. The refrain of the best-known novena to Santa Muerte reads: "Beloved Death of my heart, do not abandon me, protect me, and do not allow [name] a single moment of peace, bother him constantly, torment him, worry him, worry him, so that he will think of me always. Amen" (Gil Olmos 183).[1] This novena requests luck, happiness, and money as well as freedom from evil spells, danger, and sickness, but its primary desire is for the return of a lost or wayward lover (Gil Olmos 186).

The intimacy of the novena is remarkable. Given Santa Muerte's role as a "specialist in affairs of the heart," personal appeals to the saint to restore or initi-ate love affairs are expected (Chesnut 121). However, the novena is more than a simple request or a promise to worship the saint from a passive devotee. Instead, the novena appeals not just for the lover's return, but for total domination over him, imploring: "I want him to fall before me prostrate, surrendered at my feet, to fulfill all of his promises," and "I want you to make him beg me to forgive him, as docile as a lamb, faithful to his promises, that he may be loving and submissive for the rest of his life" (Gil Olmos 184, 186). In a sense, the female supplicant asks Santa Muerte to transfer some of her formidable power onto her. The enduring control over the lover requested by the devotee ("that he may be loving and sub-missive for the rest of his life") reflects the power she exercises as a result of her relationship of devotion and exchange with Santa Muerte.

The novena reflects a circuit of intimacy between the saint, the devotee, and the lover. Through the power of the novena, Santa Muerte touches both the devotee and the lover, transforming their relationship by literally entering their lives to bother, torment, or worry them (in the case of the lover), or protect them (in the case of the devotee). The novena also portrays a mutually constructed relationship between the devotee and the saint. The supplicant pledges an intimate relationship of devotion with the saint that resembles the one she seeks with her lover. The devotee addresses Santa Muerte like a lover ("Beloved Death of my heart") and, like a bride or groom, pledges utter, lifelong devotion to the saint in exchange for favors received. In this relationship, the devotee is not totally powerless and subservient, nor is the saint infallibly powerful. Undoubtedly, the devotee aims to assume a measure of the saint's authority over the erstwhile lover.

More importantly, however, the supplicant retains the power of negotiation with the saint. She pledges total allegiance to Santa Muerte, but such loyalty is possible only if the saint fulfills the request: "make me believe in only you by granting me this miracle" (Gil Olmos 185). Through this relationship of exchange, the devotee enters into the "consciousness" of Santa Muerte as much as the saint enters into that of the devotee. Many believers threaten their preferred saints with withholding their belief and favors, and it is common for devotees to shift allegiances between different saints. For example, in Sandra Cisneros's story "Little Miracles, Kept Promises," Ms. Barbara Ybañez of San Antonio, Texas, warns San Antonio de Padua that she will "turn your statue upside down until you send [a man who isn't a pain in the *nalgas* (ass)]" (*Woman Hollering Creek* 117–118). Although some saints, like Santa Muerte, have a reputation for being more loyal than others, this constancy frequently comes at a price. Devotees accept that if they neglect the death saint or dare to stray from her fold, they will face sacred retribution.

While the advantage in the relationship between devotee and saint may shift over time, popular devotional practices in the borderlands fundamentally emphasize the personal, intimate relationship between them. Popular rituals like spirit possession, the exchange of relics or sacred images, faith healing, and the recitation of prayers all shape relationships of exchange and identification. Since they do not require the presence of the clergy, popular rituals reorder and transcend ecclesiastical authority. The supplicants who recite novenas to Santa Muerte also appeal to Jesus Christ and recite the Lord's Prayer as part of their petition, reflecting their willingness to blend popular and orthodox spirituality. The ecclesiastical status of these sacred figures—whether they are canonized saints, folk saints, manifestations of Christ or the Virgin Mary, mystics, or faith healers, or not even routinely considered saints at all—has little impact on the masses' desire to worship on their own terms. Meanwhile, devotees incorporate a wide variety of cultural and spiritual traditions in their rituals, drawing upon various Catholic, Protestant, Evangelical, indigenous, and African beliefs.[2] Indeed, the defining characteristic of spirituality in the borderlands is its flexibility. Popular religious belief and practices may still "[serve] power as an ideological mechanism of social control, exploitation, and domination," yet there is tremendous appeal in creating one's own narratives of faith, especially for marginalized peoples who may have no other recourse to challenge the authority of church and state (León, *La Llorona's* 5).

The ritual relationships of exchange and identification between saint and devotee highlight the intersection between human and divine. This intersection, which might seem to be a contradiction in terms, in fact embodies secular sanctity. Though there is no strict definition of secular sanctity, a "secular saint" may refer to someone who is venerated for their extraordinary actions or their contribution to a noble cause, but who is not recognized as a canonical saint by a religion. In her discussion of Che Guevara as secular saint, Phyllis Passariello indicates that the Argentine revolutionary's "life story and its propagation have helped to make him not only a hero, but also a secular saint, a sacred figure, someone to be revered, emulated and even beseeched" (77). It is obvious that secular saints like Guevara are not orthodox figures, but they are not regularly considered popular saints in relation to traditional religious or spiritual practice either. Nevertheless, they are apprehended in ways similar to saints, for their images or words are frequently circulated or interpreted in a way that approximates the divine or even becomes it. Yet it is precisely because they are not traditional saints that secular saints so clearly reveal the contradiction between the human and the divine. Secular saints are defined by their human qualities—whether heroic or fallible—instead of by their canonization into a pantheon of divinities or even by popular religious belief. It is because they are accessible as fallible humans that secular saints are revered as divine mediators or as sacred figures in their own right. Although the union between secular and sacred is common to all saints, secular saints particularly foreground the simultaneity as well as the contradiction of human and divine.

It is most common for devotees to turn to saints out of the desire to manage personal issues and crises. Different saints have distinct prayers and rituals dedicated to the pursuit of health, love, employment, and countless other needs. Yet devotees' interactions with saints go beyond their individual or local desires to incorporate broader conceptions of space, temporality, memory, and identity. Spiritual beliefs and practices in the borderlands transcend both personal and ecclesiastical rituals to disrupt and destabilize the conventions of national borders and citizenship, regional space, and temporalities both secular and sacred. The saints are border crossers themselves, accompanying people from all walks of life on their travels—and especially migrants, who draw upon secular sanctity for help in deciphering their place as subjects who exceed traditional conceptions of citizenship. Yet the saints are not merely symbols of migration. Their devotees also construct national identities around them, and they also serve as markers of regional or local space. In this study I argue that secular saints such as Teresa Urrea (Santa Teresa de Cabora), Pancho Villa, César Chávez, Subcomandante Insurgente Marcos, and Santa Muerte produce and embody new forms of national, regional, and transnational identity for their devotees on both sides of the border. All of these secular saints are marginal figures in some way. While they all play an important role at the periphery of the nation-state, namely, the U.S. southern border and Mexico's northern and southern borders, they also inhabit the margins in relation to their spiritual, political, social, cultural, and gender identities. As figures that assume a sacred aura, in part because of their secular roles as political, revolutionary, or cultural icons, these saints perform and embody the contradiction of human and divine reflected in secular sanctity. Some of these secular saints remain in the margins, others insert themselves into or are appropriated by the center, and some shift back and forth between center and periphery. All of them bring the margins to the forefront, particularly during historical and political moments of crisis that shape and challenge state formation and national identity. During periods of upheaval like indigenous rebellions, the Mexican Revolution, the Chicano Rights Movement, contemporary struggles for indigenous rights, and the drug wars, saints and their followers demonstrate a certain fluidity between nation, region, and border across the U.S.-Mexico borderlands.

One recent example of the intersection between secular sanctity and national, regional, and transnational space is the erection—and subsequent destruction—of dozens of shrines dedicated to Santa Muerte along a triangle of freeways between the cities of Monterrey, Reynosa, and Nuevo Laredo (Osorno n.p.). This northern Mexican border region is one of the centers of the drug wars that have shaken the foundations of state and civil society in Mexico and are rapidly encroaching upon the U.S. side of the border. The border town of Nuevo Laredo is one of the most dangerous cities in Mexico, while the entire area that includes Monterrey and Nuevo Laredo is the locus of a violent dispute between the Gulf and Sinaloa cartels for control of drug-smuggling routes into the United States ("Santa Muerte" n.p.). The public altars to La Santísima Muerte along the freeways began to spring up in 2007. While no group has been officially linked to the shrines, many of the sites have been the scenes of shootouts and executions, and it is generally understood that the warring drug cartels are behind the finance and construction of the altars ("Santa Muerte" n.p.).

The association of Santa Muerte and her followers with the drug trade and organized crime is only one of her many attributes, but this is the main aspect highlighted in media reports (Chesnut 96). The shrines also serve as meeting places for everyday travelers, migrants, and border residents who want to worship privately or to commune with other devotees. Visitors to these shrines leave offerings of candles, fruit, flowers, liquor, and cigars and give thanks or request favors from the death saint through messages, prayer cards, and images. The presence of these shrines on the freeways in such close proximity to the U.S.-Mexico border—one of the statues of Santa Muerte was located at the base of an international bridge linking Mexico and the United States—illuminates the nomadic, transient, or liminal nature of many of Santa Muerte's devotees (Hernández, "La Plaza blog: 'Santa Muerte'"). The freeway shrines themselves also remap border space, emphasizing that the borderlands are at once a crossing point, a destination, and a home that all constitute regional, national, and transnational space.

In keeping with the liminality of the freeway shrines, Santa Muerte and her devotees challenge the limits of the sacred and the secular by demonstrating the intersection of holiness and evil. While Santa Muerte's association with the drug wars evokes the betrayal of public safety, the collapse of civil society, and the threat of a failed state in Mexico, the cult of the death saint also reflects new forms of public works and autonomous communal activism. At these freeway shrines, a cult that has been roundly maligned and largely hidden for almost a century and a half is transformed and now acts, for travelers, migrants, and border residents, as a public site of solidarity and action against the hazards of everyday life (Chesnut 121). Regardless of whether these hazards are due to the border crossing, the frequently random violence of the drug wars, labor troubles, or affairs of the heart, the open-air shrines welcome everyone equally and without judgment.

Perhaps as a result of the contradictory connotations of the death cult, those who frequent, live near, or pass by these shrines provide conflicting accounts of their relationship with Santa Muerte. Some devotees imply that their faith represents a pragmatic but potentially risky contract with the death saint, as they cite her miraculous powers and her willingness to grant difficult or even deadly favors. Others emphasize the ordinariness of their devotion, insisting that they worship Santa Muerte alongside orthodox figures like the Virgin of Guadalupe and San Judas Tadeo. Still others describe the shrines as foreboding sites where devils, presumably both mystical devils and the real-life devils of the drug trade, converge (Osorno n.p.). Throughout, the freeway shrines acknowledge and honor the mobility, flexibility, and transience of Santa Muerte's devotees regardless of their social or legal status. In this manner, the shrines exemplify the contradiction and ambivalence of secular sanctity.

Because the freeway shrines to Santa Muerte inexorably merge holy and evil, thereby disrupting church authority and national limits, it is no coincidence that over thirty of the shrines in Nuevo Laredo were destroyed in March 2009 by the Mexican military (Beaubien n.p.).[3] Military officials have provided different reasons for the destruction of the shrines, relying upon both bureaucracy and fearmongering as they cite the lack of proper permits to build on federal land and identify the altars as "narcoshrines" that must be demolished as part of the Mexican government's war on the drug cartels (Ramos Minor n.p.). The proximity of the shrines to the international border—indicating the spillover into the United States not only of drug violence but also of Santa Muerte's often marginalized and implicitly illegal devotees—was probably too much for skittish officials to bear. Adding to the complexity of the situation, the cult to Santa Muerte among the police, soldiers, and prison guards that stand "on the front lines of the Mexican government's war against the cartels . . . seems as widespread as it is among the traffickers they are fighting" (Chesnut 107). In other words, some of the soldiers ordered to demolish the freeway shrines were probably themselves devotees of the death saint, and some of them must have been terrified of her "tremendous powers of vengeance" (Chesnut 109).

Santa Muerte's devotees refused to accept the military's explanations for the destruction of the shrines, and several hundred cult members took to the streets of Mexico City to protest what they viewed as religious persecution and intolerance (Tuckman n.p.).[4] Indeed, probably the true threat to church and state is Santa Muerte's escalating popularity, for she is currently the most popular devotional figure in Mexico after Jesus and the Virgin of Guadalupe. There were no large-scale protests in the borderlands, but the Santa Muerte cult is alive and well in the region. True to the fears of the officials who ordered the destruction of the border shrines, the Santa Muerte cult is growing by leaps and bounds in the borderlands and throughout the United States, especially in areas with large populations of Mexican migrants.

Since La Santísima Muerte is so strongly associated with the profane (especially in relation to illegality or transgressivity) even as she is revered as a holy, blessed figure, she is a particularly extreme example of the collision between the secular and sacred. However, all of the figures I treat embody the dichotomy of secular sanctity, whether they are regarded as popular saints with devotional cults or they are defined primarily through their historical, political, or cultural roles. Political heroes like Pancho Villa and César Chávez function within a spectrum of secular sanctity that invests them with "special status . . . [and] perhaps even special power," not primarily because of their divine perfection but because of their fallible human characteristics (Passariello 75). All these personages instantiate the contradiction between human and divine. At the same time, all the secular saints discussed here fuse spirituality, celebrity, iconicity, and politics both in practice and in representation. While all of them are cultural icons with different levels of celebrity, some are political or revolutionary leaders who have been sacralized. Meanwhile, devotees and dominant institutions alike appropriate these figures in order to negotiate various political, social, and cultural identities. The masses and dominant institutions like the state or the Catholic Church invoke these figures for a wide variety of interests, identities, and conditions, ranging from nation-building to sexual or racial difference to migrant melancholia.

I begin this study with a focus on historical figures from the Mexican pre-revolutionary and revolutionary periods who are associated with millenarianism, indigenous and peasant rebellion, and the Mexican Revolution. Whether they desired the role of saint or not, Teresa Urrea and Pancho Villa have to varying degrees been associated with sanctity and have consequently acquired devotional cults, both during their lives and after their deaths. Although with very different historical significance, the various representations of Urrea and Villa demonstrate the extent to which religious or spiritual rhetoric, celebrity, iconicity, and political dissent are intertwined in Mexico and in the borderlands. Meanwhile, later historical icons such as César Chávez and Subcomandante Marcos demonstrate the persistence of secular sanctity, even if they neither appeal to sanctity nor are always treated as traditional popular saints by their followers. While these explicitly secular figures (*santones*, as I call them, to indicate their function as simulacra of popular saints) are committed to social and political action, they nevertheless evoke the sacred, especially since they frequently draw upon the resources of the popular saint. Chávez frequently invoked the sacrificial practices of Catholicism in his role as leader of the United Farm Workers (UFW), while Marcos strives to invert the potentially messianic or mystical associations of the popular saint in the interest of decentralized indigenous collectivism. Like many secular saints, both Chávez and Marcos are susceptible to appropriation or control by the state. Nevertheless, political movements like the Chicano Rights Movement or indigenous rights have coalesced around them as figures both secular and sacred. Finally, the encounter between sacred and secular endures in the mystical figure of Santa Muerte. Like the other figures I discuss, whether saint or *santón*, Santa Muerte embodies both contradiction and ambivalence. Yet, unlike the others, the death saint has no physical manifestation within material history. This indicates the abstraction of the hopes and desires of the subaltern but also transcends the power of the state or church to rein her in and, by extension, to tame her unruly devotees.

In this work I analyze representations of—and sometimes by—secular saints and santones that originate in, cross through, or are transformed by the borderlands. My aim is to trace the intersections among these figures, their devotees, various artists, and dominant institutions. These saints and their devotees do not simply utilize traditional spiritual practices to represent alternative spatial and temporal identities, they also construct such identities through forms of cultural production that may resemble or merge with devotional practices. Practices of popular spirituality such as the use and exchange of relics or favors, faith healing, pilgrimages, and spirit possession fuse with cultural production to exemplify the contradictions between high culture and popular culture, between the human and the divine, the secular and the sacred, that embody secular sanctity. For example, the representation and commodification of saints within cultural production sometimes resemble spirit possession in the drive to establish a personal connection or identification between saint and devotee. In turn, this personal connection signifies a variety of different possibilities concerning national, regional, transnational, racial, ethnic, religious, or gender identity. At the same time, the representation of secular sanctity often manifests in unexpected, even counterintuitive or uncanny ways in borderlands cultural production. Many of the texts and saints or santones treated here are not explicitly religious or spiritual. Even when they do reference sanctity, they often challenge received notions of the sacred. Although many of the characters, authors, and artists clearly identify with or appropriate the secular saints and santones they represent, they frequently reject or refuse them as well, in a process that José Esteban Muñoz calls "disidentification," which adds to the contradiction of secular sanctity (Muñoz, *Disidentifications* 12).

I focus upon a wide range of Mexican and Chicano/a texts from as early as the nineteenth century and covering diverse genres such as the novel, the communiqué, the play, the essay or crónica, film, and contemporary digital media.[5] I contend that these cultural texts mediate spiritual folk practices by representing and enacting popular sanctity in ways similar to spirit possession, pilgrimages, or speaking in tongues. Indeed, I argue that spiritual practice is frequently represented as narrative—while narrative, whether literary, historical, visual, or oral, may modify or even function explicitly as devotional practice. I concentrate on literary texts, yet I also emphasize the representation and circulation of saints in popular culture such as film, internet sites, and communiqués. I accentuate the extent to which literary culture in its representation of secular sanctity is infused with the popular. The saints and santones studied here embody the contradiction inherent in secular sanctity, for they are modern and non-modern, secular and sacred, human and divine. The works I analyze both rearticulate and resist the contradictory characteristics of popular saints but ultimately emphasize the simultaneous rather than the antinomical nature of their contradictions. These texts embrace contradiction rather than resisting it, demonstrating that although such ambivalence is often difficult it is ultimately a valuable part of everyday life.

Secular Sanctity and Contradiction

Before proceeding further, it is crucial to examine the concept of sanctity—both official and popular—and its relationship to secular sanctity, especially in the context of the borderlands, Mexico, and migrant communities in the United States. Scholars agree that "the saint is a familiar figure in all world religions," while many political leaders, performers, artists, royals, and cultural heroes, among others, are "candidates for 'sainthood' treatment," thus blurring the lines between sanctity, iconicity, and celebrity (Woodward 16; Hopgood xi). Echoing this multiplicity, James F. Hopgood argues that it is difficult to distinguish the "truly sacred" from "folk saints, near-saints, or saintlike personages" in any context. He concludes that it is unnecessary to hold "firm conceptual divides" between the saint, folk saint, icon, and others (xii, xvii). Hopgood asserts, "it is best to use concepts with few constraints" in an exploration of "human behavior in the area of the sacred and in religion" (xvii). Indeed, he associates the icon with the "secular saint," suggesting that any cultural figure that undergoes a process of "popular canonization" can be considered a secular saint, for he or she highlights the juxtaposition of sacred and profane (xvii).

While such spiritual and conceptual variability is certainly the norm in the borderlands, it is conspicuously absent from Roman Catholic doctrine. The Catholic Church is the only one to feature "a formal, continuous, and highly rationalized process for 'making' saints," a process that requires copious research to determine and prove the presence of holiness and miracles (Woodward 16). Yet even within official Catholic doctrine, sanctity is an inherently contradictory concept for it juxtaposes the human and the divine, the holy and the profane, the secular and the sacred. Jacques Douillet indicates that the Bible refers repeatedly to the simultaneous presence of elements both holy and profane, suggesting that one cannot exist without the other (10–11). In a sense, it follows that all sanctity is fundamentally secular, because it is always both holy and profane. Nevertheless, Douillet's analysis of the duality between the holy and the profane is decidedly orthodox, for he insists that the two poles can never be equal. He asserts that "things are holy because they are set apart from the profane world; just so, God is holy because he is not part of the world. [Although] the world is not separate from him . . . he is not a being among other beings. He surpasses them infinitely" (13). While Catholic doctrine certainly supports Douillet's assessment of the transcendence of the divine, devotional practices in the borderlands, for example, reveal much more ambivalent and flexible understandings of the duality of the human and the divine.

Saints are clearly extraordinary figures, for within Catholic cosmology they are holy, frequently miraculous men and women who, rendered sacred, have ascended into heaven. As men and women, they are like the rest of us, inherently secular. Since they are both human and divine, saints are at once different from and similar to ordinary, flawed people on earth. Saints are not gods but, rather, mediators, benefactors, and protectors. From the perspective of the faithful, the status of saints as intermediaries between heaven and earth renders them preferable to gods who, by definition, are too distant and too unlike humans, so that most devotees find it difficult to form meaningful relationships easily with them. It is the human aspect of saints and santones that renders them fallible and accessible and points toward the possibility of reciprocal relationships of devotion and exchange. By straddling the divide between divine and mundane, saints both underscore the gulf between the two realms and paradoxically blur the line that separates them. The counterpoint between accentuating and erasing the boundary between human and divine reflects the ambivalent essence of secular sanctity. The contradiction goes beyond a simple juxtaposition of two seemingly opposed poles. In Theresa Delgadillo's analysis of "spiritual mestizaje," which she defines as "the transformative renewal of one's relationship to the sacred through a radical and sustained multimodal and self-reflexive critique of oppression in all its manifestations and a creative and engaged participation in shaping life that honors the sacred," secular sanctity reveals that the divine and the mundane are deeply intertwined in everyday life (1). In secular sanctity, as in spiritual mestizaje, life "honors the sacred," while the sacred becomes a means through which to engage with secular society, signaling a "way of being in the world" (Delgadillo 4).

Secular sanctity is necessarily ambivalent. Since saints are at once both completely accessible and absolutely inaccessible, they may inspire both desire and despair in the faithful, who also may simultaneously both resist and embrace sanctity. Secular sanctity manifests the simultaneous process of identification and rejection that José Esteban Muñoz terms "disidentification." For Muñoz, disidentification is a contradictory mode that is "liberatory and horrible" and exhilarating and terrifying all at once (*Disidentifications* 18, 4). Like William Connolly, who posits that identity itself is inherently contradictory, for "to confess to a particular identity is also to belong to difference," while "identity requires difference in order to be, and it converts difference into otherness in order to secure its own self-certainty" (Connolly xiv), Muñoz suggests that identification implies a perpetual dance between association and refusal (*Disidentifications* 64). Muñoz argues that "identifying with an object, person, lifestyle, history, political ideology, religious orientation, and so on, means also simultaneously and partially counteridentifying, as well as only partially identifying, with different aspects of the social and psychic world" (8). In this manner, disidentification is flexible. It provides subjects with the agency to manage their experience of identity and identification. It is a continually shifting process that "can be understood as a way of shuffling back and forth between reception and production" (Muñoz 25). Muñoz suggests that disidentification is about accepting contradiction rather than resisting it: "To disidentify is to read oneself and one's own life narrative in a moment, object, or subject that is not culturally coded to 'connect' with the disidentifying subject. It is not to pick and choose what to take out of an identification. It is not to willfully evacuate the politically dubious or shameful components within an identificatory locus."

Rather, it is the reworking of those energies that do not elide the 'harmful' or contradictory components of any identity" (12).

Disidentification perfectly captures the vexed yet intimate relationship between devotees and saints, who are intrinsically similar but also necessarily distant from each other. Devotees routinely approach their favored saints through the lens of disidentification, refusing to elide the "harmful or contradictory components" that might arise from the duality of human and divine. Such contradiction is not an impenetrable crisis but, instead, a routine part of everyday life that is productive as well as painful.

Several theorists have examined the role of contradiction or paradox as an advantage rather than an obstacle that must be resolved. For example, by arguing that identity is inherently paradoxical, William Connolly offers a powerful reading of how paradox defines much of everyday life, and how it is ineffectively contained by various institutions and concepts that purport to manage contradiction and uncertainty. Connolly posits that a more critical acknowledgment of paradox is an important goal, arguing that those accused of performing contradiction might actually "find something positive in the very experience of paradox, as Augustine, Nietzsche, Kierkegaard, and Deleuze do when they treat paradox as a sign of something efficacious in the world that exceeds conceptual reach" (xv–xvi). In other words, the fact that paradox is incomprehensible is part of its significance. Just as secular sanctity brings together two poles—the human and divine—that purport to be separate but are in fact decisive in the development of the relationship between saint and devotee, the unsettling nature of paradox allows for a more profound understanding of identity, community, and life in general.

Gloria Anzaldúa's well-known theories of the borderlands and the "new mestiza consciousness" in *Borderlands/La Frontera* are relevant here. Delgadillo notes that Anzaldúa's analysis of the link between cultural practices and religion or spirituality, which she terms "spiritual mestizaje," demonstrates the nexus between "spirituality, on the one hand, and subject formation and material and social relations, on the other hand, as mutually informing and intersectional" (179). Delgadillo's work is an important and long overdue investigation of Anzaldúa's treatment of spirituality and borderlands cultural production. The contradiction between various forms of the sacred and the mundane highlighted by Delgadillo represents only one manifestation of Anzaldúa's use of paradox, however. For Anzaldúa, the borderlands symbolize the essence of painful yet valuable contradiction. She provides various definitions of the borderlands and the borderlands condition, which all reflect the difficulty and importance of contradiction and, above all, its fluidity. The borderlands, Anzaldúa argues, are "not comfortable, but home" (Anzaldúa, *Borderlands*, "Preface to the First Edition," n.p). Yet, while they reflect "my home / this thin edge of barbwire," they are also "in a constant state of transition" (Anzaldúa 25). Living in the border-lands requires movement, change, and an embrace of contradiction, as Anzaldúa puts it, "to survive the Borderlands / you must live *sin fronteras* / be a crossroads" (217). The "new mestiza" must develop a "tolerance for contradictions, a toler-ance for ambiguity," for to resist contradiction is to court disaster and succumb to chaos and pain (101).

For Anzaldúa contradiction is multiple and shifting, since it is always both limit and transition. Like the protean Aztec goddess Coatlicue who fuses oppo-sites ("eagle and serpent, heaven and the underworld, life and death, mobil-ity and immobility, beauty and horror"), Anzaldúa's contradiction "represents duality in life, a synthesis of duality, and a third perspective—something more than mere duality or a synthesis or duality" (68). Thus, contradiction always transcends the sum of its opposed parts. Far from signaling pure abjection, the conflict innate to contradiction is a productive one. Anzaldúa indicates as much when she describes the threshold of the borderland conflict: "I have so internal-ized the borderland conflict that sometimes I feel like one cancels out the other and we are zero, nothing, no one. *A veces no soy nada ni nadie. Pero hasta cuando no lo soy, lo soy* [At times I am nothing, no one. But even when I am not, I am]" (85). This passage epitomizes the value of contradiction—for the apparent nega-tion of the borderland conflict, which renders the subject "nothing, no one," is in fact a very strong presence capable of converting nothing into something: "even when I am not, I am" (85).

Official and Popular Sanctity

While secular sanctity reflects the contradictory yet worthy duality of human and sacred that informs all kinds of sanctity whether official or popular, ortho-dox Catholic doctrine stresses the conflict that informs this dichotomy rather than its confluence. As a case in point, Kieckhefer and Bond signal that the cen-tral paradox of sanctity is the "tension between the saint's imitability and his or her utter distinctness from normal humanity" (viii). Writing from a traditional Catholic perspective, Kieckhefer subtly laments the loss of "any vital sense of the saints as numinous beings worthy of veneration" by "Catholics living within a culture of disenchantment" (Kieckhefer and Bond 39). In contrast to Hopgood, who focuses on the multiplicity and variability of sanctity, Kieckhefer empha-sizes the decline of the sacred in the modern world rather than its transforma-tion. This hierarchical narrative of loss—in which, "if saints are important at all, it is as exemplary members of the broader Christian community" who seem interchangeable with other extraordinary figures, such as charismatic leaders or celebrities—obscures the fact that sanctity has been a flexible, shifting con-cept from the beginning (39). Even within the strict hierarchies of the Catholic

Church, where church officials have largely had the authority to influence and determine the making of saints at will, the criteria for canonization and characteristics of sanctity have shifted radically over the centuries. It is often forgotten that, in the early Christian period, all saints were effectively popular saints, for their cults rose organically through mass worship at their tombs.[6] According to the letters of Saint Paul, all of the faithful, the "newly converted people who made up the first Christian communities," were considered "saints," in the sense that they were all equally called upon to be holy (Douillet 9–10). Kenneth Woodward argues that "to identify sainthood exclusively with formal canonization . . . is to overlook the populist dimension of saint-making" (388). Indeed, the devotional practices surrounding saints' cults through at least the sixth century A.D. were essentially popular, informal, and liminal.

Peter Brown asserts that early Christians conceived of a liminal world in which Heaven and Earth joined through the body of the dead saint, for "the saint in Heaven was believed to be 'present' at his tomb on earth" (3). The graves of the saint and any associated relics, whether fragments of bodies or physical objects, were privileged sites that permitted the union of the human and the divine (3). The desire to access the frisson of the divine gave rise to the culture of the pilgrimage and the buying, selling, trading, and adoring of (frequently false) relics, as well as the reordering of private and public space through the use of tombs as communal altars for mass worship (9).

Although early devotional practices and understandings of sanctity explicitly evoke secular sanctity in their embrace of both human and divine, by the fifth century A.D. certain criteria for identifying saints were in place that officially rejected this convergence. These criteria, which eventually formed part of the process for formal canonization established by Pope Urban VIII in 1634 (Douillet 90), included the saints' "reputations, especially for martyrdom," "the stories and legends into which their lives were transmuted as exemplars of heroic virtue," and "their reputation for producing miracles, especially those worked posthumously at their shrines or through their relics" (Woodward 62). Although any local saints' cults that had existed for at least a century were permitted to stand under Urban VIII's decree, the spontaneity of the popular cult was replaced by the rigidity of formal papal procedure (Douillet 90; Woodward 75–76).

The shift toward infallible papal authority marked a transfer from "popular concern with miracles to elite concern with virtue" (Woodward 71). This does not mean that miracles ceased to matter for canonization, but proof of virtue, which frequently translated to a lifetime of perfect piety, had become the ideal. Jacques Douillet emphasizes that sanctity requires holiness, which encompasses faith, the courage to choose Christ, unified love for God, "genius" or "creative, moving forces," heroism, asceticism, prayer and contemplation, the gift of miracles, equilibrium and mental health, and martyrdom (53–74). By focusing on holiness and virtue for the process of canonization rather than the role of saints as intercessors and miracle-workers, the Catholic Church framed sanctity primarily in terms of an imitation of Christ rather than a connection to ordinary humans. As a result, the church was able to reinforce its top-down structure of authority, to establish distance between saints and humans, and implicitly to frame the notion of secular sanctity as an impenetrable paradox.

Nevertheless, saints remain alluring to the masses precisely because of their ability to fuse the human and the divine, that is, because they embody secular sanctity. Woodward contends that while saints "were venerated for their holiness, [they] were invoked for their powers" (64). These miraculous powers are what attract humans and (perhaps paradoxically) permit the closeness between saint and human. This closeness is present not necessarily because humans wish to assume the miraculous powers of saints—though there are some examples of popular ritual, like spirit possession or faith healing, that do purport to transmit divine powers, at least from the perspective of believers. Rather, devotees identify with saints because of their human qualities. While the hierarchical process of saint-making in the Catholic Church effectively severs the link between saint and devotee by distancing the saint from ordinary humanity, devotees everywhere seek ways to reinforce their connection with their favored saints by focusing on the union of human and divine. As such, even after hundreds of years of official sanctity enforced by the Catholic Church, the cult of saints is still imbued with popular beliefs and practices.

Popular and official notions of sanctity are deeply intertwined in the borderlands. Although the official markers and celebrations of sanctity have declined steadily since the mid-twentieth century as a result of shifting cultural norms and the liturgical changes instituted in 1969 after the Second Vatican Council, for example, in the borderlands, throughout Mexico, and in migrant communities in the United States, the worship of popular or folk saints has flourished.[7] Chesnut indicates that devotion to Santa Muerte, for example, has been transformed in less than a decade "from an occult practice, unknown to most Mexicans, to a burgeoning public cult that counts millions of devotees in Mexico and the United States among its followers" (4).

The formal concept of sanctity has been a part of daily life in Mexico since the Spanish conquest, while many rituals such as certain types of faith healing and votive offerings demonstrate the influence of indigenous and African beliefs and devotional practices upon Christianity. There are countless words, concepts, and aphorisms that refer to or draw upon sanctity in Mexican Spanish, demonstrating the extent to which the sacred permeates daily life in Mexico and the borderlands.[8] Some of these words, like *santito* (a diminutive form of saint, which denotes familiarity) and *santón* or *santurrón* (which denote excessive, hypocritical piety or purity) unmoor the concept of sanctity from its official, hierarchical definitions to reflect playful, disparaging, and intimate attitudes toward saints or would-be saints. It follows that many borderlands folk saints, like the Mexican faith healer El Niño Fidencio, are virtually indistinguishable from canonized saints in their miraculous or charismatic attributes (Murray 107–108).[9] Many official saints are modified and reappropriated by the masses in ways that reflect the influence of popular culture. For example, the October 28 feast day of San Judas Tadeo (Saint Jude the Apostle), the patron of lost causes and desperate cases, has been transformed into the biggest street party in downtown Mexico City, as devotees gather in front of the Temple of San Hipólito, where a famous image of the saint is housed, to worship, give thanks, listen and dance to music, eat street food, buy trinkets, and wear clothing in the saint's colors (green and white) or emblazoned with the saint's image (Hernández, *Down* 158–160). Such fluidity reinforces Hopgood's idea that it is not necessary for devotees to identify the objects of their devotion specifically as saints, "only that their activities, expressions, and devotions clearly mark the personage as sharing qualities with traditionally conceived saints" (xii).

The relationship of exchange between saint and devotee is central to an understanding of both popular and official sanctity in the borderlands. The personal relationship between saint and devotee is paramount, and many of the attributes and practices associated with popular sanctity reflect this bond, for they emphasize interaction, communication, exchange, and frequently identification with the saint. Such relationships depend upon the status of the saint as both human and divine and they reflect the contradiction inherent in secular sanctity, yet such exchange and identification are neither direct nor straightforward but instead reflect the process of disidentification with the awareness that, although the devotee can never fully approximate the saint, saints must approximate humans in order for believers to access them. As José Esteban Muñoz puts it, the "disidentificatory subject . . . tactically and simultaneously works on, with, and against a cultural form" (12). Reflecting such agency, devotees in the borderlands are not passive supplicants. They circumvent authority, for they do not primarily interact with saints through priests or in the context of the Catholic mass. They modify devotional practices as they see fit and reserve the right to seek more acquiescent patrons as necessary (though they may do so at their own risk). Devotees build home altars to their favored saints; wear them on their bodies in the form of amulets, jewelry, or tattoos; dress statues of their saints in elaborate handmade clothing; and communicate with diverse saints through prayers and offerings that range from traditional votive offerings like candles, *retablos* (votive oil paintings on tin or metal), or *milagritos* (tiny charm-like metal renderings of body parts) to more secular gifts like liquor or cigars. Luis D. León stresses the importance of gifting and the *promesa* (promise) or *manda* (obligation or errand) within the devotee-saint relationship (*La Llorona's* 67). Indeed, most devotional practices in the borderlands are predicated upon exchange, especially the giving and receiving of tangible and intangible favors. The saints might grant the return of a wayward lover or a sense of spiritual well-being, while their devotees exchange and transfer relics or images of saints, embark on pilgrimages, present votive offerings, recite prayers and novenas, construct home altars, and wear amulets, jewelry, or tattoos.

All of these devotional practices involve some sort of transfer (as in the offering of gifts to the saint in return for good health or a job), but the exchange between saint and devotee is necessarily unequal. The gift of a healthy childbirth or a son released from prison before his sentence is completed, for example, is not directly equivalent to an offering of lit candles or homemade tamales, or even to an act of sacrifice like walking to a saint's temple on one's knees. Devotees accept this disparity on the grounds that the saints are innately different from themselves in their divinity, even though they were once human themselves, or because they reflect the essential human condition. The devotees both disidentify with the saints by revering them for their extraordinary qualities and nevertheless access them because of their ordinary human characteristics. Indeed, certain devotional practices draw upon a different kind of exchange, which reflects the disidentification between devotee and saint. Rather than focusing on the chasm between ordinary human and divine saint as dictated by the Catholic Church, this type of exchange embraces the similarities and the communion between human and saint. For example, many devotees emphasize points of physical, emotional, or spiritual identification between themselves and their preferred saints or virgins. Various authors cite the link between the Virgin of Guadalupe's bronze-colored skin and that of many of her mestizo followers.[10] Meanwhile, other devotees accentuate temperamental similarities between themselves and various saints. For example, Haydé Solís Cárdenas, an impoverished Mexico City woman, asserts that Santa Muerte "understands us, because she is a cabrona like us" (Thompson n.p.).[11] These points of identification between saints and ordinary people are important for many devotees. Certain devotional practices move beyond the realm of the simile, however, to shift toward the metaphorical, suggesting that one can "be," possess, or be possessed by the saint, however fleetingly. Practices such as spirit possession, faith healing, or speaking in tongues reflect a symbolic or real transfer of the miraculous powers or sacred aura from saint to devotee. It is important to clarify that none of these exchanges or identifications, even spirit possession, implies that the saint and devotee are exactly the same. Virtually all believers would firmly reject the suggestion of equivalence. Practices like spirit possession provide the possibility of connecting with the saint at the deepest, most visceral level, for such rituals manifest the coming together of human and spiritual bodies and experiences even as they cause a disidentication with the saint's body by manifesting it in living human form.

Spirit Possession

Spirit possession is a form of folk spirituality in which the human devotee is momentarily seized by divine or demonic forces.[12] The human's personality is displaced to or otherwise joins with that of the spirit in a transcendental experience. Spirit possession can be involuntary or voluntary, and the spirits involved might be either good or bad (Lewis 110). This is a phenomenon found in many different cultures and religions, including so-called primitive societies as well as charismatic Protestant communities like the Assemblies of God, the Pentecostals, and the Spiritualist sects throughout the world. I. M. Lewis argues, "it is difficult to find a religion which has not, at some stage in its history, inspired in the breasts of at least certain of its followers those transports of mystical exaltation in which man's whole being seems to fuse in a glorious communion with the divinity" (15). Spirit possession is ubiquitous perhaps because as a mode of physical and mental exchange between the human and the divine it not only exemplifies the contradiction of secular sanctity, it comprises many other devotional practices and traditions, including faith healing, spiritual cleansing, prophecy, trance, charismatic prayer, speaking in tongues, relic worship, pilgrimage, and the production of *retablos* and *exvotos*. Some religious groups or sects believe that only marked or chosen ones may serve as mediums for the spirit world, manifesting gifts that include "sight," "clairvoyance," "hearing," "prophecy or voice," and "healing." Other groups believe that anyone can be momentarily touched or involuntarily seized by the spirit (León, *La Llorona's* 176; Lewis 110). In general, however, the *materias* (mediums) and *curanderas* (healers) who channel and transmit the spirit world are described as possessing a special gift and as constantly working to "prepare themselves to receive the beings of high light, to hear and interpret messages from the spirit world" (León, *La Llorona's* 176). The implication is that devotees must cultivate their relationship with the spirits and, in the process, improve or work on themselves.

Spirit possession elucidates the intimacy of the interaction between saint and devotee, highlighting this relationship as one of mutual embodiment. While many sources emphasize "the seizure of man by divinity," focusing on dissociation and implying a loss of self, spirit possession also signals the transformation, and frequently the return, of the supernatural entity into human form (Lewis 15). It is irrelevant whether one believes that such an exchange is possible at any level or whether spirit possession merely conveys a symbolic transfer or, more damningly, reveals psychosis or ignorance. Rather, spirit possession neatly translates Peter Brown's theories about the union of Heaven and Earth at the graves of the saints in the early Christian period to multiple spaces and temporalities, encompassing pre- or non-Christian societies, contemporary evangelical sects, and popular appropriations of Catholicism. In this manner, spirit possession reveals the presence of secular sanctity across different eras and locations. Rituals of spirit possession epitomize the "authorization of religious poetics" through popular devotional practice (León, *La Llorona's* 181). Insofar as spirit possession and faith healing confer power upon the medium or healer that performs them, they challenge and refuse the authority of the Catholic Church.

Of course, there are many other ways to resist spiritual authority. Protestant communities are founded in part on their rejection of the hierarchical model of the Catholic Church through belief in the universal priesthood between the laity and God. But practices like spirit possession bridge the gap between indigenous or African spiritual beliefs and Catholic doctrine, as well as that between popular Catholicism and evangelical Protestantism, revealing that seemingly opposed beliefs and communities may share "histories and sensibilities" as well as space in the borderlands (León, *La Llorona's* 166). Indeed, spirit possession draws upon the official pantheon of Catholic saints and adapts and creates new ones from a variety of traditions and histories, both sacred and secular. By assuming an active role in their relationships with favored saints or other spirits through spirit possession and related practices, devotees enact alternative means of authority that are open to anyone, regardless of social or cultural status. In this sense, spiritual practices in the borderlands are intrinsically egalitarian. Not every believer can attain the gifts of spirit-channeling or healing, but even the most marginalized of devotees can work to achieve the ultimate closeness with the divine by participating in rituals that draw upon the exchange and identification exemplified by spirit possession.

Secular sanctity finds its ultimate expression in spirit possession, since this reflects a corporeal and empirical exchange between the human and the divine. While the Catholic Church's process of canonization firmly distinguishes saint from devotee, in traditional spirit possession the spiritual entity actually becomes human and vice versa. In symbolic terms, the union between spirit and human that is enacted through spirit possession reflects the intersection of rational knowledge and emotion that Plato termed *nous*.[13] As Jennifer Wicke argues, "nous is thought that embraces, seduces, and impels, that relies on collectivity and on charismatic transmission" (1132). This form of knowledge is not only infused with emotion, it is driven by it. But rather than diminishing or compromising knowledge, the emotion behind nous produces a different kind of knowledge, a "non-rational intelligence linking us to the divine" (1132). Of course, spirit possession is not the only devotional or cultural practice that performs and articulates the link between human and divine encoded in nous. For example, the rise of Christian names and the cult of the patron saint reflect the symbolic union between human and sacred through the transformative rebirth of baptism and the intimacy of personal guardianship (Brown 56–58). In its potential for mutual transformation and exchange, however, spirit possession opens the door to figurative possibilities that both employ aspects of religious belief and transcend it.

Icon, Celebrity, Saint

In many ways, the desire to possess or be possessed by the divine or other spiritual entities resembles the representation and commodification of celebrity. In fact, there are many similarities between sanctity, celebrity, and the related concept of the icon.[14] The term *icon* is often interchangeable with both *saint* and *celebrity*, while all three terms may be applied in reference to "secular saints," or popular canonized figures. It is worth asking what, if anything, distinguishes these concepts. In the religious sense, *icon* refers to an image or representation, especially an image of a sacred or sanctified Christian personage; for example, the pictorial hagiographies or illustrated cycles of saints' lives of the Middle Ages (Abou-El-Haj 33). More broadly, as Phyllis Passariello argues, "an *icon* is a person whose being becomes an enduring symbol of cultural specialness, often with a tinge of religion-like awe" (75), or as Hopgood affirms, it is "indicative of a configuration of meanings associated with a particular personage" (xvii). According to Chris Rojek, *celebrity* reflects "the attribution of glamorous or notorious status to an individual within the public sphere" (10). "Celebrities are cultural fabrications" while "celebrity status always implies a split between a private self and a public self" (Rojek 10–11). Rojek emphasizes the transition from sacred to secular society in the treatment of celebrity, arguing that "although God-like qualities are often attributed to celebrities, the modern meaning of the term *celebrity* actually derives from the fall of the gods, and the rise of democratic governments and secular societies," yet he also asserts that "many of the symbols of success and failure in celebrity draw on myths and rites of religious ascent and descent" (9, 74). Indeed, both the concept of the icon and contemporary celebrity culture originate in the early Christian public religious rituals, which Peter Brown discusses in *The Cult of the Saints*. The traditional religious significances of *icon* and *charisma* are not replaced by secular versions but are instead woven into the fabric of celebrity culture. Joseph Roach discusses "the secularization of charisma" as a catalyst for celebrity culture, while Wicke draws upon Brown's work to demonstrate that celebrity is inextricably linked to "the woodcut portraits and wayside shrines . . . as well as [to] the professionally wrought iconic images of the saints" produced in late antiquity (Roach, "The Doubting-Thomas Effect" 1129; Wicke 1131). Thus we might consider that, while the terms *icon*, *celebrity*, and *saint* are clearly often interchangeable, what truly binds them is a wide spectrum of awe and devotion linking them as enduring symbols to a public.

Both saints and celebrities require the adulation of the public for their very existence. Rojek asserts that there can be no celebrity without a public (10), while Douillet concedes, "If a saint is to be known and to be recognized as a saint he must needs have a certain publicity" (118). Even the multitude of saints who might be "unknown" or "known to but a few" are publicly celebrated en masse on All Saints' Day (Douillet 122). The exchange of relics and prayer cards establishes relationships between saints and devotees, but such iconic images are also sacred in their own right. Likewise, celebrities are transmitted, but also produced, by the masses through the circulation of their images in venues that include tabloids, the internet, social media, film, and television. Rojek highlights the relationship of exchange and identification between celebrities and their public, arguing that, "other than religion, celebrity culture is the only cluster of human relationships in which mutual passion typically operates without physical interaction" (48). This lack of physical interaction does not preclude intimacy. Rojek gestures toward a secular version of spirit possession in commodity culture, indicating that "celebrities are commodities in the sense that consumers desire to possess them" (15). Wicke further evokes rituals of spirit possession and argues that celebrity "annuls the subject-object distinction," for the transfer and repetition of the celebrities' images and the endless stream of media that accompanies every aspect of celebrities' lives create seemingly intimate relationships between the public and their stars (1132).

Ultimately, the production of celebrity and sanctity confers both intimacy and agency to the masses. As Kenneth Woodward argues, "the making of saints . . . is done by others for others," especially ordinary devotees who "through prayers . . . contribute to a candidate's reputation for holiness" (17). In this sense, the making of saints, like the making of celebrities, is inherently an inclusive, democratic process. Yet sanctity, like celebrity, also harbors deep contradictions that would seem to inhibit intimacy and agency, for saints and celebrities are both tantalizingly similar to and absolutely different from the rest of us. As Joseph Roach astutely observes, "for the celebrity to remain celebrated, the contradiction that defines his or her mystery must remain in continual uncertainty" ("The Doubting-Thomas Effect" 1127). Nevertheless, through disidentificatory practices such as spirit possession, devotees are simultaneously able to bypass and to accept this contradiction freely. Devotees may know the saint through the intimate exchange inherent in spirit possession or the transfer of saints' images, but the testimonies of countless believers reveal how they understand perfectly well that they themselves are not divine.[15] Rather than resisting the contradiction between identification and difference reflected in their disidentification, the faithful understand that both poles are crucial to the formation of sainthood.

Celebrities are not the only secular figures imbued with the halo of the divine. Certain royals, heads of state, and political or revolutionary leaders have been invested with—and in many cases, have actively assumed—the aura of the sacred. In early modern England and France, as well as in other cultures throughout history, the doctrine of the divine right of kings decreed that the monarch's right to rule was granted directly by God, which implied a privileged link between the king and God. During the modern era, Emilio Gentile indicates, "the relationship between the religious and political dimensions and between power and sacredness entered a new phase that gave rise to the sacralization of politics, which . . . commenced with the birth of modern democracy and mass politics" (xv–xvi). Gentile cites "civil religion" (which "respects individual freedom, coexists with other ideologies, and does not impose obligatory and unconditional support for its commandments") and "political religion" (which is "intolerant, invasive, and fundamentalist") as the main components of the sacralization of politics (xv). Gentile stresses that "the sacralization of politics is not restricted to the cult of the charismatic leader," yet dictators around the world have mandated their own symbolic canonization as stand-ins for the state, especially through the institutionalized repetition and adoration of their image in public and private space (144).

Such obligatory hero worship leaves no space for contradiction, but the spontaneous response of the masses toward certain historical and political leaders demonstrates that these figures are revered precisely for their ambiguity and fallibility. For example, Diana, Princess of Wales, was celebrated and scrutinized during her life for her humanitarian efforts and her grace, beauty, and fashion sense but also for her troubled marriage and her vexed relationship with the royal family and its protocol. Her tragic death, which inspired rituals of public mourning around the world, solidified her standing as a sanctified icon. Similarly, Evita Perón—whose charisma "permitted her to enter a kind of 'mystical communion'" with the Argentine public, especially the poor—has undergone what Roberto Bosca terms a "political canonization," despite the fact that she was a rather controversial figure during her life (59–60). Like Diana, Evita's death at the age of 33 "raised her to a sphere of adoration like that of a saint" (Bosca 69). The masses loved Evita because she touched them. While she was renowned for literally embracing the poor and sick, her mythologized image held the entire nation in thrall. Through her touch, Evita established herself as one of the masses, yet she transcended them through her power to heal. The fact that many of the stories about Evita's healing powers are firmly grounded in myth does not diminish her link to the masses in the least. By institutionalizing Evita's canonization in order to buttress his authoritarian rule, Juan Perón and the ideology of official Peronism symbolically distanced her from the masses who worshipped her by rendering her sacralization a hierarchical process (Bosca 69). As these examples demonstrate, unlike official canonization or many instances of the "sacralization of politics," popular canonization embraces the contradiction and ambiguity inherent in secular sanctity.

Saint/Santón

Many figures that oscillate between the realms of sanctity, celebrity, politics, and revolution can be interpreted through the concept of the santón. *Santón* is a Spanish word used to denote non-Christians who live pious or saintly lives—or anyone who hypocritically assumes the mantle of sanctity. Along with *santito*, the term is sometimes also applied to popular saints in general, as in the Mexican Canal One documentary *Santitos y santones*, a television program dedicated to popular devotional practices and saints' cults in Mexico.[16] Given the concept's link to hypocrisy, which originates from the Greek word *hypokrisis* (referring to "the acting of a part on the stage, feigning, or pretence"), the santón underscores that sanctity is a performance, frequently connoting excess, irony, swagger, and playfulness (OED.com). The term is synonymous with *simulacrum*, in the sense of an image or representation, a semblance, especially a vague or insubstantial semblance, and in Jean Baudrillard's terms, "the generation by models of a real without origin or reality: a hyperreal" (3).

To understand Baudrillard's notion of a "real without origin," it is helpful to consider his analysis of the simulacrum of divinity, or the revelation of divinity in icons, "multiplied in simulacra" (5). Baudrillard refers to the possibility that "the image didn't conceal anything at all, and that these images were in essence not images, such as an original model would have made them, but perfect simulacra, forever radiant with their own fascination" (5). Rather than simply representing the divine, for example, the icon-as-simulacrum actually becomes divine, but it also breaks the link with the divine as a "sign," thus demonstrating both "the principle of equivalence" and also "the radical negation of the sign as value" (6). This simulacrum of divinity is divine on its own without referring to an original "model" of divinity. Baudrillard's notion of simulacrum is particularly useful in relation to the santón because it suggests that santones can simultaneously represent the divine, break with the divine, and become divine in their own right. In this sense, the concept of the santón is multifaceted, ambiguous, and contradictory.

Because they are simulacra, santones amplify the contradiction and performativity of secular sanctity in the borderlands. While a santón is by nature a near-saint, this is not necessarily because he or she approximates the divine through traditional channels or characteristics such as holiness, virtue, or performing miracles. Instead, the santón implies both an exaggeration of the saint's holy qualities and their total absence. By suggesting that santones actively perform sanctity, the term *santón* actually denotes the inverse of official sanctity. Douillet correctly indicates that saints require publicity in order to be recognized as such (118). Woodward suggests that this publicity is directed away from the saint, for true saints are always made by others (whether clerical authorities or the masses): "the saints themselves . . . have no need of veneration" (17). However, santones bypass external channels to claim and perform their own versions of sanctity, which frequently encompass flawed or even sinful characteristics and actions. Thus, santones embody the ambiguities and contradictions of secular sanctity, especially the disidentificatory duality of identification and rejection. Indeed, santones actively disidentify with sanctity as it is traditionally construed, frequently by overstating their own sanctity or by denouncing it entirely.

Part of the appeal of the santón concept is that it enhances the disidentificatory distance between and fusion of human and divine realms. Such disidentification is fundamentally a performance, especially in its self-conscious construction, adaptation, embrace, or rejection of the image of the saint. As Diana Taylor asserts, "performances function as vital acts of transfer, transmitting social knowledge, memory, and a sense of identity through reiterated . . . behavior" (2). Performance is both ontological, referring to an "object/process of analysis," and epistemological, an embodied practice that "constitutes the methodological lens that enables scholars to analyze events as performance" (Taylor 3). Meanwhile, José Esteban Muñoz argues that, as a mode of performance, "disidentification can be understood as a way of shuffling back and forth between reception and production" (25). In this sense, disidentification confers "an active kernel of utopian possibility" to those who produce a performance or image as well as to those who receive or perceive it, including minority or oppressed subjects who are generally "disempowered in such a representational hierarchy" (Muñoz 25). In relation to the santón, the embodied performance of secular sanctity reflects the disidentificatory shift between reception and production for santones and their followers alike.

Many secular saints share the same characteristics as santones, particularly in their refusal of official channels of canonization and their contradictory, disidentificatory performance of sanctity. Certainly, the slippery nature of the term santón could make it seem that all secular saints are santones, and vice versa. I concur with James Hopgood that it is virtually impossible to distinguish between official saints, "folk saints, near-saints, or saintlike personages," and that it is unnecessary to do so, since saints are created through devotional practices, not clerical dictates (xii). However, such practices are frequently not what we might instantly recognize as devotional or even spiritual. For example, Pancho Villa manifests bombastic, powerful, and threatening qualities in addition to fulfilling a heroic, Robin Hood persona that is more in line with the traditional saintly characteristics such as humility and empathy. Yet these seemingly opposed personae confer mass adulation and even secular sanctity upon Villa, who retains a small devotional religious cult in Mexico and the borderlands.

Interestingly, not all of the figures treated here are at the center of traditional religious cults such as those associated with popular saints, however small. Some of them openly reject all forms of spirituality or sanctity, to the point that on the surface they seem anti-spiritual. While they may reject traditional or even popular forms of sanctity and spirituality, all of the figures here perform a kind of uncanny sanctity. They are often represented and interpellated by the faithful in ways that might seem counterintuitive, that is, while some of these figures actively perform a refusal of charismatic sanctity, in the mode of disidentification such refusal nevertheless evokes the sacred. For example, Subcomandante Marcos accommodates dissent and refusal in his performance of the cult of Zapatismo, which is at once interchangeable with his iconic persona and exclusive of it. César Chávez deliberately draws upon Catholic ritual in his expression of the tenets and symbolism of the UFW, even as he is often appropriated as a symbol of rigid, exclusive Chicano perfection and martyrdom. In their performance of charismatic sanctity, political and cultural leaders like Chávez and Marcos reorder traditional modes of sacred representation and devotional practice in new and sometimes counterintuitive ways. They challenge the possibility of divine perfection and rearticulate the contradiction between sacred and human. As uncanny simulacra of saints, Chávez and Marcos break with the model or sign of the divine, in Baudrillard's terms emphasizing the "hyperreality" of the simulacrum as a divine figure in its own right (Baudrillard 6).

By examining the nuances inherent in various kinds of saints, near-saints, and saint-like figures, I do not intend to pit secular saints and santónes against each other. Regardless of what they are called, all of the figures studied here are explicitly excluded from narratives of official sanctity, and all of them demonstrate the contradiction of human and divine within secular sanctity. Figures such as César Chávez and Subcomandante Marcos are simulacra of saints, in that they do not have traditional popular cults (though they definitely have cults of personality), but they may employ official religious or spiritual practices for explicitly secular ends or they may actively disavow any notion of the sacred. As simulacra of saints, I call them "santones." Since these figures break with an original sign of divinity yet also constitute divinity themselves, as Baudrillard suggests, their followers need not refer to or even think of them as saints or santones. If a santón is inherently like a saint, more than a saint, or not quite a saint, then there can be no guarantee of purity behind the representation and spiritual practices associated with these figures. Indeed, representational practices (such as the repetition and commodification of images imbued with the sacred) and practices of popular devotion (such as spirit possession) shift meaning when read alongside the simulacrum of the santón. This does not mean that those who revere or represent these contradictory figures do not perceive them to be holy or transcendent, but rather, certain secular saints and santones and the spiritual practices associated with them always disidentify with the divine, and sometimes in uncanny ways.

Devotional Practice and Cultural Production

As a notion that is grounded in simulacra, the santón further illustrates the links between sanctity, iconicity, celebrity, and forms of political, revolutionary, or cultural leadership. Virtually all political and revolutionary leaders or heroes are renowned for their charisma and many are conflated with their causes and movements. Even those leaders who seem less than charismatic create a mystique around their image, and often their images are utilized in ways that approximate devotional practices. Many people revere or identify with these figures not only because they serve as charismatic idols, but also because they serve as vehicles for the people's own narratives of belonging. In *The Magic of the State*, a hybrid text that blends anthropology, history, and fiction, Michael Taussig describes practices of spirit possession and the cults of various saint-like figures in a fictive Latin American country (probably Venezuela) and translates them to the process of "state-making" and "stately representation" (99, 78). Taussig indicates that, in its rituals, this version of spirit possession utilizes some of the heroes and symbols of the state, like images of "The Liberator" Simón Bolívar and the national flag. Indeed, the Liberator, along with the Spirit Queen María Lionza (who is usually represented as a light-skinned woman with a crown and a cloak), African spirits such as El Negro Felipe, and Indians such as El Cacique Indio Guaicaipuro, all enter into the bodies of mediums and healers in order to commune with and touch believers (*Magic* 31–32).[17] At the same time, Taussig argues that national(ist) discourse draws upon the metaphor of spirit possession in order to imbue the state with life (*Magic* 101–102). In Taussig's view, the state initially appropriates spirit possession by physically claiming the remains of dead heroes like the Liberator: "They wanted his remains, they insisted on his spirit, and in the absoluteness of the claims to the righteousness of possession they defined the very notion of nationhood. . . . It was, in other words, the foundational act of spirit possession by the new state" (*Magic* 99–100). However, in the hands of the state, spirit possession transcends physical bodies to enter the realm of representation, symbolism, and image. Insofar as the circulation of the image of the Liberator on national currency, the naming of schools after Indian caciques, the sacralization of the Liberator's tomb, and the invocation of the spirit of the Liberator by the president as part of "the daily round of statecraft" all represent the nation-state, they solidify it as an entity (Taussig, *Magic* 139).

Taussig demonstrates that the nation-state adapts modes of spirit possession in order to claim or exclude saints and heroes for the purposes of national ideology. However, as I suggest above, marginalized people also utilize spirit possession—both as metaphor and as literal practice—in order to "destabilize [the] ideological mechanism of social control, exploitation, and domination" and assert the power they are so often denied (León, *La Llorona's* 5). While practices like spirit possession are frequently a means for marginalized subjects to articulate identities and affiliations that transcend regional constraints and have little to do with state citizenship, devotees also use them to claim national belonging on their own terms.

Much research has been conducted on spirit possession, faith healing, speaking in tongues, and other practices of spiritual exchange and identification in the fields of cultural anthropology, history, and religious studies. Luis León presents a compelling analysis of the faith communities and rituals of evangelical and Pentecostal churches in the borderlands, as well as syncretic rituals that unite indigenous, African, and Catholic beliefs. These practices appeal particularly to those who are excluded from the dominant institutions of the Catholic Church and state such as migrants, poor barrio residents, gangbangers, and other outsiders.[18] Delgadillo's book *Spiritual Mestizaje* examines the construction and representation of spiritual mestizaje in Chicano narrative. Still, as a means of addressing social inequities and of gaining agency, in general little has been said about the symbolic and representational function of popular sanctity and devotional practices. It is in the realm of the symbolic—through the resuscitation and repetition of the image and word for both sacred and secular means, through the touch and aura of the sacred within cultural production, both high and low— that I wish to situate this study.

Spirit possession and related rituals are sometimes dismissed as remnants of non-modern belief, yet they are frequently invoked and rearticulated in Chicano and Mexican cultural production. The connections between the seemingly opposed poles of sacred and secular or human and divine involved in secular sanctity are strikingly revealed through the parallels between popular devotional practices and artistic representation. Just as devotees engage in spiritual practices to establish relationships of identification and exchange with favored saints and santones, authors and artists frequently represent these figures through modes that approximate sacred communion, even when the subjects and texts in question seem firmly rooted in the secular. For example, Pancho Villa has been portrayed in literature and film as a heroic, yet threatening figure who symbolizes Mexican revolutionary nationalism, migrant nostalgia, or Mexican barbarism. As both revolutionary hero and secular saint, Villa inspires desire, obsession, personal identification, and even the possibility of spiritual synthesis in the manner of spirit possession. Authors, artists, and the characters or images they create seek a personal connection to saintly figures like Villa in order to assert a wide range of possible identities. Yet they also disidentify with Villa, at times for contradictory or counterintuitive ends that may simultaneously reinforce dominant hierarchies and invoke social justice. Spiritual traditions in the borderlands are not appropriated for purely secular purposes, and the materiality of the physical does not simply pass away into the sacred. Rather than forming rigid binaries, the sacred and secular permeate each other along the border.

Perhaps most fascinating of all is the possibility that cultural production can be a conduit for popular saints' and santones' own performances of sanctity. Certainly, saints, through the repetition of their images, have always performed the sacred from beyond the grave, for such images are icons that create and transmit sanctity. As I suggest above, part of the reason these iconic images are so revered is that they are simulacra, sacred in their own right, through which humans may touch the divine. June Macklin argues for the primacy of the image above the word in the creation of saints, claiming "the less the aspiring saint said or wrote, the more likely he or she was to leap the necessary hurdles into the ranks of sainthood" (3). Of course, some of the most well-known and most revered saints left behind copious writings such as the *Confessions* of Saint Augustine and the *Autobiography* of Saint Teresa of Ávila. But the image is a more efficient and democratic means of translating and transmitting sanctity for not all devotees are able or willing to read saints' writings, but all of them can access some version of the image. Macklin's assertion creates a false dichotomy between word and image, which is especially odd in light of the link between the Word (Logos) and Christ, which many Christians consider one of the central expressions of the divine. Indeed, saints' words are subject to reproduction and appropriation in similar ways as their images, while their images are not necessarily unified. By engaging in a variety of performative practices such as posing for photographs, traveling, migrating, or participating in tours, appearing in film and newsreels, wearing certain clothing, giving speeches, engaging in hunger strikes and marches, writing communiqués, and staging interviews and press conferences (among other activities), Teresa Urrea, Pancho Villa, César Chávez, and Subcomandante Marcos all did and still do influence, inspire, and frequently create cultural production both during their lives and after their deaths. Along with Santa Muerte, these figures elucidate the importance of the symbolic in the production of secular sanctity.

Just as popular saints and santones create and perform their own narratives of secular sanctity through images, writing, or speaking, cultural production may fuse with or resemble devotional practice. While my primary focus here is on literary texts, I am most interested in the way that narrative is constructed in various forms of cultural production. All texts, whether literary, visual, or oral, tell stories and shape narratives. Meanwhile, the saints, santones, and texts I study demonstrate that spiritual practice is represented in narrative terms. Such spiritual practice allows devotees to articulate reciprocal relationships, not only with favored saints but with symbolic communities of believers that might not otherwise coalesce. In this sense, for devotees, narratives of faith reflect temporal and spatial identities that transcend the boundaries reinforced by the state or by dominant institutions. Through the fusion of devotional practices and modes of cultural production, people from all social strata are able to engage in exchanges and identify or disidentify with their favored saints and santones. At the same time, devotional practices and cultural production provide for the articulation of spatial, temporal, social, or political identities and groups. The construction of alternate spatial and temporal identities through practices such as spirit possession is especially evident during moments of crisis related to the reordering of the state, whether via revolutions or neoliberal globalization. In this sense, whether these figures are political or revolutionary leaders or whether they serve primarily as symbols of social change, the masses are able to enunciate their own social, cultural, and political realities through those saints. The connection between devotee and saint that is evident in both ritual and cultural production helps bridge the gaps left by the breakdown of civil society and the state—for many marginalized people on either side of the border—and thus provides a way for the masses to assert their own hybrid identities and narratives.

In what follows, I consider the intersections between cultural representation, devotional ritual, charisma and celebrity, and political, revolutionary, and social action in the production and performance of secular sanctity. In every case, I examine the multiple ways in which devotees, authors and artists, dominant institutions like church and state, and even the saints themselves engage with the dichotomy of secular sanctity in their assertion of various forms of identity. Thus, in chapter 1, I focus on the struggle over the contradictory representation of the nineteenth-century borderlands saint Teresa Urrea (Santa Teresa de Cabora) and the relation of that representation with the construction of different geographic, temporal, and cultural identities. Almost all of the cultural production concerning Teresa portrays her in a paradoxical manner, regarding her status as infallible saint and flawed human or her role as a migrant border crosser. Whether these texts reject or identify with Teresa, they frequently perform a kind of disidentification by enacting versions of popular devotional practices such as ecstatic worship or spirit possession, in which an author, artist, or character symbolically or literally wishes to assume—and thus define—Teresa's powers or persona. I analyze the novels *Tomóchic* by Heriberto Frías (1893), *The Astonishing Story of the Saint of Cabora* by Brianda Domecq (1990), and other texts as examples of the intersection of popular devotional practice and cultural production, emphasizing the often contentious struggle over the saint's representation as both sacred and human.

Urrea is currently better-known as a figure of cultural representation than as a venerated saint in the borderlands, and the personal relationship that so many authors and artists represent in their works is not simply a means to revive her for the present. Instead, these practices of disidentification demonstrate the contradiction of secular sanctity by shaping cultural representation as devotional ritual.

In chapter 2, I turn to twentieth-century Mexican and Chicano texts and trace the multivalent, contradictory representations of Pancho Villa as both man and myth. At once revolutionary hero, evil bandit, military genius, quintessential macho, savior of the poor and oppressed, and icon of cinema, literature, song, and mural art, Villa is also invoked as a popular saint. Virtually all of the texts that treat the general construct him as a mythic figure who is most desirable precisely because of his flawed human characteristics. To this end, he is frequently represented through forms of symbolic spirit possession, which (particularly in the name of revolutionary nationalism) may obscure his inherently ambivalent qualities. I examine Chicano playwright Luis Valdez's work *The Shrunken Head of Pancho Villa* (1964), which mediates between representations of Villa from both sides of the border. Most Mexican texts represent Villa in ambivalent fashion, yet borderlands and Chicano representations of the general are even more complicated, for they portray him both as a conduit for Mexican nationalism and as a symbol for migrant melancholia and alienation. Many characters in the play interpret Villa through the lens of dominant Mexican nationalism, and the play's emphasis on the resuscitation of Villa's fragmented remains—rather than appealing to a unified image of the general—articulates collective forms of belonging for Chicanos/as that do not solely rely on either dominant national identities or hybrid spaces.

In chapter 3, I shift from the model of the popular saint, however atypically construed, to the santón. Such a narrative break corresponds also to a shift from the revolutionary era to the period of the Chicano Movement and its aftermath (1960s–1980s) so as to focus on César Chávez, the cofounder of the UFW union, a civil rights leader and Chicano icon. Chávez is a political and social hero and he does not have a traditional religious cult, yet he is a saint-like figure—a santón— who evokes a more conventional notion of saintliness than many popular saints. Chávez drew upon official and popular spirituality, investing his political project with a sense of justice, rooted in religious morality, as well as an aura of sacrifice. His transcendent qualities are almost always emphasized, to the exclusion of his imperfect or simply ordinary human characteristics, and produce him as an agent for rigid Chicano identities. Yet Chávez's sanctity is ambivalent. It allows for the social reproduction of his political goals and also helps shape frequently inflexible Chicano identities. The reproduction of Chávez's image and ideals in the public sphere, the nonprofit sector, in education, as well as in cultural production frequently serves as a marker of the social, economic, and cultural advancement of Chicanos/as and Latinos/as. These invocations depend upon Chávez's accessibility, yet he is often represented as unattainable because he has been consolidated as a symbol of a heroic Mexican past or a symbol of ethnic assimilation. I address the tension between Chávez's canonization as an icon—whether national American or nationalist Chicano—and his role as a borderlands santón. Focusing on representations of Chávez in Margarita Cota-Cárdenas's novel *Puppet* (1985) and the Chicano-Salvadoran theater and performance group Culture Clash's play *A Bowl of Beings* (1991), I argue that both texts contend with Chávez's duality as a marker of a heroic Mexican past and a conflicted American present. These texts ultimately disidentify with the monolithic construction of Chicano/a identity associated with romanticized images of Chávez, the UFW, and the Chicano Movement. The texts complicate the idealized view of César Chávez and reveal the limits of static Chicano/a identities and nationalisms through tactics of mistranslation, irony, and parody.

In chapter 4, I examine Subcomandante Marcos, the spokesperson for the Ejército Zapatista de Liberación Nacional (EZLN; the Zapatista Army of National Liberation) and a revolutionary icon and media darling since his debut on the world stage on January 1, 1994. There is no saint's cult around Marcos; indeed, he and the EZLN vehemently reject the possibility. Yet Marcos's personality cult renders him sacred in the eyes of many. The Zapatistas' infamous black ski masks, which emphasize the group's collective nature through individual concealment and interchangeability, also produce Marcos as a secular saint or santón. Through his writing and public persona, Marcos both challenges and performs the roles of leader and santón. I examine his multiple, often paradoxical subject positions in texts such as the "Don Durito" tales and the novel he wrote with Paco Ignacio Taibo II, *Muertos incómodos (falta lo que falta)* (The Uncomfortable Dead, 2006). I contend that Marcos deploys irony and parody in order to displace a version of the leader or saint onto other characters he constructs, especially the charismatic little beetle Don Durito. At the same time, Marcos's strategic position as novice is potentially problematic, especially in his representation of indigenous linguistic patterns. To this end, I analyze the intersection between Marcos's roles as character and author as well as the tension between his roles as both leader and anti-leader. Marcos suggests that such tension points toward the possibility of sanctity in and through the masses. But while Marcos's fragmented position as character and author rejects the traditional saint model in favor of the sanctity of the multitude, the real work of Zapatismo perhaps lies beyond representation. The true sanctity of the masses, as the EZLN suggests in the Sixth Declaration of the Lacandón Jungle (2005; Marcos and Zaptistas, *Other Campaign*), is local, global, and autonomous but will not necessarily attract attention or devotees, at least in traditional ways.

In chapter 5, I return to a more traditional conception of popular sanctity, but with a twist. I examine the contemporary culture of explicitly transgressive, sinful, or lawless secular sanctity through La Santísima Muerte, the most contradictory popular saint of all. Unlike almost every other sacred figure, Santa Muerte does not manifest in a live human form but, rather, as a skeleton. She subverts the iconographic emphasis on saints' bodies and faces. As a symbol of death (both the only certainty of life and its polar opposite), she best embodies the duality between accessibility and inaccessibility that all saints represent. I argue that La Santísima Muerte is popular precisely because of her controversial and contradictory nature. Through a study of recent cultural productions such as Eva Aridjis's documentary *La Santa Muerte* (2007), the regional Sonoran television program *Relatos de Ultratumba* (2008), the narconovela *La Santa Muerte* by Homero Aridjis, and essays, crónicas, and histories by Daniel Hernández, Carlos Monsiváis, José Gil Olmos, and others, I contend that instead of functioning as an obstacle for the faithful, Santa Muerte's contradictory and unruly character allows devotees to articulate their own narratives of equality in order to embrace their own ambiguous status within society. Ultimately, Santa Muerte fills a void in the face of the failure of civil society and the state for marginalized peoples on both sides of the border. Through the embrace of secular sanctity in their worship of the death saint, migrants, impoverished barrio residents, and even criminals may establish alternative forms of spatial and temporal communities, commerce or trade, social service, and street justice. While this secular sanctity exceeds the grasp of church and state, it transforms the abject condition of subaltern groups into a double-edged sword of empowerment and menace.

Finally, in the conclusion, I consider the ways in which devotees and non-believers alike interrogate or refuse devotional practice, and what the consequences of such resistance might be. In the process, I consider the possibility that the transcendence involved in devotion could be directed away from the register of the sacred, at least as it is traditionally construed, in order to emphasize human agency. Through a brief reading of Tomás Rivera's classic novel of migration, *. . . y no se lo tragó la tierra / . . . And the Earth Did Not Devour Him*, I examine the rearticulation of devotional practice toward the production of narrative. For the migrants in the novel and for dispossessed groups in general, the construction of narrative and cultural production reflects another version of the union of sacred and human that exemplifies secular sanctity.

1 · SAINT OF CONTRADICTION

Teresa Urrea, La Santa de Cabora

In the novel *La insólita historia de la Santa de Cabora* (1990; *The Astonishing Story of the Saint of Cabora* [1998]), Mexican writer Brianda Domecq portrays Teresa Urrea, "La Santa de Cabora" of Sonora, as she is demanding entrance at the heavenly gates shortly after her death. The ensuing scene reflects the ambiguity that surrounded Urrea during her life and after her death. The gatekeeper angel and God engage in a comical debate for they cannot find Cabora, her former home, on the registry of global place names, nor can they find her name on the official list of saints: "'She said she wanted to see you, that you would know who she was if I told you she was Saint Teresa of Cabora.' 'Doesn't ring a bell. Let's see, bring me the list of saints; maybe one slipped by without my noticing. There are so many of them now!'" (*Astonishing Story* 1).[1] Muttering that there are so many saints nowadays that not even He can keep track of them, God dismisses her as an "apocryphal saint" of the kind that arise during popular rebellions on earth. He orders the angel to turn Teresa away, instructing him not to fall prey to any feminine tricks such as tears or the display of a false hymen to prove virginity. His ultimatum is this: "If she makes a fuss, ask her for her genealogy. Women can never trace their genealogy back more than two generations. Tell her we don't admit saints without genealogies" (2). Yet Teresa defies God's contempt by boldly reciting her matrilineal genealogy to herself through more than twenty generations, flaunting her illegitimate origins while asserting her right to be called a saint.

It might seem obvious that a patriarchal God would reject Teresa Urrea, for she is a secular saint who clearly flouts orthodox Catholic tradition. Domecq's representation of Teresa embraces her secular sanctity and explicitly rejects

"Teresita Urrea, la Santa Niña de Cabora." Arizona Historical Society, Tucson. Photographic Archives. Portraits: Urrea, Santa. AHS #1671.

religious hierarchy and orthodox convention. The novel reveals that Teresa's claim to sanctity is positioned against her human qualities, especially in relation to gender. Domecq demonstrates Teresa's secular sanctity portrayed primarily as an insurmountable conflict, for she is criticized as much because of her humanity as because of her sanctity. The conflict between her humanity and her sanctity is only one of many contradictions applied to her. As the anecdote from *The Astonishing Story* suggests, there has been plenty of doubt surrounding her since she was first named a living saint in 1889 in Sonora. Teresa Urrea has repeatedly been denounced or belittled for being feminine, childlike, ignorant, closely associated with indigenous people, easily manipulated, an instigator of rebellion and revolution, a scam, or a fraud. At the same time, she has been celebrated for her intelligence, spirituality, strength, prowess as a medium, healing powers, compassion toward the poor and suffering, as well as for her resistance to corrupt authorities, especially the clergy, medical doctors, and the government of Porfirio Díaz.[2]

Unlike some other popular saints and santones, Teresa was not appropriated in any way by the state or the church during her lifetime or thereafter. While the Catholic Church roundly denounced her as a heretic, she was also anathema to any conception of the nation in the eyes of the Mexican and U.S. governments. La Santa de Cabora was frequently trivialized as a curiosity rather than interpreted as a legitimate threat to the Mexican state in much of the media and publicity that circulated in Mexico and the border region during the late nineteenth and early twentieth centuries. Yet in her heyday, Teresa was taken as a symbol of political dissent and indigenous resistance and a threat to national unity on both sides of the border. Today, she remains a border-crossing, transnational icon.

In fact, Teresa Urrea is at once a popular borderlands saint, a faith healer, a literary representation, a catalyst for indigenous and peasant rebellion, a regional legend, a subject of historical research, a media darling, a performer, a celebrity, a loving daughter and mother, a feminist icon, an "early Chicana," a symbol of transnational borderlands identity, a determined self-promoter, a hero to the poor, infirm, and dispossessed, and occasionally, an intimate companion whom devotees adore and identify with (Newell 90). The many representations of this fascinating woman are frequently at odds—in their historical veracity, their range and channels of dissemination and distribution, their ability to spin her story in a lively and complex way, their emphasis on different aspects of the saint's life, and especially, their personal or symbolic claim on Teresa Urrea. As Robert McKee Irwin argues, Teresa was always subject to outside forces, a woman who, "cast into the public eye . . . , became public property, and her image took on a life of its own" (195). Likewise, James S. Griffith refers to her as a "co-opted healer" and a "woman of many roles," alluding to the many twists and turns of interpretation and appropriation that her image has undergone (43, 57). Teresa clearly manipulated her image in various ways, yet she is often misunderstood, underestimated, and dismissed. To this day she is characterized as both visionary and hysterical, often in the same breath.

Buried in an unmarked grave, Teresa Urrea was largely forgotten in Mexico and the United States after her death. She was kept alive in the Mexican national imagination only by Heriberto Frías's novel *Tomóchic* (1893) (Vanderwood, *Power of God* 306; Irwin 248). As several critics point out, Teresa was mostly forgotten even in the U.S.-Mexico borderlands where she resided for the majority of her life (in Sonora and Arizona), except for the odd local historical or editorial publication, family and community stories and legends, and one lonely chapel dedicated to her at the Santa Teresita Ranch in Cascabel, Arizona (Irwin 253–256; Griffith 61–62; Newell 103; Vanderwood, *Power of God* 306). Irwin suggests that Teresa is so difficult to pin down precisely because she is a borderlands icon, caught between two nations, multiple languages, and multiple ethnic and racial groups. As a result, until quite recently, most historical and cultural representations of La Santa de Cabora bifurcated her life into Mexican and American halves, with Mexican authors focusing on her Mexican history and Spanish-language texts, and U.S. scholars tending "to consult only English-language texts about the period following her exile to Arizona" (Irwin 256).

These national and linguistic constraints are not the only obstacle to deciphering Teresa Urrea. Her life is well documented in history, and in periodicals from both sides of the border, yet she is most widely known as a figure of literary representation. Many sources, including Domecq, indicate that Frías's novel *Tomóchic* is where they first encountered the legend of Teresa Urrea, while others argue that Domecq's *The Astonishing Story* is "the most complete and authoritative text" (Irwin 196). Domecq herself argues that "the character from the novel [*Astonishing Story*] today turns out to be much more real and alive to me," for "history has had the luxury of overlooking" the contradictions in Teresa's life (Domecq, "Teresa Urrea" 12). At the same time, *Tomóchic* has routinely been cited in editorial pieces as if it were historical truth or factual evidence— even though it is a work of fiction.[3] Irwin points out that many historians of the Tomóchic rebellion "cite [Frías] freely, as an eyewitness source, without warning that the only thing he wrote on what transpired in Tomóchic was a novel" (222). Conversely, many historians criticize Frías for factual errors they find in his narrative, and one complains that Frías attempts to "novelize" history (Sommers 20).[4] Such claims elide the fact that many historical and editorial representations have helped shape the stereotypical readings of Teresa as a delusional child, hysterical woman, or rabid seditionist. Regardless, since its publication *Tomóchic* has generally been considered the "most authoritative source on these events" (Irwin 222). Then, in recent years, Chicano author Luis Alberto Urrea has produced two "epic novels," *The Hummingbird's Daughter* (2005) and *Queen of America* (2011), in which he recounts the "true story" of his great-aunt Teresita, introducing her to a new generation of readers "from all over the world" (luisurrea .com). These examples demonstrate that history, media, and fiction are inextricably linked in any representation of Teresa Urrea. Indeed, she is an image and icon that many agree is best—and certainly most commonly—accessed through literary representation.

For all of these reasons, it is impossible and unnecessary to speculate on Teresa's true thoughts, actions, or intentions and seek to recount her history with complete accuracy. To this end, my interest in this chapter is to examine the many transformations to which Teresa Urrea's image has been subjected. I analyze her cultural representation as a secular saint who has been interpreted and appropriated from a seemingly infinite number of spiritual, political, spatial, temporal, domestic, racial, ethnic, and gender perspectives. As a result, she is inevitably portrayed in a contradictory fashion. My point is not to condemn such representations since Teresa Urrea certainly was a contradictory figure but, rather, to examine the manner in which authors, historians, artists, and scholars attempt to repudiate or resolve such contradictions. In my view, it is more compelling to consider the multiplicity of her personas by embracing her many contradictions.

The tension between truth and fiction evident in so many representations of the saint elucidates the struggle to define her and to relate her image to different identities, interests, and conditions. Various authors, historians, artists, and scholars lay claim to Teresa's image, manipulate it, position their work against it, or even identify with it, in order to articulate diverse identities. The representations and definitions of La Santa de Cabora are so intense and imbued with meaning that in many cases they not only depict popular devotional practices but even take on the characteristics of these rituals, such as communion with the saint, hearing voices from the saint, ecstatic worship, and rituals of exchange or identification that approximate spirit possession. More than one author intimates that Teresa Urrea has spoken to or touched them in some fashion. Some authors even represent themselves, or one or more of their characters, as personally called upon to research and write about the saint's life (Díaz Björkquist; Domecq; Urrea; Vanderwood *Power of God*). It is clear that these authors and artists and the characters they create both identify and disidentify with Teresa in various different ways. Conversely, other portrayals of La Santa de Cabora, like that in *Tomóchic*, position themselves completely against her, using the contradictions to condemn the saint and silence the indigenous devotees who worship her. Whether these texts reject or identify with Teresa, they frequently emphasize or enact versions of popular devotional practice such as ecstatic worship or spirit possession, in which an author, historian, artist, or character symbolically or literally wishes to assume—and thus define—Teresa's powers or persona. Nevertheless, texts like *The Astonishing Story* reveal that it is impossible to define

Teresa Urrea without embracing her multiple contradictions. Through readings of Frías's *Tomóchic*, Domecq's *Astonishing Story*, and other texts, I argue that literary and other cultural representations of Teresa Urrea emphasize popular devotional practices such as spirit possession, and I intend to demonstrate the extent to which the saint has been defined and claimed through contradiction, especially that between her sacred and human aspects. While she is routinely attacked for these qualities, they also establish the potential to articulate numerous identities and conditions not just for the saint and her devotees but for anyone who engages with her image.

La Santa de Cabora

Since all representations of Teresa Urrea's life are necessarily fictionalized to some extent, the contours of her life can only be delineated by attending to the nuances of her representation as an image and symbol. At the same time, much of the representation of Teresa hinges on intimate, firsthand knowledge of her life, much of which is subjective or incomplete. She was born Niña García Nona María Rebeca Chávez in Ocorini, Sinaloa, in October 1873, the illegitimate child of Don Tomás Urrea, a wealthy white landowner, and a poor indigenous woman named Cayetana Chávez who lived on Urrea's property (Holden 10). Teresa spent her early years in extreme poverty, until she moved to Cabora, Sonora, in 1888 with the support of her father, who recognized her and gave her his name. At Cabora, one of the household servants, a curandera (medicine woman) called Huila, taught her the arts of healing through the use of herbs and potions. In 1889 Teresa suffered a cataleptic fit or seizure that caused her to go into a coma for thirteen days. The family, believing she had died, prepared a wake, during which Teresa awoke, sat up, and announced Huila's imminent death, which indeed took place three days later (Holden 54–56). Teresa then slipped into a trance-like state for another three months. During this trance, she began her healing ministry in earnest, claiming to be inspired by visions and voices of God and the Virgin Mary. She appeared to have acquired telepathic and telekinetic powers, and she utilized a combination of touch, herbal remedies, and mixtures of soil and her own saliva or blood to achieve cures (Vanderwood, *Power of God* 169–171). Thousands of pilgrims—especially indigenous people like the local Mayo and Yaqui Indians, but also mestizo peasants and a few wealthier Mexicans—began to worship her as a saint, flocking to Cabora to see her. In accordance with her malleable multiple identities, Teresa Urrea was approached by her followers for many different reasons, including their folk Catholicism, syncretic indigenous beliefs, anti-clericism or opposition to the Catholic Church, and spiritism, "a mystic belief system in vogue at the time in Europe and the Americas" (Irwin 197). Many of the pilgrims came to Teresa not just to fulfill their spiritual hunger or to cure their physical ills but also to realize their need for political belonging on their own terms.

Many critics scorned Teresa's mystical powers and healing works, but none was more discomfited by the activities at Cabora than the Catholic Church or the Mexican government. The pilgrimages to Cabora did not sit well with President Porfirio Díaz, particularly because Teresa was known for preaching social justice and for speaking out against the church's and the state's treatment of the poor. Cabora had become a meeting place for political dissidents (Irwin 197; Domecq, "Teresa Urrea" 19). The cult of La Santa de Cabora emerged in the 1890s, in the midst of a larger conflict in Mexico between the regional margins and the national center. At this time a bevy of living saints arose in the borderlands as popular and official sentiment was turning against Porfirio Díaz.[5] The Mexican government was particularly wary of any manifestation of indigenous difference and perceived an intrinsic link between popular devotional practices and rebellion, especially in relation to the volatile border region.

Teresa publicly denied any political involvement, but she was quickly linked to peasant and indigenous rebellion (Vanderwood, *Power of God* 184). La Santa de Cabora was highly revered by the Mayo and Yaqui Indians. The Yaquis were especially tenacious and violent in both their resistance to the Mexican state and their desire to forge autonomous indigenous communities. They identified a kindred soul of resistance in Teresa, declaring her the "Queen of the Yaquis" and identifying Cabora as a prophetic place at the core of Yaqui civilization and the key to its survival (Vanderwood, *Power of God* 197–199). While the Yaquis were particularly feared for their aggressiveness, it was the Mayos who, in May 1892, attacked Navojoa, Sonora, crying "¡Viva la Santa de Cabora!" (Vanderwood, *Power of God* 199, 196).

Of even greater significance, however, was the peasant rebellion that erupted in Tomóchic, Chihuahua, in late 1891. The rebels, who wished to challenge the state's totalitarian control over their region, fought for a year against the much larger and more powerful Mexican army (Osorio 121–124). The Porfirian government immediately attributed the rebellion to the influence of La Santa de Cabora, although in reality the rebels of Tomóchic sought Teresa's benediction and counsel only after the first full-fledged attack on their town by the federal army. Inspired by their faith in Teresa's divine powers, the rebels fought on, temporarily forcing the army to retreat. Eventually, the government crushed the rebellion, massacred almost all of the Tomochitecos, and burned the entire village to the ground in December 1892. Prior to this in June 1892, immediately following the Mayo rebellion, Teresa and her father, Don Tomás, were arrested and exiled to the United States as threats to Mexican national stability.

Teresa and Tomás Urrea initially resided in Nogales, Arizona, where she continued her spiritual ministry, remaining a symbol of revolutionary potential for

Mexicans on both sides of the border. It is unclear whether she participated in it directly, but Teresa was associated with an unsuccessful raid on a customs house in Nogales, Mexico, by a group of mostly Yaqui Indians in August 1896. She also served in a symbolic capacity for the production of revolutionary propaganda against the Mexican government (Vanderwood, *Power of God* 299–300). In 1897, under pressure from both U.S. and Mexican governments, Teresa and Don Tomás moved away from the border region to Clifton, Arizona. This period marked a turn to domestic life for Teresa and, according to both her followers and her critics, the beginning of the apparent decline of her sacred powers. Against her father's wishes, in 1900 she married Guadalupe Rodríguez, a mine laborer, who tried to take her back to Mexico by force and attempted to shoot her when she resisted. He was immediately imprisoned and later hanged himself in his cell (Domecq, "Teresa Urrea" 44–46). Shaken, Teresa returned to her family, but the rift with her father could not be repaired. Perhaps as a way to establish some independence, she traveled to California after being invited by family friends to treat the sick child of a friend in San Jose (Irwin 241). While she was in the San Francisco Bay Area, she was followed by the local press. She granted interviews and appeared at the San Francisco Metropolitan Temple to "treat the sick free of charge" (Irwin 243).

As a result of these appearances, Teresa was invited by a "bamboozling petty businessman" named J. H. Suits to embark upon a U.S. national tour with an American medical company for a purported $10,000 (Vanderwood, *Power of God* 304). While Paul Vanderwood notes that the "details of the agreement cannot be verified," it is clear that the San Francisco appearances and national tour mark not only a "shift in Urrea's image from political dissident to popular performer" but a turn away from her sacred persona (Vanderwood, *Power of God* 304; Irwin 244). There are mixed opinions as to whether her travels across the United States distanced her from or further connected her to her Mexican and indigenous followers. The tour took her to San Francisco, St. Louis, New York, and Los Angeles, where the *Los Angeles Times* reported that the "magnetic young woman from the South" was "daily besieged" by Mexican pilgrims who came to see her from all over the borderlands (15 Dec. 1902, 8). Luis D. León suggests that she used the tour to extend her ties to the *mexicano/a* communities on both sides of the border, especially in her capacity as a prophet to speak for the "poor and oppressed . . . claiming a religious poetics as if she brought a new message from God" (*La Llorona's* 148–149). However, Irwin notes that she was "now part of a business enterprise that took her to glamorous modern cities" with an audience comprised mostly of "Anglophone curiosity seekers" (245).

Teresa claimed her intention was to use her travels to determine the source of her healing powers, but the fact that she was allegedly paid a large sum to tour the country, where before she had rejected payment of any kind for her cures, and that she was becoming a bona fide celebrity rather than a humble vessel of God, surely must have resonated—not altogether positively—with her devotees. While the press continued to follow Teresa, with several articles appearing in the *Los Angeles Times*, the *New York Journal*, and other periodicals, her business career was ultimately brief and her popularity waned in the early years of the twentieth century (Vanderwood, *Power of God* 305). During this time, she fell in love with John Van Order, the much younger son of a family friend who had been serving as her interpreter on the national tour. Tomás Urrea died in 1902, but Teresa continued on tour (Irwin 246). Teresa and Van Order had two daughters, but by the time Teresa returned to Clifton in 1904, the lovers had parted ways. In Clifton she used her earnings from the medical company tour to help build a hospital. She died on January 11, 1906, of tuberculosis at the age of thirty-three (Domecq, "Teresa Urrea" 46).

Sacred and Human

Like the other popular saints and santones examined in this project, Teresa embodies secular sanctity, reflecting the tension between human and divine. Her sanctity and humanity are frequently characterized as being in conflict with each other and are thus both called into question. The doubt stems from many factors, such as her gender, her mestizo identity with its implicitly violent origins (Tomás Urrea may have raped her indigenous mother), her transgression of social class barriers, her connection to peasant and indigenous rebellion, her status as an exile, her domestic life, and her role as a performer. Teresa is a model for women's agency at a time when their options were very limited, especially if they came from origins as inauspicious as hers, and she is routinely stripped of any agency through being represented—by the state, the Catholic Church, and certain historians and critics—as an innocent child, a victim, or a lunatic. La Santa de Cabora's spiritual and revolutionary powers are frequently displaced because of her close association with folk belief and indigenous people, which, from the perspective of the state and elites, are inherently coded as ignorant.

Even some of her closest supporters tended to infantilize her. For example, Teresa is portrayed as a pawn for the revolutionary agenda of men such as Lauro Aguirre, a friend of the Urrea family and a well-known spiritist and journalist, who saw great potential in her fame and following to support his anti-Porfirian revolutionary cause (Vanderwood, *Power of God* 183–184). Aguirre was convinced that Teresa was in fact a medium, with spirits inhabiting her body, directing her actions, and granting her visions and the power to cure. Many sources suggest that Aguirre took advantage of Teresa's celebrity to incite political dissent against the government of Porfirio Díaz and possibly manipulated her into participating in revolutionary activities (Vanderwood, *Power of God* 183–184).

La Santa de Cabora is often portrayed as a relic, especially in relation to the supposedly ignorant peasants and indigenous people who worshipped her. In fact, Teresa attracted media attention from the moment she began to be venerated as a living saint and faith healer in Cabora. Many of these reports treated her as a curiosity or a freak show, or they focused exclusively on her threatening revolutionary potential or simply dismissed her altogether (Irwin 243; Vanderwood, *Power of God* 175). Time and again, Teresa Urrea is portrayed as an ignorant vessel—or a victim of others' demands for saintly counsel, faith healing, entertainment, or revolutionary action—rather than as the agent of any of these.

Despite the fact that she is frequently underestimated or belittled in historical, cultural, and media representation, Teresa authoritatively claimed agency over her own life and image. She insisted repeatedly that she was not a saint, and she steadfastly refused to accept payment for her services during most of her spiritual ministry. Paul Vanderwood argues that "she disavowed such titles and insisted that she was no saint but had only received special powers from the Divine" (*Power of God* 171). Irwin cites an article of July 27, 1900, in the *San Francisco Examiner*, where Teresa describes her healing powers: "I believe God has placed me here as one of his instruments to do good" (242). Nevertheless, she also performed—and certainly embraced—her own sanctity. Whether she was conscious of it or not, Teresa Urrea engaged in performative spectacle through her preaching, curing, performing miracles, holding meditative trances, speaking in tongues, receiving pilgrims at Cabora, Nogales, and elsewhere, traveling with the American national tour, providing interviews, and posing for pictures. She even urged her followers to believe in her more ardently in order to achieve particularly difficult cures. She clearly manipulated the gender stereotypes she was subject to by virtue of her fluctuating and contradictory persona, for she often shifts between the roles of victim and agent in literary, cultural, historical, and media representation.

According to Domecq, there is enough proof to suggest that Teresa was a primary participant in the so-called pre-revolutionary activities that developed in the decades before the beginning of the Mexican Revolution. Apart from the raid on the Nogales customs house, these activities included the publication of Lauro Aguirre's political treatise "¡Tomóchic! ¡Redención!" and the "Plan restaurador de la Constitución y reformista," a series of proposed revisions and amendments to the Mexican constitution, which, among other things, called for equal rights for women and men, regardless of racial or class background (Domecq, "Teresa Urrea" 12). Teresa Urrea is listed as co-author on these documents. However, as several critics suggest, it is impossible to determine if Teresa really had a voice in these actions or if Aguirre was speaking for her (Griffith 52; Irwin 230).[6] Nevertheless, it is clear that Teresa's spiritual powers transcend traditional devotional practices and signal political dissent against the state. As Vanderwood argues, "if she did not help to plan and finance the revolts, she surely inspired many who joined them" (*Power of God* 302). This dissent occurs not only through the assertion of regional and transnational identities such as indigenous rights or migrant subjectivity but also through the reformation of Mexican national identity, as proposed in the "Plan restaurador de la Constitución y reformista." Whether Teresa Urrea was personally involved in these actions and writings or her cult merely served as a catalyst for subversive events, she was clearly implicated in sedition against the Mexican government, even after she and her father were exiled to the United States.

Teresa Urrea has certainly been represented in myriad ways since she was first feted as a living saint in Cabora, and her contradictory image is alternately restrictive and productive. At times, she has both been confined by her sanctity and denied her human attributes. La Santa de Cabora's revolutionary activities, her femininity and domesticity, and her independence and agency have motivated scholars, journalists, writers, critics, and devotees alike to question her sanctity, even though these traits are often the very ones that inspired her followers during her life and continue to spark cultural, historical, and editorial attention. In the media and other historical and cultural representations, her supernatural powers were often stereotypically attributed to hysteria or "female problems." Teresa's human characteristics—especially those associated with her gender—potentially compromise her sanctity, yet they also contribute to her being received and represented as a popular saint. In many ways, her femininity and fallibility are crucial elements of her sanctity for, like all saints, her body is the vehicle through which her sanctity is transmitted, both literally and symbolically. Thus, pilgrims claimed that La Santa de Cabora's body and bodily fluids emitted a perfumed scent. Her miraculous hands were celebrated not just for their healing touch but as objects of veneration in their own right and were featured prominently in many images of the saint (Vanderwood, *Power of God* 169). Many of Teresa's followers emphasized her childlike femininity not in order to disparage her but, rather, to get close to her. Devotees regarded Teresa in personal, intimate terms, addressing her by pet names like Teresita, La Niña de Cabora (the girl from Cabora), or simply *la niña* or *niñita* (little child). She was revered for her warmth, compassion, and accessibility (Vanderwood, *Power of God* 161). As a secular saint, Teresa Urrea's sanctity and humanity have always been intertwined, yet many writers and critics have attempted to dissociate them. This fundamental contradiction sparks interest, rejection, and often identification with the saint that still resonate to the present day.

Heriberto Frías's *Tomóchic*

Teresa Urrea's cult and image were widely disseminated throughout the borderlands and beyond in newspaper articles in dailies such as *El Monitor Republicano, El Universal* and *La Ilustración Espírita* (Mexico City), *El Imparcial* (Guaymas,

Sonora), *El Fronterizo* (Tucson), the *San Francisco Examiner*, the *Los Angeles Times*, and the *New York Times.* Her legend was truly cemented by the publication of the novel *Tomóchic* by Heriberto Frías, however. No representation of La Santa de Cabora has been as historically important and well-known, especially in Mexico. *Tomóchic* inspired many historical, literary, and cultural responses, and many texts explicitly position themselves in relation to the novel (Aguirre and Urrea; Domecq *Astonishing Story*; Urrea).

The novel was first published anonymously in installments in the Mexico City newspaper *El Demócrata* in 1893 and was extremely controversial, especially because it was critical of the Díaz regime and treated both the peasant rebels and the federal army in relatively favorable terms, though it also at different times criticized both groups (Saborit 178).[7] Frías narrates the story of the 1892 rebellion, and the capture and destruction of the Chihuahuan town of Tomóchic, from the perspective of the Mexican army. He was a sublieutenant in the Mexican federal army and fought in the campaign against the peasants, and he relates the events through the character of Miguel Mercado, an army officer in the Ninth Battalion. The details of this uprising have been well documented elsewhere. Suffice it to say that the Tomóchic rebellion was a greater threat and embarrassment to the Mexican government than any other uprising in the borderlands to date.

This is partly due to the millenarian character of the rebellion, which, as Vanderwood argues, is implicitly linked to revolution, for "any vision that juxtaposes the promise of a better world against the present reality is an invitation to originate [revolution]" ("Tomoches" 204). Thus, in September 1892, violence erupted in Tomóchic after the villagers renounced their fidelity to the Catholic Church and federal government in the name of God and La Santa de Cabora (Griffith 52). The mestizo and criollo (white) townspeople were renowned for their "sense of independence" and their skill at warfare, honed during years of battle against indigenous tribes like the Apaches, and they shocked the much larger and better-equipped Mexican army by successfully routing their troops with cries of "¡Viva la Santísima de Cabora!" (Vanderwood, *Power of God* 116, 237). The *tomoches*' triumph was short-lived, however, for the federal army moved with a vengeance to lay siege to the town. By October 26, the army had pushed most of the townspeople into the village church, which they burned along with everyone inside and shot those who managed to get out. On October 29, 1892, the last surviving villagers—including the leader of the rebellion, Cruz Chávez, and his brothers Manuel and David—were driven out of their barracks and shot (Vanderwood, *Power of God* 276–277). Destroyed and pillaged by the federal army, Tomóchic was left in smoldering ruins.

The novel *Tomóchic* illustrates the general instability of the borderlands, emphasizing that rebellion could easily spread to other parts of Mexico or to the United States, implicitly carrying disorderly peasants and indigenous peoples with it. Indeed, the borderlands have had a history of political instability since the Spanish colonial period and have been geographically, politically, and culturally marginalized territory since before the topographical borderline and the nations it bisects even existed. As a focal point for fluctuating citizenship, the borderlands have routinely been characterized as a threat to national cohesion on both sides of the line, while their rugged geography, underdeveloped infrastructure, and fluid points of entry and exit (at least during the late nineteenth and early twentieth centuries) became synonymous with the people who lived there, especially the indigenous groups and mestizos famous for their fierce independence. The Treaty of Guadalupe Hidalgo (1848) and the Gadsden Purchase (1853), which established the present boundary between Mexico and the United States, were meant to provide freedom of movement and choice for Mexicans "now established in territories previously belonging to Mexico . . . [to be] free to continue where they now reside, or to return at any time to the Mexican Republic." These laws were seldom honored, however, and many of the inhabitants of the borderlands were never considered citizens of either nation.[8]

At the same time, the scandalous bloody events of the Tomóchic rebellion piqued the interest of Mexicans throughout the republic, and curiosity about the uprising crossed over to the U.S. side of the border as well. Historian Antonio Saborit asserts that the events of Tomóchic "are situated within the so-called appearance of the North in the history of Mexico" (14). The time was ripe for cosmopolitan Mexicans to pay attention to the borderlands, which had generally been considered either a sleepy backwater or a hotbed of indigenous rebellion. Saborit points out that, during the last decade of the nineteenth century, the residents of Mexico City entertained themselves with tales in the press of fantastic and violent occurrences from the seemingly lawless border region—stories of savage Indian tribes characterized by their scalping and thievery, of mystical living saints such as Teresa Urrea, and of indigenous and peasant rebellions (14–15). Yet the Mexican government still viewed the borderlands and its inhabitants as obstacles to national unity and, in the wake of the Tomóchic rebellion, stepped up regulation of this unruly area. Frías's novel nominally supports and occasionally even praises the rebels of Tomóchic, yet it also plays a part in regulating the borderlands to conform to a Mexican national identity.

Tomóchic is a border novel as well as a touchstone of Mexican literary history. The struggle for national construction and unity in both Mexico and the United States was waged in large part at the borderlands, for the wars against indigenous groups such as the Apaches and Yaquis, the Mexican Revolution, and the subsequent influx of Mexican immigrants into the United States, all centered on the border region. Both geographically and metaphorically, Mexico and the United States were shaped through their margins. Frías's novel reflects the fluidity of border crossing and its threat to national cohesion on both sides of the border in the late nineteenth century, particularly for marginalized groups like the indigenous people and the devotees of La Santa de Cabora. Frías ultimately condemns such groups and rejects regional difference in favor of Mexican national unity, yet his novel *Tomóchic* can be considered a borderlands text that provides a glimpse of the mobility of local groups and the fluidity of the region in general. It is also important to remember that, by the time *Tomóchic* was written, in 1893, Teresa and Tomás Urrea had been living in exile in Arizona for about a year. Attention to the novel and the rebellion itself must have been rather limited in most of the United States at the time, but the events of Tomóchic and Teresa Urrea's purported role in them surely resonated throughout the U.S.-Mexico borderlands.

The Irredeemable Saint

Even though so many authors, critics, and historians discuss Teresa Urrea's role in *Tomóchic* and several indicate that they first discovered the saint in its pages, at first glance, La Santa de Cabora seems to be nothing more than an afterthought in the novel. Teresa Urrea does not actually appear as a character in *Tomóchic*, and we never hear her voice. Instead, she exists primarily through images, gossip, and secondhand knowledge, not only for Miguel Mercado and the federal army but also for her peasant and indigenous devotees. In his representation of the saint, Frías never seems to take her seriously. He portrays her as a hysterical lunatic or a silly, misguided little girl who is easily taken advantage of by others. At the same time, he implies that she is the inspiration and catalyst for the Tomóchic rebellion, and at one point he explicitly cites her "militant opposition to the Porfirian government" and her capacity to "foment rebellion" (137).[9]

Frías appears to relegate Teresa Urrea to the background of his narrative, but the action centers on her image and symbol. Indeed, La Santa de Cabora's specter permeates the entire novel. Her presence in *Tomóchic* is especially significant when we consider how closely Frías associates her with the peasant rebels and indigenous people who worship her. She strikes awe in the hearts of the army and devotees alike with just the mention of her name or a glimpse of her image. Even though the protagonist Miguel Mercado thinks of her as a deluded or manipulated child, he spends a fair amount of time thinking about her and listening to stories about her (Frías 11–12, 22–25, 136–137). While the secondhand nature of information about the saint—and frequently, about the rebels—stands in curious contrast to the novel's standing as a firsthand eyewitness account and erstwhile historiographical source, such a contrast emphasizes Teresa Urrea's role as a transferable representation and image. Ultimately, Frías's treatment of this image is utterly ambivalent.

Miguel Mercado first encounters the saint as he listens to the chatter of a group of *soldaderas*, soldier women who accompany the federal army into battle as cooks, nurses, and lovers and who frequently also fight alongside the men. He is repulsed by the soldaderas, "those dirty, dusty women, in rags . . . wild human dogs . . . Miguel was fearful and admiring of them; they inspired pity and horror in him. They seemed repugnant to him" (Frías 11). Although these women are inexorably alien to Mercado, and he is at once disgusted and fascinated by them, he listens eagerly to their gossip about La Santa de Cabora: "Just think . . . that Teresita herself blesses the rifles, and every shot they [the Tomóchic rebels] fire is another man dead, and that the *gringos* have given them so many arms. . . . So many! Be still my heart!" (12). Mercado's characterization of the soldaderas as threatening, yet exotic, sets the tone for his eventual condemnation of Teresa Urrea and her rebel devotees. Yet he also presumes that the peasant soldier women have intimate knowledge of the Tomóchic rebels and of La Santa de Cabora by virtue of their social class. In reality, the soldaderas are relying on secondhand knowledge, just as he does, and their speech is peppered with emotional outbursts and fantastic scenarios rather than eyewitness accounts. Mercado dismisses the soldier women's excitability as proof of their peasant status, but their stories trouble him, and he frets about the "audacity" of the *tomoches*, who, because of their familiarity with the mountainous terrain and their ability to discover the army's plans, were able to ambush another battalion and steal all of their munitions (12). It seems that Mercado is only capable of managing the stories about Teresa Urrea and the rebels either by automatically dismissing them or by taking them at face value. Conversely, the soldaderas and their foot soldier companions understand and utilize these stories for many different ends. One man wryly declares, with irony: "Well, why should we leave? . . . They'll [the rebels] kill us right away . . . instead of going and going . . . and then dying like goats!" (12). Another declares, with honor: "They [the rebels] might have defeated the Fifth Batallion but the Ninth was very different!" (12). The peasant soldiers of the Mexican army are able to shift the meaning of these stories and reveal their ambivalence about their marginalized status in the federal army, through humor or by appropriating the army's own code of loyalty. In this sense, the soldiers demonstrate the malleability and transferability of the saint's image, which Mercado cannot grasp.

Frías remains conflicted about Teresa Urrea throughout the novel, attempting to control her image even as he highlights its powers of circulation and transposability. He suggests that La Santa de Cabora is an unwilling catalyst of rebellion, arguing that she is merely a "poor girl" and "tender creature whose hysteria produce[s] true cures in many nervous people," whose insistence that she is not a saint falls on deaf ears, and who has been exploited by "political ambitions" to become a "banner of protest and combat" (23). Frías further condemns the villagers of Tomóchic for misunderstanding Teresa Urrea, but he saves his highest criticism for those who use her to support their basest urges. Such is the case of José Carranza, who proclaims himself "San José" after traveling on a pilgrim-age to Cabora to seek a cure from Teresa (25). When La Santa de Cabora casu-ally mentions that Carranza resembles Saint Joseph, a maid in her household overhears "a few words" of the conversation and announces that he is the saint incarnate (25). In his new role as San José, Carranza proclaims himself "Father of the Holy Trinity" and decrees an unholy incestuous relation between his wife, his vile brother, Bernardo, and his daughter, Julia. Miguel Mercado attributes the incest to the ignorance of the Tomóchic villagers, manifest in the defective morality of the millenarian movement led by La Santa de Cabora. But while Bernardo Carranza's incestuous relationship with his niece Julia is certainly immoral, the unfortunate episode has nothing to do with Teresa Urrea's spiritual powers. Instead, it is based on misunderstanding, rumor, and abuse, for it derives equally from the gossipy rumors spread by the maid, from José Carranza's mega-lomania, and from Bernardo Carranza's lust for his niece.

Elsewhere, Frías suggests that Teresa's image assumes a life of its own, thus escaping the bounds of his authorial control. As he contemplates the possible causes of the rebellion, for example, Frías focuses on the mystical, transcendent power of her image: "Suddenly, a hot gust of religious fanaticism blows and La Santa de Cabora's name is uttered with veneration, and her miracles are nar-rated in a thousand ways, with medieval exaggeration. La Santa de Cabora!" (23). Frías's attention to the powerful, sudden gust of religious fanaticism car-rying the saint's name and circulating stories about her "narrated in a thousand ways" reflects the spontaneous, autonomous nature of her representation. Thus, even if La Santa de Cabora's history is described by her devotees in exaggerated, "medieval" or primitive terms, or if her miraculous works are misrepresented or exploited, the multiplicity of her images exceeds Frías's frequently negative attitude toward her. While Frías's dismissive, condescending representation of Teresa Urrea's transferable image is perhaps meant to malign her and her devo-tees, it also demonstrates the extent of her reach and importance. At one point in the novel, Teresa Urrea literally appears in the form of an image, a small picture of the saint found by a soldier in the rubble of the burned church of Tomóchic. The soldier happily informs Mercado that he was able to barter this "treasure of Tomóchic" for some rare, coveted cognac from one of the saint's devotees, a Pima Indian who was working for the federal army as a bodyguard. In the eyes of the soldier, this trade was "good business," if implicitly unequal, for both par-ties (Frías 136). The soldier notes that it would have been better to capture La Santa de Cabora alive, but the image turns out to be much more valuable to him than the saint herself because it is transferable, and he readily exchanges it for the cognac (136).

In the end, Frías seems uncertain as to whether Teresa Urrea is a dangerous woman capable of manipulating the ignorant rebels of Tomóchic, a simple child who is victimized by the villagers, or a "fine instrument . . . managed in the shadows by hidden hands" (136). Throughout the novel, Frías denies Teresa Urrea agency over her sacred and human qualities. Even though he briefly alludes to La Santa de Cabora's revolutionary activism, discussing her opposition to the Díaz regime and the fact that she continued her revolutionary crusade even after she was exiled to the United States, this history is relegated to a footnote. The possibility that Teresa Urrea could have been both a political actor and a sacred miracle-worker never enters into Frías's narrative.

Nevertheless, Frías emphasizes that her image takes on a life of its own through circulation and transferability. The saint's image is certainly integral to the popular devotional practices portrayed in the novel. These include the fantastic, gossipy tales of La Santa de Cabora's miraculous works that circulate among the characters, pilgrimages to Cabora, the *tomoches'* and indigenous peoples' identification of Teresa Urrea as the patron saint of their region, the exchange of images of the saint, and even the reprehensible simulacrum of the holy family that "San José" Carranza establishes with his brother, wife, and daughter. Frías criticizes many of these rituals, especially the incestuous relationships within the Carranza family, and he frequently disdains the rebels' and indigenous peoples' displays of faith in La Santa de Cabora. He certainly does not identify with Teresa Urrea, while characters like Miguel Mercado seem to engage with her primarily as a fascinating yet threatening curiosity. Yet Frías also rearticulates popular devotional practices and beliefs like those associated with the saint, especially through Mercado's relationship with Julia.

Part of the novel's lasting appeal is that it nominally supports the peasant rebellion and the rebels themselves, even though it ultimately deems them too great of a threat to national stability. The narrator praises the rebels primarily for their bravery, their loyalty to each other and their cause, and their steadfast faith in La Santa de Cabora. In addition to being credited with these desirable characteristics, the rebels are portrayed as worthy of national assimilation because of their racial/ethnic background. Frías specifically identifies them as creoles or mestizos, which distances them from the indigenous hordes surrounding them, especially the brutal, nomadic Apaches. The rebels are far more loyal than the Mexican army, for they never defect and prefer to die rather than surrender, as leader Cruz Chávez declares: "we will not surrender. Not until Our Father takes our souls will Satan's soldiers have our bodies!" (Frías 126). Finally, unlike the army, "The chivalrous sons of the mountains did not kill women!" (86). Frías definitely romanticizes and idealizes the peasant rebels, yet, as in his representation of Teresa Urrea, he frequently portrays them as ignorant, insane, or unruly. Mercado's admiration of the rebels disappears the moment they defeat his troop: "A handful of barbaric, stupid children of the mountains of Chihuahua, defeating a beautiful national army brigade!" (76). The rebels are redeemable only as long as their difference is manageable. Characters such as Mercado often assume many of the same apparently barbaric customs—including devotional beliefs and rituals—that they disparage in the rebels, though they mold them to their own purposes.

Perhaps as a reflection of his obsessive fascination with Teresa Urrea, Mercado relates to Julia, his *tomoche* love interest, in spiritual, almost transcendental terms. At the same time, he is guilty of raping her, which places him on the same level as her detested uncle. Mercado is captivated by her grace and gentility from the moment he sees her, though he focuses ardently on her "dark skin" as an exotic marker of difference (Frías 19). Their relationship is fatally flawed from the beginning, not because of their racial or class differences but because of the way Mercado exploits the religious fanaticism he perceives in the *tomoches*. When Miguel discovers Julia's shameful secret of incest and abuse, he is horrified but finds himself even more attracted to her. Despite his shock, he lusts after her beautiful face, naked arms, and dark neck. However, he consistently describes her as virginal and saintly, calling her "a girl saint, by a divine miracle," in a manner not unlike his characterization of Teresa Urrea (Frías 29). Mercado later invokes the very same religious language to lure Julia to him as her vile uncle does, proclaiming, "On my honor, I love you, I swear by God's great power. . . . You are my woman . . . God wills it!" (Frías 42). Not only does Mercado portray the rape as an extension of God's will, he reinscribes Julia as a saint in order to justify their relationship, imagining the nuptials of "the Virgin of Tomóchic with Miguel the hero" in an echo of the language of the cults of both the Virgin of Guadalupe and La Santa de Cabora (Frías 83).

The reference to Julia as a "girl saint," proclaimed "by a divine miracle," is surely no accident. Miguel Mercado's description of Julia is virtually identical to many of the descriptions of Teresa Urrea in the novel. Like La Santa de Cabora, who is regarded by Mercado as "that nervous creature, vibrant and sweet, sweet and tough," Julia is a sweet, graceful, sensitive, and beautiful child who is also highly emotional and volatile (Frías 136). While both Julia and Teresa are excessively feminized and infantilized, both retain threatening qualities. As one of the ignorant, unruly villagers of Tomóchic, Julia is acceptable to Mercado as a lover and potential wife only if she is reconfigured as a virgin and a saint. In his abuse of her, Mercado is just as barbaric and megalomaniacal as the villagers he condemns. His twisted claim on Julia draws upon the language of ecstatic worship and even spirit possession as he declares the girl his by the grace of God. In this manner, Mercado usurps popular devotional practices to rearticulate Teresa Urrea's image for his own nefarious purposes.

In the end, Julia escapes from Mercado's possessive clutches only through death, as she perishes along with the other Tomóchic rebels during the final battle. While the army burns down the church where the rebels have gathered for their last stand, the two sides exchange "vivas" (Long live . . .), as the rebels' declarations of "Long live the great power of God! Long live Santa Teresa of Cabora!" are answered by the army's cries of "Long live the government! Long live the nation united!" (Frías 114). The rebels' implicitly separatist declaration of their faith in God and Teresa Urrea is silenced by the authority of the government and national unity. In Julia's last moments, she too proclaims "Long live the great power of God!" choosing love for Tomóchic over love for Mercado and Mexico (Frías 150). While Frías portrays Julia's death as a choice, such agency is only permissible through the army's resounding victory over the rebels. Ultimately, both the rebels and Teresa Urrea are nothing more than a novelty for Frías, simultaneously romanticized and denounced. But while Frías may not really take La Santa de Cabora seriously or consider the rebels a true threat to Mexican national stability, the circulating, transferable image of the saint, symbolized by the uncontrollable gust of religious fanaticism that sweeps up the people of Tomóchic, remains.

Images of a Saint in Exile

In the summer of 1892, La Santa de Cabora was "the talk of the town" in the border town of Nogales, Arizona, where she and her father began their life in exile (Vanderwood, *Power of God* 294). Devotees and curiosity seekers descended upon the city to lay eyes on her and witness her faith healing and holy works, and a rash of media attention followed (Irwin 222). Whereas Frías's *Tomóchic* and many editorial reports had been conflicted over Teresa Urrea's identity, from the time she was exiled to the United States her life was defined by "a mix of show business, revolution, and religiosity" (Vanderwood, *Power of God* 295). Naturally, controversy still surrounded Teresa Urrea, and new debates coalesced around her, as some Anglos considered her cult an example of ignorant Mexican and indigenous beliefs, while others (mostly Mexicans, but also some Anglos) were quite sympathetic to her position as a persecuted exile. Many Anglos were especially incensed when Mexican officials crossed into the United States to harass her and pressure the Urreas to move further away from the border (Irwin 224; Domecq, "Teresa Urrea" 33). Regardless of whether public interest turned more on Teresa Urrea's political activism or her spiritual powers, no one could deny that she was now a true celebrity.

In many ways the multiplicity of her personas was finally acknowledged in exile, and her celebrity status produced new contradictions in her public image. Vanderwood indicates that representations of the saint were frequently shaped by a "sensationalist press and the bombast of politicians" (*Power of God* 295). While Frías's *Tomóchic* was a fictional eyewitness account of the rebellion and the rise of the cult of La Santa de Cabora, many newspaper articles of the time

emphasized the fantastic, lurid nature of the saint's cult. There are few existing published interviews with Teresa Urrea. The longest and most well-known
is in a feature story in the *San Francisco Examiner* from July 27, 1900, but most
newspaper accounts of the saint rely on secondhand quotes (Irwin 242).[10] The
Urreas moved frequently during their first few years of exile and often visited
and even took up residence for short periods in Yaqui settlements throughout
Arizona, where Teresa ministered to the sick and sympathized with the plight
of the Indians who had been displaced as she had (Vanderwood, *Power of God*
295). But many more residents of the borderlands (whether Spanish- or English-
speaking) would have encountered La Santa de Cabora through newspaper
accounts, if they could read, or through images or hearsay of the sort featured in
Tomóchic rather than through personal encounters. In this context, the image of
the popular saint or the media representation functions as a personal encounter
that provides access to the sacred, following Peter Brown's theorization of saint's
graves and associated relics as privileged sites that unite the human and divine
(3). Devotees and curiosity seekers in the borderlands undoubtedly sought La
Santa de Cabora's image and representation as a way to access her sacred aura, to
approach a celebrity, or simply to gawk at her. As before, the struggle for control
over the representation of Teresa Urrea's image was most intensely conducted
through literary and cultural production. In exile, it seems, her image was even
more unmoored from its already tenuous foundations as a marker of regional
identity, popular spirituality, peasant and indigenous insurgency, or social justice. Teresa Urrea continued to signify all of these things, but her image was now
further subject to the fickle ebb and flow of celebrity and national citizenship on
the U.S. side of the border.

The long-standing tension between truth and fiction in the representation of
La Santa de Cabora intensified as Lauro Aguirre (with Teresa Urrea as co-author)
published his treatise "¡Tomóchic! ¡Redención!" in installments in the newspaper *El Independiente* of El Paso, Texas, in 1896. Aguirre specifically distanced
his text from Frías's novel, asserting that it was "not the novel full of falsehoods
written by Heriberto Frías" (Aguirre and Urrea 191). More importantly, as Irwin
emphasizes, the Aguirre text is not a novel but, rather, a "'historico-philosophical
narration' addressing the 'legendary and unequalled deeds of Tomóchic'" (Irwin
228; Aguirre and Urrea 191). Despite its claim to historical and philosophical
veracity, however, this history is based on legend. In fact, rather than conceal his
ideological bent, Aguirre embraces it from the outset and situates his text as a
revolutionary treatise or propaganda. The text opens with an apocalyptic narrative, reminiscent of the Book of Revelation, referring to the "heroic Tomochitecos" as "precursors of a new era" (Aguirre and Urrea 107). Aguirre then provides
an account of Teresa Urrea's life story, emphasizing her role as a healer and a
saint and her support of the poor and dispossessed. "¡Tomóchic! ¡Redención!"

portrays Teresa Urrea as modest and steadfast, asserting that, even though she did not consider herself a saint, the rebels of Tomóchic were justified in worshipping her as opposed to the corrupt, hierarchical Catholic Church (Aguirre and Urrea 110, 124–126). In the text Teresa's spiritual biography is inseparable from the history of the Tomóchic rebellion, and sacred and secular are intertwined in the name of social justice and millenarian reckoning alike. One of the most interesting aspects of Aguirre's text is the way he personalizes it, inserting himself into its history and, as Irwin indicates, making himself "a protagonist of his version of events" (229). Of course, Aguirre knew the Urrea family intimately, but like Teresa herself, he had never been to Tomóchic and did not participate in the rebellion (Irwin 229), yet he symbolically claims the *tomoches'* story as his own: "I was a prisoner. The rages and persecutions of the most monstrous of tyrants that mankind has ever known weighed on me, because I had committed the crime of telling the truth" (Aguirre and Urrea 93). Aguirre intimates that literary representation can be construed as a "crime," and he asserts the freedom to tell the story of Teresa Urrea and the rebellion of Tomóchic, symbolically possessing this history through narrative authority. It is unclear whether the saint truly co-authored the text, and it is telling that she is referred to only in the third person, while Aguirre represents his own narration in the first person (Irwin 230). Even though "¡Tomóchic! ¡Redención!" would never reach a significant readership, the impulse toward narrative personalization as part of the struggle for control of Teresa Urrea's image continued after her death.

Symbolic Devotion

The personalization of La Santa de Cabora's image—that is, the link between the personal histories of authors, artists, and the characters they create and the saint's image—deepened after her death in 1906, though her influence waned over the course of many decades. Frías's *Tomóchic* has consistently been read as part of the canon of Mexican national literature. Meanwhile, many historians, both Mexican and American, have tackled the Tomóchic rebellion, and all discuss La Santa de Cabora to some extent in their analyses.[11] But despite the attention given to *Tomóchic* and to the rebellion itself, full-length representations of Teresa Urrea's life and work were scarce until Domecq published *The Astonishing Story* in 1990. William Curry Holden published the only book-length biography of the saint, *Teresita*, in 1978, but as Irwin notes, many scholars have criticized his archival research and his somewhat patronizing portrayal of the saint (258). Religious studies scholars have situated Teresa Urrea as part of the history of popular spirituality and living saints in the borderlands, while Chicano/a studies scholars have traced the saint's influence for Chicanos/as.[12] Scholars like Carlos Larralde fashion Teresa Urrea into a transnational icon of Chicano/a resistance. But while

Larralde declares the saint and her cult "part of our Chicano heritage" (59), other scholars such as Gillian Newell cite Teresa Urrea's failure to resonate as a source of active popular devotion among Chicanos/as, emphasizing her status as primarily a figure of academic scholarship (103). Newell is correct that Teresa Urrea has not been widely interpreted as a Chicana icon, and that most Chicanos/as, even in Arizona and the borderlands, do not worship her as a saint today. To the extent that La Santa de Cabora is known at all among most Chicanos/as, it is through literary production or scholarly research. Those living in Arizona and the borderlands may be familiar with Teresa Urrea through family and community stories or local history. In my view, however, this emphasis on tangible, active devotional practices and communities is beside the point. Instead, I am interested in the ways that Teresa Urrea's image circulates through literary and cultural production and, in the process, produces new forms of symbolic devotional practice through which to understand the saint's many contradictions.

In the past twenty years or so, there has been a resurgence of critical scholarship and literary and cultural production focusing on Teresa Urrea. Most recently, Luis Alberto Urrea has published the long novels *The Hummingbird's Daughter* and *Queen of America*, which taken together form a borderlands saga that unites La Santa de Cabora's all too frequently bisected Mexican and American life. *The Hummingbird's Daughter* ends as Teresa and her father are exiled to "great, dark North America," while *Queen of America* opens on "the other side . . . the United States" (*Hummingbird* 495; *Queen* 11). In Urrea's portrait of the saint, the moment of exile, the border crossing, is the crux of her story. *The Hummingbird's Daughter* was the winner of the 2006 Kiriyama Pacific Rim Prize and has been published in Spanish (as *La hija de la Chuparrosa*), but it remains to be seen what impact these novels will have on Teresa Urrea's critical and cultural reception on both sides of the border.

At this point, by far the most significant literary intervention into the life and image of Teresa Urrea is *The Astonishing Story* by Brianda Domecq, whose essays and novel interrogate previous representations of the saint especially those, like *Tomóchic*, that characterize her as a naïve lunatic. Domecq describes her initial discovery of the saint in the pages of *Tomóchic* as the awakening of a personal obsession to resuscitate Teresa Urrea's image for posterity, in all of its contradictions and flaws, and especially to contest condescending portrayals of her. This personal obsession originates with a seeming disparity in *Tomóchic*: on the same page where Frías describes Teresa as a hysterical victim, there is a biographical footnote citing the article by Mario Gill, who describes the saint's "militant opposition to the Porfirian government" and her revolutionary work from exile in the United States, where she inspired the Tomóchic rebellion and indigenous insurgency and directed the 1896 attack on the customs house in Nogales (Frías 137). For Domecq, the contrast between Gill's "Mexican Joan of Arc" and Frías's "poor hysterical girl" was so incongruent that it inspired her to conduct years of research in order to question what had been left out of La Santa de Cabora's story, and why ("Teresa Urrea" 12). This research culminates in the publication of *The Astonishing Story*, where Domecq writes, "Who was she? How had she achieved such influence at the turn of the century only to be forgotten a short time later?" (5).

It is especially interesting that so many authors and artists describe a personal link to or calling from Teresa, or they portray such a connection involving the characters in their texts. Whether this personal link is a rhetorical or a performative technique or whether it represents spiritual faith or belief is immaterial, especially because these personalized narratives may do both at once. Rather, the depiction of a personal connection between the saint and the author, artist, or character represents a new version of spiritual communion or transformation that links the secular and the sacred. This sort of symbolic communion with the saint through cultural representation evokes the union of human and divine through relics, holy sites, or other sacred objects (Brown 3). In a sense, texts like *The Astonishing Story* not only depict and analyze popular devotional practices such as the rituals of identification and exchange associated with Teresa Urrea, they also demonstrate that cultural production can in fact be read as devotional practice. Many authors and artists utilize these symbolic devotional practices to claim, define, and appropriate Teresa Urrea's image as a point of departure for different identities, subject positions, spaces, and temporalities, while others, like Domecq, employ such practices primarily to examine her contradictory ambiguity. *The Astonishing Story* is particularly significant because it draws upon such symbolic rituals of identification and exchange in order to represent the saint's own struggle to reconcile her multiple contradictions and define herself, at times participating in the construction of her myth or asserting control over her public image.

Possessing La Santa de Cabora

Like Domecq, Luis Alberto Urrea claims a personal tie to Teresa Urrea—in his case, one of family, for he claims that his great-grandfather Seferino Urrea was Tomás Urrea's first cousin (*Hummingbird* 497). Of *The Hummingbird's Daughter*, Luis Urrea states:

> Teresita, aka The Saint of Cabora, was indeed a relative of mine. She was always presented to me, back in Baja California and Sinaloa, as my aunt. I hunted her story down all over the US and Mexico, and even found some interesting roots for the novel in France. I learned things in sweat lodges, in kitchens, in desert outbacks and tumbledown ranchos as much or more than I learned in libraries and museums. I

even lived in a haunted house full of scary shadows. I don't know that I'll ever have the strength to undergo such a journey again. . . . People from all over the world still write to me about Teresita, and it is very moving to me to think that my aunt is known in India, or China, Israel, Italy, and France (luisurrea.com).

Luis Urrea may well be related to La Santa de Cabora. Certainly his story of discovery, investigation, and symbolic communion with the saint, which he claims originates in family folktales, resembles the personal narratives that still circulate among some Mexicans and Chicanos/as in the borderlands (*Hummingbird* 497). It is telling that he usually refers to the saint as Teresita, the diminutive, affectionate moniker used by so many of her borderlands devotees. These family or local stories, as Gillian Newell points out, "draw upon an existing reservoir of social memory that entails more than mere recollection of past experiences" to link figures like Teresa Urrea with a greater sense of collective belonging (101). The stories that circulate among some borderlands residents draw upon personal history, as in Luis Urrea's claim of family ties to the saint, as well as on collective social history, which relies on sites like kitchens and ranchos as much as—if not more than—on traditional academic sources.

Despite the intensive archival research he conducted on La Santa de Cabora, Luis Urrea emphasizes that he is not a historian but, rather, a storyteller, with the goal of writing "a story, big and wild" (luisurrea.com). Likewise, in the acknowledgments to *Queen of America*, Urrea declares, "The story is not the history" (486). Yet his possessive claim on Teresa Urrea, whether literal or figurative, serves as a way to associate his family history to Chicano and borderlands history in general. This personal and collective social history is reinforced by Luis Urrea's focus on La Santa de Cabora's mystical, indigenous heritage, folkways, and teachings. Newell indicates that Chicano "imagined communities" emphasize their Native American roots and "consider themselves indigenous to the U.S. Southwest, an area they call 'Aztlán' (the mythical homeland of the Aztecs before they moved south to settle in central Mexico)" (97). Indeed, *The Hummingbird's Daughter* accentuates the ritual customs of the indigenous peoples of northwestern Mexico, especially the herbal and mystical techniques of the curanderas and shamans that teach young Teresa the ways of faith healing (*Hummingbird* 97, 214). As part of his research, Luis Urrea also studied with curanderas and shamans, and in keeping with his focus on storytelling rather than adhering to the conventions of history, he agreed to keep some of their mystical teachings secret (*Hummingbird* 498). This recourse to the mystical and spiritual culminates in Luis Urrea's tribute and thanks to "Teresita" in several of his books, a practice reminiscent of rituals of exchange and identification.[13] By giving thanks to Teresa Urrea as part of the process of writing, Luis Urrea evokes popular devotional practices even as he grounds his work in historical research.

It is logical that Luis Urrea and Domecq, who both conduct extensive historical research yet position their work against history, would focus to varying degrees on the effects of La Santa de Cabora's mystical aura for their characters and even in relation to their own lives. But some historians invoke her supernatural presence as well, albeit in different ways. In his historical analysis of the Tomóchic rebellion, for example, Paul Vanderwood occasionally draws upon the saint's mystical and supernatural qualities, engaging in figurative devotional practices even as he underscores historical veracity. In fact, he implies that mystical identification or closeness to the saint depends upon such veracity. At one point, Vanderwood criticizes the ways that some contemporary feminists and Chicanas/os appropriate the saint, declaring, "while ratifying her claims to special powers and buoyed by Teresa's own vacillations about their origin, both feminists and Mexican-Americans have chosen to cloak Teresa in a secular garb that more resembles their own. They remember her as a fearsome fighter for social justice, but seem to be reluctant to recall the spirituality that pervaded her life" (Vanderwood, *Power of God* 323). Here, Vanderwood seems to imply that Teresa Urrea's spiritual attributes are best—or perhaps solely—approached through historical research. He further posits a dichotomy between secular and sacred by identifying feminists and Mexican Americans as secular and implying that their work, perhaps because it focuses on marginalized communities, precludes spirituality.

Aside from invoking the saint's mystical or supernatural aura, Vanderwood occasionally participates in devotional rituals as part of his historical or archival practices. For instance, in his description of the valley of Tomóchic, he highlights the wonder and respect the battleground evokes, and he reflects on the impressions of the past inscribed on the land, like that produced by the local Arroyo de Lino, which "continues to carry away thin layers of soil once soaked in blood" (Vanderwood, *Power of God* 277). Even more significant is his discussion of the remains of the burned church of Tomóchic: "Recently some random excavator dug a pit at the edge of that foundation and struck charred beams—the remains, no doubt, of the earlier structure. I have preserved a piece of that charcoal in a plastic bag, and when exposed to air it crackles as if alive" (277). Vanderwood's mystical description of the land of the Tomóchic valley establishes a sense of sacredness that transfers to him, especially since he preserves a piece of the church structure as if he is guarding a relic. Likewise, in his description of the celebration of the First Annual Santa Teresa Day, in Clifton, Arizona, in 1994, Vanderwood cites people's "hunger for a personal experience with a higher being," including, presumably, his own hunger for personal experience (323). During the festival, local tourism promoter Luis Pérez described a legendary cave in Cabora where Teresa was said to have collected soil to use in her faith healing. Vanderwood clarifies that "nothing in the historical record indicates that

Teresa utilized such a cave," but he notes that, when Pérez distributes some of the soil to the crowd, "Twenty or thirty people—one in a wheelchair, another with fearsome physical hurts, several with unrestrained tears streaming down their cheeks—requested a few grains of that soil, myself included, all for our own private reasons" (*Power of God* 327–328).

Vanderwood concludes his account on a supernatural note, implicitly communing with the saint and associating his historical research with the pilgrims who seek spiritual and physical healing. By calling upon La Santa de Cabora's mystical powers for the development of his research, in a sense he also pronounces himself a believer, and thus part of the multiple temporality of secular sanctity that she represents. At the same time, Vanderwood tacitly privileges the historian's access to Teresa Urrea, suggested by his almost territorial claim on her spirituality, as opposed to the "feminists and Mexican-Americans." For Vanderwood, it seems that historical veracity is the path to possessing La Santa de Cabora. As Domecq suggests, however, fictive representations of the saint bear a burden that history does not: the task of confronting contradiction ("Teresa Urrea" 12). While most historians do engage with Teresa Urrea's contradictions, they may not elucidate the ways in which their work may also produce narratives of personalization. History certainly may blur the line between truth and fiction, but fiction more adeptly makes that blurring visible.

Finally, performance, with its dual emphasis on archive and repertory, provides a unique glimpse into the intersection between devotional practice and cultural production in the representation of Teresa Urrea.[14] The performative representation of La Santa de Cabora not only evokes devotional ritual, it becomes it. For example, performance artist Elena Díaz Björkquist channels the spirit of Teresa Urrea in the Chautauqua performances she has presented in Arizona and elsewhere. "Chautauqua" refers to a living history presentation where a performer dresses as the historical character and assumes the persona of that character. Díaz Björkquist believes that she does not just act as a historical character but actually becomes Teresa, arguing: "It's a spiritual thing. I feel her presence. I'm myself and I'm not" (elenadiazbjorkquist.net). Díaz Björkquist employs performative techniques such as gestures, voice inflection, tonal shifts, costume change, and various props in her representation of the saint, but her appeal to an intangible spiritual presence and her assertion that she simultaneously inhabits Teresa Urrea's spirit and her own requires the very same leap of faith and belief necessary for devotional ritual. Certainly, Díaz Björkquist's invocation of Teresa draws upon rituals of communion and possession like those practiced by spiritual mediums. Dressed in early twentieth-century-style clothing and draped with a silver crucifix and assorted *milagros*, Díaz Björkquist signals Teresa's presence by taking off her glasses and shifting her tone and language to a more formal style, using some words in Spanish.[15] "Teresa" then proceeds to tell her life story to the audience and answers questions about her history. With another shift in tone and language and replacing her glasses, "Teresa" becomes Díaz Björkquist again to answer questions about her research.

In her performance as Teresa Urrea, Díaz Björkquist especially focuses on the saint's role as a Chicana feminist icon that is both transnational and local. Her performance of spirit possession focuses on the way that the gendered human body transmits sanctity through gestures, language, vocal inflection, clothing, and jewelry, thus grounding the sacred in the materiality of the body as vessel. At the same time, by channeling her spirit, Díaz Björkquist symbolically grants Teresa the agency to speak and define herself that she was so frequently denied in earlier representations. The authority of the scholar is constructed and affirmed through the authority of the saint. This authority is directed especially toward local concerns surrounding Díaz Björkquist's hometown of Morenci, Arizona, a lost town that was located right next to Clifton, where Teresa lived from 1897 until her death in 1906 (apart from the few years she spent traveling with the medical company). Although her work is based primarily in Arizona, Díaz Björkquist emphasizes the transnational nature of Arizona's history by focusing on Teresa Urrea's impact in the United States, and by extension, on her own connection to Teresa as a Chicana. Yet in Díaz Björkquist's performative, possessed state, Teresa Urrea announces, "I am glad you have come to hear the truth about me. Some reporters have written the truth about me, some have not. Truth is everything" (elenadiazbjorkquist.net). While this appeal to the truth reflects the desire to correct the historical record, it does not reveal the intense struggle behind the production and experience of the saint's many contradictions. Conversely, Domecq's Teresa Urrea understands that there is no single truth, which lends a very different perspective to the construction and interrogation of the saint's myth and public image.

The Astonishing Story of the Saint of Cabora

In *The Astonishing Story*, Domecq represents La Santa de Cabora's life as a struggle to accept and manipulate her contradictory public image. The Teresa Urrea of the novel is often just as unsure of herself and what she symbolizes to her devotees and critics as many of the authors and historians who have debated her cultural and historical significance over the years. In *The Astonishing Story*, Teresa participates in the construction of her own myth, to various ends: at times she aims to assert control over her elusive public image, at others she seems eager to succumb to it. The saint's personal struggle is portrayed throughout the novel alongside the conflicted process of identification of an unnamed woman who has been researching Teresa Urrea's life. By representing the two women's identity crises in tandem, Domecq highlights the intense desire to personalize Teresa

Urrea's life and history and suggests that the saint cannot be considered apart from her devotees or their spiritual practices, symbolic or otherwise. In the end, Domecq implies that Teresa Urrea can only metaphorically assert control over her public image through representation. This is especially true if we consider that cultural representation can also be understood as a manifestation of the saint's body and spiritual presence.

Perhaps as a nod to the malleability of La Santa de Cabora's public image as much as to the literary genre, Domecq makes no definitive claims upon the truth of her narrative. Instead, she establishes a parallel between Teresa Urrea and the researcher in the novel, as women who have been chronically misunderstood by others. Domecq's claim that she has adopted Teresa as "a sister in disgrace" through her research and writing suggests that she also identifies with her to some extent ("Teresa Urrea" 12). Indeed, the unnamed researcher in the novel bears more than a passing resemblance to Domecq. At the same time, the rituals depicted in *The Astonishing Story*—such as sacred visitations and voices, spiritual callings, and spirit possession—put Domecq's literary work into dialogue with the masses who have worshipped Teresa throughout the years and manifest the intersection between sacred and secular. To this end, Domecq establishes a connection between popular devotion, writing, and the struggle for self-representation through the relationships among La Santa de Cabora, the woman researcher, and (implicitly) her own role as an author.

Around the time of the one-hundredth anniversary of Teresa Urrea's birth, the unnamed researcher in *The Astonishing Story* dreams repeatedly of a place called Cabora and eventually comes to believe that Teresa has personally called her to research her history: "It had been like a spiritual pilgrimage for which, at times, she had felt herself chosen" (3–4). Teresa Urrea directs the narrator's actions, guiding her toward Heriberto Frías's *Tomóchic*, and the narrator describes her confusion at the saint's contradictory representation as both victim and threat. Domecq describes the researcher's identification with Teresa: "She so wanted to penetrate to the very soul of the forgotten woman and so identified with her that she ended up losing almost all notion of her own reality and was living only to retrieve the other's existence" (5). The woman researcher is so obsessed with La Santa de Cabora that her life begins to parallel Teresa's until she metaphorically and literally becomes her. The woman describes feeling possessed by "a curiosity that gnawed at her peace of mind," echoing the experience of spirit possession through the process of historical research and cultural representation (5). As the narrator gradually feels more and more alienated, she becomes increasingly unable to distinguish between her own life and Teresa Urrea's. Quotes from histories, interviews, and newspaper articles crowd out her thoughts. Eventually, she must visit Sonora in search of Cabora, where she appeals to an intimate personal connection to Teresa in order to encourage the locals to talk

to her, claiming: "She has brought me here" (68). In the midst of mystical hal-
lucinations relating excerpts from her research and visions of Teresa, the woman
arrives at the cave on the hill where the saint was said to have collected soil to
use in faith healing. After tasting the soil, like Teresa supposedly did, the woman
experiences an overwhelming sensation of déjà vu, and then, losing her footing, she slips and falls (140). In the novel, this moment definitively unites the
two women, for it is also the moment when Teresa falls into a cataleptic fit and
coma and metaphorically dies. During the fall, the two characters are fused into
one body with a common history—a dual symbolic death representing Teresa's
transformation into a saint and the researcher's transformation into Teresa: "At
that instant they felt swept away by death" (143).

The similarities are obvious between the woman's research as a personal
destiny determined by La Santa de Cabora herself and Teresa Urrea's spiritual
calling as a faith healer and saint. Both characters struggle to define themselves
through their respective callings: for the researcher, the study of Teresa's life;
for Teresa, the path of sanctity. Both of these missions are ultimately incomplete and unsatisfactory, however. In the novel, as the researcher's life unfolds
into that of Teresa Urrea, the saint must reconcile the opposing poles of sacred
and human, a contradiction she frequently resents and tries to elide (not unlike
the critics who misrepresent her). Domecq portrays Teresa as an independent
woman who rejects the societal dictates for women of her race and class, but this
independence comes at a price, for Teresa idealizes masculinity as a marker of
liberation. From an early age, she longs to be a man, especially a powerful landowner like her father, Don Tomás. Before becoming a saint, Teresa insists upon
learning to read, ride horses with a traditional saddle, and play guitar, all qualities associated with masculinity. She vows to refuse the constraints of femininity,
which she understands through the vulnerability of the female body: "she sol-
emnly swore three things: first, that she would always keep her legs together; second, she would hide in the hills every time she bled so no man would ever smell
her; and third, she would never, never get married or have children. . . . little by
little she lost her fear and strengthened her conviction that with a strong enough
desire sooner or later she would overcome so many feminine encumbrances and
become a man" (*Astonishing Story* 62).

Teresa eventually breaks all three of these vows, yet she decides at the time
that the only way to challenge the limits of the feminine is to assume a masculine persona. However, after she is reborn as a saint in the novel, she eventually
loses touch entirely with her human side. Before her sacred transformation,
Teresa disdains the humility and invisibility of her family and the other indigenous women at Cabora, and she believes that she can achieve independence by
assuming a higher level of social class after entering her father's household. She
is disillusioned after realizing that wealthy women also face restrictions based

upon social mores, and she eventually embraces her sanctity, not just to help the poor and sick but as the only true path away from the constraints of women's bodies and toward independence. She ministers as a saint against the wishes of her father, symbolically rejecting the patriarchal structure of her society. But while Teresa is liberated from her female body by becoming a saint, she also rejects her family ties and other personal relationships because of her sanctity. While the masses are attracted to her sanctity, it also distances her from them. Whether coded as masculine or feminine, Teresa is unable to engage her own human desires and frailties throughout most of the novel, and she often feels surrounded by loss. Toward the end of her life, "She thought that all of her life had been a series of goodbyes" (*Astonishing Story* 354). She initially perceives her human qualities, especially those associated with femininity, to be a prison, but ultimately her sanctity is no less of one.

In fact, in *The Astonishing Story* Teresa Urrea is simultaneously ambivalent about her sanctity and enthralled by it, often fluctuating between self-doubt and narcissism. For the most part, she acknowledges that she is a saint only through the grace of God and the devotion of others, and she is initially frightened by and uncomfortable with the idea of her sanctity. Often, her devotees have more faith in her and belief in her abilities than she has in herself. For example, Cruz Chávez, the leader of the Tomóchic rebellion, asserts, "Why are you afraid, Teresita? Isn't it true that you do the impossible? . . . We believe in you and faith works miracles, doesn't it? If you believe with all your heart in something and fight for it to happen, it can happen, isn't that true? Don't you know that too, Teresita?" (215). Likewise, a poor indigenous woman named Anastasia with advanced tuberculosis has so much faith in Teresa that she is "convinced she wouldn't die," even though the saint realizes that she is beyond recovery (242).

Nevertheless, Teresa is sometimes seduced by her own sacred powers and reputation. Early on, she feels addicted to the rush of power that accompany her miracles: "She began to crave the miraculous experience and hunger for the high it gave her. Nothing she had known was comparable to the vibrations of the mystery she experienced and shared. Anything routine began to bore her, and she was surprised to find herself actually wishing that the people who came would be struck with terrible diseases so she could perform a miracle again and feel the force that transcended her but that also elevated her above the rest" (175). Later she thinks, "Miracles became the routine and she was filled with belief in herself" and, at one point, even declares, "a lo mejor yo soy ese Cristo [Perhaps I am that Christ]" (195, 203).[16] This hubristic self-identification with Christ is totally at odds with the portrayal of Teresa Urrea as a humble vessel, innocent girl, or victim. Unlike that innocent passive girl, in *The Astonishing Story* Teresa consciously manipulates her sanctity and participates in the construction of her own myth. Ultimately, however, such control over her public image is untenable.

Teresa Urrea remains ambivalent about her sacred and political powers through-out the novel, for she is unable to reconcile the influence of these powers with their eventual failure. As she laments to a friend, "Do you know how it feels to want to do good and over and over again turn out to be an instrument of destruction?" (338).

Representational Immortality

After being exiled to the United States, Teresa realizes that her already tenuous sense of her sacred and human identity is even more transitory than she had anticipated, while the contradictions that define her life become even more extreme. In Nogales, Arizona, she loses the social privilege she had earned by moving to her father's ranch at Cabora. When she and her father are exiled, she is stripped of her home, her family and friends, and her freedom to commune with her devotees. In Nogales she is viewed as "just another Mexican" by the local gringos at the very moment that she loses her Mexican national identity: "She was just another Mexican among all the refugees who crossed the border every day, an undesirable foreigner whose customs provoked first malicious laughter and then scorn, an outcast, a cultural hybrid, an abnormality within the context of Nogales. She didn't belong there" (*Astonishing Story* 279). Far from being a revered healer and saint, in exile Teresa Urrea is lumped in with all the other "undesirable" refugees. Marked as a culturally hybrid Mexican after she is banished from Mexico, Teresa is an outsider in the United States, and she continues to be excluded from national identity. At the same time, increasingly fantastic and conflicting stories appear in the press calling her a witch, a hero, a victim, or an idiot. Teresa's customs—that is, her spiritual powers—certainly attract attention on the U.S. side of the border, but they also render her "undesirable" and "abnormal," as she complains to her friend Lauro Aguirre: "I'm a curiosity, just grist for gossip and mockery" (281).

For the Anglo residents of Nogales, it seems that Teresa's sanctity is equated with her Mexican identity and is therefore suspect. She eventually reclaims some measure of her spiritual authority by deliberately posing for photographs "dressed up as a saint" and embarking on the national tour—all practices associated with celebrity (*Astonishing Story* 282). Yet this celebrity is predictably fickle, for Teresa appears to lose her sacred aura once she participates in traditional domestic activities like marriage and childbirth. After giving birth to her first daughter in 1901, her status as a mother, which symbolizes her human qualities, especially the vulnerable femininity she so frequently disparaged, erodes her spiritual powers in the eyes of some: "they say that I no longer attract much of an audience and it bothers them that I have a daughter. They think that's what took away my aura of 'saint'" (350). In reality however, Teresa's domestic relations are far from traditional for, after only one day, her first marriage to Lupe Rodríguez ends with gunshots and chaos; her first daughter is born out of wedlock; she marries John Van Order as a mere formality; and she returns to Clifton, Arizona, a single mother with two daughters. It might seem that the problem is the fact that Teresa is now an adult, for the masses have always been attracted to her childlike tenderness and guile. In exile, even more than before, she is caught between her desire to live her life on her own terms and her frequently restrictive public image.

Ultimately, Teresa's experience with so many losses in her life—whether lost relationships, lost homes, lost citizenship, lost class and racial privileges, and even lost sanctity—associates her even more closely with the marginalized people, the migrants, peasants, and indigenous peoples who are her most fervent devotees. In the United States, she is no longer distanced from her indigenous followers because of class, race, citizenship, or even sanctity. Yet she initially recoils from the "disorder and filth" of the Mexican neighborhood she is forced to live in and considers the loyal Yaquis and Mayos who worship her "foul-smelling . . . covered with dirt, in ragged clothes, exuding misery through every pore," echoing her childhood ambivalence toward her own indigenous past (*Astonishing Story* 278). Eventually, in exile, Teresa allies herself with and even identifies with the indigenous masses: "The majority of them had arrived just as she had, fleeing from injustice, fearful of being sent to the National Valley on the Yucatan Peninsula, where they would die of hunger, malaria, and sorrow" (278). Teresa had fought for social justice for people like the destitute Yaquis and Mayos back in Cabora, and on the U.S. side of the border she is linked to them through their common status as exiles, migrants, and foreigners in a frequently hostile land. This connection appalls most of the other Mexicans in Arizona, who seek assimilation at all costs: "Other Mexican families stayed away, afraid of being identified with the motley groups of Indians. Their ambition was to conceal their mestizo traits, learn English, cover up their Latino background, and become accepted by the 'whiteys,' or at least by the 'Hispanics' who claimed to be directly descended from the Spaniards" (279). Whether she likes it or not, Teresa Urrea is bound to the indigenous people in exile. She occasionally feels like a "pariah" because she is so closely tied to them, yet she finally understands that assimilation, whether to a dominant national identity, a traditional gender ideal, or a hierarchical notion of social class, is impossible for her.

It is thus unsurprising that, in the novel, Teresa's foundational moment of loss—her exile—coincides with her radicalization against the state. Not only does she align herself with the Indians, she openly supports revolutionary activities like the raid on the customs house. Her revolutionary endeavors, like so many of her personal relationships, are doomed to failure, yet Teresa's link to the indigenous people in the United States reveals that she, too, feels a personal connection to and identifies with her devotees. By embracing a potentially threatening or uncomfortable identification with the masses, Teresa Urrea engages in practices of exchange and disidentification with her followers, just as they do with her. But these devotional practices are not always able to effect change or even to create lasting ties between saint and devotee. Even the mythical Teresa Urrea cannot help all of her devotees—as in the case of the indigenous people who are most loyal to her: "Teresa realized that the majority [of the Indians] didn't need relief from physical ailments but from spiritual ones; they wanted the identity of a community, they wanted renewed myths, they wanted to reinvent lost traditions to feel that they belonged to some place, to some history. They wanted what she couldn't give them, what had been left behind in another world, in another moment of time" (*Astonishing Story* 278–279). La Santa de Cabora is nothing if not a renewed myth for the exiled and migrant Yaquis and Mayos, but the community they seek through her is lost to them, not just in the United States but in Mexico as well, for neither country authorizes them as legitimate citizens. Despite her attempts to manipulate it, or to succumb to it entirely, Teresa is constantly confronted with the fact that her public image is out of her control.

While many of those who worship and identify with La Santa de Cabora seek to define her in order to articulate different subject positions or to achieve spiritual transcendence, like the woman researcher who is so obsessed with Teresa Urrea that she loses sight of the contours of her own life, the saint eventually realizes that she cannot always control or even understand her own myth and public image. This realization is obviously painful for Teresa as, toward the end of the novel, she laments, "My life has been a lie. I don't even know if I exist or if I'm just a fabrication" (*Astonishing Story* 338). However, while Teresa poignantly asks, "Who am I, after all?" she answers her own question by declaring that "there are no answers," for she accepts that she can only be defined through contradiction: "I have been a little bit of everything: a little saint, a little virgin, a little married, a little in love, a little idealist, a little revolutionary, a little visionary" (351). The conflict over Teresa Urrea's multiple identities continues unabated throughout *The Astonishing Story*, but by releasing the desire to control her myth and resolve her contradictions, she is freed from the vagaries of public opinion for the first time in her life. The possibility that she is just a fabrication is in fact liberating for her, because the circulating image and representation of Teresa Urrea is what persists through history. In this sense, the woman researcher's frantic attempt to "retrieve [Teresa's] existence," and her grief at the possibility that Teresa is "twice dead: first in body, then in history" is misguided (5, 116). At the end of the novel, the woman's complete and total identification with La Santa de Cabora results in her own symbolic rebirth in a hospital ward, as she emerges from a coma of several months declaring that she is Teresa, that she has been to Heaven, and that she "has come to bring kindness and justice to the world" (359). The doctors diagnose her with "psychosis induced by a death experience," echoing the claims of those who scorned and criticized Teresa Urrea's mystical powers over the years but also suggesting that the saint cannot be retrieved through reincarnation or through traditional forms of spirit possession (360).

Instead, *The Astonishing Story* demonstrates that Teresa Urrea is best summoned and embraced in all of her contradictions through cultural representation. The personal link and disidentification with the saint that so many authors, artists, and critics represent in their works are not simply ways to revive the Teresa Urrea of the past for their own times, countering years of oblivion. Instead, these practices of disidentification elucidate secular sanctity, with its fusion of divine and profane, by symbolically constructing cultural representation as devotional ritual. Just as relics, holy sites, and other sacred objects have been utilized and appropriated throughout history to invoke and possess the divine, the human and the sacred come together in new ways through the intersection of devotional ritual and cultural production.

2 · THE REMAINS OF PANCHO VILLA

$\bigwedge$S BEFITS HIS TUMULTUOUS LIFE, the earthly remains of General Francisco "Pancho" Villa, the "Centaur of the North" and leader of the División del Norte in the Mexican Revolution, did not rest in peace. In 1926, three years after his murder, Villa's head was stolen from his grave in Parral, Chihuahua (Katz, *Life* 789). As with all of Villa's actions and attributes, speculation and myth took hold of the disembodied head. Groups ranging from the army of Mexican president Plutarco Elías Calles, American soldiers of fortune, and former Carrancista generals were rumored to have stolen Villa's head. The head may have been scientifically examined in Mexico for research to determine the source of Villa's military genius, perhaps preserved as a macabre trophy for one of his former enemies, or displayed in the United States as revenge for Villa's raid on Columbus, New Mexico. There is even a rumor that Skull and Bones, a secret society at Yale University, had acquired the head (Katz, *Life* 789–790; Medina Ruiz 151). As recently as the mid-2000s, groups of Chicano/a students at Yale demanded that President George W. Bush return the head to Mexico (Taibo, *Pancho Villa* 838). Villa's head clearly holds talismanic resonance for his followers and enemies alike, suggesting the intensification of his mythic potential after his death. As historian Fernando Medina Ruiz argues, "Villa's head is more popular today than when it rested on the shoulders of that extraordinary man" (144–145). According to Taibo, the residents of Parral are still haunted by tales of ghostly apparitions seeking the lost head around the town cemetery (*Pancho Villa* 838). The fascination with parts of Villa's corpse appears in many representations of the general, ranging from Nellie Campobello's novel *Cartucho* (in which an old woman taunts the federal soldiers who are hunting Villa down, "Hey, bastard, bring me a little bone from Villa's wounded knee, so I can make myself a relic" [41])

General Francisco Villa. New Mexico State University Library. Archives and Special Collections.

to corridos such as Chalino Sánchez's "Descansa General" that refer to the power of Villa's remains.

While Villa's unruly remains are frequently celebrated within popular and literary culture, dominant institutions like the post-revolutionary Mexican state attempt to regulate the remains by converting Villa into the untouchable national hero of myth. This is especially obvious in his reburial at the Monument of the Revolution in Mexico City in 1976 where, fifty-three years after his death, Villa was granted the official recognition denied him after his assassination. His headless body now lies alongside those of his friend Francisco Madero, his bitter enemy Venustiano Carranza, and Plutarco Elías Calles, the president who was probably directly responsible for his assassination (Katz, *Life* 1–2, 789). Thus, the revolutionary factions Villa fought against in life are elided in death, further sub-suming the general's contradictory human attributes into monolithic legend.[1]

Yet the incongruity of interring the leaders of several warring factions together in the imposing monument to the revolution is not the most incredible aspect of this tale. According to Taibo, it is possible that the body in the monument is not even Villa's body at all. Instead, according to legend, in 1931 Pancho Villa's head-less body was secretly moved to another tomb in the cemetery of Parral in order to thwart further violations. As the story goes, later that year a woman who was going north to the United States to seek treatment for cancer died in a hospi-tal in Parral. Lacking identification, she was buried in the tomb that had origi-nally been Villa's. Taibo notes that in 1976 a doctor who examined Villa's newly exhumed body claimed that it appeared to have a female pelvis. So, it seems that an anonymous woman is in fact in Villa's place in the Monument of the Revolu-tion, while Villa's headless remains lie in another tomb in the cemetery of Par-ral (Taibo, *Pancho Villa* 851). Fittingly, Pancho Villa appears to have escaped the state's intractable official myth even in death.

The whereabouts of Villa's scattered remains may never really be determined, but his specter is as unruly and as compelling as ever. In fact, the fervor over Pan-cho Villa, especially the desire to possess him either literally or figuratively—whether to heal personal ills, combat evil, or simply channel his formidable power—suggests that the general is invoked not simply as a revolutionary hero but as a secular saint. It might seem strange, even heretical, to consider Pancho Villa a saint, especially since he is so often portrayed as a villainous thug. It goes without saying that Villa is not sanctioned as a saint by the Vatican, and many people, not just those affiliated with the Catholic Church, would consider him anathema to any notion of the sacred. Furthermore, given that one of the most important tenets of the Mexican Revolution was the strict division between church and state, it might seem even stranger to designate Villa a revolutionary saint, even though many peasants remained faithful to both popular and institu-tional Catholicism during and after the revolution. Nevertheless, Pancho Villa embodies practices commonly identified with popular sanctity, such as devo-tional cults, spirit possession, relic worship, faith healing, and intercession for the faithful.

In northern Mexico, along the borderlands, and among some Mexican migrants to the United States, a cult to the revolutionary general "San Pancho Villa" has been spreading for more than fifty years (Gil Olmos 173). Journalist José Gil Olmos argues, "[The spirit of Pancho Villa] is venerated by many people in the states of Coahuila, Durango, Nuevo León and Chihuahua, as well as by the Mexican migrants that live in the borderlands, all of whom consider him a miraculous saint and pray to him asking for all sorts of favors: money, protection, strength, love, and especially, justice" (173). Gil Olmos notes that the devotion for Villa is so strong that the faithful have converted a statue of the general at the entrance of his birthplace La Coyotada, Durango, into a makeshift shrine, where they gather to pray and light candles (173). There are various records of mediums (frequently women) in northern and central Mexico who specialize in channeling Villa. For example, the Escuela de Estudios Psíquicos Doroteo Arango Arámbula (Doroteo Arango Arámbula School of Psychic Studies) in La Coyotada offers counseling, prayer, social support, and faith healing through mediums who summon the spirit of Pancho Villa, often representing him in a white charro suit (Gil Olmos 173).[2] Anthropologist Ruth Behar describes very similar ceremonies in Mexquitic, San Luis Potosí, in which Chencha, a spirit medium and healer, channels Villa's spirit in order to grant wishes and perform miracles (203–222).

Alongside these more traditional expressions of popular spirituality, the general is frequently represented and invoked within cultural production in ways that approximate saints' cults and common devotion practices, especially through symbolic versions of relic worship and spirit possession, even when these texts do not explicitly identify Villa as a popular saint. In novels, films, drama, and music, the general is portrayed as a figure that diverse individuals, social groups, or institutional representatives such as politicians or intellectuals seek to decipher, understand, establish a relationship with, or otherwise get close to. In many cases, the characters in these texts or the authors and artists themselves interact with the figurative or historical Villa as a character whose aura and essence can be channeled in the manner of spirit possession. Like the spirit possession practiced by mediums, this symbolic spirit possession is not without risk, for the characters in these texts are often just as threatened by Villa as they are beguiled by him. Nevertheless, this symbolic spirit possession also transcends traditional forms of popular spirituality to signify a collective belonging that is often simultaneously regional, national, and transnational. Indeed, at different times Villa is invoked or appropriated in cultural production as a symbol of the nation, the borderlands, regions such as northern Mexico, and for popular resistance against the nation-state, reflecting the intertwined construction of border, region, and nation in Mexico and the United States.

It is important to remember that not all representations of the general that evoke popular spirituality do so in order to reflect alternative or subaltern identities or communities. Pancho Villa is also routinely appropriated by the Mexican state, while its consecration of Villa's remains in the Monument of the Revolution echoes the sanctification of relics. Such examples of popular spirituality are common throughout Latin America, as anthropologist Claudio Lomnitz demonstrates in his discussion of the relation between the official treatment of caudillos' bones and the religious treatment of relics. The relation between the two treatments influences the construction of images of national sovereignty and paves the way for the transition to a secular state (Lomnitz, *Deep Mexico* 352).[3] Similarly, Michael Taussig discusses "the magical harnessing of the dead for the authority of the modern state" through the adaptation of popular rituals of possession and reincarnation (*Magic* 3–5). In both cases, the official doctrine of church and state aims to rearticulate and control popular sanctity. At the same time, certain cultural texts represent Villa in ways that perhaps inadvertently reinforce official attempts to control his image through symbolic spirit possession. This is especially true of texts that elide the general's inherently ambivalent qualities in order to portray him as a locus of national or nationalist identities. Other cultural representations of Pancho Villa demonstrate the synthesis and inversion of the dichotomies that church and state hold so dear, such as secular and sacred, modern and non-modern, popular and elite, and region, border, and nation.

As a mediator between secular and sacred temporalities and regional, national, and transnational spaces, Villa is a secular borderlands saint who represents multiple contradictory possibilities. In cultural production, historical and political discourse, and public works, Villa is variously represented as an evil bandit, a military genius, a trickster, a quintessential macho and uneducated buffoon, a martyr for the revolution, and a savior of the poor and oppressed. Jean Franco argues that the novels of the Mexican Revolution, along with state-sponsored monuments and public works, "make the dominant ideology of post-revolutionary Mexico 'visible,'" representing Villa and the revolution in heroic terms that elide their contradictions and failings (*Critical* 447). Yet many of the novels of the Mexican Revolution such as Mariano Azuela's *Los de abajo* (1915) and Martín Luis Guzmán's *El águila y la serpiente* (1928) and films of the Golden Age of Mexican cinema (roughly 1935–1959) such as Fernando de Fuentes's *¡Vámonos con Pancho Villa!* (1935) characterize Villa as evil, even as they also celebrate him as an iconic leader. The only point on which the many historians, biographers, critics, authors, and artists who treat Villa seem to agree is that he is contradictory and ambiguous. Two of his most important recent biographers, Friedrich Katz and Paco Ignacio Taibo, ground their histories in this contradiction. Katz emphasizes the "multifaceted layers of legends and myth surrounding Villa" (Katz, *Life* xiv), while Taibo underscores the *doble mirada* (dual gaze) of Villa and villismo, which simultaneously elicits feelings of admiration, revulsion, fascination, fear, love, and hatred (*Pancho Villa* 12).

It is obvious that Villa is associated with Mexican post-revolutionary nationalism, with Mexican resistance to the United States, and even (albeit contentiously) with the Mexican state itself, but historically he has also been associated with non-nationalist and transnational interpretative possibilities. Villa's image resonates with peasant resistance against the Mexican government, northern Mexican regional identity, the migration of Mexicans to the United States, and

Chicano/a identity. Villa is officially co-opted for modernizing ends that presume to include the masses, yet despite—or perhaps because of—the fact that he is associated with rebellion against the state, he also thwarts such appropriation precisely because he is so contradictory, at once embodying grandiose myth and ordinary human fallibility. At the same time, by overturning the static myths so important to the production of hegemonic nationalism, borderlands saints such as Villa manifest the inherent contradictions of the nation-state. They demonstrate that citizenship is not always equivalent to national belonging, as is indicated by both the systematic exclusion of indigenous peoples in Mexico and the concealment of the national dependency upon undocumented migrant labor in the United States. In this sense, representations of Villa reject but also exemplify the strict boundaries between regional, national, and transnational spaces as well as those between secular and sacred temporalities.

My aim here is to trace the representation of Pancho Villa in Mexican and Chicano cultural production as a secular saint who embodies the duality of man and myth and who stands in for multiple regional, national, and transnational spaces and identities. Virtually all of the texts that treat Villa construct him ambiguously as a mythic figure who is nevertheless desired for his flawed human characteristics. In this sense, Villa can be considered a popular saint precisely because he unites heroic iconicity with physical accessibility. The focus here is on the ambivalence surrounding Villa in texts such as Guzman's *El águila* and De Fuentes's film *¡Vámonos con Pancho Villa!* and the anxiety that this ambivalence produces in the characters or artists who attempt to decipher, regulate, or emulate the general through versions of spirit possession. For example, texts such as the contemporary documentary *Los rollos perdidos de Pancho Villa/The Lost Reels of Pancho Villa* (2003) by Mexican filmmaker Gregorio Rocha, which aims in part to correct the historical inaccuracies evident in so many representations of Villa, engage in a kind of spirit possession in order to capture Villa's true essence.

The representation of Villa through spirit possession as an agent for national or nationalist identities potentially obscures his inherently ambivalent qualities. Significantly, Chicano playwright Luis Valdez's work *The Shrunken Head of Pancho Villa* (1964) mediates between the representations of Villa on either side of the border. While most Mexican texts present Villa in ambivalent terms, borderlands and Chicano representations of the general are even more fraught with tension. Chicano texts portray him not only as a locus of Mexican nationalism in the borderlands and the United States but as a symbol for migrant melancholia, with its painful existence in between cultures, nations, and identities. Although many characters in Valdez's play invoke Villa through the lens of Mexican nationalism, such efforts necessarily fail, for the Chicano/a and migrant characters are unable to access either Mexican or American national belonging. Rather, the play's focus on the resuscitation of Villa's fragmented remains, rather than on any cohesive image of the general, articulates collective forms of belonging for Chicanos/as that do not depend exclusively on either national identities or hybrid spaces.

Villa's Multiple Identities

One hundred years after the eruption of the Mexican Revolution, Villa is still one of the best-known Mexican personalities of all time. Baptized Doroteo Arango, Pancho Villa rose from an impoverished background in rural Durango to acquire worldwide fame as a revolutionary leader and cultural icon. Villa is a larger-than-life legendary figure known equally for his penchant for brutality, his loyalty to his troops, his virility, and his military strategy. He is an icon of cinema, the Mexican Revolution novel, song, mural art, and state-sponsored monuments, images, and public works in Mexico. His soldiers were legendary for their loyalty to him, and his regiment, the División del Norte, was famous for its "cavalry, its mobility, and the fighting spirit and resilience of the Mexican soldiers" (Katz, *Life* 303–304).[4] The Mexican Revolution was also the first war to be captured on film and presented to theatergoing audiences around the world. At the height of his military career in 1914, Villa became Hollywood's first Mexican superstar when he signed a contract with the Mutual Film Company to film his regiment in battle (De Orellana *La mirada* 73–75).[5] Villa was also the protagonist of countless revolutionary corridos (Mexican national folk ballads, most famously "La Cucaracha"), novels, essays, comic books, political cartoons, and news reports both during and after the revolution.[6] Finally, as Taibo and Gregorio Rocha indicate, to this day a wide range of products, services, and interests reference Pancho Villa in Mexico, the United States, and beyond (Taibo, *Pancho Villa* 841; Rocha, "*And Starring*" 142).[7]

Even though the dominant ideology of the Mexican Revolution dictates that leaders like Villa can only be understood as glorious, untouchable national heroes, Villa embodies the opposing poles that structure Mexican nationalism: he is mestizo, yet he is imbued with the prowess of Indian warriors; he is poor, illiterate, and crude, yet he is emblematic of elite, educated presidents and leaders; he is construed as non-modern, yet he employs modern technologies such as film to manipulate his image; he can be cast as a non-citizen because of his poverty, mobility, and resistance against the state, yet he is a forceful symbol of the modern post-revolutionary state and of Mexican citizenship. In this sense, representations of Villa demonstrate that Mexican nationalism is itself inherently contradictory. Perhaps because of this, he is often reduced to a caricature, as historian Ilene O'Malley suggests: "The press treated Villa as a spectacle: less than human, more than human, a 'force,' 'the Centaur of the North,' but never just a man" (87). Part of his appeal to the masses is his capacity to shift between these contradictory identities and labels.

This is especially true of Villa's embodiment of both heroic iconicity and physical accessibility. Such duality is critical for the worship of popular saints, for the general's devotees interpret him as both a mythic icon and as an ordinary man like themselves. He is naturally distanced from the common folk because of his role as a revolutionary leader and his fetishization as a popular saint, yet Villa is nevertheless often seen as one of them. His extraordinary attributes such as his legendary horsemanship and military strategy stem in part from his link to the masses—especially in northern Mexico and the border region, which has long been associated with an independent ranching and cowboy culture and with seemingly lawless, stateless indigenous groups.

Clearly, there are multiple claims upon Villa's nationality and identity, and as with almost all facets of his personality and history these are malleable. Even as he is associated with Mexican post-revolutionary nationalism and at times stands in for the Mexican nation, Villa blends in with the popular, regional masses of northern Mexico and the border region. By extension, he is identi-fied with various forms of Chicano/a and migrant identities. On the question of regional identity, Taibo indicates that there is a long-standing feud—between the inhabitants of Durango, where Villa was born, and Chihuahua, where he became a warrior—as to which province has a greater claim on him (*Pancho Villa* 16). In many ways this most Mexican of heroes is also an American product due to his standing in the mass media (Rocha, "*And Starring*" 142).[8] Eventually, of course, Villa became a villain in the American consciousness after his raid on Columbus, New Mexico, in 1916, especially since he is the only foreigner since the War of 1812 to have attacked the U.S. mainland and escaped (Katz, *Life* xiii).[9] Finally, there are even more fantastic claims upon Pancho Villa's nationality and identity. He has been claimed as Colombian, Central American, Basque, and African American by various sources (Taibo, *Pancho Villa* 17).

Virtually every aspect of Villa's background and history has been contested, whether it has to do with his childhood, his life as a bandit, his role as revolution-ary leader, his post-revolutionary life, or his death and dismemberment. Schol-ars and historians have spent considerable time and energy attempting to correct misconceptions and misrepresentations. In fact, practically every scholar, histo-rian, and author who writes about Pancho Villa seems obsessed with unearthing the true story behind his mythical image—a tendency that occasionally pro-duces tension between historical and culturalist accounts of the general. I con-tend that it is less important to decipher the truth about his life and history than to examine why the search for this truth remains so compelling.

In her essay "Caught in the Middle: Ambiguous Gender and Social Politics in Sabina Berman's Play *Entre Villa y una mujer desnuda*," critic Dianna Niebyl-ski proposes that Villa's "hotly debated public and private personae" is a cen-tral reason for his prominence (157). Niebylski quite rightly points out that "the historical man behind the myth has proven too unwieldy for easy political exploitation" (158), but this difficulty has not prevented many politicians, historians, authors, and artists from trying to manage such an ambivalent figure. It frequently seems that the efforts to determine Villa's true nature correspond to specific regional, national, or transnational identities and desires. I contend that, as a shifting and contradictory subject, Pancho Villa necessarily encompasses all of these identities. In this sense, he is simultaneously a Mexican, a Chicano, and a border subject, and his essence, within all of these identities, encompasses the duality of ordinary man and mythic hero. The symbolic struggle for possession of Villa's remains is as complex as ever, because he represents such different things within dominant Mexican, popular or regional Mexican, or Chicano cultural production.

Villa and Mexico

Although there has never been a shortage of popular and literary cultural production focusing on Villa from the moment he emerged onto the revolutionary scene in 1910, his appropriation by the Mexican state, primarily through public works and slogans, occurred more slowly. Friedrich Katz notes that, among the pantheon of revolutionary leaders, Villa was the only one who was consistently excluded from official Mexico (*Life* 790). By the time Lázaro Cárdenas was president, in the mid-1930s, Villa had been officially claimed by the PRI. As O'Malley contends, "the government probably deemed it unseemly that the most famous Mexican in the world should continue to stand outside and in contradiction of the official Revolution" (144). Although many members of the Mexican government were critical of Villa up until the 1960s, when President Díaz Ordaz proposed including his name on the walls of the Chamber of Deputies alongside Madero, Carranza, and Zapata, Villa's rehabilitation for official Mexico lent the PRI a crucial measure of credibility with the masses during times of presidential and national crisis in the 1960s (Katz, *Life* 790–791). Alongside the PRI's construction of an official narrative through substituting and replacing the frequently conflicting ideologies of the revolution in state-sponsored monuments, murals, and literature, the party distanced itself more and more from the revolutionary ideals espoused by figures like Villa or Emiliano Zapata. Villa's reburial in the Monument of the Revolution, for instance, reflects the clash between official policy and popular sentiment. Not only did the reburial obscure the rival factions that were so prominent during the revolution, it reinforced the divisions between the center and the periphery of Mexico. For example, many Mexicans celebrated the transfer of Villa's remains, but some northerners and border residents resented it, since they believed that it only further marginalized the northern region with which Villa was so firmly associated. Regardless, the Mexican state's appropriation of Villa was concerned primarily with eliding his contradictory qualities in order to construct a cohesive nationalist image.

Literary representation further shapes official Mexican nationalism, particularly through the novels of the Mexican Revolution. Narrowly defined, these are "novels written by Mexicans about the destructive, military phase of the Revolution, from 1910 until about 1920" (Rutherford 214). In general, these novels serve as firsthand accounts of life during the revolution, in terms of military events, everyday life, or both. They may also provide justification for the struggle and set the tone for the discovery of a Mexican national consciousness. These texts also require a broader definition than usual of the novel as a genre. Many significant novels of the revolution, such as Guzmán's *El águila* or José Vasconcelos's *Ulises criollo*, would be classified as autobiographies in other contexts, while Guzmán's *Memorias de Pancho Villa* could be read as a blend of biography and autobiography (Rutherford 215). According to John Rutherford, the novel of the Mexican Revolution includes "all those autobiographies, memoirs and biographies which have any aesthetic pretenses or qualities" (215). This fluidity certainly augments the tension between truth and fiction in representations of Pancho Villa. Precisely because they blend aesthetics with a representation of the truth behind the revolution or behind Villa's character, such novels may lay claim to a more authoritative truth than can be found in histories, strictly defined. This is clearly the case in *El águila*, which, like many other novels of the Mexican Revolution, presents itself as a firsthand account of revolutionary activity. Even though Guzmán purports to be sympathetic to the revolutionary cause, he ultimately portrays the general as a unified myth and obscures his many contradictions. In this sense, Guzmán's representation of Villa resembles the Mexican state's more explicit control of the general's image in the name of revolutionary nationalism.

The Battle for Villa and the Revolution: *El águila y la serpiente*

Villa is the example par excellence of the revolutionary caudillo in the novels of the Mexican Revolution. He appears as a character much more frequently than Emiliano Zapata and is arguably the central protagonist and impetus behind much of the literature.[10] Villa is generally depicted in contradictory fashion as a barbaric counterpoint to the intelligentsia, as a heroic savior of the masses, or even as mere illusion. As a result, these novels frequently represent a struggle for control over Villa's image and myth, and by extension, over the representation of the revolution itself. In Martín Luis Guzmán's *El águila y la serpiente*, for example, the central character who narrates the novel portrays this struggle for control over Villa and the revolution not only as a battle between barbaric caudillo and civilized intellectual but as a battle over national identity. Throughout

the novel, Guzmán's relationship with Villa is a force through which to concep-
tualize the inchoate post-revolutionary Mexican state, which ultimately reveals
that pre-revolutionary social and economic hierarchies remain intact. For all of
Guzmán's efforts to appropriate, possess, define, and speak for him, he does not
understand Villa at all. One of the most fascinating things about *El águila* is that
the character of Villa seems to realize this and, through this knowledge, symbolically controls both the tenor of the novel and his own image.

El águila, which was written during the revolution and published in Madrid
in 1928, records the events leading up to, during, and immediately after the Convention of Aguascalientes in October 1914, a turning point in the conflict when
the allied revolutionary factions of Villismo and Carrancismo broke with each
other once and for all.[11] Guzmán positions himself as an omniscient narrator who
shifts seamlessly between first and third person. The entire novel reflects both
his obsession and his disgust with Villa; indeed, the duality of Guzman's feelings indicates the degree to which he had trouble understanding the general.[12]
Guzmán's portrayal of Villa and his account of the events of the revolution are
frequently paradoxical and conflicted, certainly much more so than in Guzmán's
later work *Memorias de Pancho Villa* (1938), which, perhaps because of the benefit of time and distance, presents a much more positive view of the general.[13]
The conflict between Guzmán's lack of understanding and his appropriation
of Villa and of the revolution for his own purposes is the crux of *El águila*. In
sections like "La fiesta de las balas" (The carnival of the bullets) and "La araña
homicida" (Murder in the dark), Guzmán illustrates the arbitrary nature of the
politics of the revolution and the futility behind any claim to justice.[14] Nevertheless, Guzmán is always conveniently present at just the right moments in the
narrative. He provides counsel to Villa and his men before crucial battles, he witnesses the historic Zapatista occupation of the presidential palace, he observes
the Villistas' encounters with new forms of technology such as moving pictures
and modern vehicles, and he narrowly escapes death several times. Ultimately,
despite his ostensible support for the revolutionary ideals of land reform and free
suffrage, Guzmán frames the social and racial hierarchies in Mexico as inevitable
and permanent. This is evident in his association of the perceived ignorance and
barbarism of the peasant rebels with the impoverished, barren landscape of the
U.S.-Mexico border region.

To complicate Guzmán's representation of the revolution, he wavers between
portraying himself as a privileged observer of the conflict and an active participant in it. As a member of the intelligentsia, Guzmán characterizes himself
as an outsider, frequently pointing out the absurdity of his situation by calling
his revolutionary experience "a mad journey" and musing, "What was I doing
there?" (*El águila* 138–139). He is initially reluctant to accept a political position in the new Conventionist cabinet, citing his status as a civilian, though he

eventually relents and takes the job (310–311). Despite the fact that Guzmán, as an elite intellectual, emphasizes his intrinsic alienation from the revolution in either military or political terms, he fetishizes his own personal experience above intellectual theorization about the conflict. Yet, as Horacio Legrás argues, Guzmán's personal experience with the revolution is characterized by an almost total lack of action and in fact is actually predicated upon distance and disdain (449).[15] Clearly, Guzmán is not untainted by the structure of revolutionary hierarchies, and it is obvious that he is in no way an impartial observer. For example, it is clear that Guzmán's reluctance to accept the political position as minister of defense has little to do with his status as a civilian, and everything to do with his disdain for and fear of the "barbaric" peasant revolutionaries he would be called upon to guide. Like the intellectual Luis Cervantes in *Los de abajo*, Guzmán is opportunistic and eventually abandons his revolutionary ideals. Ultimately, his contradictory representation of himself as an impartial observer, an engaged participant, a champion of revolutionary ideals, or an advocate for the old guard parallels his contradictory representation of Villa and the revolution.

Like the boat and train that ferry Guzmán into and out of the revolutionary scene, Pancho Villa frames *El águila* as a point of entry and exit for the narrator, a rhetorical device that enables proximity to the revolutionary masses, and a plot device that points toward the denouement of the revolution. In his interactions with Villa, Guzmán reproduces the relation between "civilization and barbarism" that is so crucial to myths of Latin American national formation. In the section "Primer vislumbre de Pancho Villa" (My first glimpse of Pancho Villa), Guzmán sets his first encounter with the caudillo in the context of a border crossing from El Paso, Texas, to Ciudad Juárez, Chihuahua. He calls this crossing the greatest "sacrifice" and "humiliation" that human geography could ever impose upon the "sons of Mexico" (*El águila* 37). Villa is linked to the supposedly immoral environment of Juárez, but like the vice-ridden town itself, he is also irresistible to the narrator as a symbol of imminent revolutionary change. The intellectual's awe of the general's brute power is tempered by fear and his feelings of innate superiority over the barbaric peasant. But this disdain cannot compete with Guzmán's deep desire to possess and be possessed by Villa. Indeed, Guzmán's relation to and fascination with Villa resembles practices of saintly possession. His sense of intellectual superiority depends upon possessing an image of the general in the name of national unity. Yet Guzmán's image of Villa is ultimately unattainable because it cannot tolerate contradiction, whether in relation to the peasant masses, the revolution, or Villa himself.

It is clear that pre-revolutionary social and racial hierarchies persist in *El águila*, and Guzmán's relationship with Villa manifests the entrenchment of hierarchies such as those between the intellectual and the caudillo. Nevertheless, Guzmán's portrayal of Villa neither reflects solely a relationship between superior and subordinate nor one between revolutionary equals. Instead, Guzmán fluctuates between representing the general as an incomprehensible and threatening presence and representing him as someone he is fascinated with and even homoerotically attracted to. This dual rejection and attraction is certainly disidentificatory, as José Esteban Muñoz would have it. At the same time, Guzmán's desire to capture Villa's aura evokes spirit possession. Yet, while Muñoz suggests that the value of disidentification is its capacity to provide subjects with the agency to manage their identities as well as to embrace contradiction, Guzmán resists his contradictory feelings at every turn (Muñoz 25, 12). In his first meeting with Villa, Guzmán depicts the general's dark hideaway as an alien space. He assumes the perspective of a hunter approaching a dangerous animal in its lair. In this context, Villa is understood as completely other, and inassimilable, not only to Guzmán as an elite intellectual but to the Mexican state itself. Although Villa is a military man, in the novel his character bears no trace of order or duty. Instead, Guzmán describes the general as unpredictable, violent, and frightening. In his shadowy bunker, he is always on the defense and perpetually ready for battle, fully dressed and alert even though he is resting on a cot when the men arrive. Guzmán immediately compares Villa to a wild animal, "but an animal that defends itself rather than one that attacks" (El águila 43).

At the same time, Guzmán emphasizes Villa's unusual, even superhuman or unearthly characteristics. The general's visible arm is "unbelievably long," while the kerosene lamp shining on him allows him to illuminate the entire room with an ethereal smile, with "a gleam of copper around the brilliance of the whites of his eyes and the enamel of his teeth" (El águila 42–43). Villa may be surrounded by crude, ignorant peasants, hidden away in a dirty hole, and constantly under threat of attack, but in Guzmán's eyes, he is an otherworldly presence. Ultimately, Guzmán seems to reject the notion that Villa is simply an animal on the defensive. He decides that the general has "more of a jaguar about him than a man," though he is temporarily tamed for the intellectuals' revolutionary designs (44). This docility is just an illusion, however, and Villa remains "a jaguar whose back we stroked with trembling hand, fearful that at any moment a paw might strike out at us" (44). Rather than simply indicating the general's capacity for savagery, this comparison elevates him to superhuman, even godly status in the narrator's eyes, especially in light of the importance of jaguar gods in the Mayan and other Mesoamerican cultures. For Guzmán, Villa is more than human, less than human, and resolutely human all at once, reflecting the intersection of human and divine in the body of the secular saint.

Later, since there are not enough chairs to accommodate everyone in his party, Villa invites Guzmán to sit beside him. In one of the defining moments of the novel, Guzmán is perched on the edge of Villa's cot, just inches away from him, and rather sensuously observes, "the warmth of the bed penetrated through my clothes to my flesh" (*El águila* 42). This scene situates Villa's body as a "tactile presence that allows intimate moments between men" and evokes the erotic virility and homoerotic desire that pervades the novel, linking the narrator, Villa, and the revolutionary nation (Domínguez-Ruvalcava 58). While Héctor Domínguez-Ruvalcava argues that Villa's "feared and desired body creates a threshold that suspends desire without consummating it," positioning the hero's body in the "liminality between eroticism and politics that defines desire in [the] novel," Guzmán's physical absorption of Villa's body heat and essence does suggest a consummation of sorts (59).

Specifically, this moment of transfer evokes a symbolic spirit possession. As in his experience of homoerotic desire, Guzmán disidentifies with the possibility of possessing Villa's spiritual essence. He is simultaneously fascinated, appalled, and frightened by the transfer of the general's intense corporeality to his own body. But apart from signaling Guzmán's desire for the virile body of the hero and the dangerous frisson of the divine, the scene also illustrates the transfer of the revolutionary mandate from the military caudillo to the intellectual. In this sense, an erotically charged spirit possession functions as a vehicle for a new revolutionary national identity, in which theory merges with practice. At the same time, this transfer harshly indicates the triumph of intellectual thinking and politics over military action, especially in relation to the revolutionary masses. In reality, Guzmán assimilates Villa's virile force and peasant aura not to erase the differences between the two men or to embrace contradiction but to demonstrate his control over the general.

It is quite clear that Guzmán privileges rational, intellectual thinking over military force, for he thinks to himself, "[Villa] represented unrestrained brutality, which could be controlled only by wise guidance" (*El águila* 264). Indeed, throughout the novel, Guzmán emphasizes not only Villa's brutality but his recklessness, as when the general impulsively orders the execution of a group of soldiers who have surrendered to the Villistas, exclaiming, "What to do with them? What a question! What should he do except shoot them?" (294). The narrator is horrified by such barbarism and focuses on the general's "blazing eyes" and his "face [flaming] with his most terrible rage, his uncontrollable, devastating wrath" (294). Yet Guzmán is too frightened to contradict Villa and only encourages him to pardon the soldiers after much questioning: "The person who surrenders, General, by doing so spares the life of others, since he renounces the possibility of dying fighting. And this being the case, the one who accepts the surrender has no right to order the death sentence" (297). While Villa ultimately calls off the execution, Guzmán's interaction with the general reveals the difference between the intellectual and the caudillo, and how entrenched their respective social positions are. Guzmán's obsession with social categories reflects his intellectual and national insecurity, for his attempts to redefine the Mexican nation according to the ideals of revolutionary change conflict with his desire to maintain a position of intellectual superiority. Guzmán cannot escape his role as an elite intellectual, despite his erotically and spiritually charged desire for Villa and the revolution. Ultimately, the tension between the pen and the sword leads to a break at the end of the novel, as Guzmán rejects Villa as inassimilable to his national project.

Guzmán eventually decides that Villa's domestication is an illusion. Not only can he never truly possess the general either erotically or spiritually, he does not even want to. Villa's character seems well aware that the intellectual is unable to possess or control him, just as he understands that the inversion of social hierarchies in the revolution is ephemeral. Despite the authority and loyalty he commands from the Villistas and the northern Mexican populace in general, Villa knows he can never officially be a part of the Mexican government. After he is abandoned by the Conventionist government, he flatly rejects Guzmán's explanation of the situation, saying, "I don't care about those affairs of yours" (*El águila* 463).[16] Indeed, the Villistas, Zapatistas, and other peasant revolutionaries in the novel repeatedly manifest their estrangement from dominant conceptions of the nation and nationalism in order to formulate new ones. In this manner, Villa and the other peasant revolutionaries resist appropriation and possession by intellectuals and elites such as Guzmán and challenge official conceptions of the popular and dominant, the modern and non-modern, while rearticulating revolutionary ideals in unexpected ways.

Naturally, Pancho Villa is also central to the peasant revolutionaries' conception of the Mexican nation, as seen in the section "La película de la Revolución" (The film of the revolution), one of the best-known sections in the novel.[17] The episode, which takes place during the Convention of Aguascalientes, focuses on the exhibition of a film that features some of the most important battles and caudillos of the revolution, including Villa and Venustiano Carranza. As Guzmán and his friend General Lucio Blanco sit behind the projection screen in order to avoid the tumult of the crowd, Blanco bribes the operators to bring them the most comfortable chairs in the house.[18] Meanwhile, the narrator describes the escalating commotion in the theater, as competing revolutionary factions in the audience call out their approval and condemnation of the various military leaders, with cries of "Long live . . ." and "Down with . . ." (*El águila* 290). The crowd is most vocal in its support for Villa—but Carranza, the "Primer Jefe" (First Chief) of the Constitutionalist army, appears more frequently than anyone else in the film.[19] In the context of the factionalism of the revolution, especially during the divisive Convention of Aguascalientes, this suggests that the filmmaker was one of Carranza's partisans. The atmosphere in the room turns chaotic and two shots are fired, which pierce the screen where Carranza's image appears, narrowly missing the heads of Guzmán and Blanco. With characteristic sarcasm, the narrator points out that if Carranza, in the film, had entered Mexico City on foot rather than on horseback, both Guzmán and Blanco would be dead. Guzmán concludes that the arrogant Carranza would never have made such a modest entrance. If Carranza had not been so arrogant, in fact, there would have been no film viewing or bullets for there would have been no need for the Convention at all, presumably because there would have been no other dominant figure to challenge Villa and Zapata (*El águila* 291).

By emphasizing the unruliness of the crowd, as when he refers to their "savage peals of laughter," "guttural howls," and "hellish din," Guzmán implies that the shooting is the impulsive act of barbaric peasants (*El águila* 289–291). However, the revolutionary masses are neither incapable of controlling themselves nor are they simply pre-modern spectators who mistake representation for reality. Guzmán's disdain for the peasants obscures the significance of the crowd's actual response. Through the chaos of the cries and shots, the crowd articulates its own brand of collective national identity in order to reject Carranza's film.

Film as a genre is central not only to the representation of the Mexican Revolution but to the development of revolutionary policy and even to the course of the battles themselves. For example, it is well-known that revolutionary battles, especially those involving Villa and his troops, were routinely filmed and photographed by U.S. filmmakers and photojournalists (De Orellana, *La mirada* 20–26). Many of the peasant soldiers at the Convention would have been familiar with the use of film as official propaganda, and some might even have been filmed or photographed themselves. Although all of the generals, including Carranza and Victoriano Huerta, developed their own propaganda through print media, largely through the financial support of Mexican and U.S. publications, Villa was the marketing champion and media darling of the revolution (Anderson 8). Villa, not Carranza, was produced as an international movie star by American film companies such as Mutual Film. Thus, the fact that the film focuses on Carranza implies that he is trying to garner support among Convention participants or to impose his leadership upon the masses. As Margarita de Orellana argues, "*caudillos*, generals or dictators were capable of doing anything the film-maker asked of them, if they thought that they would in turn receive a favorable representation of their movements" (*Filming* 2). By promoting Carranza, the film implicitly coerces the revolutionary masses to support him, and they were surely aware of this manipulation.

Indeed, the peasant soldiers clearly have a sense of their own role in shaping and performing the revolution. Like Villa, they understand that the social hierarchies purported to be overturned by the revolution are destined to endure. By piercing the screen separating them from Guzmán and Blanco, the crowd symbolically rejects the hierarchies represented by the intellectuals' physical distance from the peasants and their use of bribery to secure privilege. Ultimately, the shooting has no effect on the tension between Villa, Carranza, and their supporters, or on the politics of the Convention in general. Nevertheless, it articulates peasant agency. By creating chaos, the peasant revolutionaries symbolically reject the definition of the revolution as imposed by generals and intellectuals. The peasants who shoot at the film screen assume the intellectual's function of defining revolutionary ideals, marking one of the only times that anyone other than Guzmán takes on this role in the novel.

Despite his condescension toward the revolutionary peasants and as in his interactions with Villa, Guzmán attempts to define them so as to possess their simultaneously alluring and threatening aura. However, the masses subtly refuse Guzmán's and other intellectuals' representations of revolutionary hierarchies and social change. As in their violent reaction to the film, the peasants refuse to be appropriated or possessed by elite intellectuals such as Guzmán. Unlike him, the peasant revolutionaries in novels like *El águila* and *Los de abajo* know that their social position will not change as a result of the revolution, at least not in the way decreed by the intellectuals. Although the masses may desire Villa just as much as Guzmán does, they more consciously disidentify with him, for they recognize that they are not on his level. Furthermore, unlike the intellectuals, the peasant revolutionaries realize that all of the revolutionary leaders could well be interchangeable. For instance, in *Los de abajo* the troops are initially confused and frightened by Villa's decline and defeat in several battles, and eventually one of them thinks, "Villa, Obregon, Carranza . . . What's it to me?" suggesting that the revolutionary factions are transposable and ultimately pointless (Azuela 198). The leader of one of the irregular bands of peasant soldiers in *Los de abajo*, Demetrio Macías asserts, "Villa defeated was a fallen god. And fallen gods are not gods or anything at all"—thus articulating the futility of the iconography and power structures of the revolution (199).

Similarly, in *El águila*, the guard who encounters Guzmán and his companions at the entrance to Villa's lair seems resigned to his fate. Guzmán imagines that the guard conveys a sense of "humble pride" as befits "victorious revolutionaries," but his dragging limbs and the enormous sombrero that squashes and overshadows his body, weighed down under a heavy rifle and scores of cartridge belts, reflect his abject condition compared to both the intellectual and the general (*El águila* 40–41). Following his characterization of the border region and its people as vulgar and barbaric, Guzmán defines the peasant masses through landscape in *El águila*, particularly in relation to the mountainous, inhospitable desert terrain of the northern Mexican borderlands. He describes the border region as a desolate, uncivilized area filled with bare, squat adobe hovels, a sea of dust and filth that infiltrates every corner, and shadowy, hazy air (37–40). Echoing the language used to define the body of the Villista guard, the air, dust, and filth are untamable, and poised to stifle revolutionary change. In contrast to the intellectual's attempts to define and possess the revolution, the peasant troops, and the general himself, the representation of bodies and landscape in *El águila* demonstrates the permanence of social and political hierarchies in Mexico.

In his final meeting with Villa, Guzmán's emotions oscillate between fear, pathos, and awe. The caudillo described as a jaguar earlier in the novel has now been betrayed by his most trusted men, defeated, and confined to the town of Aguascalientes. Yet Villa retains his threatening power and air of unpredictability. Guzmán is clearly still afraid of him and describes his encounter as being trapped in the "Lion's Mouth" (*The Eagle* 362). He is on tenterhooks as they talk, since he knows that the general could shoot him at any moment (384).[20] At the same time, Guzmán expresses the desire he has always felt for Villa, in his attention to the general's face, body, clothing, and gestures. As Villa approaches him on his "splendid sorrel," Guzmán says, "He was wearing a brown sweater that revealed every movement of the muscles of his breast and arms. His broad-brimmed hat was pushed back from his forehead by his thatch of curly hair. I could not analyze any more. His torso grew and grew, as his horse ambled toward me until its expanse flooded my eyes" (382). Guzmán suggests that Villa's bodily presence exceeds his intellectual powers of representation ("I could not analyze any more"). But rather than signaling the end point of their relationship, this scene emphasizes the symbiosis between Guzmán and Villa, especially in regard to the integration of their bodies. Villa's image "floods" Guzmán's vision, while the narrator's focus on the movement of the general's "breast and arms" is sensual and all-consuming. Villa's approach causes Guzmán's heart to beat so fast it "[fills his] whole breast, [his] throat, and [throbs] in his temples" (382). The two men's bodies merge even more completely when Villa greets the narrator with a powerful hug: "Then I felt myself lifted a foot off the ground in his arms, and his breath and mine were intermingled" (383).

Although it might seem as if the general's seductive, virile allure has disappeared by now, in fact the narrator is as bound to Villa as ever. The final scene echoes Guzmán's first meeting with Villa, for once again the men's bodily essence—corporal warmth and breath—is exchanged, and the narrator cannot determine where his body ends and where Villa's begins. Such mutual embodiment obviously distresses Guzmán, but his anxiety is superseded by his desire for and visceral link to the general. It is the symbolic physical union between caudillo and intellectual that suggests that Villa is not merely a hero to admire, or a scoundrel to fear, but a secular saint whose essence can be invoked, inhabited, or possessed. The bodily exchange and possession between Villa and Guzmán is inherently ambivalent. Despite the link between the two men, the stark contrast between Guzmán's mobility and Villa's lack of action at the end suggests a bleak, cynical result for the masses' hopes for lasting social, economic, and political change through the revolution. At the same time, even though he initially insists that Guzmán remain with him to be his personal secretary, it is Villa who allows

the narrator to escape in the novel, even securing his passage on a train to El
Paso. Although Villa enjoins Guzmán, "Don't desert me, friend; don't do it, for
honestly, I'm your friend. You're not going to desert me, are you?" the general
seals his own fate by allowing his last political ally to flee (El águila 386). Unbe-
knownst to Guzmán, Villa's character gets the last laugh in the novel by controlling his image, even in defeat. By hastening Guzmán's departure, even though
he knows exactly what it will cost him, Villa demonstrates that he understands
intellectuals like Guzmán far better than they could ever understand him. Villa's
character symbolically seizes control of the representation of his image from the
narrator in El águila. In the process, the general denies Guzmán the possibility of
symbolic spirit possession.

Losing Pancho: Villa in Film, Past and Present

Like Guzmán in El águila y la serpiente, many of the filmmakers who treat Pancho Villa are deeply invested in representing the myth, whether in the service of
Mexican nationalism, American exceptionalism, or the exoticization of the peasant revolutionary. The audience for revolutionary novels (even when they were
serialized in newspapers) was far smaller than that for popular film, however. As
Friedrich Katz argues in his prologue to Margarita de Orellana's La mirada circular, rather than novels, histories, or even the famous murals by Diego Rivera
or José Clemente Orozco, film was the primary means through which U.S. and
European audiences experienced and understood the Mexican Revolution
(Katz, "Prólogo" 7).[21] Film, especially Hollywood film, produces Villa as global
and transnational, beyond his status as a Mexican or regional border subject. The
Hollywood films of the revolution studied by De Orellana (that were produced
during the armed phase of the revolution from 1910 to 1917) are important not
only for their representation of Pancho Villa and the revolution but for dissemi-
nating the image of Mexico throughout the world. Katz notes that only a small
fraction of the American-produced newsreels and fictional films on the Mexican
revolution were ever shown south of the border, due to their frequently racist
portrayal of Mexico and Mexicans ("Prólogo" 7). Indeed, De Orellana demonstrates that Hollywood films on the revolution are largely responsible for the
construction of stereotypes of barbarous Mexico and the savage, shifty "greaser"
(La mirada 11). Villa was often the focal point for this racist portrayal, though as
usual he was presented in a contradictory fashion.

Film scholar Zuzana Pick argues that many Mexican films produced after the
revolution portrayed the conflict in stereotypical ways, particularly in folkloric
or exoticist representations, a trend that reinforces the Mexican state's particular
brand of mestizaje-inflected, modernizing nationalism even as it reiterates Mexico's inherent difference from the United States or Europe (3).[22] Of course, there

were some exceptions, especially among films produced during the Golden Age of Mexican cinema (roughly 1935–1959) that "managed, in imperfect and sometimes surprising ways, to reflect on the revolution as a disruptive and contradictory event" (Pick 4). Yet, perhaps because Mexico has always been imagined at least to some extent as the exotic other in relation to the United States, Hollywood portrayals of the revolution have not always been so nuanced. Certainly, some early Hollywood films and newsreels portrayed Villa as a heroic Robin Hood, but after his raid on Columbus, New Mexico, in 1916, he became the very essence of the bloodthirsty Mexican bandit (Pick 107–133). Villa continues to be an alluring subject for American filmmakers, although as Katz, de Orellana, and filmmaker Gregorio Rocha demonstrate, he is often represented through the stereotype of the Mexican bandit and "greaser" even today, as in the 2003 HBO film *And Starring Pancho Villa as Himself* (Rocha, "*And Starring*" 143).[23] Many Mexican films are critical of dominant portrayals of Villa, even as they may reiterate his mythic properties. Two disparate examples of this duality are *¡Vámonos con Pancho Villa!* (1935) and *Los rollos perdidos de Pancho Villa/The Lost Reels of Pancho Villa* (2003). Both films explicitly reject Hollywood's claim on Mexico and the revolution and seek to examine the man behind the myth, albeit in very different ways. Both films are clearly critical of mythic representations of the general, but they occasionally portray him uncritically as a heroic icon and evoke his role as a secular saint through the lens of spirit possession. This is particularly true of Rocha's film.

¡Vámonos con Pancho Villa! was directed by Fernando de Fuentes and adapted by the poet and playwright Xavier Villaurrutia from the novel by the same name by Rafael Felipe Muñoz. Although the film is widely considered to be one of the best Mexican films of all time, it was initially a box office failure, partly because it does not reproduce an optimistic vision of Villa and Mexico, drawing upon sentimentality and represented by the folkloric cowboy and hacienda past (Pick 86, 96). Instead, the film focuses on a group of six friends—known as Los Leones de San Pablo—who join the revolution after the youngest, Miguel Ángel del Toro (Ramón Vallarino), narrowly escapes execution by a federal army officer. Angry at the treatment of peasants by the federal army the group, led by Tiburcio Maya (Antonio R. Frausto), meets with Villa and his army at a rail crossing. Villa (Domingo Soler) accepts the Leones into his army but emphasizes that they must display bravery and valor. He jovially taunts the group, "Just how macho are you guys?" and exclaims, "Let's see if your bite is as big as your roar, my lions," after hearing about the group's moniker.[24]

As Villistas, the Leones de San Pablo fight in several battles, perform heroic deeds, negotiate on the general's behalf with the federal army, engage in a game of "the circle of death" (a Mexican version of Russian roulette) in a cantina, and generally ponder death and the meaning of revolution. In the midst of these endeavors, one by one they die: some randomly, like Rodrigo Perea (Carlos López, called Chaflán), who is killed by a stray bullet during a rescue attempt after the federal army sentences the Leones to hang; others valiantly, like Máximo Perea (Raúl de Anda), who falls after capturing a machine gun from the enemy and presenting it to Villa. Ultimately, only two Leones remain—Tiburcio Maya and the young Del Toro (christened Becerrillo [Little calf] by Villa). Then Becerrillo is suddenly struck down by smallpox. Tiburcio is determined to nurse Becerrillo back to health, but when Villa finds out about his illness, he sends General Fierro (Alfonso Sánchez Tello) to order Tiburcio to dispose of his friend. Tiburcio reluctantly complies by shooting Becerrillo and burning his body, but Villa orders him to stay behind, for fear of infection. Disillusioned and alone, Tiburcio walks into the night, away from Villa and the revolution.[25]

Despite the film's reference in its preamble to the "loyalty and courage" that the general inspired in his troops, ¡Vámonos con Pancho Villa! emphasizes the barbarism of Villa and the revolution. Notably, the preamble does not speak of Villa's loyalty and courage, but that of his men. Indeed, as Pick argues, in the film Villa "personifies the revolution but is not its leading protagonist," which reinforces his antiheroic role and transfers the focus, and viewer identification, to the Leones of San Pablo (85). The Leones are unquestionably brave and absolutely committed to Villa, but above all, they are devoted to each other. Such loyalty culminates in Tiburcio's tender ministrations to Becerrillo during his illness, even when he is forced to follow the impossible orders to kill the sick boy. The contrast between the valor and camaraderie of the Leones and the ruthlessness of Villa is obvious, suggesting that the film rejects the routine conflation of Villa and the revolution with the Mexican people. This is evident in the preamble, which, calling to mind the concurrent battles of World War I, refers to the revolutionary period as a "tragic epoch" during which "a field called Flanders" and the "peaceful valleys of France" were bloodied just as much as "the hills of Mexico." As a result, "the blame for the cruelty that occurred [during the revolution] cannot be put on any [one] group of people."

The film does not equate the horrors of revolutionary violence with the Mexican people in general, and as Pick notes, it shifts away from "glorifying mythical figures" like Villa in favor of representing the "communal quotidian of war" (96). In this sense, ¡Vámonos con Pancho Villa! is critical of dominant portrayals of Pancho Villa in several ways. While it clearly rejects the symbol of the barbaric Mexican "greaser," it reinforces the myth of Villa as a ruthless scoundrel. But a closer reading of Villa in the film, and of his representation in the eyes of the Leones, reveals a more nuanced, ambivalent character. Much of this ambivalence has to do with the fact that the masses who follow Villa construct his image but also challenge it. The Villa portrayed in the film administers arbitrary justice. He is a hypocrite who promotes the rules of war, as when he supports the primacy of the troop above individual soldiers, yet he distances himself from his men. Like a popular saint, he inspires complete devotion in those who surround him, particularly the Leones. At the same time, Villa consistently promotes his own heroic myth in the film. When we first encounter the general, he is theatrically distributing corn to a crowd of peasants from an open boxcar, exclaiming, "Look what Pancho Villa fights for! So you can all eat! Now I give you corn. When we have won, I'll give you land! Everyone will have a ranch. Nobody will be working as a peon." At first glance, this scene reinforces the perception of Villa as a benevolent champion of the poor, as he calls out to the throng, "Come my sons. Come for your corn." The camera shifts focus from Villa to the adoring crowd, especially the women among them. Villa obviously delights in singling out the women among the crowd, and at one point he even ignores a group of peasants in the front to fill the basket of an especially attractive woman with all of the remaining corn. His jovial, lascivious attitude as he sizes up the pretty woman certainly reinforces his role as the quintessential macho, but it also disrupts his position as a selfless Robin Hood figure by revealing his egotism. While the peasants definitely idolize the general, this scene demonstrates the ambivalence inherent in his sanctity. In many ways Villa and the masses who worship him are at odds with each other, and his self-congratulatory machismo does not mesh with his professed altruism.

Other examples of Villa's hypocrisy and random brutality in the film include the scene where he angrily orders the Leones to steal a machine gun from the enemy federal army: "It's time to show you're lions, and not pussycats!" Villa is belligerent as he goads the Leones to make good on their promise that they are truly macho men, though he softens, when Máximo Perea returns with the gun, and says, "Now I believe you are everything you say." When Máximo is subsequently shot and falls at Villa's feet, the general ostentatiously pats his back and congratulates him for his valiant deed. Yet no one expects Villa to risk his own life crossing enemy lines. While he is likely shielded from this possibility as the leader of the División del Norte, the derisive tone he takes on when dealing with the eternally obedient Leones smacks of hypocrisy and destabilizes the machismo that characterizes Villa and motivates the Leones' actions and their view of themselves and the revolution. Villa's insistence on honor and the rules of war is further belied by the scene when he promotes the Leones to the rank of Dorados (the golden ones), who serve as his escorts. After the Leones leave, an officer informs Villa that General Urbina has captured a band of musicians from the enemy and wishes to execute them. Villa replies, "No, man, how barbaric. Poor musicians, have them join one of our brigades."[26] When the officer protests that every brigade already has its own band, Villa coolly reverses the order: "Is that so? Then go ahead and execute them. Why are you bothering me with this?"[27] Actor Domingo Soler's deadpan delivery reinforces the arbitrary nature of war and the everyday character of life and death decisions. The horror of the randomness in war revealed by this scene contrasts with the notions of honor and machismo that Villa insists upon elsewhere.

The emphasis upon machismo and honor is finally put to rest by the disparity between the Leones' commitment to each other and Villa's hypocritical, frequently capricious behavior, which epitomizes the revolution in the film. The apex of this conflict occurs in the scene when Villa learns of Becerrillo's illness. Villa's reaction to the threat of smallpox is swift: "Get the sick from the train at once! Otherwise they'll infect the rest." Informed that Becerrillo is one of the infected, he calmly says: "This is war. Soldiers come first." In contrast, Tiburcio clings to the ideals of individual honor and brotherhood and clashes with General Fierro over Becerrillo's fate, exclaiming: "So you'd leave him here to die like a dog?" Although Tiburcio eventually agrees to follow orders, he is incredulous when Fierro orders him to burn everything, including Becerrillo's body. Tiburcio naturally protests, calling out, "Is this an army of men or of dogs?" but he finally complies. Meanwhile, the camera shifts to Fierro, who, out of Tiburcio's earshot, orders another soldier to burn down the boxcar if he does not exit in five minutes. This scene demonstrates that Tiburcio's existential struggle between following orders and his devotion to his friend, as well as the tenderness he displays when he finally shoots Becerrillo, are all pointless. No matter what Tiburcio does, General Fierro's orders will be carried out. Finally, when Villa arrives, Tiburcio approaches him with a wild look on his face, saluting as he indicates Becerrillo's burning corpse. In the ultimate act of hypocrisy, Villa fearfully shrinks from Tiburcio and angrily orders him to stay behind until he sends for him. In the end, Tiburcio decides to walk away from Villa and the revolution, perhaps realizing (unlike the crowd of peasants who beg Villa for corn) that everything he believes in—Villa, the revolution, and his devotion to the Leones—is a farce. Tiburcio's remorse is probably also due to the fact that, in an earlier scene, he had convinced the reluctant Becerrillo to stay with Villa, even as the boy tried to persuade Tiburcio that the revolution marches to its own inevitable rhythm. By walking away, Tiburcio symbolically refuses the heroic myth surrounding the general that the Leones had adhered to throughout most the film.

At every turn, ¡Vámonos con Pancho Villa! demonstrates the futility of heroic myth and ultimately elevates the common man over the mythical leader, as is evident in Tiburcio's admittedly belated decision to reject Villa and the revolution. Yet, although the film appears to favor the loyalty and honor of peasant soldiers like the Leones above the ideals of war espoused by leaders such as Villa or General Fierro, in the end, the intense camaraderie of the Leones and their hopes for the revolution amount to nothing. Despite Tiburcio's decision at the end of the film to walk away and take control of his own destiny, ¡Vámonos con Pancho Villa! suggests even more clearly than El águila that there is no destiny at all left for the peasant masses, and certainly no hope for real social or personal change as a result of the revolution. Far from being an idealized secular saint— even one who is typically flawed—the Pancho Villa portrayed in *¡Vámonos con Pancho Villa!* is merely a hypocrite who lectures others about loyalty and honor while his actions demonstrate ruthlessness, pride, and cowardice.

Like *¡Vámonos con Pancho Villa!* the experimental, first-person documentary *Los rollos perdidos de Pancho Villa/The Lost Reels of Pancho Villa* by Gregorio Rocha explores the Pancho Villa behind the myth and contests foreigners' frequently condescending representations of Villa, the revolution, and Mexicans in general. As in *¡Vámonos!* Villa is the catalyst of the film but not its protagonist. Rather, *Los rollos perdidos/The Lost Reels* centers on the role of film as archival object and Rocha's personal quest to find the missing film *The Life of General Villa*, a biography of Villa filmed in 1914 by the Mutual Film Company that combines actual combat with dramatic scenes. The documentary follows Rocha, both through his on-camera presence and off-screen first-person narration, as he travels across continents researching foreign depictions of Villa and the revolution found in archives in Europe and North America. In the process, he meets with film historians and archivists, historians of the Mexican Revolution, and the descendants of Charles Rosher, a Mutual Film cameraman, and Edmundo Padilla, a Texas film exhibitor. Rocha also holds a humorous casting call with local actors in Durango, Mexico, to re-create the lost Villa film, and contemplates his own relationship with his project through the subjects—both anonymous and well-known—who populate these films. In the end, Rocha does not find *The Life of General Villa*. However, in El Paso, among the stash of old film reels and documents kept by the family of the itinerant movie exhibitors Félix and Edmundo Padilla, Rocha discovers *La venganza de Pancho Villa* (The vengeance of Pancho Villa), a previously unknown film made up of segments of old silent films of Villa and the revolution—including one from *The Life of General Villa*—and newly filmed dramatic footage. The Padillas' film, which was produced in the 1930s, rejects the default American characterization of Villa after the Columbus raid as an archetypal Mexican bandit and, instead, presents him as a heroic figure. *La venganza de Pancho Villa* thus reclaims a specifically Mexican heroism—which is also a Mexican American, border, and migrant heroism— and lends new meaning to the concept of vengeance in the context of the U.S.-Mexico border region during the post-revolutionary period.

Throughout *Los rollos perdidos/The Lost Reels*, Rocha struggles against the representation of Villa as a barbaric villain, reflecting a very different perspective from that of *¡Vámonos!* which resists Villa's portrayal as a heroic Robin Hood. Although *Los rollos perdidos/The Lost Reels* and *¡Vámonos!* are both Mexican films, they exemplify contrasting representations of nationalism and national identification. *¡Vámonos!* primarily wrestles with an interior Mexican view of

Villa and the revolution, while *Los rollos perdidos/The Lost Reels* challenges the foreigner's perspective of Mexico. Both films emphasize Villa's role vis-à-vis Mexican national identity. Although Rocha's portrayal of Villa is situated in an international context, for example, one of his main goals is to correct the historical record on Villa, the Mexican Revolution, and the representation of Mexicans by Americans and Europeans. In the midst of his painstaking scholarly research in libraries and archives, his interviews with historians, and his extensive travels across Europe, the United States, and Mexico, however, Rocha rather subjectively identifies himself as a stand-in for the Mexican people—and, in an echo of spirit possession, even for Villa himself. The film is clearly "ironically humorous" (Johnson, "Pancho Villa" n.p.). Yet given how earnest Rocha's research and efforts are to correct biased or inaccurate representations of Villa, it is difficult to ascertain how much of his identification with Villa is sincere and how much is ironic or performative. It is best to consider Rocha's symbolic possession of Villa a mixture of both—especially in light of the many tongue-in-cheek gestures in the film, such as the dramatic casting call with actors in Durango and Rocha's comical reenactment of the telephone call that directs him to the presence of the lost reels in an El Paso library, which he conducts on a phone in the shape of a Coca-Cola can. At times Rocha exudes solemnity. Upon his arrival in Paris, Rocha quite seriously declares: "Today, in the city of the Manifestoes, I proclaim my right to challenge the demeaning image the foreign film industry has projected of me. I proclaim my right to see myself through the stereotypes they made of me; my right to recover the images of the past; to make them mine and bring them back to life. I am the savage, the half-breed, the 'greaser.' I am the rebel whom you never understood and who you were never able to catch."[28]

It might seem obvious that Rocha is distinguishing between foreign and Mexican national representations of Villa, and it even appears that he identifies Villa as the symbolic speaker of this passage, since he is the rebel that General John Pershing and the Americans were never able to catch in the punitive expedition after the Columbus raid. However, the ambiguity of the pronouns Rocha uses and the implied shift between his physical location in Paris and symbolic locations prevent any clarity. Instead, this scene reveals the slippage between Rocha's own voice and the imagined voice of Pancho Villa. Rocha approximates spirit possession by metaphorically assuming Villa's persona. Through the use of the first person and vague pronouns, Rocha becomes Villa and, by extension, all Mexicans who have been characterized through denigrating stereotypes. Unlike *¡Vámonos!* where Villa is effectively distanced from the masses, Rocha links him to the common people as the quintessential "savage," "half-breed," and "greaser." From the perspective of the "foreign film industry," Villa, the Mexican masses, and Rocha are all potentially greasers. Although Rocha's assessment of the foreign film industry is largely accurate, his conflation of himself, Villa, and the Mexican masses contrasts with his presumably objective focus on deciphering the truth behind Villa's myth and his efforts to parse the construction of this myth.

Los rollos perdidos/The Lost Reels is actually about the absence of those reels and of the possibility of transforming their remains into something else entirely through film. In an interview recorded by Magdalena Padilla with her father, Edmundo Padilla, Rocha says of the film *La venganza de Pancho Villa*, "People loved that movie, especially the Mexicans." This, of course, is most likely because of the Mexican-centered perspective of the Padillas' film, which counteracts the dominance of Hollywood films on Villa and the revolution. As Rocha discovers in an editing logbook and among the outtakes of *La venganza*, the Padillas cut blatantly racist scenes and titles, edited footage from silent films such as *Liberty, A Daughter of the U.S.A.* (Jacques Jaccard and Henry McRae, 1916) in order to recast heroes and villains, created bilingual Spanish- and English-language titles, and used real names for characters and events. Thus, as Rocha notes in the *Los rollos perdidos* subtitles, "Pancho López became Pancho Villa, the Mexican hero. [The town of] Discovery was changed back to Columbus." In the Padilla film, Villa is humanized rather than portrayed as a caricature, Mexicans are presented as brave and noble, and perhaps most importantly, the Americans' potential for brutality is illustrated, especially in relation to the invasion of Veracruz in 1914. Pick refers to the Padillas' film as a gesture of "resistance through recycling" (65) while in *Los rollos perdidos/The Lost Reels*, Rocha calls it "an act of cultural resistance, a revenge against the stereotypes imposed on Pancho Villa and the Mexicans. A celebration of David defeating Goliath with a sling shot." While the Padillas' film obviously rejects the bandit or "greaser" stereotype that is frequently projected onto Villa and the Mexican people, perhaps unwittingly and more interestingly, the film—and *Los rollos perdidos/The Lost Reels* itself— demonstrates the impact of the migration of Mexicans into the United States after the revolution and the development of new border identities. It is no accident that the Padillas' act of cultural resistance is a bilingual film produced in El Paso by two Mexican American Texans. Although Rocha aims to challenge the foreigner's perspective of Mexico, ultimately his failure to find the lost reels is transformed into a view into the Mexican American or nascent Chicano perspective on Mexico and the United States.

Rocha is circumspect about the possibility that the cultural resistance he discusses in his film is inherently linked to Chicano/a or border identities, although elsewhere he does discuss the role of *La venganza* as a border film, and the fact that the Padillas had "unknowingly [become] the first Mexican American filmmakers" ("La Venganza" 57). But in his film Rocha never seems to consider the possibility that when Edmundo Padilla speaks of the Mexicans who loved *La venganza*, he was probably referring to Mexican Americans in Texas. That is, Rocha's focus on the foreigner's view of Mexico, as well as his own intermittent identification with Villa, occasionally obscures the fact that the distinctions between "us" and "them" in the film do not neatly correspond to fixed Mexican and American national identities. Instead, *Los rollos perdidos/The Lost Reels* reveals the dual gaze of border subjects like the Padillas, positioned within and against both the United States and Mexico. Yet the film nevertheless manifests the tension between the interrogation of Villa's myth as a Mexican national hero and Rocha's ironic or inadvertent rearticulation of this myth. The rearticulation of Villa's myth as a nationalist hero is most evident through Rocha's identification with Villa.

Pick argues that Villa "haunts the film's discourse: its dialogue with an elusive subject in danger of melting away . . . and an absent agent of his own representation waiting to be rediscovered" (59). Indeed, the film portrays Villa in multiple ways: as a historical figure, as a spectral presence and voice that follow Rocha throughout his journey—especially evident through Villa's ghostly appearance on the window of a Paris subway car and as an image that morphs into the face of a jaguar superimposed onto a metal container filled with old film reels—and as an extension of Rocha's own voice and quest. It is clear that Rocha is extremely self-reflexive about his own relationship to filmmaking, as when he narrates at the beginning of the film, "I like to ask questions of old pictures. Who are you standing there in front of the camera? Who took your picture? Where were you? What was going through your mind?" Rocha's treatment of Villa is not completely analytical, however, for he frequently treats the general like an old friend, reinforcing his identification with Villa and evoking the intimacy inherent in spirit possession. Rocha constantly addresses the general throughout the film, with questions that range from the merely inquisitive, "So, General Villa, what happened to the movie you shot in 1914?" and "General Villa, what power did you find in moving pictures? What made you decide to make a film with the Americans?" to the apprehensive, "General Villa, who did this to you?" and "Where are you, general? Where did they hide your picture?" and the disappointed, "Oh, Villa, why did you lend yourself to this manipulation?" While Rocha's blurring of the lines between Villa's various personae is surely deliberate, his ventriloquizing—or symbolic possession—of the general sometimes calls his self-reflexive portrayal into question. This is especially evident in the friction between Rocha's representation of Villa as a disembodied historical voice and his own appropriation of this voice.

Rocha's ventriloquizing of the general is most obvious when he equates himself with Villa and the Mexican masses against the colonizing influence of foreign representations of Mexico. The scene that best exemplifies Rocha's struggle between portraying Villa critically and identifying with him occurs in Rochester, New York, after Rocha meets with film historian Pablo Cherchi Usai. Here Rocha enacts the self-reflexive perspective of the filmmaker by looking directly into the camera while pointing another camera at it. But the question he asks of the film—while filming its purported response—is, "What is it that I am looking for in you, Pancho Villa, that I cannot find in myself?" This question acknowledges Rocha's symbiotic relationship with Villa in the film, but it also underscores his deep longing for Villa, and the absence that he seeks to fill through his quest for the lost reels. This gesture resembles narratives of spirit possession that demonstrate the intersection between secular and sacred, and with this question Rocha suspends the critical, self-reflexive perspective that otherwise propels the documentary. In a sense, Rocha's appeal to Villa for personal guidance—even if it is meant ironically—is not unlike the rapt devotion of the peasants who beg for corn from Villa in ¡Vámonos con Pancho Villa!

Although there is nothing wrong with identifying with one's research subject, I am especially interested in Rocha's idealization and symbolic possession of Villa in the midst of his critical inquiry. Rocha's shifts between first person and third person, between different national identities (us versus them), and between the representations of Villa as agent and Villa as subject, all help destabilize fixed boundaries and identities, while ultimately, his identification with Villa and his potentially problematic association between himself, Villa, and the Mexican masses also reproduce these boundaries. At the end of Los rollos perdidos/The Lost Reels, for example, Rocha seems to back away from destabilizing fixed boundaries. After discovering the Padillas' film, rather than the lost reels he initially hoped to find, Rocha declares, "There is no more to discover of the imaginary Pancho Villa. Maybe he is lost to us forever." In a way, Rocha implies here that there is only one "imaginary Pancho Villa" to be found, contrary to the cultural resistance that the Padillas perform through their recycled images of the general. Even if Rocha is referring to the literal absence of images of Villa in film, as when he proclaims, "The images [in film] are true, even if neither of the stories around them nor the facts they claim to represent are. They tell us the stories the filmmakers want us to see," his closing statements contrast with the multiplicity of images and the many "imaginary" Pancho Villas that Los rollos perdidos/The Lost Reels presents us with.

Borderlands Villa, Chicano Villa

Although Los rollos perdidos/The Lost Reels certainly intimates that Villa is a borderlands or Chicano icon, Rocha does not emphasize this fact. Instead he focuses on the general as an agent for Mexican nationalism. However, Villa has always been a crucial symbol of the U.S. Mexico borderlands, especially in terms of the region's marginalized status and its fierce independence. Representations of Villa that reflect a border or Chicano perspective proceed from the assumption that there are necessarily multiple, contradictory versions of Pancho Villa.

But since the Mexican Revolution, like Villa himself, is always already contradictory, it cannot be interpreted solely through the lens of Mexican nationalism. One of the most important and sometimes overlooked characteristics of the Mexican Revolution is that it was fundamentally a border revolution, the only social revolution ever to occur along the U.S-Mexico border region (Katz, *Life* xiii). Although the revolution is clearly linked to the consolidation of Mexican national identity, it also had lasting effects on U.S. national identity, influencing Mexican migration and the construction of citizenship on either side of the border. The revolution was instrumental to the integration of the borderlands within the national consciousness of both Mexico and the United States, even as it reflected the independent spirit of the border region. The Mexican Revolution produced a new generation of migrants in the United States: by some estimates, more than one million Mexicans crossed over to the U.S. Southwest between 1910 and 1920, though some returned after conditions stabilized in Mexico. These were both voluntary and involuntary migrants who came from many social classes, including braceros seeking work, political and economic exiles (including former supporters of Porfirio Díaz), and uprooted Villista and Zapatista peasants (Meier and Ribera 105–109). Many Mexican nationals already living in the United States were inspired to join the revolutionary armies, demonstrating the fluidity of regional, national, and transnational identities during the time. Although entrenched class and social hierarchies largely persisted after the revolution, a number of them were blurred in different ways.

To date, little attention has been paid to Villa's representation in the borderlands or in the Chicano context.[29] The threat—both real and symbolic—that Villa posed to dominant national identities in the United States and Mexico made him extremely appealing to border-crossing migrants and Chicanos/as in the United States, who often carried his image across borders. Much like Chicanos/as themselves, and despite all efforts to rein him in, Villa challenges both the dominant Mexican and American national traditions. The Chicano texts that invoke Villa, like Silviana Wood's *And Where Was Pancho Villa When You Really Needed Him?*—a one-act play about the clash between a class of poor Chicano sixth-graders and their judgmental white teacher—emphasize Villa's role as figure of resistance even as they link him to a sense of loss or nostalgia. In Wood's play, the applicant/narrator character, who recalls overhearing two teachers discussing the students' low achievement and laughing at their Spanish-inflected accents, waits expectantly "for Pancho Villa to come charging into the room" to rescue him and his peers but ultimately realizes that he is waiting for nothing (191). Wood's play demonstrates the deep desire to claim Villa as a Chicano hero, and the concomitant difficulty, and even occasionally the hopelessness, of invoking his spirit for Chicanos/as and migrants. It is impossible for Villa to cross the border into the Chicano context as an unadulterated Mexican nationalist icon.

Nevertheless, many Chicano texts represent the characters' attempts to claim or invoke the general as a unified symbol of Mexican revolutionary nationalism. The association of Villa with Mexican (or, in some cases, Chicano) nationalism suggests a desire for a real or imagined ancestral home. Yet given the contradiction between Villa as both a symbol of the lost Mexican homeland and of the rootless nature of the Chicano borderlands, in these texts the general actually personifies the melancholy of the migrant. In this final section I examine Luis Valdez's play *The Shrunken Head of Pancho Villa* as an example of the contradictory representation of Villa as a symbol both for the nation and migration across borders and for the struggles that ensue over the general's remains.

The Shrunken Head of Pancho Villa

The Shrunken Head, produced in 1964 by the theater department of San Jose State University, is the first-full length play written by Luis Valdez (Valdez 146–147). Valdez was the son of migrant farmworkers and grew up in California's San Joaquín Valley. He is one of the founders of El Teatro Campesino.[30] *The Shrunken Head* tells the story of intergenerational and transborder conflict within an impoverished *mexicano* family in a central California barrio in the 1950s. Valdez notes that the play "is not intended as a 'realistic' interpretation of Chicano life" but, rather, "reflect[s] the psychological reality of the barrio" (154). The fantastic nature of the play is emphasized through the contrast between the stereotypical representation of most of the characters and the surreal portrayal of the same characters and their surroundings. While the disembodied head is certainly uncanny, its insatiable appetite and disgusting habits (such as constant growling and burping) clearly serve as a metaphor for the hopelessness of the family, which is sucked dry not only by the head but by the uncontrollable forces of economic and social stagnation, racial prejudice, and the lack of official citizenship on either side of the border. Furthermore, Valdez presents a variety of racist Chicano/a or migrant stereotypes, including the drunken father, the long-suffering mother, the pregnant unwed daughter, the shell-shocked veteran, the juvenile delinquent son, the unemployed freeloading son, and the whole family on welfare. Meanwhile, the family suffers from head lice and their home is infested with cockroaches. Valdez situates two of the sons as archetypal Chicano opposites. While Joaquín, the youngest, is described as "a vato loco and a Chicano," signaling his potential for Chicano activism, Mingo, the second son, is described as a "Mexican-American," reflecting his role as a *vendido* or "sell-out" to his people, a familiar negative trope in Chicano theater. Indeed, after returning from the Korean War, Mingo becomes a corrupt farm labor contractor, exploiting the young Chicanos/as he recruits, including his brother Joaquín and his sister's boyfriend, Chato (Valdez 153).

Alongside such Chicano/a archetypes, the family also includes Belarmino, the oldest son, who has no body—he is just a disembodied head that initially does not even speak, except to sing "La Cucaracha."[31] After Mingo returns from the war with plans to drag the family out of their barrio and into middle-class respectability, Belarmino begins to speak in Spanish, insisting that he is the lost head of Pancho Villa. Yet Belarmino is only one of several characters in the play who channel Villa, sometimes claiming to be him or otherwise appropriating aspects of his iconic persona, in an echo of both relic worship and spirit possession. For example, in the midst of his many drunken stupors, Pedro, the father, calls out, "Señores, I am Francisco Villa!" while elsewhere he touts his role as a Villista soldier in the revolution (Valdez 156). Meanwhile, late in the play, Joaquín, who has learned about the head's "true" identity as the head of Pancho Villa, adopts the general's bandit, Robin Hood, or revolutionary persona as a reaction against Mingo's exploitation of poor Chicano/a laborers as a "crooked farm labor contractor" (172). Joaquín dresses "in the traditional costume of the Mexican charro, complete with a pair of cartridge belts crisscrossed on his chest," carrying a 30-30 carbine and two large sacks of (stolen) flour and beans, not only to provide for his family but as an extension of Villa's quest for social justice (192, 194). Finally, toward the end of the play, Cruz, the mother, shakes off her abject guise to break up a fight between Joaquín and Mingo, grabbing Joaquín's rifle and ordering him to return the food he stole, declaring that she, not their father, was the true Villista soldadera (194–195).

For his part, Belarmino not only claims to be Pancho Villa, he specifically assumes his personality through a representation of the general's lost head, which has never been found and which could possibly have ended up on the U.S. side of the border. It is significant that Belarmino's Villa is a fragment— and a fragment of Villa's remains, at that—rather than a unified whole. In this sense, the Villa head resembles a relic; a part of the saint's body to be worshipped. At the same time, many of the characters in the play invoke and channel Villa through the head in the manner of spirit possession. Such spirit possession is necessarily fragmented, for it evokes the struggle for embodiment between the general's oscillating personae as a revolutionary hero, a bandit, a Robin Hood figure, a marker of nationalist Mexico, a harbinger of Chicano pride and community, or a symbol of migrant melancholia. At the same time, the metaphor of spirit possession extends to Belarmino's performance of the shrunken head in the play.

The prologue to the play describes the historical Villa's rise and fall but quickly shifts from the heroic icon to emphasize the story of his followers. Thus, the play's focal point is the story of the masses who interpellate, appropriate, or worship Villa after his death and beyond his role as a Mexican national icon: "July 23, 1923: Pancho Villa is ambushed and he dies in the streets of Parral,

Chihuahua. His body is dumped into an unmarked grave. Three years later it is disinterred and the corpse is decapitated. The head is never found. This is the story of a people who followed him beyond borders, beyond death" (Valdez 155). From the beginning of the play, a link is established between the lost head and Mexican migration to the United States. In the play, the migrants and Chicanos/as embrace the head as a symbol of the broken or fragmented condition they inhabit; a representation of the social, cultural, and national belonging that they lack but have never really possessed to begin with. In *The Shrunken Head*, the poor migrant family locates their desire for the two lost homelands—Mexico and the United States—with the loss of the heroic Villa head.

The characters in the play are caught in an uncertain present, since neither a Mexican past nor an American future is a viable option for them. Despite this bleak outlook, Pedro and Cruz, the parents of the family, sing hopefully on different occasions, "Ya vino Francisco Villa / Pa' quitarles la frontera / ¡Ya llegó Francisco Villa / A devolver la frontera! [Francisco Villa is here / To take the border from them! / Francisco Villa has arrived / To give the border back!]" In singing, they express their desire to see the border taken from the gringos and returned to its rightful owners, the Mexicans (Valdez 179 and 199).[32] But both instances represent moments of abjection and loss: Pedro is in a delusional stupor just one scene before his death, and Cruz, near the end of the play, has lost two of her sons and is mired in the physical decay of the crumbling house. The family is unable to access Gloria Anzaldúa's "new mestiza consciousness," an identity that encompasses a "tolerance for contradictions" and the potential to turn these contradictions into something else, "greater than the sum of its severed parts" (Anzaldúa 101–102).

For the family in the play, hybridity cannot even be conceived of, let alone considered in positive terms. Consequently, the family can only understand and access citizenship and belonging as a deficiency symbolized by remains, such as the shrunken Villa head and the headless body of one of the sons that appears at the end of the play. The lack that these remains symbolize is actually a presence, however, a new Chicano/a identity forged through fragmented remains. It is important to note that this fragmented identity is fraught with the contradictions that attend secular saints and their followers. This Chicano/a, borderlands, and migrant identity is frequently painful even as it confers agency upon the characters in the play; as such, it is melancholic. Alicia Schmidt Camacho describes the melancholia of the migrant as a "discordant mod[e] of representation" that reflects ambivalence rather than "simple autonomy from the strictures of national citizenship" (12). Migrants are neither "failed citizens" nor "belated arrivals to the national community"; instead, they "oppos[e] or modif[y] the assimilative narratives of Mexican and U.S. nationalism" (Schmidt Camacho 12). Likewise, the characters in *The Shrunken Head* do not simply reject national citizenship; rather, they rearticulate it through Villa's remains, even as they sometimes yearn for the promise of belonging that citizenship confers. As a symbol of a separate Chicano/a identity, Villa's fragmented remains are a more accurate portrayal of migrant melancholia and fractured belonging than the false unity of a revolutionary Mexican or a middle-class American identity.

It is precisely because Villa represents both heroic Mexican nationalism and migrant melancholia that the characters in the play possess, invoke, channel, or otherwise identify with him rather than with other Mexican revolutionary leaders like Emiliano Zapata or borderlands heroes like the anarchist Flores Magón brothers. However, despite the appeal of his fragmented character, the family in *The Shrunken Head* nevertheless struggle over Villa's remains throughout the play, in a futile effort to make them whole again. Many of the characters in the play invoke or attempt to possess Villa as the typical Mexican revolutionary icon, as in Joaquín's adaptation of him as heroic revolutionary bandit. Paradoxically, they often seem unable to imagine a migrant or Chicano Villa, or to consider the ways that the representation of the iconic Villa changes as he crosses into the borderlands and over to the U.S. side of the border. Throughout the play, Villa's remains haunt and grace the family as a symbol of their own migrant loss and nostalgia. The tension in the play between the representation of Villa as a Mexican nationalist, revolutionary hero and Villa as a symbol of migrant melancholia and ambivalence is enacted through the characters' various efforts to possess or invoke the general.

Joaquín, Pedro, Mingo, Cruz, and Belarmino all invoke or possess the spirit of Villa in different ways. The characters' attitudes toward Villa range from antagonistic to skeptical, to indifferent, to matter-of-fact, to celebratory. But despite the different ways in which they invoke Villa, most of the characters in the play, including Belarmino himself, are unable to understand the multiple sides of the migrant or Chicano condition of existing in between cultures, languages, nations, and identities, and the general's link to such diverse possibilities. Mingo is the clearest example of the inability—or refusal—to understand Villa's multifaceted character and his relationship both to Mexican nationalism and to migrants and Chicanos/as in the borderlands, for Mingo's attitude toward the general, like his attitude toward all things he perceives to be Mexican, is deeply hostile. When Mingo returns to his family from the Korean War, he is newly assimilated and upwardly mobile. However, for Mingo such assimilation is possible only by rejecting his previous life and family history. Hence, he forgets every aspect of his shameful past, including the existence of the Belarmino head and the fact that his father supposedly fought with Pancho Villa in the revolution. Mingo is disdainful of the head and horrified to hear that his father killed "Americanos" in the revolution: "Mira [Look], when I was with Pancho Villa, we kill more Americanos than . . ." (Valdez 163). Mingo is unable to perceive that

Villa and his family might represent something other than a Mexican identity, for he generally views the distinction between Mexico and the United States in absolute terms. For Mingo, Pancho Villa signals all that is negative about Mexico and Mexicans; in particular, he believes that his father's constant appeals to Villa merely expose his lazy, drunken, barbaric, or lower-class tendencies.

Pedro, for his part, invokes Villa's spirit with a mixture of reverence and nostalgia. When he is not drunkenly imagining that he actually *is* Pancho Villa, Pedro fondly recalls his participation as a loyal Villista in the Mexican Revolution, either re-creating battle scenarios in his dreams or attempting to educate his sons about Villa's heroism and his betrayal, murder, and lost head (Valdez 161). Despite (or perhaps because of) Pedro's drunkenness and general inefficacy as the man of the house, he is acutely sensitive to any criticism on the part of his wife or sons, especially in relation to his masculinity. For Pedro, Villa is very much a heroic, infallible saint. The general is a link to Pedro's past glory and proof positive of his heroic machismo; the only connection to power and authority he has ever experienced in his life. Through his presumed link to Villa, Pedro performs the role of the stereotypical, patriarchal father figure, despite the fact that, in reality, he cannot provide for his family either financially or emotionally. As Cruz reveals to her shocked sons near the end of the play, Pedro's celebratory portrayal of Villa and his own heroic masculinity is belied by the fact that he never even fought in the revolution in the first place. Meanwhile, although Pedro's triumphant idea of Villa seems diametrically opposed to Mingo's disdainful one, like Mingo, Pedro can only regard Villa as a Mexican nationalist icon, and Mexico (and Mexicans) as completely separate from the United States, despite his own migrant history and his children's Chicano/a identities. For example, when Joaquín expresses an interest in escaping to Mexico with his father, Pedro exclaims, "For what? You din' come from over theres, you was born heres," suggesting a clear distinction between Mexicans and Americans (Valdez 181). In Pedro's view, Villa definitively represents the Mexican side of the border. However, rather than simply indicating a heroic reiteration of the general's Mexican nationalist identity, Pedro associates Villa with the migrant nostalgia and melancholia that he feels so deeply.

Joaquín, meanwhile, is initially indifferent to his father's impassioned appeals to Pancho Villa. He is also largely ignorant about both the general's role in Mexican history and his family's Mexican past. Joaquín's first mention of Villa is dismissive, as he describes beating up "some vato" who was looking to start trouble with him: "I even take Pancho Villa at first, which was bad enough, but then he call me a lousy Pancho, and I hit the stupid vato in the mouth" (Valdez 157). The implication is that the "vato" is a "gringo" and that "Pancho," along with "Pancho Villa," is a slur for a dirty Mexican. Later, Joaquín continues to be critical of Villa, claiming "Aah, he wasn' a giant" after father praises him as a "revolutionary giant"

(160). However, it soon becomes clear that Joaquín's indifference hides his true ignorance about Villa, Mexico, the Spanish language, and his family's history, as Pedro points out, "You see, you don' know nothing" (160). As he listens to his father's stories about Villa and the revolution, Joaquín becomes more and more interested, especially after he hears Pedro claim that the "gavachos" cut off Villa's head, and that it could be somewhere on the U.S. side of the border (161). Pedro's stories appeal to Joaquín's inchoate sense of justice, and soon after hearing them, he begins singing Villista corridos like his father. Moreover, the possibility that Villa was killed by Americans, and that his head is located in the United States, functions as a point of identification for the beleaguered and alienated Chicano Joaquín.

Joaquín's inclination toward social justice influences his marijuana-fueled hallucinatory encounter with Belarmino/Villa, in a comical scene that also reveals the tension between Villa's role as Mexican nationalist icon and his role as symbol of border, migrant, or Chicano nostalgia and loss. As Joaquín sings a version of "La Cucaracha," Belarmino begins to speak coherently for the first time, in Spanish. But when Joaquín urges Belo to show their mother that he can talk, the head refuses—hissing at Joaquín, "Si todo el mundo se da cuenta que puedo hablar, van a saber quien soy. O mejor dicho, quien fui . . . ¿Qué no sabes que estamos en territorio enemigo? [If everyone realizes that I can talk, they're going to know who I am. That is, who I was. . . . Don't you know that we are in enemy territory?]" (Valdez 178). Belarmino finally reveals to Joaquín that he is Pancho Villa's head, but he also demonstrates that the two fundamentally cannot understand each other as a "Mexican" and a "Chicano." While Belo can only speak Spanish, Joaquín informs him—in Spanglish, no less—"Sorry, man, I don' speak it. No hablo español [I don't speak Spanish]" (178). Irritated, Belarmino complains, "Mendigos pochos. [Damn pochos] (Pause.) Mira, chavo [Look, kid] ah, you . . . mexicano, ¿no?" Meanwhile, Joaquín responds, "Who me? Nel [Nah], man, I'm Chicano" (178).

Although the brothers find common ground in Belo's derogatory portrayal of Mingo as a "gringo" and "gavacho," the head chides "No seas pendejo [Don't be an idiot]" when Joaquín claims to be a Chicano, insisting, "ahh, you Mexican, me Mexican . . . ahhh, this one familia Mexican, eh?" (178). Like Pedro, Belo perceives "Mexican" and "Chicano" to be distinct identities and seems to equate Chicanos/as exclusively with "Americanos," although both the head and Joaquín agree that the "gringo" Mingo is a very different kind of "Americano." Belarmino's insistence that Joaquín is *mexicano* is a well-intentioned attempt to teach him his family history, but it obscures the fact that this identity is not open to Joaquín and suggests that the head is incapable of understanding the contradictions of Chicano/a identity. Belo's resistance to Joaquín's Chicano identity also suggests that the iconic Villa cannot cross into and over the borderlands as a purely

Mexican nationalist hero. The misunderstanding between Belarmino/Villa and Joaquín is mutual, for Joaquín cannot accept the contradictions and melancholy embodied in the fragmented Villa head, a Mexican migrant cut off from a homeland he deeply longs for.

Ultimately, Joaquín's relationship to Villa resembles that of his father, for the version of the iconic Villa that he embraces is the revolutionary, Mexican nationalist one, evidenced by his channeling of Villa's Robin Hood or bandit persona, complete with a Mexican charro costume (Valdez 192). Joaquín's unyielding loyalty to the Villa head, as when he brings Belarmino/Villa a stolen box of cigars, conceals his inability to understand the head and its relation to Mexico, the borderlands, or the United States. For Joaquín, the possibility that Villa lives again seems to be the solution to his family's fractured identity, especially since this resolution—in the form of the head—is literally a part of his family's past and present. Yet the fact that the head itself is a fractured part renders Joaquín's newly acquired Mexican identity incomplete. Furthermore, Joaquín's understanding of the Villa head is incomplete. While he obviously recognizes that the head is a fragment, Joaquín takes the existence of this one piece of Villa's remains as evidence that the general is resuscitated as a unified whole. For example, when Pedro states categorically, "General? He's dead. . . . What do you mean hombre? They kill him," Joaquín replies, "Not all of him . . . Pancho Villa lives!" (Valdez 181) More importantly, Joaquín is unable to accept the head's moments of lament and nostalgia, as when it humorously complains about its disembodied status: "Qué feo no tener cuerpo, verdad de Dios! [It's horrible not to have a body, by the word of God!]" (179). Joaquín cannot believe that the head might want to be something other than a fragment, while the head cannot understand what it means for Joaquín initially to claim a Chicano/a identity over a *mexicano/a* identity. While Belarmino/Villa represents the heroic Mexican past Joaquín desperately longs for but can never truly attain, the possibility that the head could represent an entirely different sort of Chicano/a identity is not legible to Belarmino/Villa himself.

Joaquín's direct appropriation of Villa as a symbol of Mexican national identity is doomed, since it does not account for the general's concomitant role as a symbol for fractured Chicano/a and migrant identities. In many ways, Joaquín's symbolic possession of a Mexican nationalist Villa resembles the version of American assimilation that Mingo undertakes, for neither Mingo's assimilation to middle-class American life nor Joaquín's re-creation of Villa's revolutionary past can incorporate the characters' former identities. When Joaquín and Chato, Lupe's boyfriend, burst into the house armed with guns and stolen sacks of food for the family, Mingo condemns Joaquín's theft, threatening to call the police. But Joaquín attacks Mingo for being a much worse kind of thief: "You're the one that oughta be in jail for cheating the jefitos, the family, La Raza! You pinchi sellout traitor!" (Valdez 193). Meanwhile, Cruz's efforts to reason with her sons and maintain the peace are in vain. Joaquín and Mingo's argument escalates until she yells out: "¡Hijos de su chingada madre! [Sons of your fucked mother!]" (194). The "fucked mother" here is Cruz, recalling the symbolism of La Malinche, the "mother" of Mexico, as dual victim and betrayer. Yet Cruz also identifies herself as the Villista soldadera who will no longer play the role of the long-suffering passive mother, thus refusing the role of victim. Cruz orders her incredulous sons to obey her, expressing her disapproval both of Joaquín's actions and of Mingo's desire to turn to the police. Unlike Mingo, Cruz knows that obeying American laws will not change her family's social or economic status in any way, and although she is proud of Mingo's service as an army veteran, she rejects his blind faith in the U.S. government. She also understands that Joaquín's conviction that the family will achieve prosperity and a sense of national belonging through the return of the Mexican Revolution and the iconic nationalist Villa is equally false. As the only character in the play who has any tangible link to Villa in both the past and the present, Cruz rejects Joaquín's direct assimilation of Villa in favor of her own experience: "your padre never was in the Revolución. . . . I use [the 30-30]. . . . Sí, mis hijos, your madre rode with Pancho Villa! And tha's how I'm certain Belarmino ees not the general" (194–195). Cruz refuses Joaquín's appropriation of Villa's Mexican nationalist persona not because it is an inaccurate portrayal of the iconic Villa but because it excludes his contradictory representation within the migrant and Chicano context and his association with borderlands nostalgia and loss.

Toward the end of the play, we realize that Cruz has never been silent, although her broken English cannot compare to her fluent Spanish. Despite her passivity and stagnation, Cruz is the only one who understands that the family's Chicano identity both depends upon and is distinct from dominant versions of Mexican and U.S. identity. While Lupe inevitably repeats her mother's past by giving birth to yet another head, Mingo and Joaquín finally return to the family, but both seem to have broken with their past entirely. In his role as "Mr. Sunday," the welfare man, Mingo no longer has any memory of his family as he rejects his Spanish name (Domingo) and contributes to the exploitation of Chicanos/as in the United States. Joaquín, newly released from prison, is physically broken—he is now just a headless body, unable to speak or think. The comical struggle that ensues between Belarmino/Villa and Lupe for the body represents the desire finally to unite Chicano and Mexican history and make Villa's remains whole again. Belarmino/Villa declares his intention to wait as long as necessary for the body in order to complete his head, at which time "Pancho Villa [will] pass among you again" (Valdez 207). But Cruz knows it is impossible for Villa's remains to become whole in the context of the play, just as she understands that the family cannot ignore the duality of his nature. He is not simply a Mexican icon but also a borderlands, migrant, and Chicano icon. She puts a halt to the battle between Belarmino and Lupe, for she has other plans for Joaquín and a very different perception of the family's Chicano/a identity, even if it must remain fractured: "Neither his nor yours or nobody but me. Joaquín is mine" (207). Cruz knows that Villa does not have to be literally made whole for the family to possess his spirit, as Belarmino believes. Instead, Cruz understands that the family has possessed a version of Villa all along. This version may be a fragmented relic, but as such, it is a symbol for the migrant loss and longing that the family endures—and that also provides the possibility for positive change in the future.

Villa's Remains

Although I do not mean to suggest that *mexicano/a* and Chicano/a identities must necessarily preclude each other, in the context of the play they cannot function together, for the family has never been able to feel at home in either Mexico or the United States. Despite Mingo's best efforts, he is unable to become American or to access the American dream by denying his family and his past. Instead, to outsiders, like the gringo police officer who refers to Mingo as a "boy," he cannot avoid being either Mexican or Chicano and is instantly returned to his rejected past. Nevertheless, he is impervious to the police officer's insults and is incapable of understanding that he can never be unequivocally American. Similarly, Joaquín does not understand that he cannot possess Villa, for the Villa head does not represent a return to a Mexican nationalist past (which the family never had access to in the first place) but, rather, a shift toward a new borderlands identity.

At the close of the play, Villa's head remains a fragment, and so does Joaquín's headless body. Nevertheless, the Belarmino/Villa head continues to plot ways to purloin the body, arguing, "But tha's okay cause I still have time to wait. Sooner or later, the jefita gots to come across wis Joaquín's body. . . . Those people don' even believe who I am. Tha's how I wan' it. To catch 'em by surprise" (Valdez 207). Here, Belarmino's characterization of Villa approximates his stealthy bandit persona, perhaps as a gesture toward the general's link to a Mexican nationalist identity. As in his earlier confusion about Joaquín's Chicano identity, Belarmino seems unaware that Pancho Villa might represent very different things to the various members of the family. Ultimately, the spirit of Pancho Villa that the family possesses or invokes does not celebrate Mexican nationalism as redemptive macho heroism, as Joaquín envisions it, nor does it represent a link to a shameful Mexican past, as Mingo understands it. Instead, as Cruz demonstrates with her maternal, loving claim on Joaquín's body, the spirit of Villa in the play belongs to female heroism, symbolized by Cruz's role as a revolutionary soldadera. Like the real-life severed, lost head of Pancho Villa, the head in the play represents the popular disruption of dominant nationalism and national identities on both sides of the border, rather than exclusively signifying dominant Mexican nationalism or even a nationalist Chicano identity. As a Chicano text, *The Shrunken Head* manifests the conflict between the desire to possess a much-longed-for (though always already unattainable) Mexican national identity, assimilation to American culture, nationalist *Chicanismo*, and the pain and potential for transformation inherent in a borderlands migrant identity. Ultimately, the play demonstrates that the attempts to possess Villa's spirit or remains exclusively as a symbol for national identities are destined to fail, because they ignore his contradictions as a secular saint that straddles the boundary between human and sacred. Rather than signify impenetrable myth, Villa's remains point toward an alternative understanding of the family's transnational migrant and Chicano/a identity, which links region, nation, and border as it shifts between national identification and the disruption of the nation-state. It is only by embracing Villa's contradictions that he can be apprehended as a secular saint.

3 · CANONIZING
CÉSAR CHÁVEZ

THROUGHOUT HIS NEARLY FORTY YEARS of labor and civil rights organizing, César Estrada Chávez, the co-founder of the United Farm Workers Union (UFW), civil rights leader, and Chicano icon, drew upon various modes of official and popular spirituality, investing his political project with a sense of justice rooted in religious morality and an aura of sacrifice. His spiritual practices included his famous fasts, pilgrimages, and prayer vigils, but they also encompass nonviolence, peaceful boycotts, vows of poverty, and the use of religious imagery such as the Virgin of Guadalupe (Griswold del Castillo and García 36).[1] Chávez is certainly a political, social, and cultural hero for Chicanos/as and other marginalized groups in the United States and elsewhere. When he founded the UFW in 1962, in "the long organizing journey that was to be called *La Causa*," he "concomitantly inspired the Chicano political movement and largely occasioned its attendant cultural renaissance" (Levy "Prologue," n.p.; León, "Chavez" 857). Indeed, Gloria Anzaldúa links Chávez to the actualization of Chicanos/as in the United States: "Chicanos did not know we were a people until 1965 when César Chávez and the farmworkers united" (85). He remains the most well-known Chicano public figure in history.[2] Yet he is not solely a political or cultural leader, for he is frequently mythologized as a sacred figure that at first glance appears to evoke a more conventional notion of saintliness than many popular saints. Though he does not have a traditional religious cult, Chávez is akin to a popular saint; as Stephen R. Lloyd-Moffett asserts, "Five hundred years ago, this man would be seen as a living saint. . . . Once his actions are read through the prism of his religious life, Chávez emerges as a classical Catholic saint whose closeness to God led him to be seen as a Prophet by his people" (106–107). Lloyd-Moffett distinguishes between the representation of Chávez as a secular activist and a

Portrait of César Chávez and his "Huelga" car taken during the Delano Grape Strike, J. D. Marlin Ranch, Tulare County, California, circa 1965. Walter P. Reuther Library, Wayne State University, United Farm Worker Collection.

spiritual figure, arguing that he is often erroneously secularized, in that "his faith is usually presented as merely incidental to his action" (117).

Lloyd-Moffett is correct that the secularized version of Chávez was warmly embraced by the American public, even though, for the labor leader, the poles of secular/political and sacred/spiritual were always intertwined (118, 120). However, by situating Chávez as a figure of mainstream secular representation whose spirituality is only widely acknowledged by the farmworkers and some members of the Latino community, Lloyd-Moffett obscures the fact that Chávez's transcendent qualities are almost always emphasized to the exclusion of his imperfect or simply ordinary human characteristics. Rather than read Chávez as a figure widely received as a secular hero whose true spiritual essence must be retrieved, it is more productive to consider him through the contradictions of secular sanctity. Chávez is indeed lionized as a saint, a Messiah, or a moral figure in historical narratives, popular corrido ballads, and children's books.[3] Whether as saint or political activist, he is linked to orthodoxy in all aspects of his life, in terms of religion, ethnicity, nation, and social class, that is, whether Chávez is interpreted through the lens of the secular, the sacred, or both, his contradictions are elided and subsumed. Like other mythologized heroes, especially "racialized public leaders," he is "not allowed to develop and change" over the course of his life or as an icon in death (León, "Chavez" 863). Authors, journalists, politicians, historians, and educators have been variously invested in portraying Chávez as a simple, humble "common man from common origins" who is not only a champion of the poor but one of them, a devout Roman Catholic, an American hero, a symbol of Chicano/a nationalist identity, a marker of commodifiable ethnic difference, a community organizer, a crusader for environmental rights, a spiritual leader, and a representative of Mexicans in the United States (Jensen and Hammerback xxii; León, "Chavez" 860). The representation of Chávez as simple, humble, sacrificial, devout, and heroic is particularly persistent, to the point that it has become the basis of his myth and informs his standing as the quintessential public image of the Chicano. Indeed, Chávez's transcendent, sacred qualities produce him as a force for rigid Chicano/a identities in many historical, cultural, and editorial works, frequently establishing an impossible standard for ordinary Chicanos/as to live up to.

While César Chávez encompasses these identities, he is also a complicated and contradictory figure who strategically shifted his political and spiritual views over time in order to advance the cause of the UFW. He certainly emphasized different aspects of spirituality, religion, ethnicity, race, social class, nationalism, and transnationalism in his speeches and writings. At times, he appealed to religious or ethnic orthodoxy; at others, he rejected essentialism in any form. Chávez was also no stranger to controversy from both conservative and liberal perspectives; he has been criticized as much for the internal conflicts within the UFW and his support of immigration control as for his supposed radicalism. Most sources tend to characterize his selflessness and humility as being integral to his conception of the collectivity of the UFW. Chávez's son Paul F. Chávez, the president of the Chávez Foundation, asserts, "My father was always uncomfortable with personal recognition," and he appeals to the public to honor his father by "embracing . . . the enduring work of the movement he created on behalf of the people for whom he sacrificed," rather than by focusing on his individual significance (*Cesar Chavez Legacy Awards*).

Nevertheless, Chávez remains the central organizing figure of the UFW, and he is often portrayed as a synecdoche not only for the union but for Chicanos/as in general. Gary Soto argues, "In the course of this movement, César became— whether he accepted this status or not—a spiritual leader for all Chicanos" (qtd in Léon, "Chavez" 858). Indeed, Chávez's selfless collectivity is not incompatible with his position as a spiritual leader and secular saint. In many ways, César Chávez performed a version of charismatic sanctity in his expression of the spiritual tenets and symbolism of the UFW. At the same time, he rearticulated traditional modes of spiritual representation and devotional practice in order to challenge the possibility of divine perfection. Chávez's contradictory, often conflicted public image reflects the intersection of spirituality, politics, and celebrity that is consonant with the ambivalent simulacra of sanctity embodied by the santón. Chávez would have been the last person to identify himself as a saint, but in his role as both a labor leader and a "spiritual leader for all Chicanos" he nevertheless drew upon and performed sacred discourse and acts. As befits a borderlands santón, the sanctity associated with César Chávez is highly ambivalent, for it facilitates the social reproduction of his political goals even as it constructs an idealized, and frequently unattainable, Chicano/a identity. The reproduction of Chávez's name, image, and ideals in the public sphere, the nonprofit sector, and in education as well as in cultural production, signals the social, economic, and cultural advancement of Chicanos/as and Latinos/as. But while all of these invocations depend upon his accessibility, Chávez is often represented as unattainable because of the consolidation of his myth. Although he is certainly all too human, representations of Chávez often obscure his nuances, and he is frequently lionized, trivialized, and resented at the same time.

An example of the contradictory logic that regularly accompanies representations of César Chávez is evident in Richard Rodríguez's essay "Mexico's Children" in *Days of Obligation* (1992), in which Rodríguez addresses the tension inherent in negotiating a Chicano/a identity, an uncertain American identity, and a lost Mexican identity. He states, "In the late 1960s, when César Chávez made the cover of *Time* as the most famous Mexican anyone could name, he was already irrelevant to Mexican-American lives insofar as 90 percent of us lived in cities and we were more apt to work in construction than as farmworkers. My mother, who worked downtown, and my father, who worked downtown, nevertheless sent money to César Chávez, because the hardness of his struggle on the land reminded them of the hardness of their Mexican past" (67).[4] It is notable that Rodríguez focuses on César Chávez as both a locus of contemporary Chicano/a identity and a symbol of the Mexican past. Rodríguez's conception of Chicano/a identity, especially in relation to Chávez, is extremely fragmented, for he suggests that the farmworkers (and other working-class migrant Mexicans, for that matter) have nothing in common with more economically successful or assimilated Chicanos/as, except for the memory of a shared past.

His description of two very different events centering on the image of Chávez—the farmworkers' 1966 Lenten Pilgrimage through California's Central Valley from Delano to Sacramento and a black-tie benefit he attended in honor of Chávez in the early 1990s—both imply that Chicanos/as primarily view Chávez as a link to their lost Mexican past or to their difficult migrant origins rather than as someone who speaks to their contemporary, frequently urban existences in the United States. Rodríguez repeatedly cites the religious metaphors that Chávez and the UFW wielded so adeptly. Yet, although he identifies Chávez as a folk hero and spiritual authority for the present day, he describes the farmworkers' pilgrimage to Sacramento as a remnant of the past, particularly in terms of its intersection of land and spirituality. In

Rodríguez's view, the pilgrimage is an example of "private people praying in public" and bearing "the most compelling symbols of the pastoral past," such as the land, the flag, the procession in song, and the Virgin Mary (68). Meanwhile, in his reflection on the black-tie benefit, he contemplates the contrast between Chávez's fragility and the substance of the "Mexican-American haute bourgeoisie" and somewhat condescendingly calls him "our little saint," who reminds "us . . . of who our grandparents used to be" (70).

Rodríguez is clearly critical of the upwardly mobile Chicanos/as (including himself) who appropriate Chávez as a symbol of their Mexican heritage yet seem to feel no bond to the Mexican waiters who serve the group champagne. In relation to both the pilgrimage and the benefit, he suggests that Chávez and the farmworkers can only be understood through a narrative of the past. This nostalgic narrative is especially pronounced because Rodríguez emphasizes the deterioration of the UFW even as he romanticizes Chávez: "Criticized in the liberal press for allowing his union to unravel, Chávez became a quixotic figure; Gandhi without an India" (68). In this manner, Rodríguez symbolically dissociates Chávez from the struggle of the UFW and points toward his canonization as a Chicano icon and an American national hero. At the same time, even though Rodríguez suggests that Chicanos/as' economic, social, and cultural progress depends upon painful assimilation, he implies that Chávez escapes such assimilation ("he was already irrelevant to Mexican-American lives"). But while his description of the benefit and Chávez's commemoration on the cover of *Time* is awkward and disconcerting, these examples reflect the labor leader's inclusion into mainstream American society and his function as a symbol of progress in the eyes of many. In fact, Chávez is a symbol of assimilation as well as a marker of the past. Rather than representing solely the past (reflecting Mexico, the land and pastoral life, or versions of traditional spirituality), César Chávez embodies the present and future of Chicano assimilation to a U.S. identity, urban life, and economic, social, and cultural advancement. In other words, as Lloyd-Moffett implies, Chávez epitomizes both secular and sacred (120).

While Chávez embodies both sides of the duality between a Mexican past and an assimilated American present, this duality nevertheless overlooks his flaws and contradictions. The duality between past and present or between sacred and secular cannot account for Chávez's shifting, occasionally problematic political and spiritual views, his radical theorization of flux in his articulation of the goals and strategies of the UFW, or his understanding of the multiplicity involved in spirituality, space, and temporality. These ambiguities are the very ones that render him a borderlands santón, even as he is canonized as an American national or a Chicano nationalist icon. The tension between these multiple roles frequently plays out through cultural production, especially in Chicano representations of Chávez. Focusing on representations of Chávez in Margarita

Cota-Cárdenas's novel *Puppet* (1985) and the play *A Bowl of Beings* (1991; in Montoya, et al.) by the Chicano-Salvadoran theater and performance group Culture Clash, I argue that both texts contend with César Chávez's duality as a marker of a heroic Mexican past, generally corresponding to the sacred, and a conflicted American present, denoting the secular. Both sides characterize different aspects of Chicano/a identity. The representation of the past, with its emphasis on Mexican or indigenous history and culture, the land, and spirituality, frequently informs Chicano nationalism, while the portrayal of an assimilated American present signifies the arrival of Chicanos/as into mainstream U.S. society. These Chicano texts ultimately reject the monolithic construction of Chicano/a identity that is associated with romanticized images of Chávez, the UFW, and the Chicano movement. Indeed, through tactics of mistranslation, irony, and parody, they complicate the idealized view of César Chávez in order to reveal the limits of static Chicano/a identities and nationalisms.

Theorizing Flux

César Chávez's canonization depends in part upon the framing of his life as a narrative of orthodoxy, especially in terms of his humble origins, his long years of hard migratory farm labor and privation, his political stances, and his religious faith. But the labor leader's story is far more complicated than this. Throughout his life, Chávez cycled between periods of flux and stability, sometimes by choice and sometimes not. He structured his political and spiritual views—especially concerning the mission and tactics of the UFW—around such fluctuation. Chávez's childhood was touched equally by the stability of landownership and by the displacement of migration. He was born in Yuma, Arizona, on March 31, 1927, in a ranch that his father and grandfather built in the desert. From the beginning, Chávez's family confronted a clash between cultural tradition and the American legal system. He describes a trade where his father offered to clear eighty acres of a neighbor's land in exchange for forty acres, an informal business deal surely born out of economic necessity as well as community ties. Chávez's father Librado held up his end of the bargain, but "the property already had been sold to a man named Justus Jackson" (Levy 8). Librado Chávez took out a loan to buy the land outright, but as Chávez notes, "later on, when [he] couldn't pay the interest on the loan, the lawyer bought the land from him and sold it back to the original owner. It was a rotten deal all around" (Levy 9). The Chávez family was ultimately unable to pay the taxes owed on their land and unable to qualify for a loan; the state took legal possession of the ranch in 1937 (Levy 33). The family was driven from their ranch entirely in 1939, an event Chávez describes as follows: "When we left the farm, our whole life was upset, turned upside down. We had been part of a very stable community, and we were about to become migratory workers. We had been uprooted" (Levy 42).

From this point on, the Chávez family lived a migrant existence, spending years following the crops and alternating with periods in the aptly named barrio of Sal Si Puedes (Escape if you can) near San José, California (Griswold del Castillo and García 3–7). Chávez never forgot the importance of the land. As León indicates, "the ground base of his struggle was a longing to return to his childhood home" ("Chavez" 859). Yet he was cognizant of the paths not taken in his life, and their possible consequences, reflecting, "Landownership is very important, and my dad had very strong feelings about the land. If we had stayed there, possibly I would have been a grower. God writes in exceedingly crooked lines" (Levy 42). In many ways, the instability he lived as a child forms the basis of his union organizational strategies; indeed, he understands that instability and insecurity can be a path to freedom. On his decision to leave his post as national director of the Community Service Organization (CSO) in East Los Angeles and found the UFW, Chávez recalls, "Only my financial security had me tied up and kept me from moving. . . . So I resigned my job and set out to found a union. At first I was frightened, very frightened. But by the time I had missed the fourth paycheck and found things were still going, that the moon was still there and the sky and the flowers, I began to laugh. I really began to feel free. It was one of my biggest triumphs in terms of finding myself and of being able to discipline myself" (Levy 3–5). Thus Chávez rearticulates economic insecurity and migration as a source of freedom rather than of fear and abjection. This flux permits both his journey of spiritual discovery ("finding myself") and political constancy ("being able to discipline myself") and informs his strategies and tactics as the organizational leader of the UFW.

In contrast to the archetypal stagnation of his public image, Chávez's goals and tactics tended toward a focus on change and instability. In fact, one of his primary tactics of union organization is the theorization and rearticulation of instability. Chávez was inspired by Gandhi's theory of "moral jujitsu," a practice that involves "always hitting the opposition off-balance, but keeping [one's] principles" (Levy 92). The essence of "moral jujitsu" is change and instability; trying many tactics and approaches without being certain of their effects. At the same time, maintaining one's principles requires a willingness to fail or to be disregarded. The UFW's strategy of combining strikes with economic boycotts harnesses the power of public participation and media visibility to support the sacrifice and risk of the farmworkers who put their livelihood (and sometimes their lives) on the line for the good of La Causa. As Chávez argued, "Alone, the farm workers have no economic power; but with the help of the public they can develop the economic power to counter that of the growers" (Levy 201). The risk the farmworkers face in striking is very real, for their economic power depends upon public participation, but the principles of sacrifice demand that they continue whether or not they attract mass attention. In fact, the personal risk for the farmworkers is so great that at times the theorization of sacrifice supersedes their economic, political, and spiritual needs, leaving them vulnerable not only to the growers' demands but also to the organizational tactics of the UFW itself (Bardacke "Looking Back").

In terms of Chávez's theorization of flux, nowhere is the embrace of instability and change more evident than in his famous fasts. At the same time, the fasts are one of the most visible signs of his mythologization and symbolic canonization. Chávez's three major fasts in 1968, 1972, and 1988 each lasted almost a month. The fasts reflected Chávez's willingness to sacrifice his body and soul for his fellow farmworkers. They were physically and emotionally painful endeavors that surely contributed to his ill health in later years and probably accelerated his death. However, they were also transcendent mystical experiences that provided "direct and extraordinary encounters with God," which Chávez "employed as the basis for his major decisions about the life of the UFW" (Lloyd-Moffett 108).

Lloyd-Moffett emphasizes that Chávez's goal in fasting was not "to incite change in others—which would be consistent for a protest fast—but a personal spiritual transformation" (108). Yet the fasts were also highly publicized undertakings in support of nonviolence during UFW strikes, to protest state laws curtailing union activity, to protest the use of pesticides on table grapes, and to publicize the union's organized boycotts (Jensen and Hammerback 158–159). Indeed, the fasts brought much needed exposure and support to the UFW, as many union members, politicians such as Robert Kennedy, and celebrities such as Martin Sheen joined in for part of the fasts in order to demonstrate their solidarity with Chávez. Predictably, many of the labor leader's opponents suggested he was a fraud and implied that he was not really fasting (Levy 274).

The fasts were also a catalyst for dissent among some UFW members and volunteers, who "saw [Chávez's] fast as a waste of his and their precious time" and, more damningly, accused him of harboring a "messiah complex" (Jensen and Hammerback 158). These accusations persisted despite Chávez's insistence that his fasts were spiritual acts that rejected personal celebrity. In a letter to the National Council of Churches during his 1968 fast, he wrote, "[My fast] is not intended as a pressure on anyone but only as an expression of my own deep feelings and my own need to do penance and to be in prayer" (qtd in Lloyd-Moffett 108–109). Nevertheless, it is especially because of the fasts that Chávez has been mythologized as saintly, pure, and untouchable.

A closer examination of his fasts reveals that he conceptualized them in the spirit of refusal and change. Drawing upon Gandhi's philosophies of nonviolence, civil disobedience, and moral jujitsu, Chávez embarked upon his first fast in 1968 as a leap into the unknown: "I thought that I had to bring the Movement to a halt, do something that would force them [the UFW membership] and me to deal with the whole question of violence and ourselves. We had to stop long enough to take account of what we were doing.... Then I said I was going to stop eating until such time as everyone in the strike either ignored me or made up their minds that they were not going to be committing violence" (Levy 272). For Chávez, the fast represented a stop, halt, or break in the trajectory of the movement, a way to reflect upon and change its course in order to refuse the threat of violence. The fast was not an end in itself, in the sense that its primary goal was not to encourage other UFW members to support Chávez or to join in the fast with him, nor was it for him to attract outside attention, although Chávez acknowledged that the good effects of the fast, such as the renewed strength of the grape boycott, "were way beyond [his] dreams" (Levy 274). Instead, being ignored or unappreciated was a crucial part of Chávez's strategy, as he explained to his wife, Helen: "She told me I was crazy, and nobody would appreciate what I was doing. I said I didn't want anybody to appreciate it" (Levy 273). He insisted throughout that he had no idea how much "spiritual and psychological and political good" would come from his fast (Levy 275).

Certainly, Chávez's strategy of being unappreciated reflects traditional spiritual penance and atonement. But his refusal to conform to either his family's desire to protect his health or to the union members' desires to respond to government and grower violence in kind rearticulates the fasts as a political act. In his willingness to die, Chávez's fasts reflect a politics of the unexpected, attracting attention through refusal. In this fashion, Chávez unites spirituality and politics in an incredibly powerful way. Rather than adhering to dogmatic orthodoxy, Chávez theorizes both spirituality and politics in terms of change and fluctuation.

Canonizing César Chávez

In a way, Richard Rodríguez is correct that César Chávez's putative power was fading even as he could be considered "the most famous Mexican anyone can name" in the United States, thus paving the way for his secular canonization (67). Although Chávez continued to be feted for his commitment to social justice, by the 1980s and early 1990s the organizational and financial power of the UFW had greatly declined. National awareness and support for the UFW's tactic of organizing boycotts against certain growers' products, particularly grapes, had diminished. As Frank Bardacke suggests, the decline of the UFW's power was due to inherent structural flaws within the union. He argues that the union rank and file—the "farmworker soul," as he calls it—could never attain true leadership within the UFW, because the union was primarily dependent upon outside funding rather than membership dues, which "did the union in" ("Looking

Back"). Indeed, the UFW had long suffered from financial troubles, infighting among its leadership and ranks, several confrontations with the Teamsters Union over strikebreaking contracts, lawsuits from growers, and a large decrease in membership (Griswold del Castillo and García 172–173). Chávez was criticized for his demands for "utter loyalty," for primarily directing the UFW toward fundraising, and for discouraging dissent within the union (León, "Chavez" 863; Bardacke, "Looking Back"). Some sources intimate that Chávez had an occasional rivalry with UFW cofounder Dolores Huerta and reportedly at times criticized her independent personality (Griswold del Castillo and García 60–61).

Meanwhile, Chávez continued to be construed by many critics as a threat to American democratic values. He was condemned by conservatives for his alleged communism and anti-Americanism, feared as the "scourge of California," and subjected to death threats (Matthiessen 361; Levy 442–443). At the same time, he was criticized by supporters for his fluctuating stances on topics ranging from immigration control to racial and ethnic politics, to religion, to the democratic process.

One of the most controversial issues concerns immigration control. Chávez vehemently protested the collusion between growers and the U.S. government that led to the institution of the Bracero Program, and the use of braceros as strikebreakers (Griswold del Castillo and García 157).[5] At the same time, he was well aware that most of the union members were of Mexican descent and that many were Mexican citizens. In fact, some of the first UFW members killed while defending the union were Mexican migrants (Griswold del Castillo and García 166–167).[6] Chávez was certainly aware that union members and braceros alike faced many of the same threats to their health and economic power because of exploitation by the government and the growers. Perhaps because of this disparity, the UFW ratified a new constitution in 1973 that established a bill of rights for all members, regardless of citizenship. The union also increased its social and community services for migrant workers. Nevertheless, Chávez continued to support strict immigration control for the rest of his life (Griswold del Castillo and García 166–167). While this stance surely reflected his desire to keep the union solvent by restricting "scab labor," it drove a wedge between more recent migrants and Chicanos/as or *mexicanos/as* with a longer history in the United States, regardless of citizenship.

Despite these conflicts, since his death in 1993 César Chávez has been awarded several national honors from the U.S. and Mexican governments, including the Presidential Medal of Freedom, the Mexican Premio Benito Juárez, and the Mexican Aguila de Oro Award. He has been nominated for the U.S. Congressional Gold Medal and commemorated in an official U.S. stamp. Despite criticism from some Republicans in Congress, the navy named a cargo ship after Chávez in 2011. In California and seven other states, he is celebrated in an official state

holiday on his birthday, March 31, and he was inducted into the California Hall
of Fame in 2006. Many public and private works, including streets, parks, community centers, housing facilities, plazas, public schools, institutes, scholarships,
and university programs and centers have been named after him.[7] Meanwhile,
the nonprofit César Chávez Foundation continues to provide social, community, and cultural services for farmworkers and low-income Latino families and
has recently opened the National Chávez Center in Keene, California, which
includes the Memorial Gardens around Chávez's gravesite.[8] These often controversial projects provide an allegory of the entry of Chicanos/as and Latinos/as into
the U.S. public sphere through the remapping and rearticulation of local, national,
public, and private space. Many of these works specifically promote the social, economic, and cultural advancement of Chicanos/as and Latinos/as. Finally, there
is an ongoing effort to establish a national holiday on Chávez's birthday, which
is supported by President Barack Obama, who used the UFW's slogan "Sí Se
Puede/Yes We Can" during his 2008 presidential campaign (cesarchavezholiday
.org). As Luis D. León suggests, "this honor would be the equivalent of reaching
full U.S. sainthood . . . trumping in significance even the ongoing efforts to can-
onize [Chávez] as an official Catholic saint" ("Chavez" 857).

Chávez is most readily accessible to the U.S. national consciousness as
a marker of Chicano assimilation to dominant American identity—or as
a figure that symbolizes a Mexican national past rather than the continu-
ing migration of Mexicans to the United States. The process of canonization
rearticulates Chávez for mainstream American consumption, situating him
within a national canon of ethnic heroes who represent fragments of compos-
ite American identity. This process of canonization also elides the contradiction, controversy, and change associated with his image. At the same time, he
is ensconced as the mythic symbol of the Chicano, reflecting a different sort
of canonization, especially in relation to Chicano nationalism, which often
focuses on the link between Chávez and a mythical Mexican or indigenous
past. Both the Chicano nationalist and the assimilationist American perspectives on Chávez tend to represent him as a monolithic icon, despite the fact
that they privilege his accessibility to the masses.

The contradiction between accessibility and impenetrability is especially
evident in the most powerful symbols of Chávez's canonization—his awards,
honors, and memorializations. Chávez undoubtedly anticipated the perils of
personal memorialization, for when asked "if he wanted to be remembered by
statues and public memorials, [he] replied, 'If you want to remember me, organize!'" emphasizing the collectivity of the UFW rather than his own leadership (Tejada-Flores 312). Many of Chávez's commemorations have been quite
controversial, reflecting the enduring discomfort with his public image. These
memorializations implicitly or explicitly dissociate Chávez from his most radical

stances on labor and environmental rights while also concealing his own problematic stances on topics like immigration. They also tend to dilute his power as a cross-racial, transnational hero who was more than just a Chicano icon.

In many cases, these memorializations privilege Chávez's individuality above the collectivity of the UFW or characterize collectivity as a homogenous block. Regardless of what Chávez might have intended, as Frank Bardacke argues, the history of the UFW is frequently reduced to "just an aspect of César's biography," while the farmworkers in general are subsumed into his legacy ("Looking Back"). Naturally, it is much easier to celebrate, admire, and identify with one person rather than with a group. Chávez has certainly been individually commodified to some extent, with his image repeated on t-shirts, posters, and even some advertisements like Apple Computer's 1998 "Think Different" campaign.

Yet his public image as a Chicano spiritual leader and symbol denoting cultural, social, economic empowerment for Chicanos/as depends upon his expression of collectivity. Works and services such as city streets, nonprofit organizations, or schools draw upon his image in order to promote a collective identity. This identity is not specifically based on race or class but, rather, evokes community ties and implicitly promotes local activism, service, and civil rights. Nevertheless, Chávez's name and image have especially been utilized to promote the Chicano and Latino community through schools, cultural centers and educational programs.[9] The scholarships and grants in particular aim to offset the decline in affirmative action programs and funding, while many of the cultural and educational programs link Chávez to Chicano studies and Chicano history and cultural production.

Yet even as these memorializations establish Chávez's legacy as an emblem of Chicano community service, social action, and economic progress, they sometimes position him at the crux of a homogenous—and thus unattainable—Chicano/a identity. Such homogeneity is particularly evident in relation to certain manifestations of Chicano nationalism. César Chávez is an extremely important symbol for the development of Chicano and Latino studies. He was obviously aware of his status as a Chicano icon and role model, and he encouraged it even as he emphasized class solidarity over race or ethnicity. Like Jackie Robinson, Chávez did not "compromise or remake himself. He was proud of his background" as a Chicano (Bardacke "Looking Back"). He frequently risked censorship and even imprisonment by speaking to groups and conducting strikes in Spanish, and he also asked La Raza to celebrate their ties—whether past or present, symbolic or tangible—to the farmworkers (Jensen and Hammerback 123). Chávez certainly drew upon Mexican nationalist and religious symbolism in his speeches. He is often associated with Chicano nationalism, and his myth and image inform the nationalist perspective that has historically been privileged within Chicano studies. Although "the Chicano movement developed from a multitude of community-based political and civil rights struggles . . . its histo-riography has been organized around a cosmology of male heroes that reifies the 'great man' narrative and interpretive structure" (Blackwell 28). Indeed, as Maylei Blackwell argues, the representation and historicization of figures such as César Chávez have "eclipsed a fuller historical understanding of [multisited local community and labor struggles], especially women's participation," producing a "monolithic portrayal of the Chicano movement" (28).

Likewise, although Chicano studies in the United States is clearly progressive for it is rooted in community activism and must be understood as a social move-ment as well as an intellectual endeavor, "an extension within the academy of the movements against racism and on behalf of immigrant rights," it still sometimes positions itself as a nationalist endeavor in relation to concepts like Aztlán or the Chicano movement of the 1960s and 1970s (Flores 193). Chicano nationalist identity is especially symbolized by the claim on the U.S. Southwest and Mexican north as Aztlán, an "indigenous nation historically anterior to the founding of the United States" and Mexico (Saldaña-Portillo 279). Some of the most prominent Chicano poets and authors of the movement, such as Octavio Romano-V., Rudy Espinosa, and Alurista, typically represented Chávez, the UFW, and the farm-workers as integral to the contemporary mythology of Aztlán. These authors often employ Chávez and the symbolism of the UFW, especially the stylized black eagle on a white circle and red background, to articulate a myth of Chicano origins that specifically privileges a Mexican and indigenous past.[10]

To this end, Chávez and the farmworkers are also associated with the Mexi-can Revolution and indigenous groups like the Aztecs. For example, Romano-V. refers to the black eagle as a symbol of the Mexican Revolution, which now "hovers over California fields and California cities," both figuratively and literally transferring revolutionary potential to a U.S. context. He calls the Chicanos/as inspired by "a man in Delano shouting '¡Huelga!'" (Strike!) "descendants of the Aztecs" (77–82). But this cohesive Mexican and indigenous past is unsustainable for contemporary Chicanos/as, while the myth of Mexican solidarity rings false for several reasons. It should not be forgotten that many Mexicans, especially those from the middle and upper classes, either ignored Chávez or were simply unfamiliar with him. The Mexicans who were familiar with Chávez's deeds and legacy often criticized him, interpreting his support of immigration controls as an affront.

María Josefina Saldaña-Portillo astutely criticizes the "continued use of mes-tizaje as a trope for Chicano/a identity and the presumed access to indigenous subjectivity that this biologized trope offers us," which stems from Aztlán-based Chicano nationalism (279). Thus, the parallel that Romano-V. draws between the Aztecs and Chicano/a or migrant farmworkers not only privileges a mythic indigenous past, it excludes present-day indigenous groups on both sides of the border, especially those that do not clearly fit a nationalist paradigm, like Oaxa-can indigenous migrants to California or groups that straddle the border like the Tohono O'odham Nation. As Saldaña-Portillo indicates, the trope of mestizaje often reduces the presence of indigenous ancestry to an irretrievable past and "always already places indigenous people under erasure" (280).

At the same time, Chicano nationalism along with other forms of Latino national affiliation have played an important role in rejecting the archetypal melting-pot narrative of immigrant assimilation in the United States, and in "countering the tendency of U.S. social science and public policy to reduce Lati-nos to an ethnic group experience," as Juan Flores suggests (198). Flores argues that the distinct concept of Latino studies provides a way to improve under-standing of the current global and transnational flows and their relation to the Latino population of the United States. This type of critical practice accounts for the limits of national Latino/a identities, based upon the diversification and geographic dispersal of the Latino population in the United States, as well as the external and internal migration provoked by the economic restructuring of global capitalism.

César Chávez and the UFW also embody a transnational, transracial perspec-tive, even as they draw upon national symbols or are utilized for nationalist ends. Chávez recognized that the U.S. agriculture, service, and manufacturing indus-tries would be impossible to sustain without Mexican migrant labor. As a master of symbolism, he was cognizant of the power of Mexican national and religious symbols to infuse La Causa with meaning and attract mass attention (Bardacke, "César's Ghost"). Thus, in the "Plan of Delano," the manifesto issued during the 1966 pilgrimage from Delano to Sacramento describing the union's history, demand for reforms, and struggle for "social justice in farm labor," Chávez and the UFW declare that they carry "La Virgen de Guadalupe" because she is "all ours, Patroness of the Mexican people." However, they "also carry the Sacred Cross and the Star of David because [they] are not sectarians, and because [they] ask the help and prayers of all religions." While Chávez and the UFW emphasize the multiplicity of spiritual belief in their appeals to "all religions," they also rec-ognize that La Virgen is both a religious and a national or nationalist symbol, which suggests that such symbols are inherently variable and interchangeable.

It is no surprise, then, that despite the fact that Chávez and the UFW are central to the representation of Chicano nationalism and are often portrayed as agents for Chicano/a identity, Chávez insisted that the UFW did not represent a specific race, ethnicity, or nation. Indeed, as Griswold del Castillo and García suggest, he had never thought of La Causa as "a movement that would be moti-vated primarily by appeals to race or nationality" (56). Instead, Chávez aligned the union according to class lines broadly representing the poor and working class, calling collectively for racial and ethnic harmony in the "Plan of Delano":

We know that the poverty of the Mexican or the Filipino worker in California is the same as that of all farm workers across the country, the Negroes and poor whites, the Puerto Ricans, Japanese, and Arabians; in short, all of the races that comprise the oppressed minorities of the United States. The majority of the people on our Pilgrimage are of Mexican descent, but the triumph of our race depends on a national association of all farm workers. (Jensen and Hammerback 17–18)

The union's main platform was based upon the idea that individual minority groups can only truly assert themselves by uniting with other "oppressed minorities." Yet it is clear that the UFW does not primarily establish a link between these groups based on their abjection but, rather, formulates poverty in the spirit of revolution. To this end, they also proclaim themselves "sons of the Mexican Revolution, a revolution of the poor seeking bread and justice." Yet this is not a direct relationship, for they renounce armed revolution and foreground their nonviolent difference. Finally, they lay claim to their role as national and transnational historical actors, asserting, "in this very same [Sacramento] valley, the Mexican race has sacrificed itself for the last hundred years. Our sweat and our blood have fallen on this land to make other men rich" (Jensen and Hammerback 14). These proclamations are deliberately contradictory. It is precisely these conflicts that rebut Chávez's canonization as a symbol of a unified Mexican past and of Chicano assimilation to a U.S. "ethnic group experience" in the present (Flores 198).

Margarita Cota-Cárdenas's *Puppet*

As a corollary to the "great man" narrative that Blackwell identifies within Chicano movement historiography, Chicano representations of César Chávez continue to grapple with his canonization as an agent for a Mexican past and an assimilated U.S. present. Such duality is especially fraught with tension because it informs both Chávez's accessibility and his impenetrability for everyday Chicanos/as. The portrayal of Chávez as a symbol of saintly perfection conveys an unattainable ideal of Chicano/a identity. Texts such as Margarita Cota-Cárdenas's *Puppet* and Culture Clash's *A Bowl of Beings* wrestle with Chávez's iconic image, and with iconicity in general, in order to refute a monolithic Chicano/a identity based upon a nostalgic past or an assimilated present. In *Puppet*, the protagonist's conflicted Chicana identity is defined in relation to the sacred, seemingly perfect image of César Chávez. *Puppet* is an extremely rich, dense novel that contains multiple narratives, voices, and temporalities, including the story of the protagonist, Petra (Pat) Leyva and her struggle with her Chicana identity. Pat is a single mother of two girls, an instructor of Chicano literature and Spanish at a community college, and a part-time secretary at a construction company, who confronts clashing ideologies of class, language, and ethnicity. The novel is set in the early to mid 1980s, though many of its events occur in the late 1960s and early 1970s, narrated partly through flashbacks and daydreams that are written in the present tense. The novel's central narrative is the story of a young impoverished Chicano nicknamed Puppet who has been unjustly shot and killed by the police in Southwest City, a mostly Mexican town somewhere in the southwestern United States. Puppet's murder is the catalyst for Pat's narrative of self-doubt and redemption in relation to both her private life as a hard-working single mother and her public life as a member of the Chicano community. Although César Chávez is not a character in the novel, his specter influences Pat's divergent feelings about Chicano/a identity throughout.

The context for *Puppet* is the aftermath of the Chicano movement, symbolized particularly by Chávez and the farmworkers. Cota-Cárdenas wrote *Puppet* in the 1980s, during Chávez's "difficult last decade," when the UFW was losing ground on a national scale and their organizational and financial power was steadily decreasing (Jensen and Hammerback 111). Rodolfo Acuña and Carlos Muñoz Jr. argue that the decade of the 1980s also corresponds to the decline of the Chicano movement, in terms of internal division and repression within activist groups like La Raza Unida Party, and reflecting the depoliticization and containment of Chicanos/as through the use of the term *Hispanic* and the displacement of radical activist groups by middle-class business and mainstream political groups. However, Blackwell astutely points out that this periodization, which typically "historiciz[es] the emergence of Chicana feminism within the decline of el movimiento Chicano," is extremely problematic and erroneous, constituting a "historiographic device that denies Chicanas or women of color historical agency in social transformation by consistently depicting their role or importance as occurring after the 'real revolution' or period of social change" (14, 30).

Women were very much a part of movement leadership from its inception, while "the role of women and gender ideology were hotly debated" during the movement (Blackwell 7). Nevertheless, the conceptual frames utilized by social movement scholars frequently rendered women's participation and leadership "unintelligible or invisible" (Blackwell 29). Indeed, Cota-Cárdenas's post-movement reflection on Chicano/a identity still reflects a general lack of support for women's participation in the movement, whether in terms of social activism or cultural production. As was the case for many Chicana writers, Cota-Cárdenas's novel was not published by a mainstream press. Instead, *Puppet* was originally published by Relámpago, a small self-established Chicana press in 1985 (Rebolledo xiv). Because of the novel's limited distribution and probably also because it had been written in Spanish, a marginalized language in the United States, *Puppet* was out of print for many years. Although it has been known as an underground classic, to this day very little criticism has been published on the novel.[11] It was translated and republished in a fully bilingual edition by the

University of New Mexico Press in 2000, suggesting that the novel is finally gaining some prominence in the Chicano literary canon.

Although *Puppet* responds to the cultural narrative of the Chicano movement and grapples with the representation of nationalism, the novel's use of multiple languages and alternative narrative temporalities reflects the overlap and clash between regional, national, and transnational identities of Chicanas/os positioned between the United States and Mexico.[12] It also references the economic and social uncertainty of working-class Chicanos/as and Mexicans from both sides of the border. *Puppet* was originally written primarily in Spanish, but it is essentially a bi- or multilingual text, for Cota-Cárdenas constantly switches between languages, wielding formal Spanish, Mexican, and Chicano Spanish slang, Spanglish, formal English, and broken English. In the text, she utilizes different fonts and typefaces such as bold letters, capitals, italics, and indented type and even approximates the ringing of a phone. These narrative techniques demarcate shifts in time and space and characterize the overlap between stream of consciousness and descriptive prose, and between fantasy and reality.

Yet the heterogeneity of this temporal and linguistic multiplicity contrasts with the rigid formulations of identity evident in the novel. Pat believes in authentic Chicano/a identities, particularly centered on the iconic image of César Chávez and the farmworkers. The Chicano/a identities available to Pat—or more precisely, that she perceives to be available—are extremely limited, revolving around idealized conceptions of the farmworker, the working-class urban laborer, the political activist, the Chicana feminist, or the traditional housewife. In *Puppet*, Pat fulfills none of these familiar roles. However, she does ultimately disidentify with such rigid Chicano/a identities: not only is she unable to inhabit them, she realizes that she does not even want to.

Pat does not fit either a narrative of Chicano assimilation to a mainstream American present or a nostalgic embrace of a Mexican and indigenous past. She is alienated from both her educated friends that support the Chicano movement and from her construction worker friends, several of whom are illegal immigrants from Mexico who do not speak English well. She is uncomfortable about her childhood as the daughter of a farm labor contractor among migrant farmworkers, while during college she is a reluctant participant in movement and UFW activities like the 1966 Lenten Pilgrimage from Delano to Sacramento. Pat does not fulfill the role of the traditional wife and mother for she spends much of her time imagining romantic scenarios with her former lover, even as she refers to their relationship as "dirty linens" and scolds herself for indulging in "others' fantasies, not yours" (Cota-Cárdenas 46, 123).[13] Furthermore, although Pat's daughters are not as fluent in Spanish as she is, her college-age daughter, María, is radicalized by her exposure to Latin American Marxism and liberation theology and travels to Nicaragua to support the Sandinistas, which frightens Pat.

Of course, all of the characters in *Puppet* are much more complicated than Pat's idealizations suggest. Many of them are torn by internal conflict and confronted by hypocrisy or otherwise defy a limited conception of identity just as much as Pat does. Nevertheless, it is clear that Pat also refuses such strict conceptions of identity. Perhaps the clearest example of the tension in *Puppet* is the fact that the novel appears to promote fixed Chicano/a identities yet bursts with multilingual tricks and slips that challenge the limits of identity at every turn. Through a radical interrogation of language and translation, *Puppet* provides a critical perspective on the ongoing struggle between fluid and essentialist Chicano/a identities. Although Pat persists in her desire for a fixed, authentic Chicana identity, largely centered on the iconic image of Chávez, *Puppet* constantly challenges the institutionalization of identity through this interrogation of language.

The Limits of Chicano/a Identity

Pat's anxiety over identity is best reflected by her obsession with César Chávez and with farm laborers in general. For Pat, Chávez is neither a viable symbol of the Mexican past nor a marker of Chicano assimilation. She seems unable to understand or accept his contradictions. Instead, she shifts between formulaic representations of Chávez, reflecting on his character as a threatening "Communist," a revered spiritual leader, a sellout to the cause, and a fixed Chicano icon (Cota-Cárdenas 60, 110, 77). Above all, she believes that Chávez and the farmworkers represent an authentic Chicano/a identity comprising all of the characteristics she lacks, especially those associated with an activist, working-class, immigrant, and community-oriented identity. As she struggles to decipher and record Puppet's story, thoughts of Chávez, farmworkers, and other symbols of the UFW are never far from her mind, both disturbing and inspiring her.

Pat's tautological reasoning is unsustainable, for just as she constructs Chávez and the farmworkers as impervious icons of Chicano/a identity, she also thinks of Chicano/a identity in terms of iconic perfection. Conversely, she also associates those icons, and her own conflicted subject position, with abjection. At times, Chávez is an ominous presence in her life, as she ponders "who is this Chávez anyway? What does he want?" (109). But more often, Chávez represents the model of spiritual purity and selflessness that Pat can never approximate. She greatly envies the political clarity of Venus, her "redheaded college friend from the 60s," a UFW lawyer who "works with the very same Chávez" (76). It is quite clear that the redheaded, Spanish-speaking, and presumably Chicana Venus is far more assured of her ethnic legitimacy than Pat is, even though she breaks with the stereotypical notions of what a Chicana might look like. Pat interprets Venus's claim "Of course I marched with Chávez," as proof of her friend's unwavering commitment, contrasting with her own reluctance and uncertainty about the Chicano movement and La Causa (76).

Pat's self-doubt extends to her relationship with her daughter María, for she is troubled by María's questions about her role in the farmworkers' movement. Reading a letter from her daughter, Pat imagines her saying, "It's just that I remembered that you were finishing your last years at University when César marched through the Valley. . . . Mom did you meet César Chávez? . . . didn't you tell me that you had friends that worked with him? . . . And you?" (Cota-Cárdenas 63). Later, Pat recalls another letter that illustrates her inability to answer María's questions about her activism: "Mom, you still haven't answered about César and the March of Delano. . . . weren't you there . . . ? Write me" (73). Pat feels like a bad mother and a bad Chicana because she cannot fulfill María's expectations, yet she is unable to explain herself. Perhaps because of these guilty feelings, Pat reserves her highest compliment for Venus, who remains committed to the Chicano movement and to farmworkers' rights, thinking to herself, "No mijita, ella nunca perdió el hilo she never lost the thread . . . (y tú y tú y tú and you and you and you and you)" (76). This sense of constancy is precisely what Pat has been lacking her entire life, while the repetition of "y tú/and you" implies that she doubts her role as a Chicana in relation to her community and her family. She does not think she should blindly follow all of the tenets of César Chávez and the UFW or the Chicano movement, but Pat fears that her lack of faith in their ideals brands her as a traitor both to her daughter and to the community in the tradition of La Malinche.[14] By associating herself with Malinche, Pat further distances herself from the cohesive narrative of authenticity and belonging that she associates with Chávez and the UFW.

Pat's association of Chicanos/as with radical politics and activism reinforces Chávez's canonization as a symbol of Chicano redemption in the novel. Predictably, Pat's attitude toward Chávez is conflicted. On the one hand, she implies that Chávez and the UFW are a threat to national stability, especially in relation to Cold War communism and Latin American Marxism. Perhaps echoing criticism she has heard elsewhere, Pat thinks "CHÁVEZ? OH THAT TROUBLE-MAKER MUST BE A COMMUNIST!" (Cota-Cárdenas 60). On the other hand, even though Pat clearly interprets the labor leader as a threat, she dismisses the validity of the Chicano movement for the present day, thinking, "(Mira, boliche pinhead all that stuff about campos [fields] and braceros and that EL MOVIMIENTO THE MOVEMENT, doesn't it seem that it's a bit . . . behind the times . . . ? . . . I'll give you some advice . . . Don't get involved, te lo aconsejo, no te metas in things you don't know much about. . . . Or you'll start remembering other little things that years ago)" (32). Although she tries to convince herself that "all that stuff about campos [fields]" is no longer relevant to her life and to that of the immigrant laborers she knows, echoing Richard Rodríguez's claim that Chávez was already irrelevant to the lives of "Mexican-Americans" in the late 1960s because "90 percent of us lived in cities and we were more apt to work in construction than as farmworkers," Pat's true fear is of the contradictions she finds buried in her past (Cota-Cárdenas 67). César Chávez threatens her because she fears that her discordant feelings about him, and about farm laborers in general, reveal the truth about her own betrayals. As the novel progresses, we discover that her father was a farm labor contractor, and that her family rented rooms to the farmworkers. As such, the family occupied a higher social position than the farmworkers they lived among. In Pat's mind, news headlines about the exploitation and deaths of migrant farm laborers are interwoven with memories of her childhood, such as her description of Wimpy, one of her mother's boarders, and his death in a car wreck while traveling to pick tomatoes. Consistent with a child's imagination, these memories reflect an uncomplicated view of class and ethnic solidarity and provide a linear narrative of social and economic advancement. Yet immediately after recalling her childhood adventures, Pat suggests that her story about Wimpy might have been invented, at least to some extent: "(That wasn't you, I know you already and it just couldn't have been you. . . . Where'd ya get that story from, you romanticizing liar?)" (31). Whether her perception is accurate or not, she clearly worries that her relationship with the farmworkers is inherently unequal.

Pat's nostalgia for the farmworkers of her childhood does not translate into similar feelings toward César Chávez and the UFW in the present. Although Pat thinks of Chávez as the iconic Chicano hero who represents everything she cannot be, she constantly tears him down from his perch, simultaneously creating and negating him as an icon or secular saint. At times, her fluctuating opinions of Chávez seem strident and accusatory, at others, they reveal her anxiety about her own inability to commit to activism and the Chicano movement. Rather than understanding community and individual agency as intertwined, Pat conflates them entirely, framing community as a monolith that determines individual agency. Thus she occasionally situates political activism and farm labor on opposite sides, reflecting her desire to choose between the laborers and those who hire them, lead them, support them, or study them. She also implies that the masses are unable to produce their own course of struggle autonomously in relation to the Chicano movement or the UFW. While Pat occasionally echoes the idea that Chávez is a communist, she also suggests that he is a "vendido" (sell-out) who has lost touch with his people, a claim laughingly dismissed by her friend Venus (Cota-Cárdenas 77). These claims reiterate both liberal and conservative criticism of Chávez. The notion that he is a sell-out echoes the complaints of many on the left who criticized him for his unyielding control of the UFW and his insistence on total loyalty, while the characterization of the labor leader as communist reflects his ongoing power to irritate the state through civil and labor rights activism, especially in relation to the hysteria surrounding Cold War communism and Marxism. Furthermore, Pat draws upon both Christian iconography and indigenous spirituality to characterize her relationship to Chávez, thinking, "YOUR MUD-FEETED GODS BUT TUS DIOSES CON PIES DE BARRO PERO PERO ESTUVISTE TÚ??? OH WERE YOU THERE WHEN THEY" as she recalls the march from Delano to Sacramento that took place during her last year of university (109). But this narrative of syncretic spirituality reflects only absence and guilt, since Pat was not there "when they" marched to Sacramento, symbolically representing herself as one of those who (in the words of the American spiritual) stood by and watched "when they crucified my Lord" (109).

While Pat's thoughts are decidedly fanciful, as when images of singer Joan Baez, author Jorge Luis Borges, President John F. Kennedy, and Chávez blur together in her mind, causing her to imagine a conspiracy between them as "troublemakers," she also has more concrete reasons to be suspicious of political activism in the United States and Latin America (Cota-Cárdenas 74–76). Most obviously, these have to do with her fear for María's safety in Central America, but Pat also understands that the state has the power to criminalize social activism by conflating it with communism. This institutionalization can lead to deadly consequences. For example, as Pat reads a letter from María stating that she has fallen in love with a Chilean exile with whom she later travels to Nicaragua, the words of the letter merge with a list of names of the disappeared from the 1968 Tlatelolco massacre in Mexico City, provided by her friend Medeiros, whose son Chema was involved in the student protest (78–79). Pat emphasizes Chema's desire to reveal the truth to the world about Tlatelolco, a truth that was famously obscured by the PRI-led Mexican government.[15] Pat correlates her quest to reveal the truth about Puppet's murder with Chema's publicizing of the truth behind the massacre, but the implication later in the novel is that Chema is killed for exposing the truth. Pat believes that she does not have the courage to risk her life in the same way (128).

In the Mexican government's crackdown on the Tlatelolco protesters, Pat recognizes the same conflation between Marxism and political protest that she perceives in her own life, and she realizes that her feelings about Chávez resemble the authoritarian discourse of the state. This is especially evident in her encounter with UFW members who are participating in the march from Delano to Sacramento. Like her description of Wimpy, this story blurs the line between fantasy and reality, but unlike in her childhood memories, Pat positions herself against the laborers:

> you sat while the couple dressed like farm workers talked they've come to represent the others . . . the silent professors and students listening and when the two dressed in working clothes bandannas the flag with the red and black eagle

you jump you accuse and you make you encourage the other students to follow you because you can perform so well and they applaud your frenetic questions ARE YOU COMMUNISTS? WHO GIVES YOU ORDERS? WHO ARE YOU PEOPLE? you, the daughter of a contractor know how to represent, like an educated woman THAT HAD MADE IT you knew really well OR NOT OR NOT OR NOT . . . ? (Cota-Cárdenas 114–115)

Pat's vitriolic reaction is specifically directed against the UFW, for the "flag with the red and black eagle" provokes her to disrupt the meeting. She conveys many contradictory emotions in her outburst, ranging from the fear that the UFW might take advantage of poor laborers for political purposes to condescension toward the farmworkers, implying that they must be taking orders and cannot think for themselves. Her sense that she is "performing" this outburst for applause suggests that she is imagining the entire encounter, but it also demonstrates the way she feels that she is constantly on display; as she puts it, someone who must "represent" as an educated Chicana to the crowd. While she is unable to reconcile her ideas about farmworkers and the UFW with her fear of political activism, she believes that her education and her comparatively privileged background irrevocably separate her from them, removing the possibility of collaboration and collectivity.

The only time when Pat does participate in support of Chávez and the UFW, she portrays it as a complete failure. She remembers Venus encouraging her to contribute some food for the marchers when they pass through the university town, pausing upon Venus's incredulous reaction to her reticence: "Come on, Pat . . . sooo much **compañerismo** in the club, and now you tell me that you don't believe that those people are right . . . !" (Cota-Cárdenas 110). Drawing upon Chávez's own strategy of spiritual authority through folk and orthodox Catholicism, Venus attempts to convince Pat that the marchers are authentic because "some priests are marching with them and . . . they are carrying the Virgin at the front," implicitly countering Pat's accusations of communism since "if they believe in God, pues, how can they be like you say . . . ?" (110). Yet when Pat finally agrees to contribute a pot of chili beans to the marchers, no one eats them "because **it was a Friday and you put meat in them!**" demonstrating her disconnection from their Catholic practices (115). Later, Venus jokingly tells Pat, "oh yeah, they asked if you were Catholic or not, ha ha . . . ," exposing Pat's religious and cultural anxieties, in this case stemming from her mother's conversion to a Pentecostal church (114). Pat is clearly insecure about her Chicana identity, yet she firmly rejects its institutionalization. To this end, she is suspicious of expressions of identity politics and community solidarity within higher-education circles (such as MEChA) and UFW hierarchies.[16] Pat rejects her teaching assistant Elena's discourse about the Chicano movement, with its foundational texts such as the "Plan of Aztlán," and the meetings, conferences, and poetry readings she attends led by people who are "committed to the Movimiento [the Chicano movement]" (136). She mistrusts any hint of militancy, citing the potential for movements carried out in the name of a "prophet" or a "crusade" to destroy their people either literally or figuratively (138). She even compares the policing of dissent within the Chicano movement to the surveillance tactics of the CIA (138). However, rather than signaling a refusal to engage with such groups, or an indifference toward their concerns, Pat's unease indicates resistance to what George Yúdice calls "the increase in governmentalization" behind identity politics, reflecting the turn by the early 1970s within Chicano and other activist groups from "political action" to "political brokering in increasingly institutionalized settings," such as university centers and institutes, bilingual education programs, and community cultural programs (54). The mythologization of Chicano/a identity in *Puppet*, particularly through the portrayal of César Chávez, corresponds to these forms of institutionalization.

Ultimately, Pat's obsession with Chávez stems from the fact that she believes he, like the farmworkers and other laborers, has no need to question his identity. Since Chávez and the farmworkers seem effortlessly to embody Mexican or Chicano/a identity, they aren't compelled to represent it, either. By contrast, Pat is constantly trying to explain and represent herself to everyone, even though she repeatedly shifts between identities as a Chicana and *mexicana*. Pat defends her cultural background to her students, who frequently present stereotypical questions and attitudes, such as those about the preoccupation with death in Mexican and Chicano literature (Cota-Cárdenas 37). She is compelled to justify Chicano/a identity to her migrant Mexican friends, as when she confesses to her friend Memo that her children cannot speak Spanish well: "There's all kinds of mexicanos, Memo" (21). It is notable, however, that when she speaks to Memo, Pat identifies herself as a fellow Mexican but notes that Memo's kids "also don't speak Spanish very well" and suggests that "Yes, Chicanos is better" as a term to describe their mutual experience in the United States (21). Conversely, when some of Pat's middle-class Mexican friends browse through her Chicano journals, they laugh at them and ask, "What does the Chicano want, Petra?" immediately distancing her from their experience as Mexicans who mock the fact that "people live very comfortably in the States" (116).

Pat's responses to her students and her middle-class Mexican friends invoke the narrative of tradition that she rejects elsewhere in the novel. She prattles to her American students about the Mexican "dance with death" and its roots in indigenous culture, while rambling to her Mexican friends in vague noncommittal terms about Chicanos/as' desire for a "better life, better treatment, you didn't recall exactly what" (Cota-Cárdenas 117). In both cases, she is unable to respond in the context of the present tragedy and hardships facing poor Chicanos/as and migrants, symbolized by the life and death of Puppet. While Pat resents having to be accountable for the Chicana perspective to both Mexicans and Americans, she is also unsure of herself before other Chicanos/as. She interprets both identity and community as exclusive and static and yearns for the seemingly safe boundaries of ethnic legitimacy.

Yet while Pat's conception of Chicano/a identity is essentialist, it also resists essentialization. Despite her anguish and victimization—especially in relation to Chávez and the farmworkers—Pat reveals an alternative identity from the margins that is neither essentialist nor hybrid. This alternative identity is expressed most clearly through her relationship with the utterly marginalized character of Puppet, expressed especially through linguistic play.

"BREAK THE TIES TO YOUR MYTHS"

In contrast to the representation of César Chávez in the novel, with his apparently effortless embodiment of Chicano/a identity, Puppet is resolutely imperfect. Disfigured by a bone disease, he walks with a limp (hence the nickname "Puppet") and is doubly silenced because he is not fluent in English and has a speech impediment that causes him to stutter and mispronounce words. His father has abandoned the family, his mother has recently died, and he is left to care for several younger brothers and sisters who are neglected by their stepparents. As the lost child of Mexican immigrants and the impoverished urban heir to Chávez's farmworkers, Puppet is excluded from both dominant American and Mexican identities. He is marginalized even in death, for his murder is falsely portrayed as self-defense by the police. While the police initially claim to have found an old rifle in Puppet's car, they later change their story for the press: "POLICE CLAIM YOUTH CONCEALED WEAPON IN HIS LEG" (Cota-Cárdenas 118, 133). However, Pat agrees with Memo that "el chamaco nunca traiba arma never [the kid never carried a gun]" and realizes that Puppet's limp causes the police to jump to conclusions: "the batito limped, so that was it" (118, 133). Furthermore, she discovers that, just before his murder, Puppet had fought with the same drug dealers who were responsible for another friend's death; the implication is that the dealers tipped off the police to wait for him. Puppet's murder exposes the cycle of corruption and collusion between the police and the criminals, both of whom are equally capable of harming poor Chicanos/as. Because of her commitment to uncover and publish the truth about Puppet, Pat faces reprisals from the police and the drug dealers in the community. She is followed, the gas line in her car is mysteriously severed, and her home telephone is wiretapped. Pat's real-life experience with police and criminal surveillance contrasts with her fear of the inchoate threat of César Chávez's communism. As opposed to her paralysis throughout much of the novel, which is typically associated with Chávez and the UFW, Pat is finally able to take control and act because of Puppet, even though the actions she takes are risky.

Puppet becomes a new model of the Chicano who resists fixed identities and nationalist discourse. While it is difficult to imagine that Puppet could ever be officially assimilated or canonized, in some ways he is characterized as a secular saint like César Chávez. Unlike Chávez, however, Puppet is sacred precisely because he is ordinary and imperfect. His unjust murder makes him a martyr, complete with the mark of a cross tattooed on his body that reappears throughout the narrative. His martyrdom is simultaneously local and global, representing the community of Southwest City but also extending to all marginalized people, symbolized by Cota-Cárdenas's dedication of the novel to "the powerless, who like Puppet, must struggle daily for their small share of human dignity and self-respect." Pat's writing about Puppet resembles traditional hagiography, with its emphasis on his selflessness (working two jobs without complaint, and caring for younger siblings who are abused by their stepparents) and his suffering, both physical and emotional (evident through his limp and his desire to reunite with and forgive the father who abandoned him). Above all, Pat idealizes his physical beauty, perhaps as a way to suggest the perfection behind a flawed veneer: "Cojea . . . he limps when he walks. La verdad, really no one pays attention to it because right away people notice instead the beauty. . . . Dark hair somewhat long and curly, a thin face, naturally dark skinned and even more bronzed 'cause of his work, and lovely dark eyes. . . . Very bright eyes" (Cota-Cárdenas 10). Finally, the act of writing Puppet's story demonstrates Pat's faith in his powers in death to redeem and unite the community that failed him in life.

Nevertheless, Pat does not simply appropriate Puppet as a new model of ideal Chicano/a identity in place of César Chávez. Instead, in life and in death, Puppet actively inserts himself into the consciousness of Pat and others in the community, reflecting a kind of spiritual transfer or possession. Through both intentional and unintentional linguistic slips and tricks stemming from his speech impediment, his difficulty with English and formal Spanish, and his facility with slang and humor, as well as visual signs, Puppet rearticulates Chicano/a identity as multiple, malleable, and flawed, rather than the monolithic perfection Pat associates with César Chávez. At first glance, everything about Puppet's language and communication seems defective. He favors informal language and linguistic hybrids like Spanglish, his speech impediment causes him to repeat or mangle words, and he mistranslates Spanish, as when he triumphantly, and comically, announces to an inquisitive "*gabachita*" (white woman) that his new girlfriend Inés's name translates to "Inerest" (interest) in English (Cota-Cárdenas 11). Of course, the joke is on the *gabachita* who asks for the translation even more than on Puppet, since the name Inés does not properly translate at all. Doris Sommer emphasizes the need to reformulate the linguistic trickery and mishaps that arise from bi- and multilingualism such as Puppet's as "supplement, not a deficiency," not a sign of immigrant abjection but of an enthusiastic role in "the game of shuttling between insider and outsider" (3). In this sense, Puppet's linguistic misadventures bespeak a cognitive agility that exceeds standard or formal language use. Perhaps Puppet mistranslates Inés, but the *gabachita* does not even realize that the name requires no translation.

True to this sense of play, Puppet enters Pat's life through fragmented, frequently incorrect or flawed phrases, thoughts, and images. His murder forces her to question the ingrained beliefs and patterns of behavior—stagnant myths, icons, and phrases relating to Chicano/a identity—that she clings to throughout much of the narrative. For instance, as she attempts to organize information about Puppet's life and death, she recalls a poem she has written inspired by the death of her friend Félix from a drug overdose. She simultaneously reimagines the poem in the context of Puppet's murder. It is unclear when Pat wrote the poem or which of the two deaths more directly inspired her to write it, but the poem becomes a recurring symbol of Puppet's presence. The poem expresses her frustration: "THERE IS A CHICANO SUCIO / WHOM NOBODY WILL NAME / TAKES LITTLE BLACK AND BROWN CHILDREN / AND MURDERS THE SPARKLE IN / THEIR BEAUTIFUL BROWN EYES," yet as words from the poem recur throughout the narrative, they are alternately fearful and hopeful (Cota-Cárdenas 34). The image of Puppet's eyes appears most often, primarily as a call for accountability: "CHOCOLATE LIVELY EYES . . . HE WANTED TO TELL US SOMETHING BUT HE COULDN'T"; "DARK EYES OF AN OLD MAN IN THE BODY OF A YOUNG KID GRANITE EYES THAT ASK YOU THEY ASK YOU SOMETHING . . . ARGO . . ."; and "YOUNG EYES BRIGHT HOPE" (25, 39, 79). Along with the exhortation "ARGO"—a rendering of the Spanish word "algo [something]" in Puppet's voice, with the lisp that causes him to mispronounce the letter "L"—the dark eyes call for recognition of and resistance toward powerful forces such as Puppet's stepparents, the police, drug dealers, and even some of Pat's friends who threaten to silence his memory or simply forget him.

Pat describes Puppet as clever, and though he occasionally seems like a figure of fun to the other construction workers, he always strives to make the best of a bad situation through humor. After his death, he appears as a ghostly spiritual image to Pat, urging her and the community to "do somethin', ask questions to yo'self an'ta others" in order to expose the collusion of the police and drug dealers and to ask everyone to recognize their complicity with the situation (Cota-Cárdenas 53). The ghostly Puppet is neither frightening nor didactic but instead demonstrates humorous resistance. At his funeral, while his friends laugh about his three fiancées (as Memo puts it, "Y tan calladito el chamaco . . . and so quiet!"), Puppet's ghost calls for social change and self-reflection while displaying comical defiance over the three women: "ain' nuthin' wrong whit dat, whad'ya jealous or somethin'?" (56). At the same moment, Pat imagines Puppet appearing as a Hamlet figure, delivering a soliloquy on disempowerment and violence in the barrio. Puppet-as-Hamlet shifts from Shakespearean soliloquy: "Vivil o no vivil, ésa e la plegunta . . . To live or not to live, das' the question" to call for community action and accountability: "Whad' those two cops shoot me for, das' what I wanna know, pala qué" (52). Later, he urges, "Thus conscience does make cowards of us all . . . Why don' you ask the cops something useful argo güeno . . . Cause there's somethin' argo güeno . . . don't preten' ya' don' gettit" (55). Puppet flaunts his linguistic difference by insisting on Spanish and mispronouncing the words "algo [something]" and "bueno," transforming these errors into a mode of resistance against police brutality. Emblematic of the bilingual bind of excess and deficiency described by Sommer, Puppet defiantly proclaims the advantages of excess language (and knowledge of different cultural traditions) over the supposed deficiency of his speech impediment and linguistic errors (12–13). Unlike the representation of César Chávez as a romanticized yet threatening secular saint and the concomitant essentialization of Chicano/a identity, Puppet's return through spiritual haunting or possession demands self-reflexivity on the part of the entire Chicano community.

Puppet's murder forces Pat to examine her own entrenched beliefs and behavior. Although she yearns to define Chicano/a identity through a linear narrative of tradition, the brutality of Puppet's death and its subsequent cover-up preclude this: "You could write about his death first since it was the most shocking . . . you throw out that idea because then it would be giving it a meaning that it didn't have. . . . You didn't want the story in chronological order either, since that wasn't how the facts of the case had been perceived or brought to light" (Cota-Cárdenas 37). Although Pat resorts to her usual beliefs and behavior throughout the narrative, such as engaging in nostalgic fantasies, Puppet's murder and his saintly martyrdom constantly disrupt her perception of fixed identities. Puppet's murder juxtaposes the modern with popular tradition, by creating a barrio secular saint who stands up to drug dealers and the police. At the same time, his secular sanctity is a corrective for the celebration of *La Raza* through tradition, which is often predicated upon a glorified indigenous past that subsumes its marginalized present. For example, Pat's lecture to her students about the Mexican obsession with death as a manifestation of its indigenous culture contrasts in her mind with the cruel reality of Puppet's murder, demonstrating the incongruity of her celebratory narrative (37).

In this manner, Puppet inspires Pat to reinterpret the traditional symbols and myths of Chicano and Mexican culture that she alternately desires and rejects, like César Chávez. Such myths contribute to the production of limited, inflexible Chicano/a identities. By writing Puppet's story, and through her relationship with him as a symbol of collectivity, Pat is able to overhaul the stagnant symbols and identities that she struggles with. In the end, she is able to "BREAK THE TIES TO YOUR MYTHS," and accept her own accountability for their perpetuation (Cota-Cárdenas 96). In the chapter titled "Malinche's Discourse," Pat recalls events that reinscribe her not solely as a traitorous Malinche figure but as one who has been betrayed as well. Pat feels that she betrays her community by not being authentically Chicana, but she is also betrayed by them when they question her identity or force her to fit into an essentialist mold. Likewise, all of the traits ascribed to Malinche are flawed, for the mother is also a murderer, since mestizo national creation is defined in part through the loss of the indigenous culture. She thinks, "Are you Malinche a malinchi? Who are you (who am I malinchi)? seller or buyer? sold or bought and at what price?" and reveals only negative possibilities: the fear of being either a sellout or a victim (93). At the same time, Pat's double-edged representation of Malinche recalls Anzaldúa's protest against the patriarchal condemnation of Malinche as traitor and betrayer: Anzaldúa states, "Not me sold out my people but they me" (Anzaldúa 43). While Anzaldúa calls for Mexican and Chicano culture to take responsibility for denying the "Indian woman in us," Pat more clearly provides for the possibility of agency as well as victimization in the persona of Malinche (Anzaldúa 44). Imagining herself as Malinche, she protests being "sold" against her will but also admits her own complicity in the situation:

> why don't they want to understand that I did it all because of **love** and not because of any hate nor any ambition . . . A traitress . . . ? Because of our language, that I helped them that I sold my people . . . You know what, you know a lot about —isms and —acies but I advise you, my children, to look for the answers **inside** and to look further than the labels implanted . . . Because from what I've seen . . . is that we go on being, in the name of every cause, **chingones y chingadas** . . . those who fuck you and those who are fucked. (Cota-Cárdenas 95)

As Pat links herself to Malinche, she considers the way that she inhabits multiple sides: victim, agent, traitor, translator, lover, and critic. Pat's reframing of betrayal—the "selling out" of "my people"—as an act of love may seem stereotypical, but it nevertheless reclaims the contradictory aspects of Malinche's character.

In this reading, Malinche is not just a passive victim or a ruthless traitor. Instead, Pat entirely rearticulates the dichotomy of "seller or buyer" by envisioning a powerful representation of Malinche as a feminist confidante who refuses to participate in the patriarchal model. She imagines herself as Malinche fusing with La Llorona, the "weeping woman," yet another iconic figure of simultaneously dangerous and victimized Mexican motherhood. In Pat's fantasy, these two sides of her personality (Malinche and Llorona) join forces as friends, establishing a bond designed to negotiate the pitfalls of their symbolic roles as both embodiment of and threat to nationalist identity, whether Mexican or Chicano: "MY COMADRE LLORONA IS CALLING ME I STILL HAVE TO TEACH HER TO NOT PUT UP WITH SHIT TO OPEN HER EYES BECAUSE THERE'S SOMETHING REALLY GOOD" (Cota-Cárdenas 99). Although Pat's thoughts trail off here, the phrase "something good" is clearly an echo of Puppet's voice as he clamors for justice from the police, Pat, and the community. In this case, "something good" might refer to the dirty secret of internal divisions between Mexicans and Chicanos/as, or between educated Chicanos/as and working-class laborers that implicates the community in Puppet's death. Pat invokes some of the most negatively mythologized symbols of feminine national (and nationalist) identity in order to expose the complicity between the state and the popular in the production and perpetuation of these myths.

Finally, César Chávez, the epitome of the authentic Chicano in *Puppet*, is also transformed through Pat's struggle to rearticulate Chicano/a identity. The transformation is directly referenced through Puppet's association with Hamlet during his funeral. Like Hamlet, Puppet is an outsider for whom "something smells in Southwest City," referencing the link between the police and the drug dealers that leads to his murder and the lack of accountability of the community as a whole (Cota-Cárdenas 100). However, unlike Hamlet, Puppet receives another chance to redeem his people in death. The red-and-black eagle of the UFW appears on Puppet's chest, symbolically reinscribing Chávez in relation to a more radical identification with disempowered peoples than Pat has been able to imagine. This is the same symbol that follows and threatens her throughout the novel, provoking her to condemn "the couple dressed like farm workers" in the earlier fantasy (114). Rather than symbolizing a link to an indigenous Mexican past or assimilation to a mainstream American present, here the eagle represents the heterogeneity of Chicano/a identities. Although Pat initially resorts to her characteristic evasion and guilt in relation to Chávez and the UFW, thinking "what you didn't want, you didn't say, you didn't do. . . . Render unto César what is his, ha ha ha ha . . . !," Puppet forces her to confront the red-and-black eagle (57). He implores, "why don' you lookit me, siñola. . . . You did not say nothing 'bout my águila colora'a colorful eagle . . . ," demanding that she expose the truth about his murder but also that she recognize her own prejudice in construing homogenous Chicano/a identities (55, 57). In this sense, the eagle is a symbol of resistance and accountability, not only from outsiders but from the Chicano community itself.

For Pat, Puppet becomes the emblem of Chicano resistance that César Chávez can never be, but he does so in unexpected ways. Through multilingual misadventures, *Puppet* explodes dominant representations of Chicano/a identity, yet rather than simply rejecting stagnant myths—from La Malinche to La Llorona to César Chávez—the novel transforms them into markers of heterogeneous Chicano/a identities. Although these heterogeneous identities are contradictory, signaling pain as well as redemption, their strength lies in their ability to shift between and inhabit both exclusion and inclusion. In the end, Pat is transformed through Puppet, as his fragmented, multilingual speech permeates her thoughts and his face merges with her own in the mirror ("it's no longer your face in the espejo it's PUPPET's face"), and she is determined, at any cost, to heed the call to action through writing (Cota-Cárdenas 145). It is precisely the act of fragmented, flawed, and multilingual writing that permits Pat to participate wholeheartedly in a collective endeavor—her only uncompromised action in the entire novel and a collective act that simultaneously reframes her notion of individual agency and identity.

A Bowl of Beings: Extreme Chicano/a Identities

While *Puppet* contests reductive Chicano/a identities in the aftermath of the Chicano movement, Culture Clash's play *A Bowl of Beings* is simultaneously nostalgic for the movement and transforms it through parody. Like Richard Rodríguez, Culture Clash addresses the fragmentation of Chicano/a identity symbolized by the decline of César Chávez, the UFW, and the Chicano movement, but unlike Rodríguez, their goal is to revive them, albeit in new forms, to "face the dragon and make carne asada out of him or her," while "slay[ing] a few sacred cows along [the] way" (Montoya et al. 61, 59). In the introduction to the published version of the play, Richard Montoya, one of the three founding members of Culture Clash, states, "*A Bowl of Beings* was our Valentine card to the Chicano Movement. But it wasn't all about love and feeling good—there were healthy doses of rage, confusion, criticism, hope, despair and the eternal search for the perfect pizza" (59). The comical quest for pizza in the play is juxtaposed with a serious awareness of the contradictions of the Chicano movement, demonstrating Culture Clash's particular brand of tragicomedy, which merges the absurd with social and political commentary.[17] A crucial part of this tragicomedy depends upon tearing down fixed Chicano/a icons and identities, as Clash member Ric Salinas argues: "We would cut down those icons that were protected, from Frida Kahlo to Che Guevara to Julio Iglesias. That's one thing we always did; we always swung swings at the Left as much as the Right" (xiv). In this manner, Culture Clash interrogates seemingly untouchable icons, or secular saints, in order to expose their appropriation and commodification from both dominant and marginalized perspectives. Although they mock canonized figures, they also restore lost humanity to secular saints such as Che Guevara, as in the scene "The Return of Che!" in which Chuy, a Berkeley Chicano activist, brings a bewildered Che back from the dead and urges him not to be so depressed about the collapse of communism, because after all, he makes "a handsome silk-screen poster" (89). The spectacle of Che dramatically weeping over his own commodification humorously underscores the alienation of his radical politics from his sanitized, canonized persona. The scene implies that alienation and ambivalence are necessary consequences of canonization.

To this end, *A Bowl of Beings* parodies a variety of stereotypical Chicano/a and Latino/a identities, from the activist to the cholo, to the hippie stoner, to the salsa dancer and *santero* (Caribbean witch doctor). Fixed identities like the ones that paralyze Pat in *Puppet* are taken to outrageous extremes in *A Bowl* and are ridiculed even by those who embody them. The play appropriates numerous icons for Chicano culture, even those who are not specifically identified as Chicanos/as, like Che Guevara, who is celebrated as a much needed miracle that will "shake things up" by reviving the Chicano movement. As Chuy exclaims when Che appears in his house, "Oh man, wait till MEChA finds out" (Montoya et al. 62, 84). La Llorona and El Coocui, the bogeyman who hides under children's beds, are jokingly called "the ultimate Chicano couple," while the birth of the first mestizo to Don Colón and the indigenous woman America is refashioned as "history's first Chicano" (96, 72). In the scene "Don Colón (The First Chicano Opera, 1492)," the link between the "first Chicano" and Christopher Columbus confers legitimacy upon maligned Chicanos/as in the vein of the embrace of Aztlán and Aztlán-based nationalism. The connection to the "first Chicano" and Columbus suggests that Chicanos/as' roots go so far back that they precede modern nations and are interchangeable with the mestizo in general. Of course, Culture Clash does not adhere to traditional Aztlán-based nationalism. Vinnie, the "first Chicano," is predictably contradictory: he is torn between his indigenous mother "America" and his father Don Colón. His father calls him a "monster," and he is "confused and full of rage" (72). However, Vinnie also sarcastically proclaims that his people will triumph through consumption, commodification, and assimilation: "You will eat your words, Don Colón. One day my people will populate this new world. We'll own legitimate businesses. One day a dark little Indian will sit on the county board of supervisors" (73). While it appears that Chicanos/as can encompass virtually any identity in the play, Culture Clash suggests that they are impossible to define, as demonstrated by the initial exchange between Che Guevara and Chuy:

CHE: "Sos Mexicano?"
CHUY: "No, Chicano."
CHE: "Chicano? What is a Chicano?"
CHUY: "I don't know!" (84)

By simultaneously appropriating and celebrating iconic or stereotypical Chicano/a identities and by deconstructing them from within, Culture Clash parodies the very notion of the Chicano or Chicana.

At first glance, the play appears to romanticize César Chávez as an infallible Chicano hero. For Culture Clash, as for Pat in *Puppet*, Chávez and the UFW are central to the Chicano movement and represent an authentic Chicana/o identity. The play is not only a tribute to icons such as Chávez, the UFW, the Virgin of Guadalupe, and Che Guevara, it is framed as an extension of their struggle and the beliefs they represent, as Montoya indicates at the end of his introduction: "The struggle continues. Se puede? Sí se puede! We can do it. Viva César Chávez!" (62). Chávez in the play is often portrayed as interchangeable with the Chicano movement. As in *Puppet*, Chávez does not appear as a character but, rather, as a specter that pervades the play with nostalgia for an archetypal Chicano/a identity. For example, in the scene "Chicano on the Storm," the self-described "primal scream" of the play, Richard (Montoya, playing himself) delivers a monologue recalling a true story from his youth, in which César Chávez honored his family by coming to dinner but then did not eat because "he was fasting that night" (97). Chávez appears at the height of his sanctity through the sacrifice of the fast, augmented by Richard's mother's effort to prepare an incredible Mexican feast in honor of such a respected guest. Young Richard mischievously disrespects the sanctity of the fast by trying to take the labor leader's untouched food: "I asked César if I could have his chile relleno. It was mistaken as a sexual advance. I was sent to my room with no dinner. So, in solidarity with César, I fasted too" (97). Predictably, Richard's parents censure him for disrespecting the labor leader, but not because he tries to eat while Chávez fasts. Instead, Richard's parents histrionically interpret his request as a "sexual advance" (97). This scene brilliantly demonstrates Culture Clash's ironic juxtaposition of absurdity and solemnity. While critics and supporters alike often questioned Chávez's motives for fasting, his fasts are so linked to his sanctity and spiritual purity that it is shocking to think anyone could poke fun at them. Especially in relation to the implausible and comical "sexual advance," Culture Clash deliberately crosses a line in order to interrogate Chávez's sanctity and canonization, and by extension, the sanctity and canonization of other protected icons (xiv). In this sense, their ironic representation of these icons and histories is more in tune with César Chávez's theorization of flux and ambivalence than with his canonization as a rigid icon.

The play is similarly irreverent in its treatment of Chicano/a identity, in general, and challenges the narrow conception of both Chicano nationalism and Chicano assimilation to mainstream American culture. For example, Chuy, who is presented as a stereotypical MEChA-style activist, mocks the militancy of the group, telling a friend over the phone:

Obviously you haven't been listening to me carnal, ese, I already told you. . . . I can't make it to the U.S. out of East L.A. Rally, homes. Because I'm busy that day, ese. Something heavy is coming down for La Raza that day. Something that is going to have impact on La Comunidad, ese. (Pause) The Forty-Niners are playing! . . . Órale. We shall overcome, carnal. Boycott everything, aye, everything toxic: lettuce . . . grapes . . . strawberries . . . just say no. Hey ese . . . boycott your culo! (Montoya et al. 78)

Regardless of whether Chuy is just too lazy or stoned to participate in political meetings or rallies, he mocks the entrenched Chicano/a political activist who is so prominent in *Puppet*, who is defined through unyielding support for causes like the UFW or Chicano studies. To appease his friend (and to rush off to watch the football game), Chuy repeats a string of slogans and clichés—"Viva La Raza, Chicano power, ¡Qué viva la mujer!, We shall overcome, Power to the Native Americans, Boycott everything"—that have been reiterated so often they are utterly trite (78). Chuy laments the decline and commodification of the Chicano movement, but he also bolsters it, particularly through the image of Che Guevara. Surrounded by Che memorabilia such as banners and t-shirts, Chuy looks to Che to salvage the spirit of revolution: "What happened to El Movimiento? . . . How are we going to get back Aztlán? The only way to get our land back is the way Che did it. Total liberation through armed revolution. ¡Qué viva Ché!" (79). But when Che actually arrives on the scene, encouraging Chuy and his friend Frankie, the pizza deliveryman, to join him in fomenting revolution by overthrowing Domino's pizza franchises, Chuy prefers to opt out:

CHE: "Compañero, Frankie. Are you ready to struggle?"
FRANKIE: "I'm down!"
CHE: "Chuy, are you prepared to die?"
CHUY: (Nodding yes) "No." . . . (Che and Frankie exit with weapons. Chuy remains behind.)
CHUY: "Compañeros, I'll be right there! I've got to prepare myself for the revolution. I'm going to do some push-ups, make sure I'm ready, 'cause I'll probably be the first one to go down when the chingasos start. Am I ready to die? That vato takes himself pretty seriously. Comandante! I'm right behind you! I'm just gonna watch the Forty-Niner highlights first." (Montoya et al. 91–92)

Once again, this scene mingles absurdity and solemnity in an ironic jab at canonized icons like Che Guevara and mythologized histories like that of the Chicano movement or the Cuban Revolution. While Chuy comically questions Che's sanity, "That vato takes himself pretty seriously," he also implicitly interrogates his canonization as a rigid icon of Chicano/a identity (92).

Nevertheless, Chuy also reconfigures the parameters of Chicano/a identity and the Chicano movement. He tells his friend on the phone, "Excuse me, homes, don't ever question my commitment to La Raza. I've been a Chicano longer than you have, since 1985. I stopped in '90, but then I started again in '92" (Montoya et al. 78). Recalling Anzaldúa's statement about Chicano actualization through political awareness, like that conferred through Chávez and the UFW, Chuy rearticulates the term as inherently fluid (85). While "Chicano/a" sometimes seems to be an essentialist concept for Chuy, it is above all a choice that can be assumed or rejected. In *A Bowl*, such fluidity constantly inflects seemingly rigid Chicano/a identities. For example, in the scene "Stand and Deliver Pizza (The Last Chicano Movie, 1992)," we encounter two supposedly opposite types of Chicanos, a cholo and a rocker. The cholo accuses the rocker of being assimilated or having sold out; the rocker derides the cholo for being too stereotypically Chicano: "you jalapeno-eating, lettuce-picking, para bailar la bamba loser" (100). The character of Jaime Escalante tries to stop the fight, citing the two men's intrinsic similarity: "You see, gente . . . Two brown brothers, different from each other. But both not seeing the reality of their own ignorance" (101). At the end of the scene, the cholo and the rocker are united—not through their common mestizo origins, Aztlán-based Chicano nationalism, or solidarity with Chávez and the farmworkers but through their assimilation into the middle or upper-middle class. As Jaime Escalante says: "Well, the Cholo and the Rocker, they went on to become real good buddies. . . . The cholo went on to become a famous Republican Hispanic politician for the Southwest. . . . The rocker went on to become a famous brain surgeon from Malibu" (103–104). This economic and social mobility is satirized as a commodifiable, stereotypical Chicano/a identity in the play, but it also represents a different kind of liminality, suggesting that one archetype, like the cholo, can easily morph into another, like the "Republican Hispanic politician."

A Bowl reveals that there is no truly authentic Chicano/a identity; indeed, none of the characters would ever lay claim to such authenticity in the first place. While the characters are frequently conflicted and unsure about their identities, in the end they do not emulate or attempt symbolically to possess icons like César Chávez or Che Guevara (Montoya et al. 72). Instead, they disidentify with these secular saints through a contradictory blend of absurdity and solemnity. As Jaime Escalante argues, after witnessing the assimilation of the cholo and the rocker and their commodification as new archetypes, "it just goes to show you that not all stories end happily, because that's reality, Raza—or is it comedy? But then again we're Chicanos and *we're confused and full of rage*" (104). By reiterating the words used to describe Vinnie, the "first Chicano," Escalante appropriates an apparently negative characterization in order to reject the possibility of authentic or ideal Chicano/a identities. In the same manner, Richard in "Chicano on the Storm" must contend with the inevitable fall of his consecrated icons and ideals. He reflects, "the Chicano movement ended for me the day my parents got a divorce. . . . My old man was César Chávez to me, he was Che Guevara, too." Richard reveals the capriciousness of nostalgia in its power simultaneously to confer and revoke iconicity or sanctity (97). Through the portrayal of secular saints like Chávez and Che Guevara, *A Bowl* suggests that the only way to see beyond their myths and preserve their intrinsic contradictions is to approach them through parody and ambivalence.

A Borderlands Santón

Although he is often portrayed as a symbol of saintly perfection and he strategically employs many practices associated with spiritual purity, such as the penance and martyrdom of the fasts and pilgrimages, Chávez's own attitude toward sanctity and canonization clearly rejects traditional notions of spiritual perfection. In describing his understanding of the perfection of Gandhi, his spiritual model, Chávez asserts: "I don't mean he was perfect like a saint in the sense that he didn't move. I said he was perfect in the sense that he wasn't afraid to move and make things happen" (Levy 92). This description is critical, for it recalls Chávez's articulation of the strategies and goals of the UFW through flux and change. For Chávez, sacred perfection is undesirable because it is stagnant and impervious. Instead, although he insists that Gandhi is incomparable, Chávez seeks a dynamic kind of perfection, which in its willingness to "move and make things happen" allows for the possibility of imperfection, unpredictability, and even failure (Levy 92). Such dynamism is also reflected in the concept of moral jujitsu that Chávez derives from Gandhi, which fuses consistent principles and morals with variable tactics and erratic outcomes (Levy 94; León, "Chavez" 870–871). In my view, the embrace of instability, fluctuation, and unpredictability in the pursuit of spiritual and political constancy is truly what marks Chávez as not only a secular saint but also a borderlands santón. Chávez is indeed a spiritual leader for Chicanos/as—and even a symbol of Chicano/a identity itself, as many authors and critics argue. However, his expression of every aspect of this identity, encompassing spirituality, politics, ethnicity, region, nation, and temporality, is essentially contradictory and ambivalent. In closing, I want to suggest that César Chávez rearticulates canonization through his conception of temporality and its relation to the role of the UFW and his own status as a secular saint.

One of the primary criticisms levied against Chávez toward the end of his life was his emphasis on fund-raising, which, for better or worse, shifted his focus from the struggle of labor and land to economics, bureaucracy, and development. As with most aspects of Chávez's history and character, this point is ambiguous. Luis León rightly points out that Chávez "never claimed that he would remain forever in the fields, organizing workers, picketing and fasting," emphasizing the labor leader's self-professed role as a teacher ("Chavez" 864). At the same time,

Frank Bardacke argues that the focus on fund-raising also correlates to the structural flaws of the UFW, for there were no locals in the union leadership and "the staff had sources of income independent of union dues," ultimately deemphasizing the importance of membership ("Looking Back"). Certainly, by the time of Chávez's death, the UFW was primarily a fund-raising effort rather than an engine for farmworker organizing; as Bardacke notes, today the union has only about five thousand members, "who work in conditions not much different from the current low standards in the California fields" ("Looking Back"). Although Chávez knew that money was crucial, he also knew that it tied him and the UFW to linear, inflexible conceptions of history, progress, and value, that is, money inevitably inflects the perception of Chávez and the UFW's worth, whether in terms of the union's historical and cultural impact or his consumable, canonized image.

Alongside Chávez's practical and apparently conventional emphasis on fund-raising, however, he formulates a much more radical conception of temporality that reflects the variability and malleability of moral jujitsu. For Chávez, time was the most important element for the success of the union, surpassing money: "An individual who is willing to give his time is more important than an individual who is willing to give his money" (qtd in León, "Chavez" 863). He also exceeds linear conceptions of time to suggest that the UFW and the poor constitute an alternative temporality. Chávez argues that time itself is the provenance of the poor, claiming: "We know that most likely we are not going to do anything else the rest of our lives except build our union. For us there is nowhere else to go. Although we would like to see victory come soon, we are willing to wait. In this sense time is our ally. We learned many years ago that the rich may have money, but the poor have time" (Jensen and Hammerback 97).

Chávez's formulation of temporality challenges the time of history and global capital. As Dipesh Chakrabarty argues, this time may be linear or cyclical but is always continuous and represented as "natural," for his formulation suggests that events "happen in time, but time is not affected by them" (73). In other words, the time of history encompasses all events but is unaffected by them, for the time of history seems to exist prior to them (Chakrabarty 73). Chávez proposes a time in which waiting and disruption are the norm. The idea that building the union will take more than a lifetime is not an admission of defeat but, rather, a new definition of success, of "outlasting the opposition and defeating them with time if necessary" (Jensen and Hammerback 65).

Indeed, the possibility that a different understanding of temporality might become a tool for the oppressed relates to Chávez's theorization of the UFW's goals as well as to his standing as a secular saint and santón. Waiting and disruption are the basis of the political and spiritual tactics of the strike, the boycott, the pilgrimage, and especially, the fast. The notion that time is not continuous but, instead, encompasses waiting and disruption also challenges the narrative of decline that Chávez and the UFW are subject to. As he argues: "If we're so weak and unsuccessful, why do the growers continue to fight us with such passion? Because so long as we continue to exist, farm workers will benefit from our existence even if they don't work under union contract" (Jensen and Hammerback 125). Chávez's emphasis on waiting and disruption allows for the possibility that the UFW will change and grow throughout time, even if it becomes more meaningful and visible as a fund-raising effort or as a symbol. Ultimately, one measure of the value of Chávez and the UFW lies in persistence and patience, for "time accomplishes for the poor what money does for the rich" (Jensen and Hammerback 35).

This emphasis on waiting is clearly ambivalent and perhaps unsatisfactory, for it does not correspond to dominant notions of history and capital, but Chávez's transformation into a spiritual and political symbol also rearticulates concepts of value. Despite the fact that he is canonized as a fixed icon, Chávez's focus on disruption, waiting, and change challenges the possibility of sacred perfection. As a contradictory secular saint and borderlands santón, César Chávez changes through time, yet he also challenges dominant conceptions of time. Ultimately, his value as a spiritual and political icon does not lie in personal canonization or memorialization but in the frequently unacknowledged or invisible legacy and achievements of the UFW, and of Chicanos/as in general. As Chávez argues: "At the end of the trail, we [the UFW] seek . . . not recognition, but strong contracts, good wages, [and] a strong union" (Jensen and Hammerback 39). In this sense, the legacy of Chávez and the UFW is reflected neither through appeals to a nostalgic past nor to an assimilated present but, rather, through alternate forms of resistance—developments in environmental justice, workers rights, social services for the working poor such as cooperatives, housing development, and banks, cultural production, and educational attainment. This is the true marker of his spiritual and political significance.

4 · "TODOS SOMOS SANTOS"
Subcomandante Marcos and the EZLN

SUBCOMANDANTE INSURGENTE MARCOS, the spokesperson for the Ejército Zapatista de Liberación Nacional (EZLN; the Zapatista Army of National Liberation), has been a revolutionary icon and the "champion of the anti-neoliberal-globalization movement" since January 1, 1994, the very day that NAFTA went into effect (Henck 1). On that day, the Zapatistas declared war on the supreme government of Mexico, occupied seven cities in the southeastern state of Chiapas, and announced "their struggle for democracy, liberty, and justice for all Mexicans" (Muñoz Ramírez 105). From the beginning of the revolution, Marcos has been the center of national and global attention—for his charisma, media savvy, eloquence, sense of humor, intelligence, sex appeal, ability to mediate between indigenous traditions and cosmopolitan sensibilities, and general mystique as an iconic masked man, all coalesce into a cult of personality that marks him as a secular saint in the eyes of many. This cult of personality ultimately has less to do with Marcos's status as a traditional political or revolutionary hero than with his role as a master manipulator of his own endlessly transferable word and image. The armed phase of the Zapatista revolution lasted only twelve or thirteen days.[1] However, Marcos and the EZLN launched a "masterful media war" that unleashed a torrent of words and images from countless writers and artists (most notably by Marcos and the EZLN themselves) that continues to this day (Henck 211). It is not for nothing that performance artist Guillermo Gómez-Peña has dubbed Marcos the "Subcomandante of Performance," both because of the Zapatistas' "self-conscious, highly theatrical, and sophisticated use of the media," and because of Marcos's ability to inhabit multiple, ever-changing subject positions (223).

One characterization that Marcos and the EZLN have consistently challenged from the beginning is that of the traditional revolutionary leader or caudillo.

Marcos smokes his pipe as he stands in front of the U.S. Embassy in Mexico City, Mexico. Marcos joined calls to boycott U.S. goods in what was dubbed "A Day Without Gringos," an action timed to coincide with a call for immigrants to boycott work, school, and shopping in the United States. AP Photo/Moises Castillo, May 1, 2006.

Marcos and the Zapatistas emphasize his status as a sub-commander, a ranking below that of the many indigenous *comandantes/as.* Although Marcos has served as the primary mediator of the Zapatista message, in recent years other members of the EZLN have joined him in issuing communiqués, while collective organizations such as the Juntas de Buen Gobierno (Councils of Good Government) have taken on a greater role in the local communities in Chiapas and in the media.[2] Moreover, the indigenous leaders of the group stress that even though Marcos is the designated spokesperson because of his linguistic skills in Spanish he is not the primary political theorist or organizer. In an early interview they claimed: "Well, Marcos is like a subcomandante. Marcos has the facility of the castilla. We still make a *chingo* [fuck of a lot] of mistakes. . . . We are in charge of the political and organizational questions" (Rabasa 572).[3] Later, at the close of the March for Indigenous Dignity in March 2001 (dubbed the "Zapatour" by the international media), it was Comandanta Esther, not Marcos, who addressed the Mexican houses of Congress in the capital. She stated, "Some might have thought that this tribune would be occupied by Sup-Marcos. . . . You can now see that it is not so. Subcomandante Insurgente Marcos is that, a subcomandante. We are the comandantes, those who command jointly, the ones who govern our people, obeying. . . . Now it is our hour" (Hayden 196).[4] Finally, in "Mexico City: We Have Arrived, We Are Here," the speech presented by the EZLN and later signed by the CCRI-CG in the Zócalo at the opening of the March for Indigenous Dignity, the indigenous Zapatistas distanced themselves and their group completely from the roles of both leader and spokesperson, proclaiming: "We are . . . that which unveils and reveals the many Mexicos that hide and suffer under Mexico. We are not their spokesperson. We are one voice among all those voices" (Marcos, *Speed* 124).

Despite the Zapatistas' claim on collectivity, Marcos has undoubtedly been the focal point of the EZLN. Both Zapatista supporters and antagonists such as the Mexican government have firmly situated him as their leader. Historian Nick Henck argues, "the Zapatista movement has from the start been inextricably caught up with the personality cult of Marcos, but it is perhaps an unpalatable truth that the vast majority of humanity finds it easier to identify with a single individual (even if he is masked) than a committee" (5). Indeed, Marcos is not only the de facto leader of the EZLN and an international icon, many also consider him a secular saint.

Marcos and the Zapatistas are clearly uncomfortable with the idea of Marcos's sanctity, even as they perform and interrogate this role in the interest of political praxis. Although Marcos actively distances himself from the possibility of sanctity, especially in relation to his prominence within the EZLN, it is in the interest of supporters and antagonists alike to perceive him as the focal point of the organization. In particular, many critics, perhaps unwilling or unable to see the ambivalent and ironic nature of Marcos's cult of personality, have accused him over the years of not being "indigenous" enough, of appropriating indigenous beliefs and language, of duping the indigenous people, or of being a fame whore or megalomaniac. However, it is important to note that the Mexican government (perhaps Marcos and the EZLN's main antagonist) is especially invested in representing Marcos as the leader of the insurgency, and in endeavoring to demystify him by exposing his racial and class status as an educated, cosmopolitan mestizo who is removed from the everyday struggles of the indigenous peoples he lives among.

To this end, in February 1995, the Mexican government unmasked Marcos, announcing that he was really Rafael Sebastián Guillén Vicente of Tampico, Tamaulipas, a former university lecturer at the Xochimilco campus of the Autonomous Metropolitan University (UAM) in Mexico City. At the public unmasking, a government official held an enlarged transparency of the masked Marcos in front of a plain identity-type photograph of a bearded man with dark hair and eyes, joining and separating the two images for the media to record. By unmasking Marcos, the Mexican government sought to reclaim its control over the construction and dissemination of national identity and imagery (Taussig, *Defacement* 236–237). In the eyes of the state, an ordinary, provincial, slightly stocky, large-nosed son of a furniture salesman could not possibly inspire adulation among the masses. As cultural critic Alma Guillermoprieto, who was present at the unmasking, argued, "the masked idol is a Clark Kent" (34).

Nevertheless, the state's attempt to demystify Marcos backfired, for in many ways, he and the EZLN became even more popular after the unmasking. Marcos promptly reclaimed his mystique by signing the first communiqué published after the unmasking, "The Sup . . . rearranging his mask with macabre flirtatiousness." The masses responded to the unmasking by assuming his identity for themselves (Taussig, *Defacement* 237). A few days after the official unmasking, thousands of people gathered for demonstrations in Mexico City's Zócalo (city center), all wearing black ski masks and chanting "Todos somos Marcos" (We are all Marcos).

The EZLN's use of the black ski mask or balaclava is inherently paradoxical. Of course, the mask serves a protective function for it conceals the identities of Marcos and the indigenous members of the EZLN, but it also renders them interchangeable and transferable. This fungibility is not the repressive gesture of the Mexican government, which has historically treated indigenous peoples as disposable commodities or as faceless fragments of a romanticized past. Instead, the concealment and transferability provided by the mask reflects the collective voice of the EZLN, as Marcos argued on the first day of the uprising: "This masked person today is called Marcos here and tomorrow will be called Pedro in Margaritas or José in Ocosingo or Alfredo in Altamirano or whatever he is called. Finally, the one who speaks is a more collective heart, not a caudillo. That is what I want you to understand, not a caudillo in the old style, in that image. The only image that you will have is that those who make this happen are masked" (Marcos, "Testimonies" 209–210). However, despite the Zapatistas' refusal of the caudillo model, Marcos is repeatedly reinscribed as a leader through the mask. Even as the mask symbolically rearticulates and rejects the characterization of the indigenous peoples as forgotten, generic Others in order to produce the collective voice of the EZLN, it is also a conduit to Marcos's iconicity, and especially, his sanctity.

It might seem obvious that neither Marcos nor the Zapatistas identify El Sup as a secular saint. As a political activist for indigenous rights, he is explicitly secular, not sacred. However, while there are no traditional religious cults to Subcomandante Marcos, El Sup's secular sanctity is expressed through digital and print media, and through the repetition, commodification, and repetition of images like that of the black ski mask. Marcos is clearly an icon or, following Phyllis Passariello's definition, "a person whose being becomes an enduring symbol of cultural specialness, often with a tinge of religion-like awe," but he transcends iconicity to attain an aura of sanctity, especially since he is invested not only with "special status" but with "special power" (Passariello 75). This special power is conveyed in particular through the ski mask, which as an image "is dynamic and generates even more interest and involvement than mere representation and display" (87). The ski mask is not just a symbol of Marcos and the EZLN. As a "marker," it "may even overtake" the Zapatistas "in specific cultural meaning" (87). The mask is an icon in its own right, in the sense that it is a representation that ascribes sanctity and is itself sacred as a symbol of the EZLN. As an agent for concealment and transferability, the mask also allows supporters symbolically to possess Marcos and Zapatismo. That is, by putting on the ski mask, anyone can become Marcos, symbolically possessing him or being possessed by him, and signaling the transformative fusion of divine and human that is conveyed by spirit possession.

Naturally, the fungibility of the ski mask encompasses all of the Zapatistas, not just Marcos, especially because of the EZLN's insistence upon El Sup's subordinate position. Yet, while the mask stands on its own as an icon of Zapatismo and indigenous rights, it also always evokes Marcos. For example, it is significant that the chant at the Zócalo after the unmasking was not "Todos somos Ramona" or "Todos somos Esther." Those indigenous comandantas could not inspire the same sort of spirit possession or sacred transference as Marcos does, perhaps because of their obviously indigenous identity.[5] Although the EZLN firmly rejects the old-style conception of caudillo leadership, Marcos remains the focal point of the group, and he is symbolically situated as a secular saint by the masses of supporters chanting "Todos somos Marcos" in the spirit of Zapatista and indigenous solidarity.

A large part of Marcos's strategy of refusal of the leader or caudillo model involves the dismantling of hierarchies of race, gender, class, and language, for he privileges diverse voices and groups and blends political language with literary references and indigenous orality in his writings and speeches. By extension, he criticizes the conventional categorization of the indigenous peoples through traditional, essentialist markers of race, language, and class, as when he insists that the state itself must remove its mask of progress and unity (Marcos and Zapatistas, *Shadows* 86).[6] The Zapatistas' mask literally obscures visible traits such as race. At the same time, it reflects the unity and transferability of the group, since all members, regardless of class, race, or linguistic preference, wear the same mask—and as such, any one member can potentially stand in for or replace another. The mask illustrates the Zapatistas' refusal of the leader or caudillo model and their rearticulation of sanctity toward a collective register, that is, the sanctity that is generally located in an individual figure or icon is here transferred to a collective group, which is unusual.

At the same time, Marcos's role reflects the Zapatistas' embrace of paradox. He is truly both leader and anti-leader, though he is constructed as such in obviously paradoxical ways. Marcos's cult of personality—his charisma, showmanship, and eloquence—produces him as a secular saint, but he is equally saintly because of the mask, which provides concealment, interchangeability, and the flouting of potentially essentialist markers of identity such as race, gender, or sexuality. While Marcos is represented as flexible and transferable because of the mask (in short, as a character with no fixed identity), he is also often reduced to an essentialist identity, as the person who can be unmasked. Since all Zapatistas wear the mask, and the mask represents the collective, Marcos's singular, apparently sacred characteristics are subsumed into the group as a whole. However, because Marcos is celebrated as the leader and secular saint of the group, he is also the figure that the Mexican government and others are desperate to unmask. Through the mask, Marcos is as transferable as any other Zapatista, becoming a character with no fixed identity. Yet because he is the person that can be unmasked, his singularity or essential difference from the other Zapatistas is foregrounded. Ultimately, the mask epitomizes Zapatista paradox, for it renders Marcos sacred even as it points toward the sanctity of the collective.

Like some of the other secular saints I treat, Marcos does not possess the traits so common to popular sanctity, such as humility, healing powers, or traditional markers of virtue. Instead, he signals charisma, wit, and even pride while displacing more modest or collective traits onto the Zapatistas as a whole. Yet Marcos's representation of sanctity is very much in keeping with the contradictions of secular sanctity. While all secular saints manifest contradiction, especially regarding the relationship between human and divine, Marcos goes even further, both actively performing and interrogating sanctity in the manner of a santón. Drawing upon his paradoxical roles as leader and anti-leader, and as both character and author, Marcos performs sanctity as a shifting, variable construct—an identity that can be assumed, interrogated, rejected, and transferred at will. As a santón, Marcos performs sanctity as simulacra (breaking the link with the divine as a sign, as Baudrillard describes it), but he is also sacred in his own right (Baudrillard 6). His performance of secular sanctity, evoked by the iconic mask, signifies collectivity and mass political action, however his performance also denotes Marcos's authority as the only Zapatista who at the same time is able easily to inhabit and challenge sanctity, even as he denies that power. Marcos's performance of secular sanctity reflects his role as a marginal figure in relation to the nation-state and through his political, cultural, and social identities, but it also reinforces his centrality to the EZLN. In order to understand Marcos's shift between identification with and rejection of sanctity, it is crucial to recognize the sometimes unspoken contradiction between individual and collective sanctity in an analysis of Zapatismo.

Marcos as Character and Author

The disclosure and performance of contradiction is one of the most compelling aspects of Zapatismo. Marcos's contradictions specifically contribute to, rather than detract from, his sacred persona. Marcos is clearly fully conscious of his multiple often conflicting personae, evident in his writing and in many interviews. He frequently jokes about his contradictory personae, as when he mockingly associates himself with the famous comedians and actors Cantinflas and Pedro Infante instead of with revolutionary leaders like Che Guevara: "And then there is the one who is said to be their leader, one Sup Marcos, whose public image is closer to that of Cantinflas and Pedro Infante than to Emiliano Zapata and Che Guevara" (Marcos, *Speed* 200). José Rabasa alludes to Marcos's fragmented subject positions, arguing that his "multiple subject positions fulfill tactical and strategic functions within his discourse"; the subject positions that Marcos inhabits include shifts between character and author, leader and follower, and teacher and student (577–578). Yet Marcos's authorial voice frequently clashes with his portrayal of himself as a character in his essays, communiqués, stories, and other texts, especially in the pieces that are explicitly signed not by Marcos himself, but by the CCRI-CG (Henck 165). As a character, Marcos frequently portrays himself as a bumbling, self-deprecating fish out of water. He emphasizes his humility, his personal and physical flaws, and his errors in comparison to the indigenous Zapatistas, despite his decades of extensive experience and privation in the jungles of Chiapas and his probable ability to speak at least some of several indigenous languages.[7]

Nevertheless, Marcos wields the power of an author who is fluent in multiple literary, linguistic, historical, political, and theoretical registers. Following Rabasa's suggestion that Marcos's subject position is constantly changing and fragmented, the only real constant in his character is the contrast between his neophyte persona and the authority of a prolific, highly literate writer who seeks to educate the world about the history of the indigenous peoples of Mexico, and to publicize the goals of the EZLN. Indeed, it is the juxtaposition and tension between uncertainty, discomfort or subordination, and authority or control that helps produce the ironic voice Marcos is so famous for.

Several critics caution that Marcos is best considered from a distance and cite the danger involved in taking inventory of his many subject positions and author functions (Henck 7; Rabasa 578). Marcos himself, in characteristically tongue-in-cheek fashion, claims in an interview with Manuel Vázquez Montalbán, "believe me, we still do not have the distance or the objectivity to sanction that character, that Subcomandante Marcos, the one who is behind the black ski mask" (150). However, the distance contained in Marcos's persona simultaneously obscures and emphasizes his paradoxical roles as character and author, and as leader and anti-leader. In fact, although El Sup's commentary skirts the question of what the interplay between Marcos as character and Marcos as author might mean in the context of his dual role as leader and anti-leader, it does suggest that the author and public figure Marcos is also very much a character—as he asserts in the same interview with Vázquez Montalbán: "Look, the truth is that we realize that

Marcos is a character" (150). It is quite clear that Marcos helps fashion his own mutable image, especially through tactics of self-deprecating humor, irony, and "obfuscation, dissembling, and projecting a mysterious image of himself . . . [as] part of his character" in his writing and in interviews (Henck 7). It is less evident, but no less true, that Marcos does not simply reject the notion that he is a leader or even a secular saint but instead recognizes, shapes, and performs these roles in his writing. In fact, the more Marcos denies his sanctity, the more he embraces it—certainly in order to promote the EZLN's ultimate goal of collective leadership, even collective sanctity, but also perhaps to interrogate and manipulate his position of centrality.

In the spirit of Marcos's ironic obfuscation, in this chapter I examine El Sup's paradoxical role as leader and anti-leader through an analysis of his function as both character and author in texts such as the "Don Durito" tales and his co-written novel with Mexican detective writer and historian Paco Ignacio Taibo II, *Muertos incómodos (falta lo que falta)*, first published in installments in the Mexico City newspaper *La Jornada* between December 5, 2004, and February 20, 2005 and then in English as *The Uncomfortable Dead (What's Missing Is Missing)* in 2006. Although there is no way to quantify Marcos's fragmented identities and subject positions, as Rabasa indicates, I argue that he consistently deploys irony and self-deprecating humor in order to displace a version of the secular saint onto other characters that he constructs, especially the charismatic, bombastic little beetle Don Durito of the Lacandon jungle, who serves as both antagonist and sardonic alter-ego for El Sup. At the same time, I contend that Marcos's strategic position as novice is occasionally problematic, especially in his representation of indigenous language and linguistic patterns. A close analysis of some of his writings reveals a curious conflation or elision between his representation of himself as a character in the texts and certain markers of indigeneity (particularly language and race), which ultimately calls attention to the very categories he intends to challenge.[8] This elision is especially evident in *Muertos incómodos*. Although the novel, like all of Marcos's texts, underscores his role as both character and author, El Sup's representation of syncretic indigenous language occasionally raises questions about the nature of Zapatismo, especially concerning whether it is supposed to speak for or through the indigenous peoples; about the conflation of Subcomandante Marcos with *lo indígena*; and about his own status as leader and anti-leader. In the novel, Marcos portrays himself ironically as a foolish novice, even as he displaces the role of leader or secular saint onto other characters, whether indigenous members of the EZLN or political sympathizers.

Ultimately, my analysis of the intersection and conflict between Marcos's roles as character, author, leader, and anti-leader focuses on the possibility of the sanctity of the collective, signaled by the EZLN's essays and manifestoes. But while Marcos's fragmented position as both character and author rejects individual secular sanctity in favor of the sanctity of the multitude, I propose that the real work of Zapatismo lies beyond representation—and even beyond reception. The true sanctity of the masses, as the EZLN suggests in their most recent declaration to date, the Sixth Declaration of the Lacandon Jungle (2005), is local, global, and always autonomous, despite its potential inaccessibility.

Zapatista Paradox

Marcos and the EZLN consistently embrace paradox in their discourse, while their organizational and political structures and goals are frequently paradoxical in and of themselves. These paradoxes transcend Subcomandante Marcos's fragmented personae to cut to the very core of Zapatismo itself. Many of the EZLN's proclamations and objectives would seem to preclude the possibility of individual leadership and particularly the cult of personality that has sprung up around Marcos, such as their famous slogan "para todos todo, nada para nosotros" (Everything for everyone, nothing for ourselves) or their desire for "un mundo donde quepan muchos mundos" (A world in which many worlds fit). From their earliest communiqués, Marcos and the EZLN indicate that their central command is interchangeable and dispensable by design, describing a rhizome-like structure: "If [the Mexican army] are successful in destroying our central command, nothing fundamental will change: through our chain of command and the omnipresence of the Clandestine Committees of Indigenous Revolutionaries, we will eventually rise up again after any attack, no matter how spectacular or crushing it may appear" (Marcos and Zapatistas, *Shadows* 83–84). Indeed, the structure of the EZLN is based upon the transposability and omnipresence of the collective, defying the Mexican state's expectations that the group must necessarily rely on an indispensable leader and that the interchangeability of the indigenous peoples renders them invisible.

The Zapatistas utilize paradox to promote indigenous rights in Mexico as well as the rights of other marginalized peoples throughout the world through a rearticulation of race, class, gender, and sexual hierarchies. Such a rhetorical move calls for a redefinition of received notions of national identity and ethnic difference. The EZLN aims to make visible the human cost of global capital.

One of Marcos's most powerful communiqués, "Who Should Ask for Pardon and Who Can Grant It?" was issued January 18, 1994, as a response to President Salinas's offer to pardon the Zapatistas in the wake of the uprising. This communiqué spectacularly illustrates the primacy of the indigenous peoples to the nation. The Zapatistas argue that the indigenous people are not a foundational myth but, instead, form the backbone of local, national, and even global prosperity and progress, thus rejecting the Mexican national discourse that situates indigenous people as voiceless subjects who should "[accept] humbly the historic burden of disdain and abandonment" (Marcos, *Our Word* 38). In doing so, Marcos turns the offer of pardon into an eloquent assertion of indigenous rights by revealing the disingenuousness of the Mexican state. Such an authoritative statement deserves a lengthy citation:

Why do we need to be pardoned? What are they going to pardon us for? For not dying of hunger? For not accepting our misery in silence? For not accepting humbly the historic burden of disdain and abandonment? For having risen up in arms after we found all other paths closed? . . . For showing the rest of the country and the whole world that human dignity still exists even among the world's poorest peoples? For having made careful preparations before we began our uprising? For bringing guns to battle instead of bows and arrows? For being Mexicans? For being mainly indigenous? For calling on the Mexican people to fight by whatever means possible for what belongs to them? For fighting for liberty, democracy, and justice? For not following the example of previous guerrilla armies? For refusing to surrender? For refusing to sell ourselves out?

Who should ask for pardon, and who can grant it? Those who for many years glutted themselves at a table of plenty while we sat with death so often, we finally stopped fearing it? Those who filled our pockets and our souls with empty promises and words?

Or should we ask pardon from the dead, our dead, who died "natural" deaths of "natural causes" like measles, whooping cough, breakbone fever, cholera, typhus, mononucleosis, tetanus, pneumonia, malaria and other lovely gastrointestinal and pulmonary diseases? . . .

Should we ask for pardon from those who deny us the right and capacity to govern ourselves? From those who don't respect our customs or our culture and who ask us for identification papers and obedience to a law whose existence and moral basis we don't accept? From those who oppress us, torture us, assassinate us, disappear us for the grave "crime" of wanting a piece of land . . . just a simple piece of land on which we can grow something to fill our stomachs?

Who should ask for pardon, and who can grant it? (Marcos, *Our Word* 38 39).

Marcos's cry against the marginalization that indigenous peoples have suffered for hundreds of years confronts the Mexican government with its responsibility for their misery, exposing the practice of government aid as a strategy to silence the Indian peoples and obscure their rights to human dignity and to a place in the Mexican nation. As George Yúdice indicates, the Zapatistas "not only lay claim to a prioritary place in the nation, [they affirm] that democracy will come when the culture of the nation is refashioned from the perspective of indigenous peoples" (99). In this sense, Marcos demonstrates that the nation and the history of the indigenous peoples are intertwined. National belonging for indigenous peoples is possible only through self-governance and respect for indigenous customs and culture. Likewise, by emphasizing the "table of plenty" from which the indigenous peoples have been excluded in Mexico, Marcos evokes the contribution the indigenous have made to this abundance and prosperity (*Our Word* 39). Shortly after the publication of the communiqué, Mexican intellectual Octavio Paz pointed out that Marcos was implicating not only the government but the entire country, in the Zapatistas' call for pardon: "Almost all of us, to one degree or another, are guilty of the iniquitous situation in which the Indians find themselves, since our passivity and indifference have permitted the extortions and abuses of the cattlemen, coffee growers, caciques and corrupt politicians" (qtd in Henck 223). By demonstrating the complicity of everyone, even Zapatista supporters, with the marginalization of the indigenous people, Marcos alludes to the discomfort inherent in identifying with the EZLN—and especially, the discomfort with himself as a leader or secular saint.

Ambivalent Appropriations

Marcos suggests that support of or identification with the EZLN must necessarily be both critical and ambivalent; in other words, it must be disidentificatory. This is perhaps a strange pose for a global revolutionary icon who clearly enjoys attention, but it is completely in line with the EZLN's paradoxical discourse and objectives. The Zapatistas and especially Marcos himself are routinely commodified and appropriated, often uncritically, through black ski masks, t-shirts, cartoons, dolls, posters, key chains, framed photos, fair trade Zapatista coffee, and even condom wrappers (Collier and Quaratiello 4). The commodification of Subcomandante Marcos contributes to his being represented as a secular saint or a santón, for this tangible repetition of his word and image allows for EZLN supporters to possess him both literally and figuratively, to identify with him or otherwise demonstrate their faith in him and the Zapatistas. Like relics, religious totems, or icons, the ski masks, t-shirts, and dolls symbolically ensure Marcos's perpetual resuscitation. The Mexican state, of course, chooses to emphasize an uncritical view of Marcos and the Zapatistas' appropriation and commodification, as when President Ernesto Zedillo labeled the EZLN's first- and metropolitan third-world supporters "revolutionary tourists," a moniker that surfaced again in relation to the March for Indigenous Dignity. By using the language of commodification and tourism to marginalize Zapatista supporters, Zedillo seeks to undermine the power of the group's political praxis by converting it into a "repetition of outdated 1960s political activism" that has failed to produce concrete results in Mexico (Day 108–109).

While many critics focus on the radical chic that the Zapatistas supposedly provide as a means to delegitimize them, however, these critics also overlook the intrinsic ambiguity implicated in the commodification of Marcos and the Zapatistas or in identifying with or possessing their word and image. This ambivalence is evident in the production and reception of Zapatista memorabilia, such as the Marcos or Ramona cloth or wood dolls handmade by impoverished Chiapan peasants (who are frequently not Zapatistas) presumably for the same first- and metropolitan third-world public that consumes Marcos's communiqués (Estey and Fuller). These dolls transcend both mass marketing and traditional indigenous *artesanías* (arts and crafts), for their sale depends upon an aura of indigenous authenticity even as they trade traditional Mayan garb for the black masks and wooden guns of the EZLN. Whether these dolls are individually fashioned by actual indigenous people is beside the point. The "capitalizing of the anti-capitalist Zapatistas" is a savvy business practice, to be sure, but it is also a gesture that is potentially as ironic and alienating as Marcos's acerbic writing (Estey and Fuller). The EZLN dolls rearticulate traditional indigenous artesanías. They make visible the gap between production and reception or consumption, in which indigenous peasants make arts and crafts for comparatively wealthy tourists, but they also estrange the producers from the objects of the representation, since the peasant artisans are not usually Zapatistas. The production and sale of objects such as the Zapatista dolls reveal the tension inherent in possessing or identifying with Marcos and the EZLN.

Todos Somos Marcos, Todos Somos Indios?

The underlying conflict behind the commodification, identification with, and possession of Marcos and the Zapatistas is especially apparent in the disjunction between the slogans "Todos somos Marcos" (We are all Marcos) and "Todos somos indios" (We are all Indians) that supporters have chanted at pro-Zapatista rallies over the years. One conjures hero-worship, the other collectivity and reclaimed national pride. As Carlos Monsiváis argues:

> "We are all Indians." The slogan . . . is unobjectionable insofar as it assumes pride . . . in a basic component of nationality. But what can one say about "We are all Marcos"? The phrase seems excessively rhetorical, a product of militaristic passion, romantic frenzy or of messianic scenery. Undoubtedly, it is just that in some cases, but in the face of the official party line . . . opposition to the war and McCarthyism it signals something very simple: if they condemn Marcos for wanting a better world, then let them condemn me and all of us for wanting the same thing. ("¿Todos somos indios?" 334)

Monsiváis suggests that the distinction between "we are all Indians" and "we are all Marcos" might be blurred as long as the seemingly "unobjectionable" collectivity of the first slogan informs the meaning of the second, that is, insofar as "we are all Marcos" is not primarily utilized to signal messianism but, rather, to indicate collective unity and shared responsibility for the Zapatista struggle. But the terms are not interchangeable, for the messianism of "todos somos Marcos" is almost always implied in the slogan, even if the messianism is subsumed by collectivity and activism, demonstrating the fundamental ambiguity of identifying with Marcos and the EZLN. Indeed, Marcos and the indigenous people are frequently conflated in various representations of Zapatismo, whether in sympathetic or critical terms.

For example, in her observations from the Zócalo during the March for Indigenous Dignity, Canadian writer and social activist Naomi Klein discusses the Zapatistas' popular appeal. She focuses on Marcos's representation as a "self-promoter" who is engaged in a "war of inflated egos" and a brand or image war with President Vicente Fox (n.p.). She concludes that the abundance of Marcos and EZLN memorabilia for sale in the Zócalo trumps Fox's "marketing tricks" and "Coca-Cola politics," because such memorabilia reflect "genuine, utterly anachronistic folklore" rather than embodying "radical chic branding." This conclusion is unsettling at best. As she puts it, "folklore appears to be winning [the brand or image war]," suggesting that the success of Marcos's particular form of branding lies in its connection to indigenous tradition. Marcos certainly uses indigenous tales and legends to great effect in his communiqués, and he adheres to the indigenous collective tradition in EZLN governance, but Klein's analysis is naïve, because it overlooks the EZLN's pointed rejection of the characterization of indigenous people as folkloric remnants of tradition standing outside of modernity. In Marcos's speech "Paths of Dignity: Indigenous Rights, Memory, and Cultural Heritage," presented at an intercultural meeting during the very same March for Indigenous Dignity, he argued: "The power wants to ensnare the indigenous struggle in nostalgia, chest beating, and the 'boom' in folk crafts. It wants to fence the Indian struggle within the framework of the past, using fashionable marketing language like 'The past reaches out to us with its unpaid accounts.' . . . In the struggle for dignity, there is an apparent turn to the past, but—and this is fundamental—the final horizon is the future. . . . In short, we indigenous aren't part of yesterday. We're part of tomorrow" (Marcos, *Speed* 132–133). Marcos and the EZLN consistently maintain that the Zapatistas are both traditional and modern, emphasizing their role in the present and the future of Mexico. Klein's association of the indigenous peoples (and, implicitly, of Marcos) with tradition, particularly artesanías, is a loaded gesture, for it retains the binary division between modernity and tradition that the EZLN refuses.

Mexican writer Vicente Leñero takes a more critical view of the intersections between Marcos and the indigenous peoples in his 1995 play *Todos somos Marcos*. One of the protagonists in the play, Raúl, an ostensibly leftist bohemian who is also sexist and patriarchal, is describing to his friend Miguel his recent breakup with Laura, who has departed for Chiapas to join the Zapatista struggle. In the wake of the mass demonstrations in the Zócalo after the government's unmasking of Marcos and the chants of "Todos somos Marcos," Laura, wrapped up in revolutionary frenzy, becomes a fervent Zapatista supporter. As Raúl derisively puts it: "She became a total leftist. Fist in the air and all that shit. . . . She became a whole-hearted Zapatista" (Leñero 53).[9] Laura's activism is beyond the pale for Raúl, especially because she is thinking with her heart. In his mind, she chooses love for Marcos and the EZLN over love for him. From Raúl and Miguel's perspective, Laura's crime is not just her leftist activism but her conflation of Marcos, the indigenous people, and herself, for she gets carried away by her activism, as Miguel puts it: "As if she were an Indian, right? Now everyone feels like an indigenous person, way to go, feel the Chamula vibes man, and all that shit" (Leñero 54).[10] Although Raúl and Miguel are nominally leftist, they ultimately cleave to the status quo of neoliberal progress in Mexico. Leñero's play emphasizes the discomfort behind the idea that Zapatista supporters necessarily "all feel like indigenous people," and that Laura in particular represents the continuum between Marcos, the indigenous people, and Zapatista supporters.

As Stuart Day argues, Raúl and Miguel abhor Laura's decision to become a wholehearted Zapatista "as if she were an Indian," because her choice ignores ethnic categories, disrupting entrenched racial categories while demonstrating that the category *indígena* is more a "marker of social class," which they are not prepared to relinquish as privileged, educated, well-connected members of the upper middle class (109). Nevertheless, the conflation between "we are all Marcos" and "we are all Indians" is not one that the Marcos and the Zapatistas easily or routinely make. Certainly, the EZLN's endeavor to upend racial and class hierarchies extends to its use of racial, ethnic, and class-based linguistic categories. But whether we read *indígena* as strictly equivalent to race/ethnicity or not, there is discomfort inherent in the association of the slogans. Whenever Marcos and the EZLN do suggest a link between the two slogans, it is always with a critical, ambivalent, or ironic bent. For example, in the epigraph to his play, Leñero quotes from an interview with Marcos in February 1994: "If Marcos disappears with the ski mask on, any one of us can put on a ski mask and that person becomes Marcos" (Leñero 45). Marcos's use of the third person to refer to himself is quite deliberate, emphasizing his role as a transposable character rather than a fixed entity and suggesting that the "nosotros" (we) of Zapatismo transcends race, class, or gender.

Even more significant is the occasional articulation of "Todos somos Marcos" by the indigenous members of the EZLN, as in the introduction to the collection *The Speed of Dreams* (2007), where the editors Canek Peña-Vargas and Greg Ruggiero describe a young medical student who has come to Oventik, a

Zapatista *caracol*, to help with the cause."¹¹ The earnest student, who is clearly depicted as a representative of the sort of cosmopolitan activist who travels to Chiapas to live and work with the Zapatistas (and who, in other contexts, might be labeled a "revolutionary tourist"), asks a group of indigenous *compañeros/as*, "Have any of you actually *met* Marcos?" evoking the outside world's sustained fascination with the masked spokesperson (Marcos, *Speed* 8). The response, "Of course . . . we are all Marcos," is important for its tongue-in-cheek humor as well as for its inclusivity (8). Everyone present, including the aspiring doctor, laughs, "and there was an understanding" (8). There is no hint of the messianism that characterizes Raúl and Miguel's perception of the slogan in the play *Todos somos Marcos*, and even less of the racial or ethnic hierarchies they seek to propagate. Rather, the laughter that leads to understanding includes the indigenous Zapatistas as well as the medical student within the collective rubric of "we are all Marcos."

Nevertheless, it is much more common for the cosmopolitan supporters of the EZLN to assert "We are all Indians" than it is for the indigenous Zapatistas to declare "We are all Marcos." It is generally unheard of for outsiders to single out other Zapatista comandantes/as such as Comandanta Esther or Coronel Moisés, delineating a difference between the masked Indians and their masked spokesperson that transcends his superior Spanish linguistic skills. This difference has less to do with Marcos's identity behind the mask than with the fact that he is much more readily situated and apprehended as a secular saint than any other member of the EZLN. Ultimately, the point is not whether Marcos has the right to articulate the "we" of Zapatismo when discussing indigenous affairs, as in the "Paths of Dignity" speech during the March for Indigenous Dignity ("we indigenous aren't part of yesterday. We're part of tomorrow"), any more than whether Indians should declare "We are all Marcos" (Marcos, *Speed* 133). Such binary thinking overlooks the EZLN's purpose to reject racial, ethnic, sexual, or gendered hierarchies and obscures the vital interchangeability provided by the mask. Instead, we must examine Marcos's ability to shift between the roles of character and author in his texts and speeches—recognizing that this is a power that is denied to the other Zapatistas—and the link between this ability and his position as leader and anti-leader.

Disidentification

To this end, I am especially interested in Marcos's negotiation and performance of his own privileged position as a leader and a secular saint. Naturally, he is fully aware of his status as the focal point of the EZLN's word and image and of the way he shapes this role through his writing and gestures. Although he interrogates, mocks, and officially rejects this privileged role, he also promotes it in a contradiction reminiscent of the paradoxes that permeate Zapatista thinking. Once again, Marcos's ironic humor serves as a tool of both inclusion and distancing, indicating the ambivalence of identifying with his privileged position and even with Zapatismo itself. In one of his most famous early pieces—the postscript "Majority-which-disguises-itself-as-untolerated-minority-P.S.," which is part of the May 28, 1994, communiqué "Old Antonio Tells Marcos Another Story"—Marcos metaphorically projects himself into a variety of different, sometimes conflicting identities:

> About this whole thing about whether Marcos is homosexual: Marcos is gay in San Francisco, black in South Africa, Asian in Europe, Chicano in San Isidro, Anarchist in Spain, Palestinian in Israel, Indigenous in the streets of San Cristóbal, bad boy in Neza, rocker in CU, Jew in Germany, ombudsman in the SEDENA, feminist in political parties, Communist in the post–Cold War era, prisoner in Cintalapa, pacifist in Bosnia, Mapuche in the Andes, teacher in the CNTE, artist without gallery or portfolio, housewife on any given Saturday night in any neighborhood of any city of any Mexico, guerrillero in Mexico at the end of the twentieth century, striker in the CTM, reporter assigned to filler stories for the back pages, sexist in the feminist movement, woman alone in the metro at 10 P.M., retired person in *plantón* in the Zócalo, campesino without land, fringe editor, unemployed worker, doctor without a practice, rebellious student, dissident in neoliberalism, writer without books or readers, and, to be sure, Zapatista in the Mexican Southeast. In sum, Marcos is a human being, any human being, in this world. Marcos is all the minorities who are untolerated, oppressed, resisting, exploding, saying "Enough." All the minorities at the moment they begin to speak and the majorities at the moment they fall silent and put up with it. All the untolerated people searching for a word, their word, which will return the majority to the eternally fragmented, us; all that makes power and good consciences uncomfortable, that is Marcos. (Marcos and Zapatistas, *Shadows* 214–215)

The postscript, which was written as a cheeky response to claims about Marcos's sexuality in several newspapers during the early months of the rebellion (with the intent to "unmask" or otherwise delegitimize the idol), engages with the concept of difference by parsing the limits of minority and majority status and pushing against them. The questions about Marcos's sexuality in the media, meant to tear down the sex symbol, might well have been serious—recall Leñero's representation of Raúl and Miguel's reaction against Marcos's desirability—but the postscript is clearly tongue-in-cheek. Yet amid the irony, Marcos reiterates some truths about Zapatismo and his own role as leader. He appears to emphasize and even endorse his own omnipresence, seemingly validating the kind of uncritical appropriation that some have criticized as messianism. However, his ironic stance is immediately apparent, and we understand that not only are many of his identities conflicting and potentially incompatible, these identities are themselves multiple. Marcos performs an inversion of the mantra "Todos somos Marcos," which suggests that many are reflected in one, and instead asserts that each individual is multiple and malleable.

There are darker sides to the apparently inclusive multiculturalism of the postscript, which, although almost always cited in a celebratory manner, embodies "all the minorities who are untolerated, oppressed, resisting, exploding, saying 'Enough.'" A closer look at the passage reveals that several of the groups that Marcos lays claim to do not correspond to the progressive views generally associated with the EZLN (Marcos and Zapatistas, *Shadows* 215). While most of the groups mentioned fulfill the expected role of "untolerated minority" striving for equal rights and recognition, some are oppressed *majorities* ("black in South Africa") and others are reactionary minorities ("sexist in the feminist movement"), which presumably few progressive thinkers or Zapatista allies would support. The groups that Marcos identifies do not reflect liberal multiculturalism, since they do not correspond to a cross-cultural union of "untolerated minorities," as some have occasionally suggested.[12]

Instead, they comprise a series of frequently opposing differences. By emphasizing the diversity of these groups, including attention to their internal conflicts, Marcos implicitly questions the universalization of difference frequently advocated by both the opponents and the supporters of Zapatismo. Furthermore, while Marcos aligns himself with "all the minorities at the moment they begin to speak," he also identifies with "the majorities at the moment they fall silent," perhaps in a gesture toward his iconic, and thus majoritarian, status (Marcos and Zapatistas, *Shadows* 214). Indeed, the postscript's title, "Majority-which-disguises-itself-as-untolerated-minority," is probably a mischievous, self-critical recognition of Marcos's conflation with the indigenous people. Marcos understands that he represents the majority to the outside world as the Zapatista leader and admits to sometimes disguising this majority status under the cloak of the minority. In this sense, Marcos demonstrates that he recognizes, negotiates, and performs his privileged role as a leader and secular saint or santón.

Once again, however, Marcos is the only Zapatista who is able to shift easily between majority and minority status, whether this shift is mocking and self-critical or not. One mode that proves much more inclusive and complete, if still difficult, is disidentification. As José Esteban Muñoz puts it, disidentification is a "survival strategy" that is employed by minority subjects as a "mode of dealing with dominant ideology . . . that neither opts to assimilate within such a structure nor strictly opposes it; rather, disidentification is a strategy that works on and against dominant ideology" (5, 11). In other words, disidentification is a way for minorities of all kinds who are excluded from identification with dominant

ideologies—what Muñoz calls "the fiction of identity"—simultaneously to perform, resist, and confound "socially prescriptive patterns of identification" (5, 28).
Of course, Marcos would be the first to admit that he is not at all the same kind
of minority subject as the other Zapatistas, and not only because most of them
are indigenous. While Zapatismo ideally transcends race and class, he recognizes
that he is able to shift between the various roles of leader, anti-leader, character, and author; the other Zapatistas are not able to do this. Furthermore, many
EZLN supporters would certainly not fall into the category of "minority subject"
in terms of their position vis-à-vis dominant ideologies, no matter what their
politics and level of commitment to the cause. Most of the minority subjects
that Muñoz refers to in his analysis are U.S.-based homosexual, ethnic, or racial
minorities, and it is important to recognize that minorities in the United States
of any kind are necessarily different and differently interpellated by the dominant culture from the indigenous peoples who reside in the mountains of the
Mexican Southeast.

Nevertheless, Muñoz's formulation aptly describes the ambivalence and discomfort that Marcos advocates in any relationship to Zapatismo, including his
own. For Marcos and the EZLN disidentification is both strategy and warning,
a practice that is performed by those in the know, like the indigenous Zapatistas
who slyly counter the earnest medical student's unwittingly essentialist queries
about Marcos's identity by proclaiming "We are all Marcos," but a practice that
also confronts hegemonic powers like the Mexican state whether those powers
like it or not. As Muñoz argues, disidentification embraces contradiction, for it
"is not to pick and choose what one takes out of an identification. It is not to willfully evacuate the politically dubious or shameful components within an identificatory locus. Rather, it is the reworking of those energies that do not elide
the 'harmful' or contradictory components of any identity" (12). Marcos and
the EZLN understand all too well that most appropriations of Zapatismo "from
above," including most examples of the "Todos somos Marcos" chant, do not
incorporate "politically dubious or shameful components" such as indigenous
misery and death; thus, the Zapatistas bring those components to the forefront.
For example, in the postscript "The 'Mercantilist Postscript' Section" of the letter "Cynical Agony: The Sup Prepares to Exploit Himself" from February 1994,
Marcos writes, "P.S. without monetary value: And for our dead, how much pain
will it take to pay for them? How much money will it take to fill their pockets?
How much more blood so that their silence won't have been in vain? Who wants
the exclusive on their grief? Nobody? So be it" (Marcos and Zapatistas, *Shadows* 143). Marcos knows that most identifications with Zapatismo, or with his
role as the leader of the group, are predicated upon a neatly packaged version
of indigenous difference, which ultimately refuses to take responsibility for
indigenous suffering.

At the same time, in the letter "Cynical Agony," Marcos satirizes the appropriation of the Zapatistas by jokingly selling out, as he offers himself and the EZLN to the highest bidder from the outside world. The letter, written in February 1994 just prior to the EZLN's dialogue with a peace envoy in San Cristóbal de las Casas, is interesting for its portrayal of Marcos's negotiation of his contradictory but ultimately privileged roles. Marcos pretends to agonize over which clothes to wear to the dialogue, finally settling on his usual uniform consisting of "a brown shirt (the only one), a pair of black pants (the only ones), a festive red bandanna (the only one), a pair of dirty boots (the only ones), and the ski mask, a discreet black (the only one)" (Marcos and Zapatistas, *Shadows* 142). Marcos plainly understands that his performance of his iconic image, with its recognizable guerrilla costuming and the endlessly transferable ski mask, frequently trumps his politics or the EZLN's collective dialogues and actions. By alternating between embracing costuming as essential and rejecting it as frivolous (even if both acts are meant in jest), Marcos simultaneously privileges and refuses the power of the guerrilla's image. For Marcos, disidentification necessarily includes both a celebration of and rejection of his own iconic image. This is not a simple refusal of his iconicity and sanctity, as he and the EZLN insist upon elsewhere, but a willingness to embrace the potentially politically dubious (and possibly megalomaniacal) aspects of his privileged role, even as he accentuates his position as a subordinate spokesperson.

Don Durito of the Lacandon Jungle

Disidentification with Marcos and the EZLN requires those who engage with Zapatismo, whether as supporters or critics, to simultaneously embrace and reject their contradictory organizational structure, political aims, and potential for individual and collective sanctity. Of course, there are many examples of the disidentificatory shift between identification and refusal in Marcos's writing and the communiqués of the CCRI-CG, as when the indigenous Zapatistas irreverently assert "We are all Marcos." As always, however, Marcos is much more easily able to articulate this shift from his privileged position as leader, anti-leader, character, and author. It is often through his tactics of ironic obfuscation, his self-deprecating humor, and his self-styled position as an outsider that Marcos most clearly represents and constructs his role as a secular saint or santón. This is especially true in his representation of other characters in his stories and letters, particularly the wise-cracking beetle Nebuchadnezzar, or Don Durito of the Lacandon Jungle, who with respect to Marcos fulfills a disidentificatory function as both double and consummate rival.

Marcos incorporates many different characters and voices into his writing, including his mentor and father figure El Viejo Antonio (Old Don Antonio);

indigenous children like Andulio, Héctor, Toñita, and Pedrito whom he plays with and learns from; his possible lover "La Mar"; and other indigenous Zapatistas (Henck 358).[13] However, Durito's character is unique for his sustained performance of disidentification with Marcos and his exchange between a conscious celebration of iconicity and celebrity and support of a distinctly transnational solidarity among marginalized groups throughout the world. As usual, in the Don Durito tales Marcos represents himself as a novice, a fish out of water in the jungle and in relation to Zapatista discourse. But even more than usual, in these stories Marcos appears to be stripped (and to strip himself) of any possibility of secular sanctity. Instead, his apparently messianic characteristics are transferred to the little beetle. At the same time, even more than Marcos himself, Durito has the capacity to shift between multiple, often conflicting identities and subject positions, opening up the possibility of identification and transference in the manner of spirit possession.

Marcos first introduced Durito to the world in a letter to Mariana Moguel, age ten, who sent him a drawing of himself in the ski mask in the early months of the rebellion (Marcos, *Our Word* 291–293). Since 1994, Durito has appeared in many of Marcos's writings, often in speeches and letters explicitly directed at children or students—as in his speeches aimed at "the boys and girls of the Isidro Favela Neighborhood" or students at the Autonomous Metropolitan Universities Azcapotzalco and Xochimilco in Mexico City during the 2001 March for Indigenous Dignity (*Our Word* 135, 140, 147). While Marcos has written other stories for children, often derived from indigenous legends or tales (like the bilingual *Story of the Colors/La Historia de los Colores*), these tend to focus on the intersection between the natural and the spiritual worlds, demonstrating the synthesis of animals, plants, the environment, gods, and indigenous struggle (*Our Word* 373).[14]

Because they are representations of ancient Maya myths (as in *The Story of the Colors*, narrated by Old Don Antonio), they lack the ironic tone that is so prominent in Marcos's Don Durito tales. This irony accentuates the degree to which Durito's lessons are imparted to adults, particularly those who are in power, and especially to the Mexican state. As Kristine Vanden Berghe and Bart Maddens argue, because of this irony and the tales' "more cosmopolitan frame of reference," the Don Durito stories "[deviate] in certain respects from the [EZLN's] mainstream rhetoric" of Mexican revolutionary nationalism and the rights of indigenous peoples (138). The Don Durito tales are uniquely positioned to interrogate Zapatismo and Marcos's role as leader because of their irreverence, but they also establish solidarity with marginalized peoples throughout the world in a manner that transcends Mexican nationalism and the individual indigenous groups of Chiapas.

Although he is a small, vulnerable beetle, Durito's identities are multiple, fragmented, and transferable, like those of Marcos himself. Marcos describes Durito as a "self-dubbed knight errant" in the tradition of Don Quixote, a "little smoking beetle, very well read and an even better talker, who gave himself the task of giving his company to a soldier, El Sup" (*Our Word* 289). In an echo of the "Majority-which-disguises-itself-as-untolerated-minority" postscript, Marcos variously describes Durito as a detective, a political analyst, a pirate, a "miner in the state of Hidalgo and an oil worker in Tabasco," a mariachi in East Los Angeles, an undocumented *mojado* in the United States, a wanderer, an entrepreneur, an intellectual, a consummate lover and Don Juan, border crosser and migrant, mediator between jungle and city, writer of epistles, as well as a knight-errant (*Our Word* 306, 332–333). In fact, Durito is even more malleable than Marcos, because he assumes personalities that are closed to El Sup or that appear to go against dominant Zapatista discourse. For example, Marcos suggests that the little beetle is equally capable of symbolizing regional (he is "a miner in the state of Hidalgo and an oil worker in Tabasco") and transnational identities (he is an undocumented *mojado*) as well as Mexican nationalist possibilities, in contrast to most Zapatista discourse, which sometimes seems to valorize the Mexican nation even above indigenous autonomy (Vanden Berghe and Maddens 133).

Marcos portrays Durito as both antagonist and teacher, and in many ways, the little beetle seems to function as El Sup's alter ego, reflecting the tension within Marcos's contradictory representation of himself as well as his ironic commentary on his role as the spokesperson of the EZLN. From the first day that Durito arrives to the Zapatista camp, a few years after the start of the rebellion, the little beetle steals Marcos's tobacco, orders him around, corrects him, and ridicules and harasses the "big-nosed" Sup about everything—from his looks to his intellect, to his fame. At the same time, Durito conveys important lessons of compassion and subaltern resistance to Marcos and the other Zapatistas. As Marcos puts it: "[he] touched the best in us: our astounding capacity for human tenderness and our hope of growing better together with others," even as he exposes the injustices of the world by "righting wrongs . . . instructing the ignorant, humbling the mighty, and exalting the humble" (*Our Word* 289). Marcos also describes Durito as "the child we all have inside . . . whom we've completely forgotten because it shames us," projecting a sense of innocence as well as immaturity and playfulness as well as repression (*Our Word* 289).

In a possible—though by no means definite—glimpse at Marcos's personal history, El Sup asserts that Durito "studied at the UAM and . . . was a professor there," just as Rafael Guillén, Marcos's alleged unmasked identity, was a lecturer at the UAM-Xochimilco campus (Marcos, *Speed* 140).[15] Frequently, Durito is situated as the true interlocutor and writer of the letters, communiqués, and speeches. Durito insists that he, not Marcos, is the one who actually exchanges letters with and grants interviews to literary giants such as Gabriel García Márquez, José Saramago, Manuel Vázquez Montalbán, Carlos Monsiváis,

Bertolt Brecht, and Dario Fo. Indeed, on more than one occasion, Marcos is symbolically divested of his authorial role by Durito, as when he concedes, "And here I, the Sup, stop writing, because Durito has taken the word by force" (*Speed* 148). Furthermore, Durito appears to usurp Marcos's role as heroic figure and sex symbol. Marcos describes Durito's iconic status in language virtually identical to that used to define Marcos in the press and elsewhere—claiming, "news of [Durito's] deeds has circled the world. Millions of women sigh for him, thousands of men speak his name with respect, and hundreds of thousands of children worship him" (*Our Word* 289). Thus, like Marcos, Durito evokes the transferability and potential for spirit possession conveyed by the Zapatistas' ski mask through his multiple, malleable identities.

Unlike Marcos, however, Durito is free to openly embrace the *protagonismo* or self-promotion and the desire to be the center of attention that many outsiders have accused El Sup of. In this sense, Durito's role as Marcos's antagonist is a parody of his own messianic image through an ironic blend of humor, realism, exaggeration, and sincerity. These qualities are present in much of Marcos's writing but are especially evident in the Don Durito tales. Through frequent put-downs and pretentious lectures, Durito amplifies Marcos's bumbling, foolish characteristics and reinforces his status as novice. For example, Durito constantly criticizes Marcos's appearance and intellect, as when he scolds, "Don't think those scoundrels [the hard-liners of the Mexican Congress who refuse to engage in dialogue with the EZLN] are refusing you the ear and the word because of that ghastly mask, since it's common knowledge that you'd be even more ghastly without it" (*Speed* 141). Even more damningly, in a reference to Don Quixote de la Mancha, the beetle insists that Marcos is the true subordinate in their relationship, serving as his Sancho Panza or shield-bearer. Of course, this reference reflects another ironic twist, for Don Quixote is famously idealistic—even delusional—about his status and abilities. The fact that Marcos's disidentificatory alter ego Durito is so closely associated with Don Quixote denotes more lighthearted criticism of Marcos's role as an iconic secular saint. Finally, as I have already suggested, Marcos often struggles to maintain control of his authorial role (but to no avail) in the face of Durito's penchant for revising, appropriating, directing, and otherwise inserting himself into Marcos's writing and speeches. For example, at one point he laments, "[I try] to avoid the inevitable, which is that Durito will get a hand into what I'm writing, because for this purpose he's got too many hands and too much impertinence" (*Speed* 167). While the struggle over authorial control is obviously symbolic for Marcos always retains the power of authorship, it emphasizes the degree to which he is uncomfortable with his own authority.

Yet Durito's criticism of Marcos transcends this discomfort and occasionally seems to suspend all parody or irony, for the little beetle quite seriously aims to spread and reinforce the goals and morals of Zapatismo, whether

Marcos-as-character is able to recognize them or not. True to his neophyte persona, Marcos often portrays himself as someone in need of a refresher course on Zapatismo, and the little beetle is only too happy to oblige. To this end, many of the Don Durito tales are structured as parables. For example, the little beetle explains his study of "neoliberalism and its strategy of domination for Latin America" allegorically, as in the 2003 letter "Durito on Trains and Pedestrians" (*Our Word* 292):

> Durito (who was once a railroad worker) says the politics of power under neoliberalism . . . is like a train. Durito says that, in the train of neoliberal politics, the forward coaches are foolishly fought over by those who think they can conduct better, forgetting the fact that it is the locomotive that drives the coaches, and not the other way around. . . . Durito says that everyday people travel on foot. . . . Durito says that, among the people on foot, there are some who are rebels. These not only criticize the destination of the journey and the ridiculous, arbitrary distribution of the tickets. They even question the train's very existence and they ask themselves if trains really are necessary. Because, yes, certainly they arrive more quickly and more comfortably, but one arrives where one does not wish to arrive. Durito says we Zapatistas are some of those rebel pedestrians . . . and we are the object of mockery by those who criticize the fact that we do not want to buy a ticket and travel at top speed . . . to catastrophe. Durito says we Zapatistas are some very otherly pedestrians. Because instead of watching the train's arrogant passage with indifference, a zapatista just approaches the track, smiling, and puts his foot on it. . . . Durito says that the zapatistas will not be done walking the night until all those on foot can decide not just the train's existence and path, but also, and above all, until there are, in the walk of the pedestrians of history, many chairs under an apple tree full of fruit . . . for everyone. (*Speed* 173–175)

Durito's story, an allegory about neoliberal politics and capitalism, is a metaphor for the simple strategies of the EZLN that resemble that of the "otherly pedestrian" who approaches the track with a smile, and puts his foot on it. These strategies include teaching through stories and parables, speaking through silences, and simultaneously distributing their word through local and global channels like the Zapatista caracoles, pirate or independent radio, regional, national, and global media, and the internet.[16] Another strategy is waiting, but rather than "watching . . . with indifference," the EZLN advocates continued activism, as Marcos suggests in *Muertos incómodos*, when the protagonist is asked how long it takes to become a Zapatista: "Sometimes, it takes more than 500 years" (*Speed* 174; Marcos and Taibo, *Muertos* 21).

   Like the tactic of the Zapatista who puts his foot on the track, these strategies are deceptively simple. By maintaining local, national, and international attention despite—or perhaps because of—sustained periods of silence, and by shifting their struggle between local community issues and the international media, the EZLN assure their continued relevance. At the same time, the EZLN also understand that most, if not all, of their achievements regarding indigenous rights and the refusal of neoliberalism must be accomplished through incomplete or unexpected channels. For example, in "Durito on Trains and Pedestrians," the beetle alludes to the defeat of the PRI in 2000, a momentous event that ended over seventy years of single-party rule in Mexico: "in the dawn of January 1, 1994 . . . a zapatista indigenous put down his foot in order to derail the all-powerful train of the PRI . . . six years later, the PRI was left lying in the bottom of the gully, and its remains are being fought over by those who yesterday mocked that indigenous" (*Speed* 174). Although the EZLN are certainly partly responsible for the defeat of the PRI, with their unexpected armed rebellion in the most historically impoverished state in Mexico and the worldwide media attention they subsequently attracted, they realize that their work is nowhere near finished (*Speed* 14–15). Indeed, since 1994 the Zapatistas have consistently refused to accept the various terms of negotiation or settlement that have been offered to them by those in power; as Durito puts it in another letter, "all the multiple options being offered by power conceal a trap" (*Speed* 197). Furthermore, in the Sixth Declaration of the Lacandon Jungle, issued in 2005, the Zapatistas flatly reject all alliances with electoral organizations and denounce the "bad governments" and politicians of Mexico from all political parties—for "neither their hearts nor their words [are] honest"—in favor of an "other" national campaign, which is grassroots rather than electoral (Marcos and Zaptistas, *Other Campaign* 75, 141).

One of the most prominent themes of the Don Durito narratives is the contradiction inherent in different ideologies, especially those that purport to structure the logic of globalization. This emphasis on internal contradiction is present in much of Marcos and the Zapatistas' writings but is even more obvious in the Durito tales because of the beetle's own contradictions, especially his irreverent shifts between humility and arrogance. The little beetle does not apologize for inhabiting seemingly discordant subject positions; in fact, he is able to defuse potentially problematic situations through irony and hyperbole. Because of this, Durito is able to embrace the disjunction between authority and submission that Marcos's character often seems so uncomfortable with. For example, part of Durito's criticism of neoliberalism involves a representation of grassroots decentralized capitalism as a very small but savvy entrepreneur. Marcos writes that one day the little beetle appeared in the camp riding a turtle, a substitute horse called Pegasus, "a name that seems pure madness" (*Our Word* 303–304): "So that there is no doubt, Durito has written on the turtle's shell, in large and decisive letters: 'PEGASUS. Copyright reserved,' and below that, 'Please, fasten your seat belts' . . . one can read on Pegasus' left flank: 'Smokers' Section,' 'Union

cowboys not allowed,' 'Free advertising space. For information call Durito's Publishing Company.' I can't make out much free space, the advertising covers Pega
sus' entire left flank and rear" (*Our Word* 304). In some ways, Durito's one-man
entrepreneurial operation could be read as neoliberalism stripped down to its
core. The little beetle seems to promote the tenets of neoliberal economies as
described by David Harvey in his eager support of intellectual property rights
and "private enterprise and entrepreneurial initiative . . . [as] the keys to innova-
tion and wealth creation" (Harvey 64). Yet Marcos insists that Durito's "ultra-
mini-micro entrepreneurial vision" is the "only way to survive the failures of
neoliberalism and NAFTA" (*Our Word* 304). The little beetle mocks the Mexican government's attempts to throw off its third world shackles through neoliberalism by exposing a makeshift, alternative economy of entrepreneurship,
commerce, and advertising. In fact, Durito's entrepreneurial vision operates in
unexpected ways and occasionally draws upon apparently contradictory ideologies in order to expose the paradox of neoliberalism.

For example, in the original Spanish version of the above passage, the terms
referring to copyright and business names are rendered in English: "Copy Rights
Reserved" and "Durito's Publishing Company" (Marcos, "Durito III"). Here,
Durito is most likely pragmatically and cynically acknowledging the role of
English as the global language of business, a gesture that is lost in the English
translation. At other times, Durito inhabits seemingly opposing perspectives
and subject positions, as in his commentary on the corruption and infighting
in Mexican union politics. Before introducing his "horse" Pegasus to Marcos,
Durito brandishes a lance (a "stretched-out paper clip"), arrogantly declaring,
"my indefatigable sword . . . is anxious to feel the necks of independent unions"
(*Our Word* 302–303). Meanwhile, Pegasus' left flank reads "Union cowboys not
allowed" (*Our Word* 304). In the original Spanish, the warning is "Prohibido
el paso a charros sindicales," a pun on the word *charro* (cowboy) that refers to
corrupt trade union leaders ("Durito III"). Since the pun does not translate it
might seem that Durito's entrepreneurial vision rejects unions, when in fact it
refuses to condone corrupt union bosses. At the same time, while the beetle's
threat against the independent unions suggests he is assuming the guise of one
of the "charros sindicales" or union leaders, his grandiloquent tone, especially
in the context of his ironic Don Quixote persona, indicates further criticism
of the union bosses. Ultimately, Durito plans to ride Pegasus into Mexico City
(where prior to the March for Indigenous Dignity, the government had barred
the Zapatistas from entry) to attend the May Day parade and fight for workers'
rights (*Our Word* 303). It is clear that corrupt labor bosses could violate these
workers' rights just as easily as the Mexican government could.

In their embrace of *protagonismo*, authorial control, and arrogance, on
one hand, and humility and resistance, on the other, the Don Durito tales

demonstrate the exchange between apparent support of certain versions of power and incisive criticism of such power. Through his parody and rearticulation of neoliberalism and capitalism, Durito emphasizes the disidentification with all forms of power and authority that Marcos and the EZLN advocate. Whether this power and authority refers to the Mexican state, to neoliberal globalization, to racial, ethnic, class, or gender hierarchies, or to Marcos's role as a leader or secular saint, Durito's shift between celebration and refusal of authority reveals the importance of disidentification and ambivalence as strategies not only for combating such power but for understanding Zapatismo.

Muertos incómodos: falta lo que falta (The Uncomfortable Dead)

Marcos innately understands the importance of discomfort in relation to Zapatismo and his role within it, even—or especially—when he is the one producing the discomfort. Whether such discomfort is intentional on Marcos's part is immaterial; what matters is that it is as constant a companion to Zapatismo as social activism and the struggle for indigenous rights. The Don Durito tales convey discomfort and disidentification with forms of power encompassing the Mexican state, global capital, and Marcos's privileged position as a leader and a secular saint or *santón*. However, Marcos and Paco Ignacio Taibo II's cowritten novel *Muertos incómodos* (The uncomfortable dead) delves even more deeply into the messy and occasionally problematic production of such discomfort. The novel's title is apt in more ways than one, for not only do the titular dead—whether victims of Mexico's *guerra sucia* (dirty war); the perpetrators of war crimes; or Marcos's indigenous protagonist, the Zapatista "commisión de investigación" (investigation commission) Elías Contreras—convey discomfort from beyond the grave, some of the strategies of disidentification with power and authority employed in the novel are uncomfortable as well.[17] In particular, although Marcos is a minor character in the novel, his representation of himself and his portrayal of the indigenous Zapatistas are sometimes uncomfortable in light of his privileged authorial and leadership role. This discomfort is especially evident in the occasional conflation between Marcos and markers of *lo indígena* in *Muertos incómodos*, particularly through his representation of syncretic indigenous language.

Muertos incómodos is a detective novel written *a cuatro manos* (by four hands) in alternate installments by Marcos and Taibo (who had never met in person), with Marcos providing the odd chapters and Taibo contributing the even chapters. The novel was published in installments by the center-left Mexico City newspaper *La Jornada* between December 5, 2004, and February 20, 2005. According to the prologue published in *La Jornada*, the novel originated in a letter written by Marcos to Taibo, where he proposed that they write a detective novel "designed like a game of ping-pong in which each author and his protagonist reacts to what the other has written, in a story that promises to insert itself in the entrails of the national disaster" (Marcos and Taibo, "Prólogo"). Perhaps because of its multiple voices, the novel is difficult to summarize. The basic story of the novel concerns the simultaneous and convergent investigations of Elías Contreras and Taibo's well-known Mexico City detective Héctor Belascoarán Shayne into multiple sources of Mexican and international corruption all pointing to a mysterious figure named Morales. While Belascoarán investigates a series of disconcerting phone messages supposedly coming from a student militant with links to Morales who was assassinated in 1971, Contreras examines the papers that the family of the late Manuel Vázquez Montalbán sent to the EZLN, which target Morales as a source for international crime in Barcelona, Mexico City, and Chiapas. Belascoarán and Contreras eventually meet up in Mexico City to pool information and plan their respective operations in Mexico City and Chiapas against "Bad" and "the Evil." In addition, one of the novel's main themes, especially in the chapters written by Marcos, is the solidarity of marginalized peoples around the world through direct and indirect links to Zapatismo.

Although Marcos routinely incorporates legends, tales, and stories into the EZLN communiqués, *Muertos incómodos* is one of the few examples of pure fiction written by El Sup. As such, it emphasizes Marcos's role as character much more than his communiqués and declarations, despite the fact that he is a rather minor character in the novel. Marcos's authorial control is on full display in *Muertos incómodos*, especially in light of its barrage of occasionally competing, sometimes apparently extraneous literary techniques. Perhaps as a gesture toward the novel's subtitle "falta lo que falta" (what's missing is missing), it contains many characters and narratives that appear only briefly, especially in the sections penned by Marcos, like that of the "Club del Calendario Roto" (Broken Calendar Club), a group of foreign Zapatista sympathizers who live and work in one of the EZLN caracoles and meet with Elías Contreras. Moreover, in the chapters written by Marcos, *Muertos incómodos* gestures toward the genre of meta-narrative, in which some characters reflect upon their status as characters in the novel and upon a reading of the novel itself. Meanwhile, Elías Contreras is actually dead, although he is fully aware of his deceased status and narrates or participates in the action as if he were alive. Nevertheless, there is no explanation as to how Contreras died or how he continues to function among the living. This technique is probably a nod to the modernist Mexican writer Juan Rulfo's novel *Pedro Páramo* and is completely in line with Marcos's penchant for intertextuality as he highlights and even exaggerates his many literary influences.

Muertos incómodos has been celebrated as the first instance of a literary collaboration between a well-known revolutionary guerrilla and a prominent novelist as well as for its rapid translation and dissemination throughout Latin America, Europe, and the United States.[18] It has also been widely criticized, especially for the segments written by Marcos, in part because of its possibly superfluous multiculturalism, the random insertion and disappearance of characters and narratives, and the frequently unaccounted-for elements of meta-narrative. In fact, many reviewers suggest that the novel's only real literary merit is in the chapters written by Taibo. Critic Glen S. Close suggests that this is partly because Taibo's narrative is "comfortably familiar, since it revives the characters and scenario of Mexico's best established detective series," the Belascoarán Shayne novels (n.p.).[19] Other reviewers are not quite so generous, as one critic declares, "the subcomandante . . . is simply not a talented fiction writer; it's sometimes hard even to know what his sentences mean" and notes that Marcos's chapters "ramble on" while pronouncing Taibo's chapters "written with skill and wit" (Slivka).

An especially scathing review in the Mexican journal *Letras Libres* argues that while Taibo "tried to . . . provide some literary technique (suspense, creation of plausible characters), Marcos, for his part, provided the exaggeration, the diversion, and the chaos" (García Ramírez n.p.). Several critics accuse Marcos of allowing politics to take over the narrative: as Andrey Slivka of the *New York Times* puts it, "*The Uncomfortable Dead* is thoroughly overdetermined" (n.p.), while Close calls Marcos's narrative "a revolutionary cant tending toward absolutism" (n.p.). Fernando García Ramírez of *Letras Libres* is even more forthright, asserting that Marcos's purpose was not to write a novel at all but simply to produce just another strategy of communication, claiming "Marcos conceive[d] of the novel as a vehicle to disseminate his discourse" (n.p.). García Ramírez damningly concludes that the novel is a "failed exercise" that represents the "[expression] of a masked Narcissus" (n.p.).

But perhaps what gives critics the most pause is Marcos's representation of indigenous language and linguistic patterns. The protagonist Elías Contreras's language and speech patterns, as well as those of the other indigenous Zapatistas, feature a blend of Spanish and native syntax that Taibo has favorably referred to as "Tzotzil-inflected Spanish" while praising Marcos's "very good ear" for his use of such syncretic language (qtd. in Close n.p.). García Ramírez of *Letras Libres* is far less charitable, as he affirms of Contreras, "Marcos makes him talk like 'La India María'" (n.p.).[20] To be sure, Contreras constantly uses colorful, non-standard Spanish phrases like *un poco bastante* (a little enough), *aluego pues* (later on then), *ya vine ya* (now I'm here now), while repeating other phrases over and over again, such as *que sea* (that is), *o sea* (that is), *tal vez* (perhaps), *de por sí* (for real) and *y entonces* (and then) (Marcos and Taibo, *Muertos* 37, 10, 61).[21] Furthermore, like the character of La India María, Contreras is often comically baffled by urban life. García Ramírez even implies that Contreras's explanations of unfamiliar things and events are embarrassing and absurd, as when he encounters the Mexico City traffic for the first time: "it's as if the cars get pissed off and want to gore people as if they were male cows, that is, bulls and oxen" (Marcos and Taibo, *Muertos* 79).

True to Marcos's meta-narrative style, however, Contreras is fully aware of the impact of his unorthodox language, which he refers to as a "very other" form of speaking, in a clear reference to the "Other Campaign" the EZLN launched in 2005. Indeed, far from being a source of shame, this "very other" language is a point of indigenous pride that extends to the latest Zapatista writings and declarations and culminates in "The Sixth Declaration of the Lacandon Jungle" (2005). The Sixth Declaration, which promotes an alternative or "Other" politics that goes beyond elections and national boundaries and situates the indigenous peoples as integral to a unified global Left, is much more colloquial than any of the previous Zapatista declarations, and contains some of the same unorthodox language as *Muertos incómodos*. Above all, the Sixth Declaration emphasizes collectivity and popular language by reiterating the theme of "our simple word," as in its opening paragraph: "This is our simple word which seeks to touch the hearts of humble and simple people like ourselves" (Marcos and Zapatistas, *Other Campaign* 61). Following this rhetoric, Contreras says of Belascoarán, "according to him my language was very 'other,' and, whenever he felt like it, he would correct my way of speaking. But instead of correcting myself, I kept at it" (Marcos and Taibo, *Muertos* 11). It is clear that Contreras is not ignorant about proper or standard speech but, rather, deliberately chooses to speak his "very other" language while refusing Belascoarán's corrections.

Marcos's representation of indigenous language is indeed problematic, particularly because it conflates the voice of the indigenous peoples with his own authorial voice, which exacerbates the ever-present tension between his roles as character and author, and leader and anti-leader. Clearly, Marcos's linguistic abilities are crucial for the dissemination of the EZLN's message. But despite his incorporation of native folktales and his frequently irreverent, colloquial tone, Marcos's formal, educated Spanish also threatens to distance him from the indigenous Zapatistas who may still make many mistakes in their adopted tongue. He repeatedly alludes to this possibility throughout his writing, as in *Muertos incómodos*, where several characters jokingly grumble about El Sup's highhanded language: "Yeah, you know, some of the communiqués sent by El Sup are very complicated and I don't always understand what he's saying, because he uses very cultural words" (Marcos and Taibo, *Muertos* 220).[22] Marcos's representation in the novel of "Tzotzil-inflected Spanish," as Taibo describes it, also challenges the linguistic distance between himself and the indigenous masses and is part of a strategy of self-criticism of the overly complicated, pretentious language employed in many of his writings (Close, n.p.).

However, Close argues, "what is problematic in the literary construction of *Muertos incómodos*, in the context of Marcos's campaign of reemergence as the voice of the voiceless, is the suspicion of ventriloquism of the voiceless which haunts the reader" (n.p.). Although the question of "speaking for" the indigenous peoples is a topic that is frequently addressed by Marcos and the EZLN (as in the humorous anecdote where the indigenous Zapatistas cheekily proclaim, "We are all Marcos"), it is worth revisiting in the context of *Muertos incómodos*. Close notes that Marcos "confidently enunciates the indigenous 'we' in his written communications and in his public appearances," suggesting that this is understandable in view of El Sup's nearly thirty years of living in the mountains of Chiapas among the indigenous peoples (n.p.). Likewise, historian Nick Henck rejects the essentialist, identity-based criticism that is frequently leveled at Marcos, claiming "That Marcos is not himself indigenous seems to me irrelevant" (3). Given that one of the major objectives of Zapatismo is to transcend identity-based hierarchical categories such as that of race or gender, Henck's point is exactly right. Yet it remains true that some of Marcos's contradictory, awkward slips into essentialist lines of thinking, especially through his representation of syncretic indigenous language as in *Muertos*, are difficult to swallow. While we—and Marcos—understand that the linguistic distance between him, in his position as spokesperson, leader, or author, and the indigenous masses always remains, he occasionally obscures this fact.

In an interview with Manuel Vázquez Montalbán, Marcos argues that, in the Zapatistas' writings, "a certain syncretism is produced between urban and indigenous language. This suggests that it is possible to do other things, without establishing an alternative model of the nation, or of society" (Vázquez Montalbán 142–143). Marcos proposes that the kind of syncretic language he employs in *Muertos incómodos* can be utilized not only to interrogate the hierarchical distinction between elite and popular language but also to work within the nation and society to open up a space for all groups and languages. Vázquez Montalbán certainly recognizes that the production of syncretic language in the EZLN's writing is a joint endeavor that depends as much upon the indigenous voice as on Marcos's skill as a writer. He addresses this by referring to the EZLN's collective project, using the informal plural Spanish "you" (*vosotros*): "You offer [*Ofrecéis*] a new linguistic proposition, which depends upon indigenous metaphors, and the capacity to represent through the symbolic" (Vázquez Montalbán 142). But when Vázquez Montalbán asks Marcos about his own individual performance of linguistic and cultural syncretism in his writings, using the informal singular "you" (*tú*) construction, "you add [*le añades*] elements of high culture, creating a sort of linguistic syncretism," Marcos responds, as he does throughout the interview, with the collective "we" of Zapatismo: "What we want [*Lo que queremos*] to do is to give the word another use" (142). Vázquez

Montalban's shift might seem imperceptible or arbitrary. However, given that he primarily uses the informal plural "you" when speaking to Marcos, thus encompassing the EZLN as a collective, the moments when he employs the informal singular "you" are clearly addressed to Marcos alone. Marcos's persistent refusal to respond in kind, instead answering in terms of the group, is consistent with the EZLN's insistence upon collectivity and the subordination of El Sup. It also suggests, however, that it is easy to conflate the EZLN with Marcos, whether in terms of individual iconicity, group collectivity, or language and linguistic patterns. Whether the blurring of the linguistic lines between Marcos and the indigenous peoples is intentional on his part is irrelevant. Rather, I am interested in the sometimes seemingly arbitrary shift between Marcos as a spokesperson for the EZLN and for indigenous affairs, and Close's suggestion that he occasionally appears to serve as a ventriloquist for "the voiceless" (n.p.).

As in the Don Durito tales, Marcos generally casts himself as a novice and a character who is secondary to the development of the narrative in *Muertos incómodos*. Frequently, he is a humorous foil for the indigenous characters to position themselves against, as when he attempts to teach some of them the proper way to build a roof or to speak Spanish. In almost every case, however, Marcos's expertise is subtly mocked or even flatly rejected. Rather than reflecting incompetence or indigenous ignorance, the linguistic errors made by Elías Contreras and other indigenous characters in the novel reveal a kind of native resistance to or refusal of standard Spanish. These errors frequently seem to be deliberate, as when one of the Zapatista women, Erika, asks Marcos for his advice about compañero Noé, who is flirting with her. Erika initially claims that Noé is touching her (*toqueteando*), when in fact he is flirting with her (*coqueteando*), a distinction that is revealed when she imitates his winking at her (Marcos and Taibo, *Muertos* 56–57). However, even though Marcos corrects her language, she persists in using the "wrong" word, *toqueteando*, and dismisses him when he corrects her again. Meanwhile, Elías Contreras rejects linguistic corrections more than any other character in the novel, true to his nom de guerre "Contreras" (or contrarian), which he claims was given to him by Marcos precisely because he refuses others' attempts to correct his customs and his language. Instead of correcting himself according to the instructions of others like Belascoarán Shayne, Contreras insists on taking control of his learning process by writing the new Spanish words and phrases he learns during his time in Mexico City in his notebook in order to share them with the other Zapatistas in Chiapas. When he returns to Chiapas to plan the capture of Morales with a group of Zapatistas, Contreras encourages all of them to write the new words he has learned in their notebooks as well—an act that is portrayed as a collective and egalitarian method of learning rather than an authority-based structure of linguistic dominance (202–203). The Zapatistas thus accept standard Spanish only on their own terms and on equal footing, with the primary purpose of advancing their struggle.

Of course, only Elías Contreras and the other indigenous characters of *Muertos incómodos* utilize non-standard Spanish in the novel, not the character of Marcos himself. While Marcos is mocked, chided, and ignored by many of the other characters because of his elevated language and his failed pedagogy, he is clearly in on the joke, for unlike other characters in the novel, as an author he is able to shift seamlessly between formal and popular language. Yet even though Marcos's representation of the indigenous peoples' blending of Spanish and native syntax provides an important example of syncretism and reflects crucial strategies of native resistance to or disidentification with standard Spanish, his portrayal of this Tzotzil-inflected Spanish remains contentious. Read as a direct representation of indigenous dialect by a (presumably) non-indigenous writer (recalling Jean Franco's characterization of the Latin American indianist novel as a genre that "has inevitably suffered" because it "has been written entirely by non-Indians"), this linguistic syncretism could potentially reinforce the hierarchical borders that the EZLN purports to dismantle (*Introduction* 242).

Although the Zapatistas reject the hierarchical distinctions of race, class, gender, and language that are entrenched in Mexican society, these markers are occasionally reasserted through Marcos's representation of himself in texts like *Muertos incómodos*. Alongside the novel's multicultural inclusivity and linguistic syncretism, we are confronted by the dominance of Marcos's rhetoric as he shifts between elite and popular language and between character and author. The racial or linguistic distinction between "Indian" and "non-Indian" that is productively obscured within the context of Zapatismo (as through the use of the ski mask) is also blurred in *Muertos*. For example, there are subtle shifts in the novel regarding the nature of Zapatismo and its relation to race and language, as Marcos realizes when Contreras informs him that one of the indigenous compañeros, Genaro, has been abusing his wife. Marcos is surprised, for he thought that Genaro "seemed to be very Zapatista" (Marcos and Taibo *Muertos incómodos* 21). However, Contreras understands that to be Zapatista is a continual endeavor, one that does not depend upon race, gender, or language but, rather, on revolutionary struggle and community activism and may in fact "take more than 500 years" to achieve (21). Occasionally, there seems to be some slippage regarding what it means to be a Zapatista in the novel. At times it seems to be based on markers of identity such as race, as when Marcos invokes the indigenous "we" when comparing President Vicente Fox's appraisal of the Zapatistas ("He said that we are practically a thing of the past") with that of the conquistador Hernán Cortes, the dictator Porfirio Díaz, and other leaders who have attempted to squelch indigenous rebellions in Mexico (125). Overall, however,

Marcos clearly portrays Zapatismo as an ongoing struggle that depends upon forms of local resistance and collectivity independent of race or language. This is evident in his willingness to be educated by Contreras and others about the nature of Zapatismo, even as his attempts to impart lessons to the indigenous people elsewhere in the novel fall flat.

Yet the paradox remains: Marcos wields the authorial power to shift perspectives and subject positions in *Muertos incómodos*, but the other characters in the novel or the indigenous Zapatistas do not. Furthermore, his attempts to render himself insignificant as a character in his writing actually emphasize his position as author as well as his role as a secular saint or *santón*. In many ways, the more he negates himself, the more visible and central he becomes as the image of Zapatismo. For instance, while Marcos closes most of his chapters with "From the mountains of Southeast Mexico, Subcomandante Insurgente Marcos" (his customary sign-off in letters or messages to Elías Contreras), at the end of Chapter XI, his final chapter, Contreras assumes the authorial signature for the first time since "El Sup is not here" (Marcos and Taibo, *Muertos* 220). Glen S. Close argues that this gesture "only calls attention to the force of Marcos's ill-concealed presence in much of what has gone before," for the "face behind the textual mask" is too "recognizable" (n.p.). According to Close's analysis, it would seem that Marcos is trying to have it both ways in order to be the omniscient author that can also assume a subordinate character role when necessary.

The same argument could apply to Marcos's status as leader and anti-leader. But I want to suggest another possibility: in the context of Zapatismo and Marcos's writing, neither position can exist without the other. Like the mask, the roles of leader and anti-leader and character and author both conceal and reveal Marcos's position within Zapatismo, even as they expose the inequality of the other Zapatistas who are unable to shift sides. Rather than signaling opposition, this simultaneous negation and revelation demonstrates that Marcos's roles of leader and anti-leader and character and author actually construct each other. In the end, all of these contradictions are crucial to Marcos's persona as a secular saint and *santón* who performs his own iconicity by negating it.

The Sixth Declaration and the Other Campaign

For all of its flaws, *Muertos incómodos* can be read as an introduction to the Zapatistas' Sixth (and latest, to date) Declaration of the Lacandon Jungle and the "Other Campaign" (*Other Campaign* 13).[23] The novel—along with the 2003 report "Plan La Realidad-Tijuana," which focuses on the Mexican political struggle, and a few other related communiqués—marks the end of a period of silence that culminates in the Sixth Declaration and the Other Campaign. As I suggest above, *Muertos incómodos* is clearly an antecedent to the Sixth Declaration in terms of its informal linguistic style, right down to the use of similarly idiosyncratic phrases like *de por sí* or *que sea*. However, the novel also anticipates many of the ideas presented in the Declaration, particularly the mutual construction of the roles of leader and anti-leader, the distancing from Marcos's position as spokesperson, and the primacy of the masses. While some, like García Ramírez of *Letras Libres*, argue that Marcos's imprint is all over the Sixth Declaration, "La Sexta" foregrounds the Zapatista masses to the exclusion of Marcos. In fact, Marcos is not mentioned at all in the text of the declaration.[24] Of course, as in *Muertos incómodos*, Marcos's absence conspicuously announces his presence. But the Sixth Declaration is unique in its emphasis upon what I regard as the sanctity of the collective. That is, even more than the EZLN's other declarations and communiqués, La Sexta argues for collective solidarity between the indigenous peoples and other participants (such as workers, campesinos, students, teachers, employees) in the struggle against neoliberal globalization throughout the world (*Other Campaign* 93). While Marcos and the EZLN have gestured at such solidarity before, the aims of La Sexta explicitly refuse racial, ethnic, or gender essentialism, making the indigenous peoples part of a global struggle for change and apparently rendering moot the notion of hierarchical leadership. In the terms of the Sixth Declaration, the Zapatista struggle is no longer primarily about indigenous rights or national belonging but, rather, about the rights, leadership, and potential sanctity of a global collective located "below and to the left."

The roots of the Sixth Declaration and the Other Campaign lie in the EZLN's realization that, in spite of the rhetoric about collective leadership within the Zapatistas' group and Marcos's role as spokesperson, they had still been relying upon traditional, hierarchical forms of authority or leadership. In particular, the Zapatistas were willing to negotiate to a certain extent with the Mexican federal and local governments, even while maintaining a critical distance. But La Sexta and the Other Campaign represent a complete break from any connection with official forms of authority and leadership. In a sense, the Zapatistas are simply giving back exactly what they have received from federal and local governments. Indeed, Marcos and others have linked the Sixth Declaration and the Other Campaign to various moments of refusal, lies, and bad faith on the part of the Mexican political class, particularly the government's rejection of the San Andrés Accords.[25]

The San Andrés Accords on Indian Rights and Culture were signed in 1996 by President Zedillo and the Mexican Congress in a diluted form, with consciously changed language and terms (for example, substituting "community" for the concept of "original peoples" in order to localize the indigenous struggle), which finally "[deprived the accords] of their spirit and coherence"

(Henck 322). This version of the accords was watered down even further when, during the 2001 March for Indigenous Dignity, the Senate "considerably modified the bill . . . by restricting indigenous autonomy to the municipal [not regional or federal] level" (Henck 351). Although the Senate passed the bill in April 2001, the EZLN considered the agreements null and void, arguing in the Sixth Declaration: "It was a waste of time for us to be talking with the politicians, because neither their hearts nor their words were honest . . . on that day, when the politicians from the PRI, PAN, and PRD approved a law that was no good, they killed dialogue once and for all; they clearly stated that it did not matter what they had agreed to and signed, because they did not keep their word" (*Other Campaign* 75).

In light of this denunciation of political authority, in an interview with Aura Bogado, Marcos reiterates his willingness—along with that of all of the "known leadership" of the EZLN, such as Comandanta Esther and Comandante Tacho—to sacrifice not only their positions as leaders but their lives for the cause of the Sixth Declaration and the Other Campaign (*Other Campaign* 151). However, the absolute refusal to recognize federal and local governments and forms of electoral politics is a new stance. As the EZLN put it: "we understood that dialogue and negotiation had failed as a result of [the] political parties" (75). In keeping with their collective politics, the Zapatistas have applied this general refusal of hierarchy and authority to their own organization. Indeed, part of the goal of La Sexta is to reorganize the EZLN's own political-military hierarchy, which the group confesses is "not democratic, because it is an army" (79). Effectively, the EZLN pledges to separate "the political-military from the autonomous and democratic aspects of organization in Zapatista communities," and to no longer "[involve] itself in giving orders in the villages' civil matters," in a process of "governing by obeying" (79, 83). They also emphasize their intention to speak to the "simple and humble of the Mexican people" without "intermediaries or mediation," further acknowledging and dissociating themselves from their own practice of authority and hierarchy (137).

In many ways, the Sixth Declaration marks a clear return to the tactics of Zapatista paradox, tactics that Marcos and the EZLN have always embraced, but which are at their apex in La Sexta. In addition to refusing all forms of authority and hierarchy, the Sixth Declaration emphasizes many paradoxical possibilities. These possibilities include the sanctity of the collective, an understanding that the EZLN's grassroots methods of local organizing and talking directly to ordinary Mexicans might not reach a global audience as effectively as the internet-distributed communiqués issued by Subcomandante Marcos, and a further willingness to accept that their methods might not even work at all within established modes of representation and reception. One example of Zapatista paradox in the Sixth Declaration is the reiteration of the principle that the EZLN's tactics might not bear immediate visible results and that they might not function at all within received modes of representation and representation—in the spirit of Marcos's claim in *Muertos incómodos* that, to become a Zapatista, "Sometimes, it takes more than 500 years" (21). The Zapatistas accept that the work of visiting local communities throughout Mexico, talking to people in person, issuing communiqués, and establishing alliances with "non-electoral organizations and movements which define themselves . . . as being of the Left" will last for "an indefinite period of time" and might not gain recognition from the outside world (*Other Campaign* 139). While such grassroots activities and communiqués are regularly announced and reported on the EZLN's official website, *Enlace Zapatista*, and they are occasionally still distributed through media channels like *La Jornada*, the local, private nature of many of the meetings precludes mass media attention. Even the occasional international meetings and forums that the Zapatistas have organized under the banner of "La Sexta Internacional" (The Sixth International), like the "Encuentros Intergalácticos" (Intergalactic Encounters), have been relatively low-key affairs that are not routinely reported in the international press. Yet such local, private, and autonomous meetings and communiqués are completely in line with the EZLN's long-standing aims to "govern by obeying" (*Other Campaign* 83).

Finally, although La Sexta clearly focuses on autonomous indigenous rights, describing the work the EZLN has done to establish the Juntas de Buen Gobierno (Councils of Good Government), it looks far beyond indigenous rights, Chiapas, and Mexico to link the Zapatistas in solidarity with networks of laborers, students, mothers and women's groups, migrants, the dispossessed, and ethnic, racial, and sexual minorities throughout the world. While the EZLN has frequently gestured toward such international solidarity, its primary goals have always been indigenous rights and national identity. However, unlike the famously tongue-in-cheek "Marcos is gay" postscript, which ironically links Marcos to marginalized peoples on a global scale, the Sixth Declaration quite seriously lays out plans to assist groups that are fighting for social justice and against neoliberal capital throughout the world, such as the *piqueteros* of Argentina, the Mapuche Indians of Chile, and the people of Cuba (*Other Campaign* 123).[26] The Zapatistas' aid consists of very small, perhaps seemingly insignificant gestures such as gifts of free-trade goods and indigenous arts and crafts as well as spiritual support, but it nevertheless represents "new relationships of mutual respect and support with people and organizations who are resisting and struggling against neoliberalism and for humanity" (131). In this manner, the EZLN extends its non-electoral, grassroots Other Campaign beyond Chiapas and Mexico to encompass like-minded people throughout the world under the banner of Zapatismo. The emphasis on international, cross-racial, and cross-ethnic unity—as the Zapatistas put it, "our hearts learn that we are not alone"—further relates to the notion of the sanctity of the collective, which transcends debates about Marcos's role in the group (103). Instead, the Sixth Declaration argues that the future of Zapatismo lies with the international masses on the left, going beyond racial, ethnic, or gender essentialism but also remaining faithful to local, autonomous indigenous issues and rights. By symbolically removing Marcos from the equation, the Sixth Declaration reinforces the EZLN's original objective, which is to advance a new kind of collective, mass sanctity, initially made possible by the interchangeability of the iconic mask but ultimately residing in grassroots face-to-face collaborative action.

Difference and the Sanctity of the Collective

While I do not doubt Marcos and the EZLN's desire to reject all forms of authority, particularly within their own group, the fact remains that they can never completely avoid some form of hierarchical differentiation. Indeed, many would argue that Marcos's absence within the new organizational structure of the Sixth Declaration is merely an illusion. Even as they call to abolish such hierarchies, Marcos and the EZLN must accept that outsiders, whether antagonists or supporters, will nevertheless ascribe hierarchies to their organization. In the spirit of disidentification, the EZLN must look beyond those paradoxes it routinely emphasizes—such as the function of concealment and revelation provided by the iconic mask or the rhetorical demand for a world where many worlds fit—in order to scrutinize some of the more ambivalent, problematic contradictions of Zapatismo. In this way, the EZLN might more effectively work within and contest its own structural hierarchies as well as the authority of the state and global capital. There is occasionally a disconnection between words and practice in Zapatismo, particularly in regard to the role of women and women's rights within the EZLN, and to the potential homogenization of various indigenous groups. Left unacknowledged, such discordance precludes the possibility of the sanctity of the collective, especially if it is understood through the transposability of the iconic mask. The mask can only stand for transcendent unity if it does not obscure internal indigenous difference in the manner of Mexican state discourse.

Marcos certainly acknowledges that there is much work left to do regarding women's rights within Zapatismo, as he remarks in *Muertos incómodos*, "There's still a whole lot missing on the question of women" (27).[27] Likewise, in the Sixth Declaration, the EZLN proclaim, "little by little, there are more women going into this work, although there is still a lack of respect for the compañeras, and a need for them to participate more in the work of the struggle" (*Other Campaign* 85). Despite these official admissions about their roles, women and other marginalized groups within the indigenous groups of Chiapas (like gays and lesbians or religious minorities, for example) remain vulnerable. Such minorities are frequently coded as inferior, and their concerns are often subsumed by the larger parameters of the diverse indigenous groups. Meanwhile, Vanden Berghe and Maddens indicate that Marcos's writing, especially in his representation of indigenous myths and history, sometimes portrays different indigenous groups as a homogeneous bloc, giving the impression that "there is no conflict" or inequality within indigenous communities (131).

Marcos's elision of indigenous difference might well be a tactical move, designed to promote the most universal, transferable image of indigeneity possible, like that enclosed in the mask. As feminist critic Marisa Belausteguigoitia Rius astutely argues, it has been extremely difficult to grasp the "indigenous problem" while taking the diversity of the groups into account (300). In particular, she points to the "silence of the other" that indigenous women represent, and she questions whether Marcos is capable of "translating" women, and whether the EZLN is truly able to listen to them consistently (300).[28] Indeed, Belausteguigoitia's comments point toward the insidious beliefs that indigenous groups are all the same or that they harbor no internal conflict. Yet rather than departing from the hegemonic view of the Mexican state, which renders indigenous peoples invisible by suggesting they are interchangeable in their marginalization (and which the EZLN contests through the iconic mask), Belausteguigoitia reminds us that indigenous women are still silenced and excluded within their racial, ethnic, and linguistic group, and that they remain so even within the EZLN. She suggests that the only way to see these women and to begin to know them, even in superficial ways, is to travel to Chiapas and focus on the EZLN's local, grassroots politics. Even then, we must recognize that, for these indigenous women, "technology does not work miracles, biology reigns and the body must accompany the gaze" (300).

Through his disidentificatory, uncomfortable shift between the refusal and the rearticulation of his iconic persona, Subcomandante Marcos alludes to some of the pitfalls of sanctity, whether in terms of the individual or of the collective. Since the indigenous Zapatistas simply cannot assume the dual roles of leader and anti-leader and character and author like Marcos can, the repetition of the black ski mask as icon of Zapatismo reflects the universalization of difference even as it signals indigenous solidarity. Even if the transposable mask transcends individual iconicity and ethnocentrism in its evocation of Zapatismo, it is crucial to recognize and interrogate the mask's potential to erase indigenous difference. As Belausteguigoitia suggests, the best way to ensure this is to focus on local Zapatista and indigenous politics at the ground level, either by visiting Chiapas or by attending one of the Zapatista "encounters" elsewhere. In keeping with the aims of the Sixth Declaration, such local politics are essential to the development and functioning of indigenous communities.

It is difficult for many outsiders to participate in these meetings, however, and perhaps even harder for them to suspend their preconceived notions of organizational hierarchy and the desire for the kind of secular sanctity that conveys celebrity and charisma rather than collective unity and transposability. Thus, the medical student I refer to above is initially confused when the indigenous Zapatistas inform her "We are all Marcos," before she can grasp the humorous inclusivity of the gesture. In a letter from October–November 2011 titled "Una Muerte . . . o una Vida" (A death . . . or a life), Marcos provides a much more scathing analysis of the desire for hierarchy and centrality when he discusses the "carrion-feeding journalists" that descended upon the Zapatista caracoles after the death of Comandante Moisés. After the journalists discover that the deceased man in question was not Coronel Moisés, who has been increasingly visible in issuing communiqués and speaking in public, but Comandante Moisés, they lose interest, for "none of them cared about someone that had not appeared as a public leader, someone who had always remained in the shadows, someone who was apparently just another indigenous Zapatista" (*Enlace Zapatista*).

In the remainder of the letter, Marcos pays tribute to Moisés in the style of hagiography. Marcos informs us that Comandante Moisés joined the EZLN in 1985–1986, when its members could be counted on two hands, "with fingers left over"; that "like any other combatant," he participated in the column that took the Municipal Palace in San Cristóbal de las Casas on January 1, 1994; and that he participated in many local and national informational campaigns and delegations. Above all, Marcos emphasizes Comandante Moisés's humility and passion, affirming his importance to the group as "just another shadow among thousands of Zapatistas," that is, not as a typical public leader or speaker, or a secular saint, but as the very spirit of the collective. In this sense, Marcos indicates an inversion of the mantra "Todos somos Marcos," which suggests that many are reflected in one, instead asserting that each individual reflects the collective.

The slogan "Todos somos Marcos" is far less commonly utilized as a gesture of Zapatista solidarity than it used to be, as Marcos has physically and symbolically receded into the background of the EZLN's organizational and political structure. Yet after nearly twenty years of Zapatismo, hierarchies remain among and between the different indigenous groups in Chiapas. Such hierarchies persist despite the marginalization of the indigenous peoples in relation to Mexico and the world at large. As such, Marcos and the EZLN must never relinquish their self-critical stance, especially regarding Subcomandante Marcos's position as leader and secular saint or santón. Rather than simply casting El Sup as a spokesperson or rejecting authority and hierarchy out of hand, Marcos and the EZLN must accept their own use of such authority, in the ambivalent mode of disidentification. Perhaps even more important, we must all acknowledge that the "difference within difference" that Belausteguigoitia refers to is a potential impasse when it comes to the possibility of the sanctity of the indigenous masses. In order to honor the spirit of Zapatista paradox, we all need to ensure that this sanctity does not further obscure the differences among the indigenous peoples or Chiapas, or render them invisible.

5   ILLEGAL MARGINALIZATIONS

La Santísima Muerte

"SANTA MUERTE HEARS PRAYERS from dark places. She was sent to rescue the lost, society's rejects. 'She understands us, because she is a cabrona like
us. . . . We are hard people and we live hard lives. But she accepts us all, when we
do good and bad,'" claims Haydé Solís Cárdenas, a resident of Mexico City's infamous barrio Tepito and devotee of La Santísima Muerte or Saint Death (Thompson n.p.). Solís Cárdenas, a street vendor who sells smuggled tennis shoes for a
living, feels an affinity with Santa Muerte not as a righteous, holy inspiration but
as a tarnished outsider much like herself. Secular saints like La Santísima Muerte,
who is the unofficial patron of the poor, the criminals, and the sinners, in general,
are outsiders who straddle the line between good and evil or sacred and secular.
Although devotees from all walks of life worship Santa Muerte, she is especially
important to those who live on the margins of society, such as undocumented
migrants, taxi drivers, truck drivers, prostitutes, drug addicts, and criminals in
Mexico, the United States, and beyond. Perhaps because of her link to marginalization and illegality, she has exponentially risen in popularity on both sides of
the border in terms of media attention, cultural production, and academic studies. Many scholars attribute the death saint's increase in popularity in Mexico
to the economic crisis of 1994, also known as the *efecto tequila* (tequila effect),
during which the Mexican peso sharply decreased in value and the middle class
lost most of its buying power (Gil Olmos 91–92). The crisis intensified Mexican
migration to the United States, as many sought to escape ever more precarious
economic conditions. In the past fifteen years or so, Santa Muerte has found a
home in cities and regions of the United States with large populations of Mexican migrants, while in Mexico today only Jesus and the Virgin of Guadalupe have

A statue of Santa Muerte dressed a bride, seen outside of a shrine in Tepito, Mexico City. Copyright Jan Sochor, May 1, 2010.

more devotees.[1] Whether Santa Muerte is viewed as a solution in times of crisis or as just another manifestation of crisis, she is popular precisely because of her controversial and contradictory nature. Devotees and critics alike are simultaneously fascinated and frightened by her.

The focus here is on La Santísima Muerte as the most contradictory figure within the contemporary culture of secular, seemingly sinful or lawless, and explicitly cross-border sanctity. Santa Muerte is famous for being very miraculous and loyal but also for being a jealous, vengeful patron who requires the utmost devotion and respect and favors offerings of fruit, candy, liquor, and cigars. She is known by a variety of nicknames, such as "La Niña Blanca" (White Girl) or "La Flaca" (Skinny Girl), and many of her followers refer to her with loving, familial endearments such as "Mi Reina" (My Queen), "Mi Niña Bonita" (My Beautiful Girl), "Madrina" (Godmother), or "Holy Mother," even as they may feel a great deal of fear toward her. She is represented as a skeleton, dressed in hooded robes, as a bride, or in other elaborate, hand-made clothing, wigs, and jewelry that change depending on the calendar or on the moods of her devotees.[2] She often carries a sickle, a globe of the world, an hourglass, and the scales of justice. Like her followers, and indeed like every human, she is potentially good and bad at once. A true secular saint, Santa Muerte is not venerated for her purity or holiness but for her accessibility to the masses on both sides of the border and her resistance to the powerful forces of the state, the Catholic Church, and wealthy elites.

As a symbol of death—both the only certainty of life and its polar opposite—Santa Muerte most fully embodies the duality between accessibility and inaccessibility that all saints represent. Since all humans must face death, both that of others and their own, La Santísima Muerte is the great equalizer across class and social distinctions and racial, gender, or sexual hierarchies. Judith Butler reiterates the unifying power of death, suggesting that it is the only thing that might unify diverse people as a collective, however reluctant: "Despite our differences in location and history, my guess is that it is possible to appeal to a 'we,' for all of us have some notion of what it is to have lost somebody. Loss has made a tenuous 'we' of us all" (20). Santa Muerte's devotees certainly embrace her role as an equalizer and unifier of the human race.

At the same time, they are acutely aware that she is illegible, for she represents life's greatest mystery. While devotees might request protection from violence, pray for help finding work, love, or happiness in their personal lives, or ask Santa Muerte to bring harm to their enemies, they can never expect her to protect them from death forever. As Enriqueta Romero Romero (known as Doña Queta), the caretaker of the best-known shrine to the death saint, says: "You are born with a destiny, from the day you are born . . . your destiny is marked" (Hernández, *Down* 156). The first order of this destiny is the inevitability of death.

Nevertheless, devotees like Doña Queta take great comfort in putting their lives in Santa Muerte's hands. In the film *La Santa Muerte* by Eva Aridjis, Doña Queta affirms, "Oh Skinny Girl, I know you're the one who's going to take me away. But while I'm still in this world, take care of me, help me, keep me company."[3] In this sense, the death saint walks with her devotees in life as well as in death. Yet despite the intimacy and solace that Santa Muerte's followers find in her cult, they do not presume to understand her, identify with her, or possess her. Death remains impenetrable to humans; as such, in relation to Santa Muerte, the practice of spirit possession—that is, the possibility of assuming her image, whether literally or figuratively—is frowned upon by most of her followers. At the same time, Santa Muerte represents the universality of death and its proximity for the faithful. Reflecting the contradiction between accessibility and inaccessibility, Santa Muerte's devotees understand that, rather than their possessing death, death must possess them.

Through a study of recent cultural production such as Eva Aridjis's documentary film *La Santa Muerte/Saint Death* (2007), the regional Sonoran television program *Relatos de Ultratumba* (Stories from beyond the grave, 2010), the narconovela *La Santa Muerte* by Homero Aridjis, and essays, crónicas, and histories by Daniel Hernández, Carlos Monsiváis, José Gil Olmos, and others, I argue that—rather than functioning as an obstacle for the faithful—the ambivalent, contradictory character of Santa Muerte allows devotees to articulate their own narratives of equality. By asserting their equality and belonging through the death saint, marginalized devotees may embrace their own ambiguous status in society.

At the same time, La Santísima Muerte's ambivalent nature remains a serious threat to her critics, such as the Catholic Church, the Mexican state, and many middle- and upper-middle-class Mexicans and Chicanos/as. While such criticism is usually attributed to Santa Muerte's status as a pagan or satanic icon, in reality she and her devotees are most threatening because they disrupt the status quo of class-based, racial, gender, and sexual hierarchies on either side of the border. Indeed, the ambiguity, mobility, and transgressivity symbolized by Santa Muerte is so menacing to the dominant powers of state, church, and social elites that its true significance must be elided or denied. Ultimately, La Santísima Muerte frightens her critics because she fills a void in the face of the failure of civil society and the state for those on the margins, especially migrants, impoverished barrio dwellers, and most contentiously, for criminals, to establish alternative forms of spatial and temporal communities, commerce or trade, and social services through secular sanctity.

Fickle Death

Unlike many other popular saints in Mexico and in the borderlands, La Santísima Muerte is not clearly connected to any one specific region or village. Instead, many scholars, artists, and journalists link the death saint to Mexico itself, like anthropologist Claudio Lomnitz, who considers Death to be Mexico's national symbol and totem, while arguing that "the cult of death could be thought of as the oldest, seminal, and most authentic element of Mexican popular culture" (*Death* 23–24). Lomnitz indicates that Mexican artists and writers such as José Guadalupe Posada, Octavio Paz, Diego Rivera, Juan Rulfo, José Revueltas, and Teresa Margolles, to name just a few, have represented death for satiric, festive, and melancholic purposes as a sign of both national pride and political critique (*Death* 23–25). The illustrator and artist Posada, considered by many to be the "father" of the representation of death in Mexican visual art, is particularly famous for his political, social, and cultural satire through the portrayal of skeletons in all manner of social situations and activities (Perdigón 45). Although neither Posada nor the other Mexican artists and writers who represent death through art created the image of Santa Muerte as she is known today, all of them draw upon colonial and medieval representations as well as their own historical moments to emphasize the permanent, everyday nature of death.

In line with such diverse representations of death, Santa Muerte is a marker not only of Mexican national identity but of globalization and transnational identities. As Lomnitz asserts, Mexico's "death totemism" is currently most evident through "the emergence of the cult of the so-called Santa Muerte as a patroness of those who thrive in the underside of globalization . . . and the rise of the Days of the Dead as a key to contemporary Mexican-American identity" (*Death* 57). Although Santa Muerte is worshipped in the United States primarily by Mexican migrants, the cult to La Santísima on both sides of the border signifies very different things than the celebration of the Days of the Dead, which Lomnitz argues are crucial to the development of Chicano/a identity politics (*Death* 475). The devotees of Santa Muerte do not necessarily celebrate the Days of the Dead, at least in traditional ways. Lomnitz notes that until recently, in Mexico "urbanization and upward mobility had been associated with turning one's back on the celebration of [the] holiday," though its contemporary commodification and fusion with Halloween suggests a much wider dissemination of the holiday than in the past (*Death* 474). Instead, the celebration of the Days of the Dead and the worship of Santa Muerte are linked through the deep connection between death, migration, and identity on either side of the border, evoking migrant crossings and deaths along the U.S.-Mexico border, the femicides in Ciudad Juárez and other border towns, the casualties of the drug wars, and the deep-rooted presence of Mexican communities in the United States.

As befits Santa Muerte's contradictory nature, no one can confirm her origins or history. In fact, she has multiple points of origin throughout Mexican history. Some of these points overlap while others seem to have no connection whatsoever. Although the death saint's origins are murky, it is more important to note that most of her devotees have little interest or stake in her history and instead approach her from a purely pragmatic perspective (Chesnut 27). Many argue that the cult to Santa Muerte has existed for hundreds of years and is linked to pre-Hispanic goddesses such as Coatlicue, the goddess of life, death, and rebirth, or Micetecacihuatl, the queen of the underworld and goddess of death. Anthropologist Alfredo Vargas González affirms that the image of Santa Muerte has been present since the Spanish conquest. He cites her historical association with San Pascual Bailón (also known as San Pascual Rey or San Pascualito, as well as Santo Esqueleto [Saint Skeleton], since he is sometimes represented as a skeleton), a Catholic saint with a long cult history in Chiapas and Guatemala (Vargas González 103). Lomnitz cites Serge Gruzinski's description of colonial religious sodalities or *cofradías* in Mexico, including one from the eighteenth century that developed a cult to Santa Muerte and employed the saint's image "to gain political power" by granting the miracle "of handing [the group] the rods of justice [*bara de govierno* (sic)]" (*Death* 486).

Chesnut cites cases of "Indian idolatry" from the colonial period in Mexico, including an example from 1793 when a Franciscan friar filed a complaint against a group of Indians who worshipped "an idol whose name is the Just Judge and is the figure of a complete human skeleton standing on top of a red surface, wearing a crown and holding a bow and arrow" (32). As a result of persecution by the Catholic Church, devotees of the death saint in her various manifestations "made their devotion to her even more clandestine, to the extent that she disappears from the Mexican historical record for the next century and a half" (Chesnut 32). Chesnut also notes that several anthropologists mention Santa Muerte's role as a "love sorceress" in their research from the 1940s and 1950s, signaling the death saint's reemergence as a guide to matters of love (35).

José Gil Olmos discusses the presence of Santa Muerte in the state of Hidalgo, linked since 1965 to the skeletal image of San Bernardo in the church of Tepatepec, and in Zacatecas, where people in the village of La Noria have worshipped a skeleton figure since 1967 (64–68). Gil Olmos also cites the existence of the cult in Oaxaca, dating to the early 1990s (73). In his account, the cult of Santa Muerte in Oaxaca developed around the sculpture of a skeleton with a crown on its head and a scythe and a candle in its hands, located in the museum of the village of Yanhuitlán. The exhibit is considered a holy image of Santa Muerte by the faithful (73).

Vargas González notes that Santa Muerte is associated with Afro-Caribbean and Brazilian spiritual traditions, specifically with the goddess Orisha (also known as Oyá, goddess of war and the ruler of cemeteries and funeral rites), signaling the presence of the saint's cult outside of Mexico (104). Chesnut discusses Santa Muerte's entry into Mexican film and popular culture with an appearance in the 1976 film *El miedo no anda en burro* (Fear doesn't ride a donkey), in which she materializes as a "chilling Grim Reapress" rather than the traditional goddess of love (36). Indeed, since the 1980s Santa Muerte's association with the macabre and the criminal underworld has overshadowed all other manifestations of the death saint in the media (Chesnut 36–37).

According to Lomnitz, it is entirely possible that the contemporary cult to La Santísima Muerte is an evolution of the cult to San Pascual, although it differs in some crucial ways. First, San Pascual is a male saint, yet in the cult of Santa Muerte "Death is always feminine" (*Death* 489–490). It is common for devotees to establish kinship-like connections to their favored saints of either gender, but the fact that the death saint is specifically coded as feminine implies maternal attributes, with the potential to give life, even as she takes it away. In this sense, Santa Muerte's femininity reinforces her duality as a figure of both redemption and damnation, encompassing aspects of other feminine icons in the Mexican and Chicano community, such as La Virgen de Guadalupe, La Llorona, and perhaps most of all, the mother/betrayer La Malinche.

Second, the contemporary cult of Santa Muerte is not confined by region but has spread rapidly throughout Mexico—and, increasingly, Central America and the United States, especially in areas with large Mexican migrant populations such as Los Angeles, Chicago, Houston, Tucson, and New York City.[4] According to the *Los Angeles Times*, there are no fewer than three storefront shrines dedicated to Santa Muerte in Los Angeles, including the Templo Santa Muerte on Melrose Avenue, which offers "the full range of Catholic-like sacraments and services," including weddings, baptisms, and monthly rosaries as well as classes "derived from New Age beliefs, magic, and parapsychology" (Leovy n.p.; Chesnut 89). Journalist Gil Olmos further asserts that the growth of the cult no longer depends exclusively upon paths of migration because of the presence of Santa Muerte images, media, and churches on the Internet (102). As Gil Olmos puts it, the Internet has spurred the rapid transformation of the death cult from a clandestine practice to one that is open and readily available to anyone with access to a computer: "thanks to the internet, Death has gone from being an image hidden in obscurity on a [prayer] card to an image that is reproduced a thousand million times in cyberspace" (102).

Chesnut notes that the sale of Santa Muerte paraphernalia "sustains thousands of esoterica shops and market stalls" in both Mexico and the United States; the availability of such merchandise online further renders the death cult a borderless, transnational phenomenon (143). Online, devotees can freely access and purchase Santa Muerte images, merchandise, and prayers. They are even able to participate in public devotion online through chat threads or live-streaming webcasts featuring preachers and prayer groups.[5]

While there are competing claims on Santa Muerte within all of these spaces and temporalities, most sources link the contemporary cult to Santa Muerte most strongly to Mexico City, especially to the *barrio bravo* of Tepito, where several competing shrines and churches are located. One of these is Doña Queta's altar on Alfarería Street, which many critics, artists, and journalists identify as the beating heart of the death cult. Chesnut asserts that Doña Queta, an "unassuming quesadilla vendor," singlehandedly ended "the long period of furtive devotion" to Santa Muerte when she brought her skeleton saint "out of the closet" to the street (37). She claims to have venerated the death saint since 1964, but Doña Queta asserts that the shrine was born on September 7, 2001, when one of her sons gave her the life-sized statue of the saint.[6] Doña Queta's altar, which consists of a large glass case containing a life-sized figure of Santa Muerte, which she dresses in extravagant gowns, wigs, jewelry, and tiaras and arranges with color-coordinated displays, is certainly the most publicized shrine to the death saint. The main feast day at the altar on Alfarería is Halloween, when at midnight thousands of people arrive to pray and pay tribute to Santa Muerte. Doña Queta insists that her shrine is popular simply because she provides people with a necessary public space in which to openly express their faith in Santa Muerte (Gil Olmos 76; Hernández, *Down* 76).

Many recent cultural and media representations of the death cult feature the shrine on Alfarería prominently in their analysis, including Aridjis's film *La Santa Muerte*, Chesnut's *Devoted to Death*, Daniel Hernández's *Down and Delirious in*

Mexico City, Gil Olmos's *La Santa Muerte: La Virgen de los Olvidados*, and David Lida's *First Stop in the New World*. Lida calls the altar "the most important [shrine to La Santa] in Mexico City" (118). Hernández affirms that it is "the most famous Santa Muerte altar in Mexico City" (*Down* 153). Gil Olmos goes further by labeling Doña Queta's altar "El Santuario Nacional de Tepito" (The national sanctuary of Tepito) (75). Chesnut calls it the "most renowned Santa Muerte in the world" and identifies Doña Queta as "a legend in her own right" (41).

Certainly, the fact that the shrine is located in Tepito adds to public curiosity about the cult of Santa Muerte. Known since pre-Columbian times as a center of independent commerce and trade, Tepito is renowned for its plucky self-made denizens who eke out existences in fields ranging from shoemaker to boxer to prostitute. At the same time, the neighborhood is legendary for its lawlessness, poverty, and crime. In his photographic essay *Tepito ¡Bravo el Barrio!* (2007), photojournalist Francisco Mata Rosas chronicles the pride and ingenuity of the Tepiteños and suggests that, far from being a downtrodden, wretched barrio, Tepito is a symbol of the independent, rebellious spirit of Mexico City and by extension, of Mexico itself. Similarly, Daniel Hernández cites Santa Muerte's role in situating Mexico City as a synecdoche for Mexico: "in Mexico City, where history is an epic parade of death and bloodshed, no religious icon is more rooted in the place's essential identity. A saint of death for the land of death" (*Down* 153).

Nevertheless, while the majority of these sources emphasize that Santa Muerte is not linked primarily to any specific region or any one shrine or church, some of them perhaps inadvertently downplay her peripatetic nature. This is probably because several of the churches and public altars to Santa Muerte in Mexico City and the surrounding Estado de México (including others in Tepito, such as Bishop David Romo's church) have been locked in fierce rivalries or embroiled in corruption and scandals. While Chesnut, Hernández, and Gil Olmos discuss these rivalries in detail in their books and in media reports and blogs, it is clear that Doña Queta's altar is positioned as the ideal public face of the cult of Santa Muerte. Notably, the forthright Doña Queta roundly denies any connection between her altar and the criminal underworld, and like almost everyone else associated with the death saint, she refuses to speak openly about her relation to or conflicts with other Santa Muerte leaders and caretakers. She has also emerged as one of the positive public faces of Tepito, granting many interviews, posing for photographs as in Mata Rosas's book, and being filmed (Mata Rosas 233). Of course, Doña Queta is not the only figure associated with the cult of Santa Muerte that is featured in the media and cultural production. However, her candid personality, her pithy, dry statements, her obvious love for the saint, and perhaps most of all, her insistence that she is just an ordinary devotee like any other, all contribute to her position as a media star. Gil Olmos expresses the dual frustration and admiration common to portrayals of Doña

Queta when he claims, "she is known for two things: her bad attitude and the streak of white in her hairline" (75). For Doña Queta, the fact that her altar is openly visible and easily accessible on the street in the famous, heavily-trafficked barrio of Tepito is enough to cement its popularity with devotees and the media. In comparing her shrine to the less frequently visited one in Hidalgo, Doña Queta asserts "that altar was not on the street, it was not in a neighborhood like Tepito" (Gil Olmos 77). Most important, the public, visible nature of the shrine on Alfarería reinforces the egalitarianism of Santa Muerte. As Doña Queta says, "Santa Muerte belongs to everyone, [there is] no need for priests or churches" (Gil Olmos 79).

The focus on the Alfarería shrine situates the cult to Santa Muerte as simultaneously regional, national, and transnational. The shrine centered in Tepito has helped bring the death saint (and the barrio of Tepito itself) to prominence in national and international media and cultural production. The notoriety of Doña Queta's shrine also reinforces the implicit link between Tepito, Mexico City, and Mexico. Of course, it is difficult to characterize the cult to Santa Muerte as primarily national, because of the marginalized, criminal status of most of her devotees. In reality, the cult is at once a regional, national, and transnational phenomenon in Mexico City, linked equally—but not exclusively—to specific neighborhoods like Tepito, to the consolidation of national identity through local space, and to migration across regional and national lines. For all of the importance of the shrine on Alfarería, the representations of the altar that diminish or simply ignore other altars in Mexico City and beyond provide a less nuanced view of Santa Muerte and her devotees, for they tend to obscure the intrinsic fragmentation, transience, and malleability of her cult.

Transgressive Death

It makes sense to identify her as transnational or stateless, but La Santísima Muerte is more accurately defined through the transgression of all manner of boundaries, whether spatial, temporal, legal, ethical, sexual, racial, or class-based. One of her greatest transgressions is the fact that she is as itinerant, transient, and malleable as her followers. For instance, despite the number of public shrines and churches to Santa Muerte, she is much more commonly worshipped through peripatetic and transient images, relics, shrines, or altars. These altars are often kept in private homes, from which devotees remove images or relics to have them blessed by curanderas or preachers who specialize in giving masses or rosaries in honor of the death saint. Santa Muerte's image is also frequently seen hanging from taxis or microbuses, protecting travelers and drivers alike. Most strikingly, she is worn—and literally inscribed—upon the bodies of her followers in the form of jewelry, amulets, scapulars, and especially, tattoos. The tattoos in particular are most prevalent among criminals and prisoners, but ordinary devotees also adorn their bodies with her image to give thanks for petitions received or as a form of protection. All of these corporeal adornments reinscribe the traditional model of the shrine onto the body, further dissociating it from any fixed geographic location, and reinforce Santa Muerte's role as an itinerant secular saint.

The Catholic Church and the Mexican state attempt to contain the cult to La Santísima Muerte by linking her mobility and malleability to illegality, marginalization, and sinfulness, in terms of both human and divine law, in order to suppress her and her devotees. Nowhere is this mobility and transience more evident than among ambiguous, marginalized, or illegal spaces, like the borderlands or *barrios bravos* like Tepito, and identities, like that of criminals, migrants, or transvestites. The Mexican military and police deny that they target the death saint or her followers, yet they freely admit that they frequently consider Santa Muerte shrines, altars, and tattoos to be evidence in criminal cases. In the past, Santa Muerte has generally flown under the radar for most people in the United States, but this is rapidly changing, especially in cities with large Mexican immigrant populations like Los Angeles. The Mexican government's destruction of dozens of statues of the death saint in Nuevo Laredo, Tamaulipas, just across the border from Laredo, Texas, in 2009 certainly reflects the anxiety surrounding the internationalization of Santa Muerte. While the destruction of the shrines was officially attributed to Santa Muerte's link to the drug wars, the statues were clearly threatening because of their association with marginalized or transgressive people in general, and especially in such close proximity to the United States.

Certainly, some of the press surrounding Santa Muerte's association with *narcos* and the drug wars has a basis in fact. At the same time, some of the more salacious stories lend an aura of the fantastic and occult to the random brutality of drug violence along the border.[7] For example, Claudio Lomnitz cites the link between the death cult and border drug cartels, including the famous "narcosatánicos," drug lords who "engaged in human sacrifice and murdered a number of people" in the late 1980s (*Death* 492). In this sense, linking the death saint to the drug wars may provide some sort of rationale for the violence, in the face of its true senselessness and unpredictability.

Whether the statues of Santa Muerte primarily appeal to narcos (as many of the saint's critics charge) or simply to ordinary citizens (as her followers contend), her presence along the U.S.-Mexico border is also threatening because she influences and symbolizes two of the most transgressive, ambivalent identities from the perspective of the Mexican and U.S. states—that of migrants and impoverished barrio residents. Both groups fall outside the parameters of national citizenship and represent a form of refusal of the state. As Lomnitz convincingly argues, the recent spread of the cult of La Santísima Muerte "can be understood as a symptom of Mexico's second secular revolution—the nation's increasingly tenuous relationship to the state—for Death, in this cult, is neither a simple emissary of God nor the representative of the state. She is, from the viewpoint of her devotees . . . an independent agent" (*Death* 491). Gil Olmos reinforces the view that Santa Muerte represents hope for those who are excluded from all other avenues, claiming, "every day people request things [from her] that neither the state nor the government grant them, despite the fact that in many cases, these things are constitutional rights" (143). The transgressive, frequently mobile subjects that worship Santa Muerte are "independent agents" as well, though it is important to remember that they are often not so by choice. Rather, La Santísima Muerte's devotees are routinely marginalized and criminalized, whether or not they are actually criminals. In many cases, they are denied basic human and civil rights such as safety, health care, food, housing, work, and citizenship. Yet the saint's followers also signal the obsolescence of institutions like the Catholic Church and the Mexican state for the poor and the marginalized, for they worship, establish social services, and develop alternative communities in ways that either rearticulate state and civil society or reject them entirely.

Fear of the Naco

Officially, criticism of Santa Muerte and her followers is almost always limited either to official theological objections or to accusations of criminal activity. Naturally, the Catholic Church rejects any saint figure it does not sanction, and the news media, particularly through the infamous *nota roja* (crime news), is especially attracted to tales of sensational, illicit activity. The attention and criticism directed at Santa Muerte through cultural production, journalism, religious institutions, or the state, however, exceeds any formulation of human or divine law. The most important reason for much of the criticism of the death saint and her devotees is the pervasive prejudice and racism against the lower classes and anyone perceived to be dark-skinned or "Indian." Predictably, this prejudice is often—though not always—unspoken. The inherent mobility and liminality of these groups is particularly threatening. In the United States, such prejudice usually indicates fear of the perceived illegal alien, who is often defined reductively through racial, linguistic, or social constructions. In many cases, the racial profiling directed against undocumented migrants is further obscured, to emphasize dress or hairstyle as a substitute for or supplement to skin color or linguistic difference, as in the case of Arizona Senate Bill 1070.[8]

Meanwhile, in Mexico, such prejudice denotes fear of the *naco*, a slang term with multiple connotations that is typically derisive and generally used to denote all that is tacky, low-class, vulgar, uncultured, dark-skinned, or indigenous-looking. Carlos Monsiváis, who has written extensively about the naco, contends that the word stems from *totonaco* and argues that it is the quintessential Mexican insult (*Mexican* 51).[9] According to Monsiváis, *naco* denotes "undisguisable Indian roots and blood." The term is usually applied to the lower classes, but it also goes beyond socioeconomic status to refer to those who are "without education or manners, ugly and insolent, graceless and unattractive, irredeemable, complex-ridden, resentful, vulgar, mustachioed and shocking" (*Mexican* 53). In this sense, *naco* "violently allud[es] to the most marginalized of the nation" (*Mexican* 51). Essayist Rafael Toriz suggests that the most frightening aspect of the naco for middle- and upper-middle-class Mexicans is its very ordinariness and universality. He argues, "Currently, we are all susceptible to being nacos, or, in other words, anyone can act like a naco [*naquear*] from time to time" (n.p.), that is, given the right context, any one of us could be a naco, for it is the Other that potentially resides within everyone.

Perhaps because of rather than despite this uncomfortable proximity, in certain circles in Mexico the concept of naco has also been reclaimed as a marker of pride and "cultural self-fashioning," with "all of its class and racial connotations" (Kun 207). The celebration of naco culture is also evident in the representation of the barrio bravo of Tepito and its residents, as symbols of Mexican independence, ingenuity, and authenticity.[10] Not everyone agrees that "naco is beautiful," for the concept still has the power to wound, revealing the pervasive racism and classism of Mexican society (Monsiváis, *Mexican* 55). The correlation between indigenousness and ignorance involved in the word *naco* is especially insidious, since it is frequently obscured by the more benign, humorous connotations of the term, like the naco's supposed love of plastic furniture covers, or socks worn with sandals. In the same way, the accusations on the part of many middle- or upper-class Mexicans and others that La Santísima Muerte and her devotees are satanic or criminal conceals their true disdain for the impoverished, transient, migrant, indigenous, and naco masses who worship the death saint.

The comments on YouTube and similar websites must be taken with a grain of salt, especially since the faux anonymity and performativity of social media, particularly conveyed through pseudonyms or avatars, promote antagonism and lowered inhibitions. Nevertheless, a quick perusal of user comments for videos and images of the cult of Santa Muerte reveals extreme prejudice and racism directed toward the lower classes and indigenous people. In the YouTube comments for the regional Sonoran series *Relatos de Ultratumba*, which features the cult of Santa Muerte in an episode from 2010, a representative user opines, "Damn fucked-up people [*Pinche gente jodida*] who live in my great nation praising stupid beliefs for Indians and ignorant people. The country will never get out of our fucked-up condition as long these beliefs that only cause mental retardation exist. Poor country, in truth, poor country."[11] While the commenter, who is presumably Mexican, laments that there are so many "fucked-up people" praising "stupid beliefs for Indians and ignorant people," it is significant that he or she also cites "my great nation" and "our fucked-up condition," effectively implicating and associating his or her self with the very people being condemned. Indeed, as Monsiváis argues, the revulsion toward the naco stems from the fact that cosmopolitan Mexicans view them with terror—as their own mirror image and as a "confirmation of the inferiority of a lesser country" (*Mexican* 53). The vitriol that many cosmopolitan Mexicans feel toward people like the followers of Santa Muerte reflects a perceived personal and national assault, for in the eyes of the middle and upper classes, the "naco" devotees of the death saint, like Octavio Paz's pachuco, could easily be confused with their own image. It follows that middle- and upper-class Mexicans and others would conceal their objections to Santa Muerte under the cloak of morality, ethics, or illegality in order to maintain their occasionally tenuous sense of self and national pride.

Indeed, the discrimination and racism directed at the followers of La Santísima Muerte by cosmopolitan Mexicans and others is rarely acknowledged, even in many scholarly or critical representations of the death cult. Instead, devotees and detractors alike reiterate the doctrine of church and state when describing criticism of the cult, affirming that Santa Muerte is not a true saint, that worship of the death saint is tantamount to devil worship, or that her followers are all criminals or narcos. For example, Enriqueta Romero (Doña Queta), owner and caretaker of the shrine on Alfarería Street in Tepito, provides typical testimony in Eva Aridjis's film: "If people say this is Satanic, and that I'm a devil worshipper, and lots of nasty things, you know? And even the press, the newspapers . . . say a lot of things, like that we're Satanic, that we're devil worshippers. . . . Well, I say time will tell, and they'll eat their words, right?" Similarly, Jesse Ortiz Peña, who gives masses and hands out rosaries to La Santa at the shrine on Alfarería, says: "Lots of people have believed in Saint Death for many years. . . . But you couldn't wear an image of Saint Death before, because if people saw it . . . they would consider you a Satanist. . . . That you're a Satanist, that you're a sorcerer, that you're a witch. So you would hide your Saint Death. But not anymore. Now you can wear it more freely." Doña Queta and Ortiz Peña proudly flaunt their faith in the death saint and lay claim upon public space and open worship. However, neither of them mentions the possibility that the mass media, the church, the upper classes, or anyone else might reject them because of their marginalized status as impoverished, indigenous, migrant, lawless, or naco. Doña Queta and Ortiz Peña clearly reject the official doctrine of church and state, and by reiterating such discourse they also implicitly reinforce the dominant attitudes toward Santa Muerte and her devotees that reject them precisely because they are marginalized. The devotees of Santa Muerte are ultimately most threatening because they are marginalized and coded as illegal, not because they worship an illegitimate or implicitly illegal secular saint.

Cultural Representations of Santa Muerte

Virtually all of the cultural texts and media reports that discuss La Santísima Muerte agree that the death saint and her devotees are ambiguous and controversial. Santa Muerte's many contradictions continue to elude definition, even for critical or scholarly texts that attempt to chronicle the cultural milieu and historical, social, or geographical significance of the death cult. These sources differ greatly in their representation of Santa Muerte's contradictions, especially in relation to her position as a saint both good and evil and simultaneously fair and arbitrary.

Some texts, like the novella *La Santa Muerte* by writer, diplomat, and environmental activist Homero Aridjis, hew closely to the more sensationalist representation of the death saint as a link between the occult and violent crime. The novella focuses on a journalist, Miguel Medina, whose beat is narcos and the drug wars, and his terrifying experience as a guest at the twenty-four-hour bacchanalian birthday party of a prominent drug lord. During the party, which is attended not only by narcos but by politicians, actors, and even Catholic bishops and priests, Medina witnesses a human sacrifice in which one of the guests is killed at the drug lord's Santa Muerte home altar. As Medina puts it, "Santa Muerte is the image of violent death . . . [with] three attributes: violent power, cunning aggression, and cruel murder" (Homero Aridjis 125, 127). Interestingly, Chesnut cites a personal interview with Homero Aridjis where the author claims that the novella "is a fictionalized account of events that he witnessed at a Saint Death birthday bash" (Chesnut 157).

Whether this salacious story is true or not, it supports the dominant media portrayal of Santa Muerte as an occult figure tied to the criminal underworld. In fact, Homero Aridjis's representation of the death saint, with its emphasis on satanic ritual and human sacrifice, resembles the sensationalist stories about the "narcosatánicos." The novella is roundly condemned by devotees, who "object to [Aridjis's] portrayal of the Bony Lady as a satanic sorceress" (Chesnut 157). Yet his text is most significant for its representation of both the corruption of the upper-middle and upper classes, evidenced by the coming together of Catholic clergy, politicians, actors, and law enforcement officers at the drug lord's party, and the implicit threat posed to civil society by the figure of Santa Muerte. This threat is especially reflected through the tenuous nature of freedom of speech in the Mexican media and the perils that journalists face as they attempt to report on the drug wars. Despite the attention to the ambivalence behind the corruption of the Mexican state and civil society, Aridjis's novella portrays a very one-sided version of a dark, threatening Santa Muerte.

Conversely, other sources, like Eva Aridjis's film *La Santa Muerte*, provide a more balanced perspective on the lives of ordinary people who worship the death saint.[12] At the same time, many of the texts that question or challenge the typical image of Santa Muerte as the patron of criminals or as a symbol of Satanism tend to elide the unmistakable allure of the death saint's dark side. As such, these sources elide Santa Muerte's contradictory nature and implicitly, if unintentionally, reinforce the idea that the death saint's transgressivity is essentially threatening. For many of Santa Muerte's devotees, her dark side is what draws her to them; indeed, her threatening nature is extremely compelling to even her most ordinary followers.

La Santa Muerte (Saint Death)

Eva Aridjis's documentary film *La Santa Muerte* accurately reflects the contradictions of the death cult, which encompass faith, rage, peace, uneasiness, fear, and hope. While the film portrays the cult much more analytically than the frequently condemnatory or salacious reports in the mass media, it also downplays the power for evil that attracts so many of Santa Muerte's devotees. The film portrays Tepito and the lives and stories of several devotees in a positive light, following Aridjis's claim that her film work focuses on the theme of the misfit, with "characters [who] are always in . . . their own world, people living on the edge of society, kind of outcasts or misfits" (Johnson n.p.). However, *La Santa Muerte* scarcely addresses the critics of the saint or of the "misfits" who worship her— arguably, those who help categorize these devotees as misfits in the first place. The only opponent featured in the film is a Catholic priest who condescendingly and predictably claims, "It is interesting to see the warmth that people feel for Saint Death, and the tenderness with which they speak of her. If it was another [sort of] devotion, it would be edifying. . . . Meaning it is good people, who are searching for God. . . . I don't think they do it conscious of the fact that it is the Devil whom they are worshipping." Apart from this standard theological objection to Santa Muerte, Aridjis' film deals with the cult's ambiguous and fearsome dark side in a very limited fashion. This may be due to Aridjis's zeal to amend the many negative portrayals of the death saint and her devotees, especially those that link them to the drug trade. But for the majority of devotees, Santa Muerte's dark side is not exclusively or even primarily linked to the criminal underworld or the drug wars. Instead, it manifests itself through the death saint's purported jealousy and the price she supposedly exacts from believers who dare to use her powers recklessly or who fail to pay her proper tribute.

The few examples of the death saint's dark side in the film are subtle. Certainly, Aridjis is justly concerned with correcting the negative representations of Santa Muerte that dominate media reports and inflect the attitudes of the Catholic Church and the Mexican and local governments toward the saint and her devotees. In a segment that discusses the cult of Santa Muerte in the prisons of Mexico City, most of the inmates interviewed in the film claim that they pray to the death saint for protection from harm, for the care of their families, or for their freedom. In fact, the majority of the people Aridjis interviews in the film, including those who clearly live on the margins of society like the prison inmates and transvestite prostitutes, are distinguished by their ordinary concerns, such as the desire for lost lovers, for a reunion with a beloved mother, or for money and employment to provide for their families. And devotion to Santa Muerte is by no means limited to the inmate population. Aridjis interviews an official at the Mexico City Penitentiary who asserts that Santa Muerte is the patron of the entire penal system, encompassing prisoners, guards, lawyers, psychologists, clerks, and all of their families, thus demonstrating that worship of the death saint transcends illegality and extends to diverse segments of society. The prisons provide a much more tolerant, inclusive space for worship than many other state or civil institutions. Aridjis interviews a social worker employed at the Centro Femenil de Readaptación Social (Women's Social Readaptation Center) who, quite unlike the Catholic priest who condemns the worship of Santa Muerte, professes acceptance and respect for the prisoners' beliefs, saying, "We have great respect for this religious diversity . . . and we try to give them the space and the freedom within which to manifest it. There are no restrictions here."

Aridjis deftly portrays the nuances of Santa Muerte's criminal devotees, featuring several who are artists (both tattoo artists and visual artists) and poets who are inspired by and dedicate their work to the death saint. As always, these artists' uses of Santa Muerte are contradictory. One artist shows Aridjis an unfinished sketch titled "With her tears I pay for my sins." The poem that accompanies the sketch cites indigenous gods like Tonatiuh (the Aztec sun god) alongside the death saint, demonstrating the syncretic religious beliefs that many historians emphasize in their discussions of the cult of Santa Muerte. The poet also affirms: "The penitentiary is my university, it's the place where I received my education, and learned how to survive within the demented." This powerful statement reinscribes Santa Muerte not only as a protector or guide to navigate the treacherous world of the penitentiary but also as a teacher for those (like most of the inmates portrayed) who lack the opportunity to receive a traditional education.

At the same time, many inmates and Tepito residents portrayed by Aridjis subtly reveal uncomfortable, unpleasant, or potentially threatening emotions or actions that relate to different forms of illegality. Aridjis meets with Tepito resident Ernestina Ramírez Hernández's daughter, an inmate at the Women's Social Readaptation Center, who equivocates and nervously covers her mouth with her hands when the filmmaker asks her how she landed in jail: "For pickpocketing. Well, for robbery. Of a . . . they say I stole a wallet . . . 1,700 pesos. But I didn't do it. On Tuesday when I had my hearing, the guy kept on contradicting himself . . . him and the police. My lawyer said I'll probably beat them." When Aridjis asks her about her devotion to Saint Death, the woman animatedly describes her daily prayers and her desire for her freedom. Whether or not the woman is guilty of committing the petty theft, what is certain is that both her criminal activity and her devotion to Santa Muerte are transgressive.

While Ernestina Ramírez's daughter vacillates about her criminal past, probably in order to support her claim for her release, another woman that Aridjis speaks to is more upfront about her transgressive life. This woman, who paints murals and other images of Santa Muerte for her fellow inmates, openly situates the death saint as both an economic succor and a guardian for her drug habit. She asserts, "a lot of people have asked me to paint her for them. And from that I get some money for food . . . and to buy myself whatever I want. . . . And it's like she's my friend, because . . . when I get high, she holds my hand. She's right by my side. Because what if I overdose and die? She's there with me." It is fascinating that this woman seems to expect neither judgment for nor deliverance from her drug habit. Instead, she considers Santa Muerte a friend who will not only protect her from overdosing but will stay by her side as she gets high, perhaps implicitly participating in her illicit journey. Such a friend is certainly threatening to mainstream society and reflects the illegality that is so appealing to many of the death saint's marginalized devotees.

Only one prisoner interviewed in the film openly acknowledges that many people use Santa Muerte to harm others but then quickly affirms that she is in fact "kind . . . good and generous," while asserting "sometimes the bad one is oneself." Although the film does not elaborate upon this point, the inmate implies that the believers' own capacity for good or evil—that is, their own free will—directs the death saint. The only other detailed description of the use of Santa Muerte to harm others is the testimony of devotee Ernestina Ramírez Hernández, who describes her son's violent death on the streets of Tepito and her pleas to the death saint for retribution. Ramírez, who claims that her son never did drugs and was killed because he refused to join a gang or to "be like the other guys from here," prays to Santa Muerte in a reversal of Jesus' proverb "turn the other cheek": "You know that a tooth for a tooth and an eye for an eye . . . and those who do bad things receive bad things. So I place them in your hands. And that's what happened to them." Of one gangbanger in particular, Ramírez asks, "O Saint Death, I know that guy was involved. Mark him. How are you going to punish him? Don't let him die, but leave him so he's useless." The bereaved mother proudly asserts that her prayers have been answered. Whether her narrative of an innocent, upstanding son is accurate or not, it steers clear of the threatening possibility that the gangbangers who killed her son might have been followers of Santa Muerte as well or that he might have been involved with them in some way. In an inversion of the negative perspective typically held by many cosmopolitan Mexicans and the Catholic Church, Aridjis's film presents an optimistic, perhaps occasionally one-sided portrayal of Santa Muerte and her followers.

Ernestina Ramírez's example of the use of Santa Muerte for "bad things" is fundamentally ambiguous, for her prayers seek retribution and justice in an area where most residents completely lack legal, economic, or social justice. In other words, Santa Muerte might be the only hope for justice that these people have. The marginalized misfits featured in Aridjis's film allude to their social status in oblique, matter-of-fact terms, as when Ernestina Ramírez affirms that her dead son refused to join a gang or do drugs like all the other guys from Tepito simply because he lived there, or when Doña Queta's son (Omar Romero Romero, named only in the film credits) casually discusses his multiple brushes with death. Looking like a typical gangbanger, with a shaved head, heavily tattooed muscular arms, and a wife-beater t-shirt, Romero Romero asserts that Santa Muerte has saved his life at least three times. He claims, "Well at times when I've been unwell. About to . . . die. It's only been a few times, like two or three times. . . . The police beat me up and . . . I was dying. My mother was already going to bring a priest. The liquid was going into my brain. My skull was split open. And . . . that's when I pray to her. Because . . . I'm not going to ask her for things all the time." The matter-of-fact attitude he adopts toward his near death experiences is both chilling and logical given his dangerous environment and his possible involvement in the criminal underworld. Romero Romero's reluctance to call upon Santa Muerte arbitrarily, instead only appealing to her in truly life or death situations, reflects a code of justice and retribution that rewards those who know when and how to best summon the death saint. Since death surrounds so many of the residents of Tepito, they must be sparing in employing their pleas to Santa Muerte.

Doña Queta herself alludes to the economic privation most Tepito residents contend with when she intimates that her public altar to Santa Muerte is something of an extension of her home. When describing her decision to bring her large Santa Muerte statue out to build a street altar, Doña Queta tells Aridjis, "And since I live in a very small room, you've seen the room where I live. . . . My bed is there, but there's really not much space." For Doña Queta, the public shrine extends her private space not only because of her dedication to the death saint or her position of leadership among the community of the faithful but because her living quarters consist of just one tiny room. Rather than inhabit a subordinate role, the devotees featured in *La Santa Muerte* exhibit pride as they articulate their own narratives of equality and resourcefulness through Santa Muerte, even as they sometimes give lip service to established hierarchies such as those decreed by the Catholic Church. Much of this narrative of equality celebrates the totally democratic nature of the death saint, for many of the faithful interviewed in the film reiterate that Santa Muerte does not discriminate: she will eventually take everyone, no matter how much money they have or how dark or light their skin is, or whether they are citizens or migrants, straight or gay, good or bad, young or old.

Thus, the cult of Santa Muerte articulates equality for marginalized groups of people and spaces that fundamentally lack it. Several of the devotees in the film invoke the power of the death saint through street or home altars, amulets, jewelry, or tattoos as a kind of neighborhood watch to protect them in Tepito, where the police often refuse to tread. Many of the devotees that Aridjis interviews, including Doña Queta and Jesse Ortiz Peña, claim that Santa Muerte has protected them from danger in the neighborhood. Doña Queta asserts that the death saint protected her when she was on her way to see her critically injured son Omar late at night with a group of women friends, by covering them "with her holy shroud" so that a group of muggers would not see them. Meanwhile, Ortiz discusses an encounter with thieves and kidnappers that was defused when he informed them that he gives masses to Santa Muerte. The film also demonstrates that worship of the death saint produces much more routine, permanent benefits, such as the establishment of public social space for the inhabitants of Tepito. Thus Doña Queta's street altar expands the available safe space in which to live, pray, work, and socialize for all of Santa Muerte's devotees. The death cult in prisons or around shrines like the one on Alfarería—with its attendant preachers, dressmakers, caretakers, and especially, the congregation that attends the monthly masses—serves as confessor, social worker, therapist, friend, and family for the faithful. Furthermore, Santa Muerte is intrinsically egalitarian because devotees need only their faith to participate in her cult, not money or status. In the film and elsewhere, Doña Queta emphasizes this point, as when she proudly tells journalist Gil Olmos about a woman who takes solace in purchasing a basic candle from her store, rather than buying more expensive Santa Muerte candles sold elsewhere. Doña Queta tells the woman, "they are cheating you with the prepared candles, the important thing is your faith," thus reinforcing the accessibility of the saint and bypassing her own margin of profit (79). Doña Queta's assertion supports the equalizing power of the death saint, but it is important to recall that she is also an entrepreneur, with a shop run by her husband, Ray, that "does a brisk business in a wide array of Santa Muerte paraphernalia" (Chesnut 41). As Chesnut puts it, "between profits from the store and generous donations made by believers at the shrine, the skeleton saint has blessed her preeminent devotee with a much better income than she had as a quesadilla vendor" (41). Yet even if Doña Queta's socioeconomic status has risen significantly compared to many of her fellow devotees in Tepito, she nevertheless draws upon the narrative of equality associated with Santa Muerte to establish civil, social, and religious rights that the saint's devotees often lack due to their socioeconomic or racial status.

It is important to note that Santa Muerte's devotees do not depict her egalitarianism as an abject narrative of deferral, following the maxim that the poor will inherit the earth. Instead, as Doña Queta demonstrates in Aridjis's film, the devotees invoke the death saint in order to assert a place in a society that deeply marginalizes them, and to rearticulate the hierarchical, frequently closed structures of religious discourse and cultural capital. In a scene directly after the interview with the priest, Doña Queta argues: "Unless I am ignorant, there is only one Death and only one God. And the Death that is going to take me is going to take everyone. And the God that people believe in . . . is the same God that I pray to. So I pray to the same God as the Church. . . . And when those people are finished on this earth, well I would like to know: Who's going to take them away? . . . Well the Skinny Girl! She's the only one." Similarly, during one of his masses in honor of Santa Muerte, Ortiz Peña encourages the first-time congregants, saying, "As you can see, [the cult] is not diabolic, it is not Satanic. I am glad you decided to break the barrier . . . of ignorance." Significantly, both of these examples reverse the terms of ignorance in a society that usually accuses Santa Muerte's devotees of ignorance. Here, Doña Queta and Ortiz claim ownership over God, saints, altars, prayer, and the ritual of the mass, as much if not more than the Catholic Church does, emphasizing that the truly ignorant are those who do not believe in Santa Muerte's power. Recalling that cosmopolitan Mexicans fear the naco especially because of the possibility that it could reside within them, Doña Queta and Ortiz demonstrate that Santa Muerte's critics cannot admit that they are equal to the marginalized residents of Tepito on at least one level, for they will all die eventually.

Relatos de Ultratumba
(Stories from Beyond the Grave)

The Sonoran television series *Relatos de Ultratumba* is an example of the long tradition in Mexico, the borderlands, and among Latino communities in the United States of newspapers, magazines, films, television programs, websites, and other cultural paraphernalia devoted to spiritual or supernatural beliefs. *Relatos* focuses on all aspects of the supernatural and occult and is decidedly lurid, with a melodramatic narrator, spooky background music, candles, and theatrical reenactment scenes. The series is part of a new generation of internet programming that allows a regional program based in Guaymas, Sonora, to reach a wider audience through a YouTube channel and a separate website, complete with member groups, chat room, and solicitations for member stories to include in future episodes, making it a truly interactive experience in line with contemporary social media and fan-based marketing and distribution (*Relatos*). On the YouTube channel, the series is described as "a program [about] Paranormal investigations and Enigmatic Places [that attempts] to provide a touch of Reality to its dispatches." Besides the cult of La Santísima Muerte, *Relatos* has featured such personalities as María Matuz, "the most powerful curandera in Mexico"; and El Padre Jeringas (Father Héctor Orozco), a contemporary "living saint" and miracle worker from Culiacán, Sinaloa, who is said to have the ability to appear in two places at the same time. However, despite its sensationalism, *Relatos* seems much more comfortable with the ambivalent nature of Santa Muerte and her devotees than Aridjis's highbrow documentary film is. Rather than drawing a strict distinction between the death saint's dark and light side or between ordinary believers and criminals, the television program emphasizes that devotees frequently use her for good and evil simultaneously.

As in Aridjis's film, the devotees in *Relatos* who follow Santa Muerte agree that she is the great leveler. One curandera, Señora Bárbara, states, "Death is the only truth of humankind," while another, Señora Viky, asserts, "She doesn't discriminate about who she takes—whether they are poor, rich, children, old people. She takes all equally." From the beginning of the episode, the narrator Juan Pablo Pantoja Vela accepts the death saint's duality, citing her reputation for being jealous and vengeful as well as miraculous and giving. When Pantoja interviews botánica vendors, curanderas, and devotees in several cities in Sonora about their impressions of and experiences with Santa Muerte, he never shies away from addressing the death saint's relationship to evil and darkness. Unlike most of those who focus on the death saint's dark side, however, Pantoja does not situate it primarily in relation to Satanism or to criminals but, rather, as a fact of life for ordinary people. Several vendors discuss the meanings of different colored candles and statues of Santa Muerte and debate the ways that the saint is used for good or ill. As one claims, "Well, in the book it does not say that she should be used for ill purposes, but many people also use her to do harm. The Saint Death [dressed in black] is supposedly used for evil purposes." Others affirm that she is miraculous and generous, but only when paid her proper due: "Often [people say] that yes, [she has performed miracles], but that she asks a price." Santa Muerte's care and concern for her followers comes at a steep price, for if she is ignored or not paid proper tribute, or if her devotees carelessly terminate their relation with her, she will take revenge. In a sense, vengeance is built into the cult of Santa Muerte, even when she is used for good or holy purposes. This vengeance may take the form of ominous spectral appearances or broken furniture or household appliances, or worst of all, of illness or death inflicted upon oneself or one's family and friends. But the devotees featured in the television program agree that the devotion to Santa Muerte is serious business, and her altars and images must be cared for diligently and responsibly. The narrator concludes that "You cannot lie to Saint Death," confirming her reputation as a jealous patron and suggesting that she is much more than the benevolent miracle worker that she is often portrayed as in Aridjis's film.

Most fascinating of all, *Relatos de Ultratumba* emphasizes that, while the death saint is fundamentally just, life and death are nevertheless essentially arbitrary. The television program frequently underscores that those who invoke Santa Muerte are responsible for their own actions and beliefs, ultimately guiding the saint toward good or bad. This sentiment echoes the idea expressed by the inmate in the film *La Santa Muerte* who declares, "sometimes the bad one is oneself." In *Relatos*, the fundamental duality and ambiguity of the death saint is a central theme, evident in the testimonies of everyone interviewed. The people featured in the program reinforce that whether Santa Muerte is good or evil has nothing to do with either devil worship or her dangerous association with the drug trade, or with positive attributes such as community building or the establishment of alternative social services. Instead, the death saint simply reflects ordinary people's capacity for both good and evil, as the curandera Señora Viky argues: "The truth is that Santa Muerte is whatever you want her to be, however you use her." The curandera Señora Bárbara lays the responsibility for the cult of Santa Muerte even more squarely on the shoulders of believers, asserting, "Is Santa Muerte good or bad? . . . [she is] according to the person who uses her. . . . In this sense there are not good things [or] bad things. You make them good, you make them bad." That is, Santa Muerte and her cult are neither good nor bad as many, whether critics or supporters, would have it. Instead, as Señora Bárbara argues, people merely reap what they sow: "it is not the girl who [comes to] collect from you, it is you, your actions." As well as suggesting that the faithful direct the death saint, Señora Bárbara implies that her association with vengeance and justice comes from within the hearts of devotees themselves.

In a sense, the curanderas interviewed in *Relatos* suggest that people can explicitly unite with or direct the divine through their use of La Santísima Muerte. This possibility is simultaneously cathartic and menacing, for it demonstrates that ordinary devotees have the power to control the death cult with their own actions, intentions, and beliefs—implicitly breaking down the barrier between human and divine—while it also reveals the banality of both good and evil, insofar as both conditions depend upon the actions and beliefs of ordinary, fallible people. At the same time, many of the people interviewed by Pantoja Vela emphasize that the death saint's primary purpose is to assign justice in the name of both good and evil. For example, Señora Viky testifies, "If she sees that the person who wishes to do harm is justified, she will grant it. But if they simply want to [do harm] just for fun or to malign the person, she will not grant it. . . . If [you use] Saint Death to inflict harm on a person that hasn't done anything to you . . . [she] will return the harm to you . . . without harming [the other person]." According to these women, the death saint's manifestation of good and bad is basically fair and rewards those whose intentions are justified. In this case, Santa Muerte, not her devotees, is the final arbiter, but those who believe in her place complete trust in her judgment.

Even if Santa Muerte's followers believe that their own actions and intentions are subject to a standard of justice in which the saint fairly and systematically distributes punishment and reward, in the final instance devotees pray to her in the hopes of mitigating the capriciousness of life and death, not to change the terms of such essential human conditions. The death saint's devotees promise to worship and respect her so that she might accompany them while they are on this earth, but they understand she cannot allow them to escape death. As anyone can attest, the actual experience of justice and retribution, illness and health, poverty and wealth—and especially, of life and death itself—is necessarily arbitrary (at least to some extent). In the end, La Santísima Muerte straddles the boundary between justice and randomness in life and death, allowing the faithful to reconcile the contradictions that arise in their own lives from the frequent gap between actions and results or cause and effect. *Relatos de Ultratumba* reveals that the saint's true power lies neither in her reputation as a saint who is very reliable in her ability to produce miracles for the devoted nor in her link to threatening illegality but, rather, in her intrinsic duality and ambiguity—in that she really is whatever you want her to be, whether good or evil.

Possessing La Santísima Muerte

Recently, several high-profile stories of public disputes, scandals, and crimes concerning the cult of La Santísima Muerte have made headlines in Mexico and even, to some extent, in the United States. Among other things, these stories involve alleged kidnapping, money laundering, and murder; yet they are not about drug lords or the other criminals who supposedly form Santa Muerte's base, nor do they focus on the hopes and fears of ordinary devotees. Instead, these stories reflect the bitter rivalries and corruption that accompany the rise of competing churches, spiritual leaders, priests, or bishops within the cult of Santa Muerte. One name that comes up repeatedly is that of David Romo, a self-proclaimed bishop and the founder and former leader of a prominent sanctuary dedicated to Santa Muerte based in the Colonia Morelos in Tepito (Hernández, "La Plaza blog: Rival"). Romo's church, its status, and even the image of its devotion have gone through many changes since he established himself as leader in 1997 (Gil Olmos 87–88).[13] Most recently, the church has been known as the National Sanctuary for the Angel of the Holy Death, where Romo has installed an icon he calls the Ángel de la Muerte (Angel of the holy death), a woman with light skin and long red hair who looks nothing like the traditional skeletal representation of Santa Muerte.[14] While Romo has always been a controversial figure, this particular move has angered and turned many of the faithful against him. His many critics accuse him of pure self-interest, alleging that Romo abandoned Santa Muerte because of her supposed link to human sacrifice and murder among drug lords in Tamaulipas and especially, because the Mexican government stripped his church of recognition as a religion in 2005 and he wanted to regain its official status under a new icon (Gil Olmos 89–90). Romo

has been embroiled in public disputes with other leaders or caretakers of differ-
ent Santa Muerte churches or shrines, especially Jonathan Legaria, also known as
El Pantera (the Panther) or El Padrino (the Godfather), and Enriqueta Romero
(Hernández, "La Plaza blog: Rival"; Gil Olmos 139).

In many ways, Romo and his church are the polar opposite of the media-
friendly shrine on Alfarería and the candid, soundbite-worthy Doña Queta. In
fact, writers, artists, filmmakers, and other media outlets favor Romero and her
altar as the ideal public face of the cult of Santa Muerte, sometimes to the exclusion of other churches or clusters of devotees. Insofar as nonbelievers and outsiders have heard of Santa Muerte, it is frequently through the conduits of Doña
Queta and the shrine on Alfarería. In contrast, David Romo and his church are not
very well-known outside of Mexico City and its environs, though he has attracted
some attention in the United States in some media outlets like Hernández's "La
Plaza" blog in the *Los Angeles Times.* Yet Romo is a tabloid fixture in Mexico City
who is skilled at appealing to the news media and promoting his church. His public denunciation of other local Santa Muerte churches and his ostentatious plan
to build the "first worldwide temple" dedicated to Santa Muerte, a cathedral on
par with the Basilica of Guadalupe, have gained him notoriety in the capital (Gil
Olmos 129–130).[15] While Doña Queta seems to be the preferred choice for reporters and artists in search of a seemingly benign taste of the death cult and the barrio
bravo of Tepito, Romo is famous for dipping his toes into the very same waters
usually inhabited by Santa Muerte's criminal devotees.

It is no surprise, then, that Romo was arrested in early 2011 and charged with
participating in a kidnapping and money-laundering ring (Hernández, "La
Plaza blog: Rival").[16] Moreover, there are rumors that Romo, who frequently
clashed in the press with "El Pantera" Jonathan Legaria, the leader and "priest"
of a Santa Muerte church in Tultitlán, north of Mexico City, is somehow connected to Legaria's death in July 2008. Legaria, who was shot more than a hundred times by assault weapons in a drive-by shooting, "with all the markings
of a coordinated assassination," presided over what he claimed was the largest
known representation of Santa Muerte in the world: a statue over seventy feet
tall (Hernández, *Down* 148). Some claim that Romo was envious of Legaria's status and his rapidly growing fellowship base (Hernández, "La Plaza blog: Rival";
Gil Olmos 85). The killers have not been caught, for as Daniel Hernández notes,
the "local authorities washed their hands of the investigation . . . handing the
case over to federal authorities in a formality that all but ensured Legaria's killing
would never be solved" ("La Plaza blog: Rival"). Like Romo, Legaria had many
enemies, including the municipal authorities of Tultitlán, who have been fruit-
lessly trying to remove his enormous statue of the death saint, which remains in
place to this day (Gil Olmos 86). However, no other figure associated with the
cult of Santa Muerte has been as much of a lightning rod as Romo.

Much of the criticism of Romo is off the record, and any connection between Romo and Legaria's murder is pure speculation.[17] There are many legitimate reasons to condemn him, but it is curious that most criticism of Romo centers not on his probably very real attempts to profit economically from his devotees (as in the case of the disappearance of the donations for his unrealized cathedral) or even his well-documented link to the kidnapping and money-laundering ring, but on his relationship to Santa Muerte. There is no doubt that Romo is a megalomaniac who has taken advantage of many of his putative parishioners, whether spiritually or economically. But apart from the typical accusations that he is a Satanist or charlatan because of his link to Santa Muerte, Romo is effectively denounced for seeking media attention through the death saint, though he is far from the only person associated with her to do so. In an article in the *Los Angeles Times* about Romo's recent arrest, filmmaker Eva Aridjis argues, "It's these kinds of stories that give Santa Muerte a bad reputation" (Wilkinson n.p.). Aridjis goes on to cite the standard negative association of the death saint with narcos and thieves, claiming, "not everyone who worships her is a criminal," even though as a self-proclaimed—if corrupt—bishop of the church with thousands of supporters who have rallied to his defense, Romo is hardly the typical criminal devotee of Santa Muerte (Wilkinson n.p.). Throughout his book, journalist Gil Olmos quite openly criticizes Romo's megalomania and opportunism, although many of his sources are impossible to corroborate, since they consist of anonymous or second- or thirdhand accounts. For example, the journalist cites a lengthy letter from a "faithful devotee of Santa Muerte who helped Romo in the 'National Sanctuary, or the Parish of Mercy' on 35 Bravo Street," which he claims was delivered to him personally (Gil Olmos 133). The letter is anonymous, yet Gil Olmos transcribes it in its entirety, emphasizing the letter's detailed description of "the funneling of money and the manipulation of the cult that Romo has conducted for his personal gain" (133).[18] Elsewhere, Gil Olmos reveals a possible ulterior motive for his condemnation of Romo when he discusses the complicity of the press with the negative image of Santa Muerte. He cites historian Katia Perdigón, who granted him several interviews for his book and claims that the press purposely portrays Santa Muerte and her devotees in a lurid manner and omits information that might normalize the death cult, like the fact that some notorious criminals such as the serial killer "El Mochaorejas" maintained shrines to the Virgin of Guadalupe alongside well-publicized ones to Santa Muerte (Gil Olmos 125).[19]

Such sensationalist strategies presumably sell tabloids and advertising revenue, but like the stories about David Romo, they also potentially make studies of Santa Muerte look bad by association, like that of Gil Olmos. In this sense, the bad press extends not only to the negative portrayal of Santa Muerte's devotees as marginalized, hopelessly ignorant nacos but also to the artists, writers, and journalists who discuss and represent Santa Muerte. For Romo, however, bad press is clearly better than no press at all. Hernández astutely suggests that Romo is probably most upset about the fact that authorities did not recognize his status as a bishop, as when the prosecuting Attorney General Miguel Ángel Mancera claimed that he initially "had no idea that the señor had anything to do with any church" (Hernández, "La Plaza blog: Rival"). In reality, it seems that the erstwhile bishop is objectionable not only because of his criminal activities but because he is a magnet for media attention to the cult of Santa Muerte. But while some critics, scholars, artists, and devotees condemn Romo for attracting too much negative press to the death cult, others, including some who might have been in direct competition with the fallen bishop—like Jonathan Legaria's mother, Enriqueta Vargas, the current "Madrina" (Godmother) of the sanctuary in Tultitlán—reject him for another reason: the notion that he has assumed the mantle of the death saint for himself (De Marcelo Esquivel and Hernández n.p.).

Enriqueta Vargas's interesting claim that Romo "is not the Santa Muerte, and not the whole church" raises several issues regarding the portrayal of the death saint and her relation to her devotees (De Marcelo Esquivel and Hernández n.p.). First, it demonstrates the prevalence of battles for leadership and media coverage surrounding many of the shrines and sanctuaries dedicated to Santa Muerte. Second, it alludes to the implications of possessing Santa Muerte, and by extension, death. Although many devotees assume different positions of leadership within the death cult, frequently in an informal capacity, the fallen bishop is specifically accused of trying to institutionalize or centralize the church of Santa Muerte, implicitly re-creating the hierarchies of the Catholic Church. The common refrain among his critics is that Romo is a fraud for presuming to be the one true leader of the cult, akin to a pope. For example, the anonymous devotee who wrote the letter published by Gil Olmos accuses Romo of trying to "patent" La Santísima Muerte and of appropriating her image (Gil Olmos 137). Manuel Valadez, an associate of Doña Queta's, asserts that Romo's proposed cathedral would in fact damage the spontaneous relationship between Santa Muerte and the faithful, since the saint "is born out of people's faith . . . they pray to her wherever they are" (Gil Olmos 140). Valadez suggests that the devotees' true problem with Romo's transformation of Santa Muerte into the Angel of the Holy Death is that the fallen bishop presumes to put a human face on the saint: "Who is he to incarnate a spiritual guide? Who told him to dress her like a stripper, to make her light-skinned when she could be dark-skinned, to put a wig of red hair on her?" (Gil Olmos 141). Valadez's comment exemplifies the conflict between many devotees and leaders in the churches of Santa Muerte and the problematic implications of possessing the death saint. He emphasizes that instead of the model of European beauty that dominates in the media and advertising, Santa Muerte "could be dark-skinned," like the majority of her followers. In this sense, Romo's rendering of a fair-skinned, redheaded woman flies in the face of the agency and personal identification that La Santísima Muerte provides her most marginalized devotees.

Universal Death

One of the reasons that the death saint is so compelling to the faithful is that she eliminates the need for hierarchy or authority in spiritual worship, for the connection between the saint and her followers is direct. As Gil Olmos indicates, this direct, immediate connection also extends to the location and mode of worship, since the faithful do not need a specific church or temple to worship Santa Muerte (18, 40).[20] Of course, this situation is not unique, for the direct, transposable connection between Santa Muerte and her followers is true of all saints. Traditionally, saints serve as intermediaries between human and divine worlds, even as they also assume divinity in their own right. Gil Olmos asserts that Santa Muerte is distinct, however, because unlike other secular saints like the Santa de Cabora, Jesús Malverde, or Juan Soldado, she is not a charismatic personality but rather a symbol (153). Unlike almost every other secular saint, Santa Muerte does not manifest in a human form but, rather, as a skeleton, so she subverts the iconographic emphasis on saints' bodies and faces. Santa Muerte is not embodied, and her transferability is possible because of her symbolic nature. It is true that Santa Muerte is different from secular saints like Juan Soldado, who are identifiably human whether they actually existed or not, but she also represents that which makes everyone human and fallible, that is, our inevitable and universalizing death. Rather than diminishing human possibility by representing the end point of life, Santa Muerte's devotees find strength and agency in her malleability, mobility, and transgressivity.

By attributing a particular human face to Santa Muerte, by coding her as lightskinned or European, or by trying to assume her image and power for himself, Romo prevents the saint's devotees from worshipping her however and wherever they see fit, from taking responsibility for their own actions, and especially, from shaping her in whatever image they choose, including their own. Indeed, a great part of the reason Santa Muerte is so important to her followers is the agency and personal responsibility that she inspires in them. Both the curandera Señora Viky in *Relatos de Ultratumba* and Doña Queta highlight this agency and responsibility when discussing the saint: "Santa Muerte is whatever you want her to be, however you use her" and "You don't have to do anything special to pray to Santa Muerte, just what comes from inside of you" (*Relatos*; Gil Olmos 77). Doña Queta suggests that Santa Muerte's universality is empowering, and she claims, "She is inside of you just as she is inside of me. . . . Once you peel this [your skin] . . . you are the Muerte. You already have her . . . in you" (Hernández, *Down* 156). Doña Queta's powerful, simple image conjures the notion of a saint that the faithful do not even have to invoke, because she is always with them. In other words, everyone already possesses her inside of themselves; or more accurately perhaps, Santa Muerte possesses us. This accessibility is surely what makes Santa Muerte so threatening to her critics and popular with her devotees, for it suggests that all of her contradictions are universal. Santa Muerte's fundamental ambivalence—as a secular saint who is simultaneously sacred and profane, good and evil, and fair and arbitrary—permits her often marginalized devotees to embrace their own contradictions as the essence of the human condition.

As in the case of the occupation and expansion of public space through the establishment of street altars like that of Doña Queta, Santa Muerte's devotees articulate alternate forms of identity, community, or social and civil services in a world that frequently marks them as disposable or invisible and denies them basic human rights. Indeed, civil society and the state have failed many of the devotees of the death saint in Mexico and the borderlands. Meanwhile, the religious institutions and groups that frequently intersect with both state and civil society also exclude Santa Muerte and her followers, as Haydé Solís Cárdenas, the street vendor who sells smuggled tennis shoes in Tepito, suggests: "She said the Virgin of Guadalupe Mexico's patron saint, would not sympathize with a life like hers, tending rather to well-off people with college degrees and nice clothes" (Thompson n.p.). Solís Cárdenas's claim is especially significant because it interprets the Virgin of Guadalupe as both a symbol of religious orthodoxy, linked to the Catholic Church, and a symbol of the Mexican state. From Solís Cárdenas's perspective, the popular spirituality that informs devotional practices associated with the Virgin of Guadalupe does not seem to be a viable option. Instead, the Virgin is associated with church, state, and the middle and upper classes, while Santa Muerte is reinscribed as the patron of the dispossessed. Yet while the secular sanctity that is bound to Santa Muerte exceeds the grasp of church and state, it also transforms the abject condition of marginalized groups into a double-edged sword of empowerment and menace, that is, as Homero Aridjis argues, while most of the saint's followers "seek protection from the evil that lurks in their lives, others . . . seek darker blessings no other saint would approve" (Thompson n.p.). Santa Muerte is undeniably a refuge for criminals as well as for their victims, as some devotees "ask [her] for protection from harm even as they harm others" (Thompson n.p.). Yet all too often, the hyperbolic association of the death saint with criminals and narcos obscures the fact that her devotees are very much aware of her potential for harm, and the possibility that she could turn on them if they do not treat her with care. Ultimately, the understanding that Santa Muerte represents empowerment and menace alike reflects her accessibility and ambivalence for her followers. Whether they use her for good or ill, Santa Muerte's devotees respect and embrace her because she signifies the choices that are so often denied them as marginalized subjects in the borderlands and beyond.

CONCLUSION
Narrative Devotion

THE NARRATIVES OF SECULAR SANCTITY in the borderlands are as ambivalent as they are contradictory. Through participation in rituals of exchange, identification, and disidentification with their favored secular saints and santones, devotees shape autonomous forms of civil society, challenge the authority of church and state, and articulate diverse identities as individuals and as collective groups. In many cases, these devotees approach secular saints not exclusively through traditional spiritual rituals, whether official or popular, but through narrative. Such narratives are certainly reflected in cultural production, but they also rearticulate devotional ritual, that is, while the cultural representation of secular saints and santones manifests devotional practices, it frequently becomes devotional practice in and of itself. Cultural production highlights and facilitates the personal relationship between devotee and saint just as much as traditional spiritual practices like prayer, spirit possession, or the exchange of relics or sacred images. The link between cultural production and devotional practice is especially salient in light of the fact that many secular saints and santones also create and perform their own narratives of secular sanctity, whether through images, writing, or speaking. Cultural production and devotional ritual alike reflect the intersection as well as the contradiction between human and divine enclosed in secular sanctity.

At times, the link between traditional devotional ritual and cultural production has been translated literally. Certainly, many of César Chávez's speeches or Subcomandante Marcos's communiqués draw upon transcendent language and imagery to appeal to a blend of spiritual, political, and cultural traditions. Chávez specifically employed religious and spiritual practice in his speeches and manifestos, such as the "Sacramento March Letter, March 1966," and the UFW's Plan of Delano, which delineate the need for "pilgrimage, penance, and revolution"

(Jensen and Hammerback 15). In Chávez's eyes, social or political revolution is not possible without spiritual tribute, while devotion is a form of political praxis. Many of Chávez's and Marcos's writings also give homage to individual members of the UFW or EZLN, functioning as eulogies or elegies for the living and the dead. Ultimately, these writings—many of which are written in collaboration with or entirely by the UFW or EZLN as a whole—also pay tribute to the collective, linking these groups in solidarity to the oppressed and marginalized on a global scale.

The connection between devotional ritual and cultural production is even more apparent in contemporary versions of religious iconography, echoing the medieval pictorial hagiographies or illustrated cycles of saints' lives discussed by Barbara Abou-El-Haj (33). Some of these icons, such as the devotional candles or prayer cards dedicated to "Gran General Revolucionario Pancho Villa" or the "Spirit of Pancho Villa," are no different from other forms of popular spiritual ritual. Others such as the religious portrait *César Chávez de California* by Br. Robert Lentz, OFM, the painting *César Chávez* by iconographer Mark Dukes, or the portrait *Subcomandante Marcos as the Buddha* by Erin Currier fuse devotional practice, cultural production, and the commodification of celebrity, rearticulating these figures as secular saints for the masses. Dukes's painting *César Chávez*, created in collaboration with Saint Gregory of Nyssa Episcopal Church in San Francisco under the auspices of All Saints Company, is an especially important example of the fusion of celebrity, icon, and saint. The painting is part of the *Dancing Saints Icon*, a three-thousand-square-foot fresco that wraps around the church rotunda. The icon features saints ranging from traditional figures such as Teresa of Ávila, Francis of Assisi, and King David to unorthodox and non-Christian figures like Anne Frank or Malcolm X. Because the icon is inside the church, it is firmly situated as an object of traditional religious devotion, yet because it portrays writers, artists, scientists, political activists, and heroes alongside orthodox canonized saints, it truly illuminates the union and contradiction of sacred and secular.

Since the sacred and the secular are unified through the contradiction of human and divine, they inherently meld distance and presence, producing both joy and pain for devotees. Yet sometimes the contradiction between them may seem intolerable or untenable rather than productive and the pain may outweigh the pleasure. Indeed, for many devotees the sacred falls short in the face of the secular. The partial identification, counter-identification, and rejection that is part of the process of identifying with secular saints, who are both tantalizingly accessible and resolutely inaccessible to their devotees, is sometimes too difficult or traumatic to sustain. As José Muñoz suggests, this experience of simultaneous identification and rejection is necessary to the processes of disidentification that accompany figures like secular saints and santones (8). However, some devotional practices and cultural representations seem to dispense entirely with any sort of identification with secular saints, completely refusing the sacred instead. At times, cultural production is clearly alienated from any kind of devotion and not every narrative of faith signals autonomy for devotees. Faith occasionally oppresses, circumscribes, and fails the very devotees who so ardently desire and practice it. Meanwhile, potential devotees and nonbelievers may reject faith out of hand. Cultural production may certainly reflect or even become devotional practice, but it can also refuse traditional forms of spiritual devotion. Such refusal may also signal a rearticulation of ritual, devotion, and secular sanctity. Indeed, the contradictory nature of secular sanctity can even be emphasized through the refusal of sacred devotional practice.

The failure and refusal of sacred devotional practice is a central theme in . . . *y no se lo tragó la tierra* / . . . *And the Earth Did Not Devour Him* (1971), Tomás Rivera's classic novel of Mexican American migrant workers in the 1940s and 1950s.[1] The novel is structured through a series of vignettes, recounted through the fragmented voices of the migrant farmworkers, which emphasizes the need to construct and shape narrative in order to articulate identity. This identity is not unified but, rather, incorporates fragmentation, memory, abstract voices, visions, and dreams as part of its narration. From the perspective of the unnamed boy protagonist who attempts to make sense of his "lost year" in the fields, this fragmented narrative of identity and migration is estranged completely from both popular and orthodox forms of spirituality. The migrant workers in the novel are clearly the kinds of marginalized and transgressive subjects who engage in popular devotional practices. In relation to both dominant U.S. and Mexican culture, they are marginalized to the point of invisibility. Most of the migrants are not U.S. citizens, most of them do not speak English, their children are able to attend school only sporadically, the families are constantly on the move, and they are subject to the whims of corrupt growers and apathetic or misguided public servants and other authorities. At the same time, because of the entrenched economic, racial, and social hierarchies that persist in Mexico, they are unable to sustain dignified lives there either. In short, the state and civil society have failed these migrant workers and their families in both Mexico and the United States.

In another context, these laborers might worship secular saints like Santa Muerte. Like the impoverished residents of Tepito or contemporary border-crossers, the migrants of the novel could well articulate alternate forms of collective belonging as well as the civil, social, and religious rights they lack through devotion to the death saint. But while the migrants of Rivera's novel do not worship Santa Muerte, they frequently draw upon spirituality and devotional practice to make sense of their difficult lives and to commune with others. The boy's family is devout in its spiritual belief, but the boy asserts his own elusive, marginalized identity largely by rejecting such sacred rituals. Ultimately, the boy demonstrates that the transcendence involved in devotion may be directed away from the register of sacred, at least as it is traditionally construed, in order to emphasize secular human agency.

Not only do the migrants in . . . *y no se lo tragó la tierra* lack citizenship rights in the United States, their ostensible access to legal Mexican citizenship does not translate into political, economic, or social rights in that country either. They remain marginalized on both sides of the border. In the novel, this marginalization is evident in the migrants' inability to feel at home in either Mexico or the United States. Far from providing a safe haven or a marker of nostalgia, Mexico represents only lack to the migrants, for they have no tangible connection to either a Mexican national present or past. For them, the Mexican Revolution is nothing but a failed promise, while its heroes, like Pancho Villa, are merely betrayers. The grandfather asserts: "Then came the Revolution and in the end we lost. Villa made out well but I had to come here. No one here knows what I went through" (Rivera 150). In this reading, Pancho Villa is self-serving and decidedly not anyone that marginalized subjects like the grandfather could ever identify with. Meanwhile, the various situations that the migrants find themselves in are virtually identical in their oppression. As such, distinctions between different locations are meaningless, as one migrant complains: "When we arrive, when we arrive, the real truth is that I'm tired of arriving. Arriving and leaving, it's the same thing" (Rivera 145). While the grandfather's disillusionment with Mexico demonstrates that nostalgia escapes the migrants, the sites of migration are also impenetrable to them.

In the novel, the migrants encounter many institutions such as the Catholic Church, farming corporations, and public schools, and are confronted by many authority figures such as labor bosses, priests, teachers, and school nurses. But rather than serving as translators or guides to life in the United States, these institutions and authority figures are at best apathetic and at worst menacing or ruthless. The migrants are routinely punished, often fatally, for attempting to claim basic human needs such as drinking water, shelter from the sun, or care for their children (Rivera 86, 110, 120). In every instance, the economic and political imperatives of growers, corporations, and institutions supersede the needs and rights of the farmworkers. One migrant couple's little children, for example, are left alone to fend for themselves at home and are burned in a fire, because "the owner didn't like children in the fields doing mischief and distracting their parents from their work" (120). These injustices are so commonplace they seem almost banal, yet the migrants do not simply accept them passively even though they may not understand the economic and political imperatives behind them. Instead, as Alicia Schmidt Camacho argues, the "Mexican American migrants refuse, or fail, to incorporate themselves into the settled order of national life" (7).

Such failure or refusal is not without pain. It is important to note that frequently the farmworkers in the novel are simply unable to understand their new, inhospitable environment, just as they cannot understand the foreign language that surrounds them. When one migrant asks another, "*Comadre,* do you all plan to go to Utah?" his friend replies, "No . . . we don't trust the man that's contracting to go work in—how do you say it? . . . Because we don't think there's such a state. You tell me, when've you ever heard of that place?" (Rivera 91). Neither of the migrants knows where Utah is located, as the compadre reveals when he muses, "Well, we've never been there but I hear it's somewhere close to Japan" (91).

While an outsider like the contractor might interpret the compadre's comment as proof of ignorance, it actually emphasizes the interchangeability of the hostile routes of migration. Utah may as well be Japan for all the migrant laborers know about it. The comadre further connects her misgivings about migrating to Utah to the untrustworthy contractor, demonstrating how much oppressive authority figures impact the migrants' understanding of their environment. While the contractor is not to be trusted, neither are the routes and stops of migration.

Meanwhile, in the vignette "The Night before Christmas," the boy's mother, María, literally cannot understand or engage with her environment because she suffers from anxiety and agoraphobia. Imprisoned by fear and uncertainty, María rarely leaves her home, and "she was unfamiliar with downtown even though it was only six blocks away" (Rivera 132). When she finally decides to venture downtown to purchase the Christmas toys her children have been begging for, she becomes so disoriented and panicked that she "start[s] to hear voices coming from the merchandise," grabs some toys, and rushes out of the store (133). Predictably, she is accused of shoplifting, as the security guard declares, "Here is she is . . . these damn people, always stealing something, stealing. I've been watching you all along" (133). While María succumbs to her anxiety and loses any sense of her surroundings, later vowing never to leave the house again lest she be sent to an insane asylum and separated from her children, the security guard elides her trauma by casting her as a thief who must be controlled through oppressive surveillance. María's mental illness renders her unable to understand her environment, but in turn, others misunderstand her. Moreover, such misunderstandings are applied to all migrants, for the security guard interprets them all as a uniformly suspect group of "damn people" (133).

Even when the migrants do articulate modes of resistance, their gestures are misunderstood. For example, when the boy's class needs a button on the poster to represent the button industry, he immediately tears a button off his shirt to give to his teacher. This act greatly surprises her "because she knew that this was probably the only shirt the child had," and she assumes that he would need to preserve it (Rivera 119). Unlike almost every other authority figure in the novel, this teacher is compassionate toward her migrant student. The boy's gesture touches her deeply, and she sympathetically imagines that he might have given her the button out of a need to belong, a desire to be helpful, or out of love for her. Yet though the teacher takes the boy's poverty into account when she considers that he probably owns only one shirt, she cannot understand the "intensity of [the boy's] desire" (119). Her rootedness contrasts with the transitory nature of migrant lives. For the migrants, material possessions are few but are also necessarily disposable since they are often left behind in the course of migration.

Nevertheless, the teacher's misunderstanding is benign compared to the marginalization effected by others, like the Spanish priest who charges the migrants five dollars each to bless their cars and trucks before undertaking their migration north. The priest profits greatly from this scam, earning enough money to travel to Barcelona to visit his family and friends. Upon returning, he places postcards "of a very modern church" at the entrance of his own rural church so that the migrants "might desire a church such as that one" (Rivera 135). The priest's efforts to inspire economic and devotional progress seem to be in vain, for "words began to appear on the cards, then crosses, lines, and con safos symbols, just as had happened to the new church pews" (135). The graffiti is quite purposeful, but "the priest was never able to understand the sacrilege" of the willful defacement of church property (135). The migrants' gesture of resistance is as incomprehensible to the priest as is their coded graffiti. The crosses and "con safos" signs, which simultaneously connote respect and refusal, are legible only to the Mexican and Chicano community. They symbolize the migrants' resistance to the priest's extortion, as well as to the economic and social structure that erases their existence. More subtly perhaps, the graffiti challenges the priest's assumption that the migrants would be pleased to have new pews, which their hard-earned money presumably paid for, or that they would "desire" a modern church like the one in Barcelona, a distant city they have no hope of ever visiting or knowing anything about. Meanwhile, the migrants willingly pay the five dollars in exchange for a blessing, but they are fully aware that, as Alicia Schmidt Camacho argues, the blessing "anticipates the hardship that awaits them at the migrant camps" (8). The migrants are cognizant that the priest and the associated Catholic hierarchy take advantage of their fear and disposability, yet they still desire the blessing to protect them in their travels. The priest's bewilderment over the migrants' sacrilege and his ignorance of their ambivalent attitude toward the blessing reflects his erroneous belief that he can understand the migrants, when in reality their world is impenetrable to him.

Schmidt Camacho argues that the migrants' graffiti also constitutes an alternative faith practice, an "enunciation of presence against erasure" (8). The words and symbols scrawled on the postcard and the pews certainly rearticulate devotional practice to emphasize the agency of the migrants. Many of the other devotional practices in the novel reflect more traditional versions of popular and official spirituality, such as prayer, spirit possession, and ritualistic offerings. Yet spirituality is frequently portrayed as a false panacea, a fraud, or a mere habit, although the hope that many migrants perceive in devotional practice is very real. The mother that prays for the return of her son, missing in action in the Korean War, is well versed in both popular and orthodox spiritual practices. She consults a medium who performs rituals of spirit possession. Everyone who witnesses the ritual conforms to the conventions and practices necessary for spirit possession: "everyone, very mindful of not crossing their arms nor their legs nor their hands, watched her intensely. The spirit was already present in her body" (Rivera 89). The act of keeping all body parts uncrossed opens the devotees up to the presence of the spirit. This ritual act is collective, for it requires the participation of the entire audience, not just the medium. Despite this collective ritual effort, however, the tone of the vignette expresses cynicism rather than hope. The mother desperately reaches for such hope, telling the medium: "I'd like to know whether or not [my son is] alive. I feel like I'm losing my mind just thinking and thinking about it" (89). But the medium's response is rote and reflects only insipid promises: "Have no fear, sister. Julianito is fine. He's just fine. Don't worry about him anymore. Very soon he'll be in your arms. He'll be returning already next month" (89). The contrast between the mother's hope and the mechanical tone of the medium's platitudes reveals the cracks and flaws in belief and devotion.

In the next vignette, "A Prayer," the mother, who still has not heard word of her son, prays to a pantheon of sacred figures including the Virgin of Guadalupe, Jesus Christ, and the Virgin of San Juan del Valle. Her prayer in part reflects the migrants' need to make sense of the demands of a national identity, represented by the U.S. military, that they cannot completely inhabit or understand. The mother's prayer counters the faceless, seemingly interchangeable menace of the "Communists and the Koreans and the Chinese" who threaten her boy, as she pleas for miraculous protection: "Shield his body, cover his head, cover [their] eyes . . . so they cannot see him, so they won't kill him" (Rivera 90). As in the ritual of spirit possession, the mother is fully cognizant of the practices of exchange and identification, indicating her connection to Mexican and migrant devotional culture. She not only promises "to pay homage" at the shrine of the Virgin of San Juan, she offers her personal relics from the boy's childhood, referring to the "toys from when he was a child" and the "cards and funnies" she is saving for her son's return (90). These objects, which symbolize the mother's cherished memory of her boy as a child, are necessarily portable, like the lives of the migrants themselves. The mother offers her own heart as the ultimate, most permanent sacrifice possible: "I sacrifice my life for his. . . . Here is my heart! Through it runs his very own blood. . . . Bring him back alive and I will give you my very own heart" (90). There is no indication that her prayers are ever answered or acknowledged. Instead, it seems that she is left to ask, offer, and sacrifice with no hope of any reward or even any indication that her child is alive or dead.

Although faith, devotees, and devotional practices surround the boy protagonist, he reiterates their banality and their failure. When the boy's father is afflicted by sunstroke, his mother begs for God's help, lights candles, and places scapulars around his neck, but "nothing happen[s]" (Rivera 109). She is only able to understand the boy's anger at God as a frightening sacrilege: "You scare me. It's as if already the blood of Satan runs through your veins" (109). Concomitantly, she can only answer with platitudes when the boy asks why he and his family must suffer "burrowed in the dirt like animals with no hope for anything" (109). The boy perceives these platitudes for the empty promises that they are: "'But why us?' 'Well, they say that . . .' 'Don't say it. I know what you're going to tell me—that the poor go to heaven'" (110). The mother's unspoken explanation about the poor inheriting the earth is the very sort of cliché that Santa Muerte's devotees so firmly reject.

The clichés do not mean that her faith is not true, but they do reflect the boy's perception of the disconnection between belief and reality. At the same time, the novel hints that the mother is aware of this disconnection in much more nuanced ways than the boy is able to understand or articulate. In another vignette, the boy describes his mother's ritual of leaving a glass of water under the bed for the spirits. He claims, "What his mother never knew was that every night he would drink the glass of water that she left under the bed for the spirits. She always believed that they drank the water and so she continued doing her duty" (85). In turn, the boy's duty is perhaps to help his mother maintain her illusion of faith by drinking the water. It is unclear whether the mother truly "always believed" that the spirits took the offering of water or whether she knew all along that her son drank it. Since the vignette is narrated from the perspective of a child, it seems likely that the mother is well aware of her son's nightly act. This is especially true since the boy innocently thinks "Once he was going to tell her but then he thought he'd wait and tell her when he was grown up," emphasizing the child's trust that he can accurately represent what his mother is thinking or feeling (85). The juxtaposition between the child and the mother's perspectives reinscribes the boy's view of his mother's leap of faith as a performance of devotion between mother and child. Although the child is unaware of the mother's agency in this fiction, by perpetuating it, mother and child perform a duty of devotion and love to each other.

As the boy becomes more willing to transgress his spiritual duty, he begins to understand that the rules and conventions that order religious discourse are frequently arbitrary or baseless. Furthermore, the promised repercussions for apathy or blasphemy never come to pass. Since "the devil had fascinated him as far back as he could remember," the boy decides to call him forth (Rivera 104). He structures the ritual around the received wisdom and gossip overheard from other migrants and his experience of watching the Christmas nativity plays.

Although he fears the sacrilege of "fooling around with the devil" and the consequences of "giving up his soul," the boy puts on a devil mask, goes outside,
waits until midnight, and ponders the proper way to call the devil, demonstrating his ability to construct popular ritual (104). However, even cursing the devil
seems to bring no results: "But nothing. Nothing nor no one appeared, nor did
anything change. . . . There was no devil" (106). This absence has a very different impact on the boy than the expected supernatural punishment, for it leads
him to question everything he has been taught about spirituality. It grants him
new knowledge: "Now he understood everything. Those who summoned the
devil went crazy, not because the devil appeared, but just the opposite, because
he didn't appear" (106). This knowledge is painful because, as the boy realizes, if
there is no devil, "there is nothing," not even God (106).

While the boy's realization upends his cosmic sense of retribution and justice,
it also transmits alternate modes of resistance. These modes do not insist upon a
search for more accommodating saints, nor do they require total abandonment
of faith and devotional practice. Instead, they rearticulate ritual and spirituality
to create a new register of faith in the creation and ordering of narrative. Since
their lives are predicated upon transience, the migrants in Rivera's novel have
nothing to hold onto but their own stories and cultural histories.

These stories are initially elusive for the young protagonist. While he struggles
throughout the novel to make narrative, chronological sense of his "lost year"
and tries "to figure out when that time he had come to call 'year' had started,"
he is at a "loss for words" (Rivera 83). Nevertheless, knowledge comes to him in
other ways, such as through the reordering of spiritual practice in his call for the
devil, through the devotion of duty between mother and son, through the fragmented voices that he hears, and through the liminal, nonlinear time between
waking and sleeping during which "he saw and heard many things" (83). Indeed,
the boy's process of acquiring knowledge rearticulates spiritual practice, whether
official or popular, toward storytelling and the construction of narrative.

As his First Communion approaches, the boy strategically decides to confess
more sins than he thinks he has really committed, so that there will be "no sacrilege" and he can "be purer" (115). But on his way to the church, he hears loud
noises coming from a laundromat and peeks in the window to see a couple having sex on top of a pile of clothes on the floor. Although he realizes that the sight
might constitute the "sins of the flesh" that an overbearing nun has warned him
about, and he feels like he too has committed these sins, he deliberately refuses
to confess them (116). Ultimately, he realizes that flouting spiritual convention
brings him the gift of understanding, which he derives great pleasure from: "I
kept remembering the scene at the cleaners, and there, alone, I even liked recalling it. I even forgot that I had lied to the priest. And then I felt the same as I
once had when I had heard a missionary speak about the grace of God. I felt like

knowing more about everything. And then it occurred to me that maybe everything was the same" (116).

For the boy, narrative knowledge is like the "grace of God," indeed, it is a form of devotional practice. Yet narrative knowledge is even more significant because it allows the boy to order his fragmentary life in a way that spiritual devotion does not. When he curses God after his father's bout with sunstroke, the earth does not open up to devour him. Instead, he feels his feet planted even more firmly on the ground. With this realization, he is further able to order the narrative of his life: "There were clouds in the sky and for the first time he felt capable of doing and undoing anything that he pleased" (Rivera 112). For the first time, the boy is able to kick the earth and announce, "Not yet, you can't swallow me up yet. Someday, yes. But I'll never know it" (112).

The boy's process of structuring narrative temporality ultimately leads the other migrants to think he is crazy just like his agoraphobic mother, for he holes up under a house to escape the rooted, symbolically national space of school "because he didn't know the words" to function there (148). Instead, like a true migrant, he has "to keep moving constantly" in order to keep his wits about him (148). Under the house, all of the fragmented voices and visions come together in the boy's head as he structures the lost year: "he realized that in reality he hadn't lost anything. He had made a discovery. To discover and rediscover and piece things together. This to this, that to that, all with all. That was it. That was everything. He was thrilled" (152). The boy's capacity for narrative construction brings him the ability to lay down the roots he has been denied as a migrant, to resist the "conventions of national citizenship in both Mexico and the United States," to manage the crises of everyday life, and most of all, to articulate his identity in relation to his community (Schmidt Camacho 9). After this realization, the boy climbs the tree in his yard, spies a palm tree on the horizon, and imagines "someone perched on top, gazing across at him" (Rivera 152). For the boy, this act of communion is only possible through the structuring of narrative, not through traditional devotional practice or secular sanctity. Nevertheless, the transcendence enclosed in this act of communion reorders sacred devotion as narrative. For the migrants in the novel and dispossessed groups in general, the construction of narrative and cultural production reflects another version of secular sanctity, with its contradictory union of human and divine.

NOTES

INTRODUCTION: THE SECULAR SANCTITY OF BORDERLANDS SAINTS

1. Unless otherwise indicated, all translations are my own.

2. See Gloria Anzaldúa, *Borderlands/La Frontera*; James F. Hopgood, *The Making of Saints: Contesting Sacred Ground*; and Luis D. León, *La Llorona's Children: Religion, Life, and Death in the US-Mexican Borderlands*.

3. The military also destroyed several Santa Muerte shrines in Tijuana at the same time.

4. It is significant that the protests occurred during Holy Week in front of the Mexico City Metropolitan Cathedral, reflecting the clash between orthodox religion and popular belief evoked by the cult to Santa Muerte. The Metropolitan Cathedral is not only the seat of the Roman Catholic Archdiocese of Mexico, it is also a symbol of Mexican national identity. The cathedral is a Spanish colonial structure built atop the sacred ground of the Aztec city of Tenochtitlán in the present-day Zócalo (main square) of Mexico City, the symbolic center of the independent mestizo nation.

5. Regarding the adjective *Chicano/a* or *Chicana/o*: In (Chicano or Chicana) cultural criticism, these forms are often favored because they shift the focus away from the masculine identified *Chicano*, which, like *Mexicano* or other similar adjectives in Spanish, can be applied to a group regardless of whether there are women in it or not. In other words, a group of five Mexican women and one Mexican man would historically still be called *Mexicano*. This explains the preference in feminist circles for the feminine form *Chicana*. These usages have political significance in the Chicano context. Many departments or conferences of Chicano Studies are now called "Chicana/Chicano Studies," for example, frequently with the feminine form first, for this reason. This double form becomes somewhat confusing when applied to English gender-neutral nouns such as *text* or *community*. In this work, I have kept the dual term *Chicano/a* when referring to people (who are clearly gendered) or identities, but for general English nouns with no gender I have most often gone with the traditional *Chicano*, so as not to burden the text with extraneous gender issues.

6. For more on the early Christian cult of the saints, see Peter Brown, *The Cult of the Saints*; Richard Kieckhefer and George D. Bond, *Sainthood: Its Manifestations in World Religions*; Kenneth L. Woodward, *The Making of Saints*.

7. Kieckhefer argues: "Through the 1960s most days of the year were special feast days of saints. . . . Liturgical changes in 1969 included the deletion from the calendar of 52 saints whose very existence was questioned. . . . Although some recent saints were added, the net effect was to diminish attention given to the saints" (Kieckhefer and Bond 9).

8. Aphorisms that draw upon sanctity are especially plentiful in Mexican Spanish, for example, *Ni tanto que queme al santo, ni tanto que no lo alumbre* (Not so much that it burns the saint, or so little that it does not shed a light on him; meaning, "Don't deal in extremes"), and *Se quedó para vestir santos* (She or he was left behind to dress the saints; meaning, "She or he was left on the shelf").

9. El Niño Fidencio, born José Fidencio de Jesús Síntora Constantino (1898–1938), is a popular Mexican folk saint who is renowned as a curandero or faith healer. He believed that he received the gift for spiritual healing directly from Jesus, who appeared to him in visions. Fidencio was said to hold "distinctive personal characteristics" such as a "falsetto voice, boyish demeanor, and lack of secondary male sexual attributes," which contributed to his sanctity and earned him the nickname "El Niño" (Murray 107–111). Fidencio was linked to spiritism, and his cult manifests today through trance mediums (*materias*) who "receive his spirit and continue his healing ministry," as well as through pilgrimages to Espinazo, Nuevo León, where his spiritual ministry is based (Murray 113).

10. One of the Virgin of Guadalupe's monikers is La Virgen Morena (The dark-skinned virgin). See Sandra Cisneros, "Guadalupe the Sex Goddess," and León, who cites an East Los Angeles woman named Señora de la Cruz who feels a particular affinity with Guadalupe because "She looks like me" (León, *La Llorona's* 115).

11. *Cabrona* is a Mexican swear and/or informal slang word (the feminine form of *cabrón*). It has many different meanings and is not directly translatable, though it connotes "cuckold." In Mexico, as a pejorative term, it can mean something like "bastard," "asshole," or "bitch." It can also mean "dude" or "man," depending on context.

12. See Clarke Garrett, *Spirit Possession and Popular Religion*; Morton Klass, *Mind over Mind: The Anthropology and Psychology of Spirit Possession*; I. M. Lewis, *Ecstatic Religion*.

13. See Plato, *Plato's Cosmology, the Timaeus of Plato*.

14. Scholars have emphasized the link between sanctity and celebrity through the embrace of charisma, the importance of the public, the proliferation and repetition of the icon or image, and the conflation of subjectivity and objectivity. See Matt Hills, *Fan Cultures*; Joseph Roach, *It*; Chris Rojek, *Celebrity*.

15. See Hernández, *Down and Delirious in Mexico City: The Aztec Metropolis in the Twenty-First Century*; and León, *La Llorona's Children*.

16. The documentary features many popular saints' cults throughout Mexico and the borderlands, including those of Santa Muerte, Juan Soldado, Jesús Malverde, and El Niño Fidencio. See http://oncetv-ipn.net/santitos/. Elijah Wald further indicates that one of the appellations of Jesús Malverde, the Sinaloan patron of narcotraffickers, is El Narcosantón (The big drug saint), in *Narcocorrido* (61).

17. The racial and ethnic origins of the Spirit Queen are under dispute. According to Taussig, "Years later, Katy told me different. That the spirit queen was not an Indian but a *mestiza*, hybrid child of an Indian woman and a *conquistador* (sixteenth century) and that she had had to seek refuge in the mountain until saved by the Liberator (born late eighteenth century) who sent *el Negro* Felipe to care for her" (*Magic* 31).

18. Similarly, the recent two-volume encyclopedia *Hispanic American Religious Cultures*, edited by Miguel de la Torre, covers the full range of Latino spiritual affiliations and rituals in the United States and the borderlands, while Gastón Espinosa and Mario T. García's collection *Mexican American Religions: Spirituality, Activism, and Culture* analyzes the influence of religion and spirituality on Mexican American social practices like activism and healing as well as on popular culture and cultural production.

1. SAINT OF CONTRADICTION: TERESA URREA, LA SANTA DE CABORA

1. Translation taken from Brianda Domecq, *The Astonishing Story of the Saint of Cabora* (1998).

2. General Porfirio Díaz was president of Mexico from 1876 to 1911, when he was ousted by the Mexican Revolution. Widely considered a dictator, he was famous for his ruthlessness and

for his implementation of positivist reforms and public works in Mexico; his rule is known as the *Porfiriato*.

3. Historian Antonio Saborit argues, "Few have resisted the temptation to read *Tomóchic* as fact, instead of the literary piece which it undoubtedly is" (14; my translation).

4. See also Lillian Illades Aguilar, *La rebelión de Tomóchic, 1891–1892*; Rubén Osorio, *Tomóchic en llamas*.

5. Besides La Santa de Cabora, some of the best-known borderlands saints and healers of the late nineteenth and early twentieth centuries are Don Pedrito Jaramillo, who gained fame as a healer in the Texas border region at the turn of the century, and El Niño Fidencio of Espinazo, from Nuevo León in northeastern Mexico, the most famous Mexican healer of all.

6. Irwin points out that, with her limited education, "it is unlikely that she was able to write something on her own" (230). She may well, of course, have provided her opinions orally, while others like Aguirre could have written them down.

7. Saborit indicates that Frías's name was not officially attached to the novel until 1899, in an edition published in Spain (178). After Frías was revealed to be the author, he was tried in court and temporarily imprisoned, although he was eventually cleared of the charges of treason after the original manuscript was destroyed (James W. Brown, *Tomóchic* "Prologue" xii). Frías continued to criticize the upper classes and the Porfirian government in later literary works such as *Los piratas del boulevard* (1915), but like many other authors of the time, he was also compensated for writing pieces praising Díaz and his cabinet (Brown xiv).

8. Treaty of Guadalupe Hidalgo, Article VIII, 1848.

9. The quote comes from a footnote, where Frías recounts Teresa Urrea's history, derived from an article by historian Mario Gill.

10. Irwin points out that since Teresa Urrea only spoke Spanish, the English-language text of the interview was translated by a Mrs. A. C. Fessler and then shaped by the reporter, Helen Dare (242).

11. See especially Illades Aguilar, Osorio, Saborit, Vanderwood *Power of God*, and Vargas Valdez.

12. See Griffith, León *La Llorona's*, Larralde, and Newell.

13. Luis Alberto Urrea gives thanks and praise to Teresita Urrea in *The Hummingbird's Daughter* and in his earlier work *By the Lake of Sleeping Children: The Secret Life of the Mexican Border*.

14. For more on the hybrid nature of performance and performance studies, see Richard Schechner, *Performance Studies: An Introduction*; Diana Taylor, *The Archive and the Repertoire*.

15. *Milagros* are small metal medals or charms shaped like body parts (leg, heart, kidneys, eyes, etc.) that are in need of healing. Devotees pin the milagros to holy shrines, statues, or crosses when they pray for divine intervention for a cure.

16. Curiously, this line does not appear in the English translation of the novel.

2. THE REMAINS OF PANCHO VILLA

1. Taibo wryly claims that many Mexico City natives attribute the city's frequent earthquakes to the animosity between the reluctant neighbors who lie within the Monument of the Revolution (*Pancho Villa*).

2. According to Gil Olmos, the Escuela de Estudios Psíquicos Doroteo Arango Arámbula, located in La Coyotada, Durango, and founded by Juana Hernández Juárez in her home has existed for about thirty-two years. According to Hernández Juárez, the school offers counseling, healing, and spiritual lessons for the faithful: "The school's activities are to provide counsel, to heal, and to teach students about many things that people overlook pertaining to the psychic" (174).

3. Mexican national leaders and intellectuals have long utilized popular notions of spirituality and the supernatural to shape Mexican nationalism. See Lomnitz's book *Deep Mexico, Silent Mexico*, where he discusses the link between messianic imagery and the martyrdom and dismemberment of Mexican national leaders (89). Two examples are President Antonio López de Santa Anna, who erected a national monument containing his amputated leg that was severed in battle against the French, and President Álvaro Obregón who lost his arm during the Mexican Revolution in the battle of Celaya against Villa. The severed arm later became the centerpiece of yet another national monument. Ultimately, the martyrdom of leaders such as Obregón was used self-consciously to funnel charisma into a "bureaucracy [the PRI, Mexico's dominant national party which ruled for 71 years] that has insistently called itself revolutionary" (*Deep Mexico* 94). The PRI is the Partido Revolucionario Institucional (the Institutional Revolutionary Party).

4. Everyday life in the División del Norte differed from its heroic legend. Katz stresses that it is difficult to determine the "revolutionary consciousness" of the members of the regiment. It was primarily a volunteer army (with the exception of captured members of the Mexican Federal Army who were forced to join or be shot), and Katz notes the volunteers were heterogeneous. They had various motives for joining the army, many of which had little to do with the revolution (292–293, 295).

5. Villa famously signed a contract with the Mutual Film Company in 1914 to "provide moving picture thrillers in any way that is consistent with his plans to depose and drive Carranza out of Mexico." It is also generally rumored that Villa agreed to film fake battle scenes, fight during daylight whenever possible, and bar competing film companies from encroaching upon Mutual Film's territory (De Orellana, *Filming Pancho* 43–45). See also Gregorio Rocha, *Los rollos perdidos de Pancho Villa/The Lost Reels of Pancho Villa*, 2003.

6. In his study of Mexican drug ballads, *Narcocorrido*, music historian Elijah Wald calls Villa "the greatest *corrido* hero of them all," but Wald emphasizes that, while historians tend to celebrate Villa as a great general, the singers remember him as a man, defined as "the most macho character of a singularly macho time" (24–28). After Villa's death, his memory lived on in the borderlands primarily through popular culture, especially through the circulation of revolutionary corridos among migrants and Chicanos/as. The most popular revolutionary corridos—including many that featured Villa—celebrated the resistance of rebels, bandits, smugglers, and migrants against Mexican and U.S. authorities alike. For more on the borderlands corrido tradition, see Américo Paredes, *With His Pistol in His Hand*.

7. Taibo claims that there are 333,249 entries on the Google search engine related to Pancho Villa (*Pancho Villa*).

8. Rocha discusses the production of *The Life of General Villa* (1914), one of the first American biographical feature films, which is now lost except for some fragments ("*And Starring*" 142–143).

9. The Columbus raid was a military confrontation with the United States that established Villa's notoriety on both sides of the border. Although the raid was small and few were killed, Villa's elusion of General John Pershing, who was sent into Mexico to pursue him, became proof to many of his supernatural power.

10. Some novels of the Mexican Revolution in which Villa or his specter figures prominently are Mariano Azuela, *Los de abajo* (1915); Nellie Campobello, *Cartucho* (1931), *Las manos de Mamá* (1937), and *Apuntes sobre la vida militar de Francisco Villa* (1940); Martín Luis Guzmán, *El águila y la serpiente* (1928) and *Memorias de Pancho Villa* (1936); Rafael Muñoz, *¡Vámonos con Pancho Villa!* (1931); Francisco Urquizo, *Tropa vieja* (1943). For a

contemporaneous American perspective on Villa and the revolution, see John Reed, *Insurgent Mexico* (1914).

11. During the Revolutionary Convention of Aguascalientes, revolutionary leaders met to establish the future of the revolution. Soldiers were present but not involved in the meetings. The three main factions were the Villistas (supporters of Villa), the Carrancistas (supporters of Carranza), and a diverse group from the Division of the Northwest (Sonora) who were against both Carranza and Villa. Later, the Zapatistas arrived, and Carranza broke ties with the Convention and with Villa.

12. As Paco Ignacio Taibo II argues, it is ironic that Guzmán, who wrote two novels about the Mexican Revolution focusing on Villa and who is effectively his best-known and most-read "biographer," was never truly able to understand him (*Pancho Villa* 486).

13. Katz calls Guzmán's *Memorias* the most famous book of memoirs published about the general. The book consists of three parts; the first is based on three original memoirs dictated by Villa; the second consists of handwritten notes, possibly taken by Manuel Bauche Alcalde, a Villista intellectual; the third is a series of handwritten notebooks by Bauche Alcalde (830).

14. All English translations of *El águila* are taken from Guzmán, *The Eagle and the Serpent*, trans. Harriet de Onís.

15. Legrás equates Guzmán's inactivity with the profound antagonism between the intellectual and the revolution (449).

16. Translation mine. The original Spanish reads: "Esos enredos de ustedes a mí no me importan" (*El águila* 463). In Harriet de Onis's translation, she writes, "I don't give a damn about your little fusses" (*Eagle* 384); however, I translate this as "I don't care about those affairs of yours," which more clearly distances Villa from the revolutionary politics he disdains.

17. In *The Fence and the River: Culture and Politics at the US-Mexico Border*, Claire Fox analyzes the way that scenes from this section reappear in contemporary popular culture like the "Young Indiana Jones Chronicles."

18. Lucio Blanco was one of the signatories of the Plan de Guadalupe (1913), which disavowed the leadership of President Victoriano Huerta and chose Carranza to be the "Primer Jefe" of the Constitutionalist army. He later helped organize the Convention of Aguascalientes (Krauze 341–342).

19. When Venustiano Carranza was appointed "First Chief" in 1913, neither Pancho Villa nor Emiliano Zapata agreed to submit to his authority. Villa officially disavowed Carranza in September 1914, just prior to the Convention. Although the Convention called for Carranza's resignation, naming Eulalio Gutiérrez provisional president, Carranza refused to accept the orders of the Convention until three conditions had been fully met: (1) the establishment of a preconstitutional regime "that would take charge of carrying out the social and political reforms that the country needs before a fully constitutional government is reestablished"; (2) the resignation and exile of Villa; (3) the resignation and exile of Zapata. These conditions were not met, and Carranza seized control. In late 1914, "after negotiating the unconditional withdrawal of American occupation forces from the city, Carranza set up his government in Veracruz" (Krauze 347–350).

20. In the original Spanish, Guzmán describes himself as being in "la boca del lobo" (the wolf's mouth) rather than the lion's mouth (*El águila* 437).

21. See De Orellana, *Filming Pancho: How Hollywood Shaped the Mexican Revolution*, for a filmography of American feature films, shorts, documentaries, and newsreels produced during the years 1911–1917.

22. On the resurgence of revolutionary film in Mexico and abroad, Zuzana Pick (3) cites Soviet filmmaker Sergei Eisenstein's unfinished project *Que Viva Mexico!* (1930–1931, 1979), Mexican director Fernando de Fuentes's *El prisionero trece* (Prisoner 13, 1933), *El compadre*

Mendoza (Compadre Mendoza, 1933), and *¡Vámonos con Pancho Villa!* (Let's go with Pancho Villa, 1935), *El tesoro de Pancho Villa* (The treasure of Pancho Villa; Arcady Boytler, Mexico, 1935), *La Adelita* (Guillermo Hernández Gómez, Mexico, 1937), *Viva Villa!* (Jack Conway, U.S., 1933), *Flor Silvestre* (Wildflower; Gabriel Figueroa, Mexico, 1943), *Pancho Villa vuelve* (Pancho Villa returns; Miguel Contrera Torres, 1949), *Vino el remolino y nos alevantó* (The whirlwind came and swept us away; Juan Bustillo Oro, 1949), *Los de abajo* (The underdogs; Chano Urueta, 1939), *Rosenda* (Julio Bracho, 1948), and *La negra Angustias* (Matilde Landeta, 1949).

23. De Orellana especially emphasizes Villa's particular seductiveness for Hollywood filmmakers, even suggesting that the portrayal of Villa and the revolution—and by extension, of Mexico—is an American creation (*La mirada* 39, 69). See also Zuzana Pick, *Constructing the Image of the Mexican Revolution: Cinema and the Archive*, 3–4.

24. Except when otherwise indicated, all translations of text and dialogue are taken from the English language subtitles in the 2005 Cinemateca—Condor Media DVD of *¡Vámonos con Pancho Villa!* "Let's Go with Pancho Villa!"

25. The 2005 Cinemateca—Condor Media DVD of *¡Vámonos con Pancho Villa!/Let's Go with Pancho Villa!* also features the film's alternate ending, which was discovered many years after its original release. The alternative ending was not released until August 21, 1982, when it was aired on the Mexican television channel TV 13. In this version, an old and weakened Villa returns ten years later to Tiburcio's farm, to try and recruit him once again. When Tiburcio hesitates, the general kills Tiburcio's wife and daughter, then Tiburcio himself when he tries to resist. Villa ultimately leaves, taking Tiburcio's young son with him. It is unknown whether the director De Fuentes deleted this scene himself or whether it was censored by the Mexican government because of its resolutely negative portrayal of Villa. The alternate ending cements Villa's ruthlessness once and for all and eliminates the possibility of any redemption or agency for Tiburcio.

26. My translation. The 2005 Cinemateca DVD English translation states only "Musicians? No, have them join us," omitting the lines "N'hombre, qué bárbaros. Pobres músicos . . . [No, man, how barbaric. Poor musicians . . .]."

27. My translation. The 2005 Cinemateca DVD English translation omits the crucial line: "¿Qué me viene a preguntar a mí nada? [Why are you bothering me with this?]"

28. All translations of text and dialogue are taken from the English language subtitles from the DVD of *Los rollos perdidos/The Lost Reels.*

29. Besides Luis Valdez's *The Shrunken Head of Pancho Villa*, some Chicano texts that invoke Villa include Silviana Wood, "And Where Was Pancho Villa When You Really Needed Him?"; Dagoberto Gilb, "The Death Mask of Pancho Villa"; and Sheila Ortiz Taylor and Sandra Ortiz Taylor, *Imaginary Parents*, especially the segment "Moving Pictures."

30. El Teatro Campesino was founded in 1965 as an organizing tool within César Chávez's United Farm Workers Union, and became the best-known Chicano performance ensemble to emerge out of the Chicano Movement of the 1960s and 1970s. El Teatro performed their "actos" in the fields, in an agitprop, improvisational style, conveying political messages to farmworkers who could not necessarily read or write. For more on El Teatro Campesino and the demystification of the notion of male "creative genius" embodied by Valdez within Chicano theater, see Yolanda Broyles-González, *El Teatro Campesino: Theater in the Chicano Movement*. Valdez is also well-known as the director of the film *La Bamba* (1987).

31. On stage, the actor who plays Belarmino stands in one position covered by a black tarp, with only his head sticking out. See the Hemispheric Institute Digital Video Library at http://hidvl.nyu.edu/video/000539599.html to view a 1999 screening of *The Shrunken Head* performed by El Teatro Campesino in San Juan Bautista, California.

32. *The Shrunken Head* contains much dialogue in Spanish and Spanglish, and some of the characters, such as Belarmino, do not speak English. To preserve the multilingual essence of the play, I leave the original dialogue in Spanish with my own in-text English translation where applicable.

3. CANONIZING CÉSAR CHÁVEZ

1. I do not mean to suggest that Chávez and other farmworkers were poor out of choice. Chávez considered his poverty a political stance in support of the independence of the UFW. Many times, he refused funds and grants from private foundations because he firmly believed that the workers, not a foundation, should determine when and how to act.

2. Mario T. García states, "There is no question but that César represents the most recognized Latino figure in U.S. history, as attested by the recent issue of a César Chávez commemorative stamp by the postal service" (2).

3. For children's books about Chávez, see, for example, Rudolfo Anaya's *Elegy on the Death of César Chávez*, with illustrations by Gaspar Enríquez. For corridos about Chávez, see "El Corrido de Delano" and "El Corrido de César Chávez" by Lalo Guerrero, the "Father of Chicano Music."

4. It is worth noting that Rodríguez's preferred term is "Mexican-American," not Chicano/a.

5. The Bracero Program was begun by Congress in 1942 to import Mexican seasonal contract laborers under government supervision in order to alleviate wartime labor shortages. Congress repeatedly extended the program until 1965. During this time, almost five million Mexican workers entered the United States. The workers were often exploited through racial discrimination, violations of wage agreements, substandard living quarters, and exorbitant charges for supplies—in short, many of the same conditions Chávez and the UFW were struggling to improve among farmworkers in general. Growers, meanwhile, used braceros to break strikes and lower wages, disposing of such workers as they saw fit (Griswold del Castillo and García 28–29).

6. These were Juan de la Cruz and Rufino Contreras, both Mexican-born UFW members.

7. These projects have taken place in both urban and rural areas, although they have attracted the most attention in large cities such as San Francisco and Los Angeles. While the renaming of streets for Chávez has occurred mostly in Chicano and Latino population centers within large cities, it has also taken place in smaller cities with fewer Latinos/as, such as Lansing, Michigan. For a complete list of commemorations honoring the life and work of César E. Chávez, see www.chavezfoundation.org/uploads/commeroration_list.pdf.

8. See chavezfoundation.org for more information about the César Chávez Foundation and the National Chávez Center.

9. Some examples at the university level are the César Chávez Scholarships for entering freshmen at the University of Arizona, UCLA's César E. Chávez Center for Interdisciplinary Instruction in Chicana and Chicano Studies, the César Chávez Cultural Center at the University of Northern Colorado, and the César E. Chávez Institute at San Francisco State University.

10. For some examples of Chávez and the UFW eagle flag as representative of Chicano nationalism or the Chicano movement, see Octavio Romano-V.'s edited volume, *El Espejo/ The Mirror*, and Cota-Cárdenas's *Puppet*.

11. Cota-Cárdenas is perhaps better-known as a poet, and more attention has been given to her poetry, which is also written in Spanish. On *Puppet*, Rebolledo cites Manuel Rodríguez-Martín, "En la lengua maternal: Las escritoras chicanas y la novela en español."

12. Cota-Cárdenas is herself a product of this linguistic and cultural diversity. She was born to a Chicana mother and a Mexican father in Heber, California, in the Imperial Valley just north of Calexico and the U.S.-Mexico border.

13. Unless otherwise indicated, all quotes are taken from the English translation of *Puppet*, which incorporates Spanish language with translation in the text. Also note that *Puppet* frequently utilizes unorthodox font in the text, incorporating italics, bold type, all capitals, and other stylistic devices. I have reproduced these in the quotes.

14. La Malinche—or Marina/Malintzin—is legendarily known both as the mother of the Mexican nation and as its quintessential betrayer. The lover and indigenous translator of the Spanish conqueror Hernán Cortés, she is one of the most iconic and negatively mythologized symbols of Mexican femininity.

15. The Tlatelolco massacre took place on October 2, 1968, following months of political unrest in Mexico City. That morning, thousands of students from various universities marched in peaceful protest against the army's occupation of the UNAM (National Autonomous University of Mexico) and the Politécnico campuses. They congregated at the Plaza de las Tres Culturas in the neighborhood of Tlatelolco. As evening fell, army and police forces, armed with attack helicopters, tanks, and heavy-caliber weapons, surrounded the plaza and began firing into the crowd. The shooting continued throughout the night, as protesters and bystanders alike were wounded and killed. Thousands of people were detained as the army tried to clear all trace of the massacre by removing and burning bodies, and denying access to journalists, photographers, and even the families of the victims. The official government explanation was that the students themselves provoked the massacre by firing from buildings overlooking the crowd, to which the army responded in self-defense. See Enrique Krauze, *Mexico*, 717–723; also Elena Poniatowska, *La noche de Tlatelolco*.

16. MEChA (Movimiento Estudiantil Chicano de Aztlán) is a Chicano student group with chapters on university campuses throughout the country. The group arose from the National Chicano Youth Liberation Conference and the Santa Barbara Conference in 1969, where students voted to drop organizational names associated with a particular campus or region. MEChA's founding goals call for ties between the university and the social and political life of Mexican American communities. On campus, it "was to become a permanent, well-organized power bloc for the purpose of redirecting university attention and resources to the needs of Mexican-American students" and communities (Carlos Muñoz 80–81).

17. In *A Bowl*, pizza is a recurring trope, whether as a cure for the munchies or as a vehicle to bring Chicanos/as from opposite ends of the political spectrum together, as demonstrated in the scene "Stand and Deliver Pizza (The Last Chicano Movie, 1992)," in which former math teacher Jaime Escalante appears as a pizza parlor owner.

4. "TODOS SOMOS SANTOS": SUBCOMANDANTE MARCOS AND THE EZLN

1. The armed phase of the revolution is usually officially documented as lasting twelve days. However, in her history of the Zapatista movement, *The Fire and the Word: A History of the Zapatista Movement*, Gloria Muñoz Ramírez states, "Twelve days after the indigenous insurrection began, a mass demonstration was announced to demand that the president call a ceasefire and open up dialogue with the indigenous insurgents. . . . Under pressure from the Mexican people . . . [Mexican president Carlos Salinas de Gortari] took the first step and decreed a ceasefire hours before the demonstration. 'The army will only attack if attacked,' he said. The march was held anyway and more than 100,000 people filled the Zócalo . . . of Mexico City to protest against the war in southeast Mexico. However, twenty-four hours after the ceasefire was decreed, military troops backed up by artillery helicopters attacked a Zapatista unit in Ocosingo. The war moved to the mountains and the ceasefire held only in the cities. In spite of this, the EZLN accepted the proposal to end hostilities" (112).

2. The Juntas de Buen Gobierno (Councils of Good Government) or caracoles (snails) are five autonomous regional governments in Zapatista territory in Chiapas, named La Realidad, Morelia, La Garrucha, Roberto Barrios, and Oventic. The councils "[name] their own authorities and [take] charge of organizing education, health, and the administration of justice themselves." The councils reflect the indigenous peoples' rejection of "the fruitless struggle for autonomy through legal reforms" (Marcos and Zapatistas, *Other Campaign*, 11). Just as the Zapatistas refuse to recognize the "bad" federal and local governments, the councils are not recognized by the Mexican federal or state governments.

3. Translation José Rabasa.

4. Comandanta Esther is one of the commanders of the Comité Clandestino de Revolución Indígena–Comandancia General (CCRI-CG; the Clandestine Revolutionary Indigenous Committee–General Command) of the EZLN. Although Subcomandante Marcos essentially serves as the group spokesperson, many of the comandantes, including Esther, routinely give speeches to the group and to the public. The CCRI-CG is the ruling body of communal assembly delegates from each of the four main Zapatista language groups.

5. Ramona, a prominent Zapatista comandanta who died in 2006, was especially well-known for her role in the occupation of San Cristóbal de las Casas during the 1994 uprising, and for traveling to Mexico City in 1996 as part of the delegation that founded the National Indigenous Congress (Henck 249, 313).

6. By "essentialist," I mean that a given human trait, such as race, is interpreted as having an innate existence or universal validity rather than being a social, ideological, or intellectual construct.

7. Nick Henck notes that "there is considerable debate even now as to the extent of Marcos' acquisition of indigenous languages" (93–94). Predictably, Marcos's critics claim that he speaks almost no Tzeltal, Tzotzil, or Chol (three of the primary indigenous languages of Chiapas), instead relying on interpreters. Henck cites Marcos's interview with Yvon LeBot, in which he discusses his ignorance of indigenous languages during his early years as a guerrilla and the shock he faced in having to confront them, along with the indigenous campesinos' propensity for making fun of him in their languages. However, I agree with Henck's hypothesis that it is unlikely that Marcos remains mostly ignorant of these languages today (93–94). Given his linguistic abilities and his incentive to learn the languages, it seems likely that he is fluent enough in one or more of these tongues.

8. Here I wish to distinguish between texts that are explicitly signed by Marcos and those that are signed by the collective CCRI-CG, although Marcos's authorial voice is arguably present in the background of the pieces signed by the CCRI-CG as well.

9. Translation by Stuart Day (107–108).

10. Translation by Stuart Day (108).

11. The caracoles, established in 2003, are the organizational regions of the autonomous Zapatista communities in Chiapas. They are "centers for political and cultural meetings and exchange between the Zapatista communities and national and international civil society. They are also the headquarters of the Good Government Boards [Juntas de Buen Gobierno], recently formed as a crucial building block of Zapatista autonomy" (Muñoz Ramírez 13).

12. For an example of the use of Marcos's postscript in a celebratory, multicultural manner, see the play *Trece Días/Thirteen Days* (1995) by Raquel Rubio Goldsmith, Daniel Nugent, and Eva Tessler. The play was originally written as part of a conference on the Chiapas rebellion at the University of Arizona. It was first produced as a stage reading by Borderlands Theater of Tucson, Arizona, and later performed by Borderlands Theater and the San Francisco Mime Troupe. It illustrates the instant, worldwide dissemination of information on January 1, 1994, alongside the immediate campaign of concealment and confusion on the part of the Mexican and U.S. states, represented by President Salinas, U.S. border patrol agents, the Mexican

military, and other government officials. The play portrays the Zapatista question in the context of the United States and Chicano/a identities, depicting the EZLN rebellion alongside the persecution of undocumented migrants and the corruption of the U.S. border patrol. It is an important addition to a body of work that addresses the reception of Marcos and the EZLN by U.S. Chicanos/as, drawing especially upon the connection between indigenous people and migrants to the United States. The play ends with the triumphant recitation of the "Majority-which-disguises-itself-as-untolerated-minority-P.S.," which can be read as an example of triumphant multiculturalism.

13. "La Mar" is the possible nom de guerre of Gloria Muñoz Ramírez, a Mexican journalist, former reporter for *La Jornada*, and author of *The Fire and the Word: A History of the Zapatista Movement*, who first met Marcos during the first years of the Zapatista uprising. In September 2005, a Mexican celebrity magazine, *Quien*, published an article with rumors of a relationship (and possible child) between Marcos and Muñoz Ramírez. Henck emphasizes that there is no proof to back up these allegations, and that they must remain speculation. However, the very fact that these claims exist is proof that the outside world is still preoccupied with "unmasking" the details of Marcos's private life, even ten or fifteen years after his initial appearance on the scene, thus reinforcing his celebrity, iconicity, and sanctity (Henck 358).

14. See Subcomandante Insurgente Marcos, *The Story of the Colors/La Historia de los Colores: A Bilingual Folktale from the Jungles of Chiapas*.

15. The UAM is the Universidad Autónoma Metropolitana (Autonomous Metropolitan University). Rafael Guillén was a lecturer here from 1979 to 1984 with a few breaks in between when he may have visited Chiapas and other countries, such as Nicaragua and the United States, though nothing is known for certain (Henck 42–52). Of course, it is crucial to remember that anything Rafael Guillén might have done has no bearing on Marcos the character.

16. The EZLN operates a shortwave radio station, "Radio Insurgente: La voz de los sin voz" (The voice of the voiceless), which broadcasts "from the mountains of the Mexican Southeast" in Chiapas and is completely "unattached to the bad Mexican government." Their goal is to "cover the five Zapatista zones in Chiapas with community radio stations that will produce their own programs depending on the needs and languages of each zone." The station is available as internet downloads and streams at http://www.radioinsurgente .org/index.php

17. The *guerra sucia* (dirty war) is an internal war between the PRI-led Mexican government and left-wing student and guerrilla groups that lasted roughly from the late 1960s to the early 1980s. The number of rebel suspects killed or "disappeared" by the Mexican army during the Dirty War is unknown. For more information, see Julio Scherer García and Carlos Monsiváis, *Los patriotas: De Tlatelolco a la guerra sucia*, and Alberto Ulloa Bornemann, *Surviving Mexico's Dirty War: A Political Prisoner's Memoir*. In 2002, President Vicente Fox of the Partido Nacional Acción (PAN; one of the three main political parties in Mexico, occupying the right of Mexico's political spectrum in relation to economic and social policies) set up the first existing office to investigate possible human rights violations under the administrations of Presidents Díaz Ordaz (1964–1970), Echeverria (1970–1976) and López Portillo (1976–1982). The office presented its (unreleased) report in December 2005. BBC News, "Mexico 'Dirty War' Crimes Alleged," February 27, 2006.

18. Marcos and Taibo agreed to donate all author royalties. Proceeds of the book benefit Enlace Civil, an NGO that provides support for social services for indigenous communities in Chiapas.

19. The Belascoarán Shayne series of detective novels began in 1976 with *Días de combate* and concluded (at least until the publication of *Muertos incómodos*) in 1993 with *Adiós, Madrid*. Recently, the complete series was published in a collection titled *No habrá final feliz* (2009).

20. La India María is a popular Mexican fictional character portrayed by María Elena Velasco in many films and television programs as a typical rural indigenous woman who migrates to the big city (whether Mexico City or cities in the United States) for work. La India Maria dresses in traditional native clothing, speaks a highly accented and non-standard Spanish that she sometimes sprinkles with native language, and is frequently confused by urban life. Nevertheless, she is wise about human behavior and often imparts social or moral lessons.

21. Close sharply criticizes Marcos's discursive tics, especially one instance where "y entonces" is repeated "more than 150 times in eight pages" (n.p.). Translations of *Muertos incómodos* are my own, unless otherwise indicated.

22. Translation taken from Marcos and Taibo II, *The Uncomfortable Dead*, trans. Carlos López.

23. The Other Campaign, which Hermann Bellinghausen and Gloria Muñoz Ramírez assert is "the Sixth Declaration in practice," was launched in 2005 as a non-electoral grassroots campaign that rejects traditional, hierarchical political and electoral campaigns, whether from the Right or the Left (317). Bellinghausen and Muñoz Ramírez note that the first stages of the campaign consist of tours by delegations of Zapatistas insurgents to visit places and peoples throughout the Mexican nation, including meetings with migrants and Chicanos/as on the other side of the border (317–318). For the purposes of the Other Campaign, Subcomandante Marcos adopted the moniker "Delegate Zero."

24. "La Sexta," like most of the other Declarations of the Lacandon Jungle, is signed by the collective CCRI-CG of the EZLN. The only exception is the Fifth Declaration, which is signed by Subcomandante Insurgente Marcos and the CCRI-CG. Interestingly, however, in the book *The Other Campaign/La otra campaña*, a bilingual publication that contains an introduction to "La Sexta," both the Sixth Declaration and a separate interview with Marcos are attributed to "Subcomandante Marcos and the Zapatistas."

25. The San Andrés Accords on Indian Rights and Culture were meant to be a wide-ranging plan that agreed to a certain level of Indian autonomy, as well as "the right of indigenous people to establish their own forms of organization," though many of the points that the EZLN insisted upon—such as the reinstating of Article 27 of the Mexican Constitution on land reform and *ejidos*—were soundly rejected by the government (Henck 299–300). Ejidos are parcels of collectively owned, communal land registered with the Mexican National Agrarian Registry. In 1991, President Salinas de Gortari eliminated the constitutional right to ejidos, primarily because of Mexico's impending entry into NAFTA.

26. The piqueteros are organizations of unemployed workers who utilize pickets, road blocks, and blockades in order to promote social change and fight for their rights. Many piqueteros are women, including some of their leaders. They have also formed co-operatives for bartering systems, small-scale farming, sewing, food distribution, libraries, bakeries and even collectively run factories. See "The Piquetes," *The Dominion*, for more information.

27. Translation taken from Marcos and Taibo, *The Uncomfortable Dead*, trans. Carlos López.

28. Belausteguigoitia argues, "Within the diversity [of indigenous groups], the other that has been most silent is the indigenous woman" (300).

5. ILLEGAL MARGINALIZATIONS: LA SANTÍSIMA MUERTE

1. Journalist José Gil Olmos cites Katia Perdigón, a Mexican anthropologist whom he interviews in his book *La Santa Muerte*, on this point. According to Perdigón: "today the devotion to Santa Muerte is only below that of Jesus and the Virgin of Guadalupe, and equal to that of San Judas Tadeo" (92). Gil Olmos cites an interview with Manuel Valadez, a seller at the

Mercado de Sonora (Sonora market) a well-known traditional public market in Mexico City famous for its collection of merchandise dedicated to medicinal plants, spirituality, and the occult. Valadez claims, "of all the figures available at the market, the most sold is that of Santa Muerte" (82).

2. Many devotees, like those featured in Eva Aridjis's documentary *La Santa Muerte*, make or order new dresses and outfits for their Santa Muerte figures to correspond to religious or national holidays or simply to reflect the change in season. Journalist José Gil Olmos notes that devotees dress their Santa Muerte figures in particular costumes and outfits such as those of a *china poblana*, Aztec dancer, mariachi, or football (soccer) player. Gil Olmos argues that the wide variety of outfits and accessories manifest the agency that stems from the direct link between saint and devotee, "since the figures belong to them" (103).

3. All quotes from the film *La Santa Muerte* are taken from Eva Aridjis's English subtitles.

4. Gil Olmos claims there are fifteen Santa Muerte "parishes" (*parroquias*) in Los Angeles, as well as others in San Diego, New York, and El Paso. He notes that altars have been documented in El Salvador, Honduras, and Guatemala (102).

5. The Templo Santa Muerte features live-streaming radio and television on the site http://templosantamuerte.com/SITIO/index.html.

6. Doña Queta recounts the history of her altar in Eva Aridjis's film, as well as to Chesnut (37–41), Gil Olmos (75–76), and Daniel Hernández (*Down and Delirious* 155). She claims that she installed the altar to Santa Muerte with the help of her companion, Mr. Ray, and opened it to the public for the first time on October 31, 2001 (Gil Olmos 75). Aridjis also interviews Doña Queta's son Omar Romero Romero, who confirms that his brother gave his mother the statue of the saint.

7. See also Gil Olmos (115–116).

8. Arizona Senate Bill 1070 is a legislative act signed into law in the state of Arizona on April 23, 2010, that is the broadest, strictest anti-illegal immigration measure in recent U.S. history. In June 2012, the U.S. Supreme Court ruled on the case *Arizona v. United States*, upholding the provision requiring immigration status checks during law enforcement stops "if there is reasonable suspicion that a person is in the country illegally" but declaring three other provisions unconstitutional (Rau n.p.).

9. *Totonaco* refers to the Totonac indigenous people, who historically resided in eastern coastal and mountainous areas of Mexico and presently reside in the states of Veracruz, Puebla, and Hidalgo. They may have built the pre-Hispanic cities of El Tajín and Teotihuacán. Although they did not originate the ritual, they are best-known performers of the dance *Voladores de Papantla* (Papantla flyers), which is most strongly associated with the town of Papantla, Veracruz.

10. For more on the proud, independent spirit of Tepito, see Francisco Mata Rosas, *Tepito ¡Bravo el Barrio!*

11. YouTube user name "olearyrod," comment from November 2010 on "La Santa Muerte" Part 1, *Relatos de Ultratumba*, YouTube channel "bungolio," accessible at http://www.youtube.com/user/bungolio.

12. Filmmaker Eva Aridjis is Homero Aridjis's daughter.

13. Romo's church was originally known as the Iglesia Santa, Católica, Apostólica y Tradicional México–Estados Unidos (Holy, Catholic, Apostolic, and Traditional Mexico–United States Church), reflecting his desire to extend his church "to several states [in Mexico] and to the United States, through the immigrants that seek a Catholic base [that would be] closer to their traditions than to Vatican rules" (Gil Olmos 88).

14. Gil Olmos notes that some Santa Muerte devotees claim that Romo's Angel of the Holy Death is modeled on his latest wife (90).

15. According to Gil Olmos and Daniel Hernández, Romo eagerly shared with reporters his extravagant floor plans for the building, claiming that the twelve-hundred-square-meter cathedral would contain crypts, a baptismal font, offices, an audiovisual room, and two recording studios for television and webcasts. The projected cost of the building would be 38 million pesos (over 3 million dollars), to be collected from donations. To this day, there is no record of the whereabouts of the thousands of dollars donated by the faithful for the construction of the cathedral, which was never even begun (Gil Olmos 129–130, 133).

16. See also Tracy Wilkinson, "Mexico Has Arrested a Leader of Santa Muerte 'Church,'" *Los Angeles Times*, January 5, 2011. According to Wilkinson: "David Romo, a self-appointed bishop of the church, stands accused of running a kidnapping ring and laundering its ransoms through his personal bank account. . . . To bolster their case, prosecutors released videotape from security cameras at a bank that purportedly showed Romo withdrawing some of his ill-gotten gains" (n.p.).

17. Legaria's followers assert that El Pantera was murdered because of "jealousy and religious differences," yet they quite understandably refuse to name any names (Hernández "La Plaza blog: Rival").

18. Gil Olmos states, "A faithful devotee of Santa Muerte who helped Romo in the National Sanctuary, or the 'Parish of Mercy,' on 35 Bravo Street delivered a letter to me, which I transcribe here, where he reveals his discomfort and denounces, in detail, the funneling of money and the manipulation of the cult that Romo has conducted for his personal gain" (133).

19. Daniel Arizmendi López, better known as "El Mochaorejas" (The ear chopper), is a notorious Mexican kidnapper famous for cutting the ears off his victims in order to put pressure on their families to pay for their release. Chesnut notes that Santa Muerte first gained widespread national press coverage in Mexico in 1998 when El Mochaorejas was arrested and police permitted him to bring a figure of the death saint with him to prison (Chesnut 97).

20. Gil Olmos states, "None of the new expressions and cults can compare with this kind of belief, which, unlike other religious customs, does not require an intermediary—priest or Church—to establish a direct link between the deity and her followers" (18).

CONCLUSION: NARRATIVE DEVOTION

1. Rivera wrote . . . *y no se lo tragó la tierra* / . . . *And the Earth Did Not Devour Him* in Spanish. The English quotations are taken from the 1992 translation by Evangelina Vigil-Piñón.

WORKS CITED

Abou-El-Haj, Barbara. *The Medieval Cult of Saints*. Cambridge: Cambridge University Press, 1994. Print.

Acuña, Rodolfo. *Occupied America: A History of Chicanos*. 3rd ed. New York: HarperCollins, 1988. Print.

Aguirre, Lauro, and Teresa Urrea. "Tomóchic! Redención!" *Tomóchic: La revolución adelantada*. Vol. 2. Ed. Jesús Vargas Valdez. Ciudad Juárez: Universidad Autónoma de Ciudad Juárez, 1994. 91–193. Print.

Anaya, Rudolfo. *Elegy on the Death of César Chávez*. El Paso, TX: Cinco Puntos Press, 2000. Print.

Anderson, Mark C. *Pancho Villa's Revolution by Headlines*. Norman: University of Oklahoma Press, 2000. Print.

Anzaldúa, Gloria. *Borderlands/La Frontera*. 2nd ed. San Francisco: Aunt Lute Books, 1999. Print.

Aridjis, Eva, dir. *La Santa Muerte*. Dark Knight Pictures, 2007. DVD.

Aridjis, Homero. *La Santa Muerte*. México, DF: Alfaguara, 2003. Print.

Azuela, Mariano. *Los de abajo*. 1915. Madrid: Ediciones Cátedra, 1991. Print.

Bardacke, Frank. "César's Ghost." *The Nation* 26 July 1993. Web. 3 Apr. 2012.

———. "Looking Back at the UFW, a Union with Two Souls." *The Nation* 13 Feb. 2012. Web. 16 Mar. 2012.

———. *Trampling out the Vintage*. London and New York: Verso, 2011. Print.

Baudrillard, Jean. *Simulacra and Simulation*. Trans. Sheila Faria Glaser. Ann Arbor: University of Michigan Press, 1994. Print.

Beaubien, Jason. "Saint or Sinner? Mexico Debates a Cult's Status." NPR.org. 13 Apr. 2009. Web. 8 Feb. 2012.

Behar, Ruth. *Translated Woman*. Boston: Beacon Press, 1993. Print.

Belausteguigoitia Rius, Marisa. "Máscaras y posdatas: Estrategias femeninas en la rebelión indígena de Chiapas." *Debate feminista* 7.14 (1996): 299–317. Print.

Bellinghausen, Hermann, and Gloria Muñoz Ramírez. "The Next Step: The Sixth Declaration of the Lacandón. Jungle." *The Fire and the Word: A History of the Zapatista Movement*. By Gloria Muñoz Ramírez. Trans. Laura Carlsen and Alejandro Reyes Arias. San Francisco: City Lights Books, 2008. 317–34. Print.

Blackwell, Maylei. *¡Chicana Power!* Austin: University of Texas Press, 2011. Print.

Bosca, Roberto. "Evita: A Case of Political Canonization." *The Making of Saints: Contesting Sacred Ground*. Ed. James F. Hopgood. Tuscaloosa: University of Alabama Press, 2005. 59–74. Print.

Brown, James W. "Prologue." *Tomóchic*. By Heriberto Frías. 1893. México, DF: Editorial Porrúa, 1999. ix–xxi. Print.

Brown, Peter. *The Cult of the Saints*. Chicago: University of Chicago Press, 1981. Print.

Broyles-González, Yolanda. *El Teatro Campesino: Theater in the Chicano Movement*. Austin: University of Texas Press, 1994. Print.

Butler, Judith. *Precarious Life*. London and New York: Verso, 2004. Print.

Campobello, Nellie. *Apuntes sobre la vida militar de Francisco Villa*. México: EDIAPSA, 1940. Print.

———. *Cartucho*. 1931. México, DF: Factoria Ediciones, 2000. Print.

———. *Las manos de Mamá*. 1937. 2nd ed. México: Editorial Villa Ocampo, 1949. Print.

Castillo, Debra A., and María Socorro Tabuenca Córdoba. *Border Women: Writing from La Frontera*. Minneapolis: University of Minnesota Press, 2002. Print.

César Chávez Foundation. Web. 15 Mar. 2012.

César E. Chávez National Holiday. Web. 15 Mar. 2012.

Chakrabarty, Dipesh. *Provincializing Europe*. Princeton: Princeton University Press, 2000. Print.

Chávez, Paul F. "Welcome!/Bienvenidos to the Sponsorship Site!" *Cesar Chavez Legacy Awards*. Web. 15 Mar. 2012.

Chesnut, R. Andrew. *Devoted to Death: Santa Muerte, the Skeleton Saint*. New York: Oxford University Press, 2012. Print.

Cisneros, Sandra. "Guadalupe the Sex Goddess." *Goddess of the Americas*. Ed. Ana Castillo. New York: Riverhead Trade, 1996. 46–51. Print.

———. *Woman Hollering Creek*. New York: Vintage, 1992. Print.

Close, Glen S. "*Muertos incómodos:* The Monologic Polyphony of Subcomandante Marcos." *Ciberletras* 15 (2006): no pagination. Print.

Collier, George, and Elizabeth Lowery Quaratiello. *Basta! Land and the Zapatista Rebellion in Chiapas*. Oakland: Food First Books, 2005. Print.

Connolly, William. *Identity/Difference*. Minneapolis: University of Minnesota Press, 1991. Print.

Cota-Cárdenas, Margarita. *Puppet: A Chicano Novella*. Trans. Barbara D. Reiss and Trino Sandoval. Albuquerque: University of New Mexico Press, 2000. Print.

Currier, Erin. *Subcomandante Marcos as the Buddha*. Portrait/Collage. *Erin Currier Fine Art*. 2002. Web. 1 Dec. 2012.

Day, Stuart A. "Foretelling Failure: Questioning the Mexican Political Left from Within." *Discourse: Journal for Theoretical Studies in Media and Culture* 23.2 (2001): 102–21. Print.

de Fuentes, Fernando, dir. *¡Vámonos con Pancho Villa!* (*Let's Go with Pancho Villa*). 1935. Cinemateca—Condor Media, 2005. DVD.

de la Torre, Miguel, ed. *Hispanic American Religious Cultures*. Santa Barbara: ABC-CLIO, 2009. Print.

Delgadillo, Theresa. *Spiritual Mestizaje*. Durham: Duke University Press, 2011. Print.

de Marcelo Esquivel, Antonio, and Enrique Hernández. "¡Él no es la Santa Muerte!" *La Prensa* [México, DF] 5 Jan. 2011. Web. 5 July 2011.

de Orellana, Margarita. *Filming Pancho: How Hollywood Shaped the Mexican Revolution*. Trans. John King. London/New York: Verso, 2009. Print.

———. *La mirada circular: El cine norteamericano de la Revolución mexicana, 1911–1917*. México, DF: Artes de México, 1997. Print.

Díaz Bjorkquist, Elena. "Chautauqua: Teresa Urrea, La Santa de Cabora," and "Excerpt from 'History Live!'" *Elena Diaz Bjorkquist*. Web. 5 Jan. 2012.

Domecq, Brianda. *The Astonishing Story of the Saint of Cabora*. Trans. Kay S. García. Tempe, AZ: Bilingual Press, 1998. Print.

———. *La insólita historia de la Santa de Cabora*. México, DF: Planeta, 1990. Print.

———. "Teresa Urrea: La Santa de Cabora." *Tomóchic: La revolución adelantada*. Vol. 2. Ed. Jesús Vargas Valdez. Ciudad Juárez: Universidad Autónoma de Ciudad Juárez, 1994. 11–47. Print.

Domínguez-Ruvalcava, Héctor. *Modernity and the Nation in Mexican Representations of Masculinity.* New York: Palgrave MacMillan, 2007. Print.

Douillet, Jacques. *What Is a Saint?* New York: Hawthorn Books, 1958. Print.

Dukes, Mark. *César Chávez.* Portrait. Saint Gregory of Nyssa Episcopal Church, San Francisco. *All Saints Company.* "The Dancing Saints Icon Project." Web. 1 Dec. 2012.

Enlace Zapatista. Web. 10 Apr. 2011.

Espinosa, Gastón, and Mario T. García, eds. *Mexican American Religions: Spirituality, Activism, and Culture.* Durham: Duke University Press, 2008. Print.

Estey, Miles, and Grant Fuller. "Mexico: Capitalizing on the Anti-Capitalist Zapatistas." *Global Post* 25 Oct. 2010. Web. 11 Feb. 2011.

"Flocking to See Mystic Santa Teresa." *Los Angeles Times* 15 Dec. 1902, page 8. Print.

Flores, Juan. "Latino Studies: New Contexts, New Concepts." *Critical Latin American and Latino Studies.* Ed. Juan Poblete. Minneapolis: University of Minnesota Press, 2003. Print.

Fox, Claire F. *The Fence and the River: Culture and Politics at the US-Mexico Border.* Minneapolis: University of Minnesota Press, 1999. Print.

Franco, Jean. *Critical Passions: Selected Essays.* Durham: Duke University Press, 1999. Print.

———. *An Introduction to Spanish-American Literature.* 3rd ed. Cambridge and New York: Cambridge University Press, 1994. Print.

Frías, Heriberto. *Tomóchic.* 1893. México, DF: Editorial Porrúa, 1999. Print.

García, Mario T. *The Gospel of Cesár Chávez.* Lanham, MD: Sheed & Ward, 2007. Print.

García Ramírez, Fernando. "Muertos incómodos, de Paco Ignacio." *Letras Libres* Aug. 2005. Web. 16 Mar. 2011.

Garrett, Clarke. *Spirit Possession and Popular Religion.* Baltimore: Johns Hopkins University Press, 1987. Print.

Gentile, Emilio. *Politics as Religion.* Trans. George Staunton. Princeton: Princeton University Press, 2006. Print.

Gilb, Dagoberto. "The Death Mask of Pancho Villa." *The Magic of Blood.* New York: Grove Press, 1993. Print.

Gil Olmos, José. *La Santa Muerte: La virgen de los olvidados.* México D.F.: Debolsillo, 2010. Print.

Gómez-Peña, Guillermo. *Dangerous Border Crossers.* London and New York: Routledge, 2000. Print.

Griffith, James S. *Folk Saints of the Borderlands.* Tucson: Rio Nuevo Publishers, 2003. Print.

Griswold del Castillo, Richard, and Richard García. *César Chávez: A Triumph of Spirit.* Norman: University of Oklahoma Press, 1995. Print.

"Guadalupe Hidalgo, Treaty of." *Dictionary of American History.* 2003. Encyclopedia.com. Web. 12 Mar. 2013.

Guerrero, Lalo. "El Corrido de César Chávez." *El Chicano Inolvidable.* Warner Music Latina, 2002. CD.

———. "El Corrido de Delano." 45 rpm record, 1966.

Guillermoprieto, Alma. "The Unmasking." *The Zapatista Reader.* Ed. Tom Hayden. New York: Thunder's Mouth Press/Nation Books, 2002. 33–44. Print.

Guzmán, Martín Luis. *El águila y la serpiente.* 1928. México: Editorial Anáhuac, 1941. Print.

———. *The Eagle and the Serpent.* Trans. Harriet de Onis. Gloucester, MA: Peter Smith, 1928. Print.

———. *Memorias de Pancho Villa.* 1936–1951. 6th ed. México: Compañía General de Ediciones, 1963. Print.

Harvey, David. *A Brief History of Neoliberalism.* Oxford: Oxford University Press, 2005. Print.

Hayden, Tom, ed. *The Zapatista Reader*. New York: Thunder's Mouth Press/Nation Books, 2002. Print.

Henck, Nick. *Subcomandante Marcos: The Man and the Mask*. Durham: Duke University Press, 2007. Print.

Hernández, Daniel. *Down and Delirious in Mexico City: The Aztec Metropolis in the Twenty-First Century*. New York: Scribner, 2011. Print.

——. "La Plaza blog: Rival Santa Muerte Church Claims Captured 'Bishop' Does Not Represent the Mexican Death Cult." *Los Angeles Times* 10 Jan. 2011. Web. 5 July 2011.

——. "La Plaza blog: 'Santa Muerte Statues Removed from Nuevo Laredo.'" *Los Angeles Times* 25 Mar. 2009. Web. 5 July 2011.

Hills, Matt. *Fan Cultures*. London and New York: Routledge, 2002. Print.

Holden, William Curry. *Teresita*. Owing Mills, MD: Stemmer House, 1978. Print.

Hopgood, James F. *The Making of Saints: Contesting Sacred Ground*. Tuscaloosa: University of Alabama Press, 2005. Print.

Huerta, Jorge, ed. *Necessary Theater*. Houston: Arte Público Press, 1989. Print.

"Hypocrisy." *The Oxford English Dictionary*. OED.com. Web. 18 Oct. 2012.

Illades Aguilar, Lillian. *La rebelión de Tomóchic, 1891–1892*. México, DF: Instituto Nacional de Antropología e Historia, 1993. Print.

Irwin, Robert McKee. *Bandits, Captives, Heroines, and Saints: Cultural Icons of Mexico's Northwest Borderlands*. Minneapolis: University of Minnesota Press, 2007. Print.

Jaccard, Jacques and Henry McRae, directors. *Liberty: A Daughter of the U.S.A.* Universal Pictures, 1916. Film.

Jensen, Richard J., and John C. Hammerback, eds. *The Words of César Chávez*. College Station: Texas A&M University Press, 2002. Print.

Johnson, Reed. "An Inside View of Society's Outsiders." *Los Angeles Times* 23 Oct. 2005. Web. 14 Jan. 2011.

——. "Pancho Villa, leader of the Mexican Revolution and Hollywood movie star." *Los Angeles Times* 1 May 2010. Web. 26 Feb. 2013.

Katz, Friedrich. *The Life and Times of Pancho Villa*. Stanford: Stanford University Press, 1998. Print.

——. "Prologo." *La mirada circular: El cine norteamericano de la Revolución mexicana, 1911–1917*. By Margarita de Orellana. México, DF: Artes de México, 1997. 7–11. Print.

Kieckhefer, Richard, and George D. Bond. *Sainthood: Its Manifestations in World Religions*. Berkeley and Los Angeles: University of California Press, 1988. Print.

Klass, Morton. *Mind over Mind: The Anthropology and Psychology of Spirit Possession*. Oxford: Rowman & Littlefield Publishers, 2003. Print.

Klein, Naomi. "A Clash of Image and Folklore." *The Guardian* [London] 14 Mar. 2001. Web. 27 Apr. 2012.

Krauze, Enrique. *Mexico: Biography of Power*. New York: HarperCollins, 1997. Print.

Kun, Josh. *Audiotopia: Music, Race, and America*. Berkeley and Los Angeles: University of California Press, 2005. Print.

Larralde, Carlos. "Santa Teresa: A Chicana Mystic." *Grito del Sol: A Chicano Quarterly* 2 (April–June 1978): 1–113. Print.

Legrás, Horacio. "Martín Luis Guzmán: El viaje de la revolución." *MLN* 118 (2003): 427–54. Print.

Leñero, Vicente. *Todos somos Marcos. Teatro completo II*. México, DF: Fondo de Cultura Económica, 2011. Print.

Lentz, Br. Robert, OFM. *César Chávez de California*. Portrait. *Trinity Religious Artwork and Icons*. Web. 1 Dec. 2012.

León, Luis D. "Cesar Chavez in American Religious Politics: Mapping the New Global Spiritual Line." *American Quarterly* 59.3 (2007): 857–81. Print.

———. *La Llorona's Children: Religion, Life, and Death in the US-Mexican Borderlands.* Berkeley and Los Angeles: University of California Press, 2004. Print.

Leovy, Jill. "Santa Muerte in LA: A Gentler Vision of 'Holy Death.'" *Los Angeles Times* 7 Dec. 2009. Web. 3 Oct. 2012.

Levy, Jacques E. *César Chávez: Autobiography of La Causa.* Minneapolis: University of Minnesota Press, 2007. Print.

Lewis, I. M. *Ecstatic Religion.* London and New York: Routledge, 1971. Print.

Lida, David. *First Stop in the New World: Mexico City, the Capital of the Twenty-First Century.* New York: Riverhead Books/Penguin, 2008. Print.

Lloyd-Moffett, Stephen R. "Holy Activist, Secular Saint: Religion and the Social Activism of César Chávez." *Mexican American Religions: Spirituality, Activism, and Culture.* Ed. Gastón Espinos and Mario T. García. Durham: Duke University Press, 2008. 106–24. Print.

Lomnitz, Claudio. *Death and the Idea of Mexico.* New York: Zone Books, 2005. Print.

———. *Deep Mexico, Silent Mexico.* Minneapolis: University of Minnesota Press, 2001. Print.

Macklin, June. "Saints and Near-Saints in Transition: The Sacred, the Secular, and the Popular." *The Making of Saints: Contesting Sacred Ground.* Ed. James F. Hopgood. Tuscaloosa: University of Alabama Press, 2005. 1–22. Print.

Marcos, Subcomandante Insurgente. "Durito III: El neoliberalismo y el movimiento obrero." *Enlace Zapatista* 15 Apr. 1995. Web. 10 Apr 2011.

———. "Una Muerte . . . O Una Vida (Carta cuarta a Don Luis Villoro en el intercambio sobre Ética y Política)." *Enlace Zapatista* Oct.–Nov. 2011. Web. 11 Dec. 2011.

———. *Our Word Is Our Weapon: Selected Writings.* New York: Seven Stories Press, 2002. Print.

———. *The Speed of Dreams: Selected Writings, 2001–2007.* San Francisco: City Lights Books, 2007. Print.

———. *The Story of the Colors/La Historia de los Colores: A Bilingual Folktale from the Jungles of Chiapas.* Illus. Domitila Domínguez. Trans. Anne Bar Din. El Paso, TX: Cinco Puntos Press, 2003. Print.

———. "Testimonies of the First Day." *The Zapatista Reader.* Ed. Tom Hayden. New York: Thunder's Mouth Press/Nation Books, 2002. 207–16. Print.

Marcos, Subcomandante Insurgente, and Paco Ignacio Taibo II. *Muertos incómodos (falta lo que falta).* México, DF: Editorial Joaquín Mortiz, 2006. Print.

———. "Prólogo." *Muertos incómodos (falta lo que falta).* La Jornada 5 Dec. 2004. Web. 8 Dec. 2012.

———. *The Uncomfortable Dead (What's Missing Is Missing).* Trans. Carlos López. New York: Akashic Books, 2006. Print.

Marcos, Subcomandante Insurgente, and the Zapatistas. *The Other Campaign/La Otra Campaña.* San Francisco: City Lights Books, 2006. Print.

———. *Shadows of Tender Fury.* Trans. Frank Bardacke, Leslie Lopez, and the Watsonville, CA Human Rights Collective. New York: Monthly Review Press, 1995. Print.

Mata Rosas, Francisco. *Tepito ¡Bravo el Barrio!* México, DF: Instituto Nacional de Bellas Artes: Trilce Ediciones, 2007. Print.

Matthiessen, Peter. *Sal Si Puedes (Escape If You Can): Cesar Chavez and the New American Revolution.* Berkeley and Los Angeles: University of California Press, 2000. Print.

Medina Ruiz, Fernando. *Francisco Villa, cuando el rencor estalla.* México: Editorial Jus, 1992. Print.

Meier, Matt, and Feliciano Ribera. *Mexican Americans/American Mexicans.* New York: Hill and Wang, 1993. Print.

"Mexico 'Dirty War' Crimes Alleged." *BBC News* 27 Feb. 2006. Web. 10 Apr. 2011.

Monsiváis, Carlos. *Mexican Postcards.* Trans. John Kraniauskas. London and New York: Verso, 1997. Print.

———. "¿Todos somos indios?" *Debate feminista* 6.11 (1995): 333–36. Print.

Montoya, Richard, Ricardo Salinas, and Herbert Siguenza. *Culture Clash: Life, Death, and Revolutionary Comedy.* New York: Theatre Communications Group, 1998. Print.

Muñoz, Carlos Jr. *Youth, Identity, Power: The Chicano Movement.* London and New York: Verso, 1989. Print.

Muñoz, José Estéban. *Disidentifications: Queers of Color and the Performance of Politics.* Minneapolis: University of Minnesota Press, 1999. Print.

Muñoz, Rafael. *¡Vámonos con Pancho Villa!* 1931. 2nd ed. México: Espasa Calpe, 1950. Print.

Muñoz Ramírez, Gloria. *The Fire and the Word: A History of the Zapatista Movement.* Trans. Laura Carlsen and Alejandro Reyes Arias. San Francisco: City Lights Books, 2008. Print.

Murray, William Breen. "Spirits of a Holy Land: Place and Time in a Modern Mexican Religious Movement." *The Making of Saints: Contesting Sacred Ground.* Ed. James F. Hopgood. Tuscaloosa: University of Alabama Press, 2005. 107–23. Print.

Newell, Gillian E. "Teresa Urrea, Santa de Cabora and Early Chicana? The Politics of Representation, Identity and Social Memory." *The Making of Saints: Contesting Sacred Ground.* Ed. James F. Hopgood. Tuscaloosa: University of Alabama Press, 2005. 90–106. Print.

Niebylski, Dianna C. "Caught in the Middle: Ambiguous Gender and Social Politics in Sabina Berman's Play *Entre Villa y una mujer desnuda.*" *Revista de Estudios Hispánicos* 39.1 (2005): 153–77. Print.

O'Malley, Ilene. *The Myth of the Revolution.* Westport, CT: Greenwood Press, 1986. Print.

Ortiz Taylor, Sheila, and Sandra Ortiz Taylor. *Imaginary Parents.* Albuquerque: University of New Mexico Press, 1996. Print.

Osorio, Rubén. *Tomóchic en llamas.* México, DF: Consejo Nacional para la Cultura y las Artes, 1992. Print.

Osorno, Diego Enrique. "La Santa Muerte tiene su carretera en Tamaulipas." *Milenio online* [México, DF] 25 Nov. 2008. Web. 8 Feb. 2012.

Paredes, Américo. *With His Pistol in His Hand.* Austin: University of Texas Press, 1958. Print.

Passariello, Phyllis. "Desperately Seeking *Something*: Che Guevara as Secular Saint." *The Making of Saints: Contesting Sacred Ground.* Ed. James F. Hopgood. Tuscaloosa: University of Alabama Press, 2005. 75–89. Print.

Perdigón Castañeda, J. Katia. *La Santa Muerte: Protectora de los hombres.* México: INAH, 2008. Print.

Pick, Zuzana. *Constructing the Image of the Mexican Revolution: Cinema and the Archive.* Austin: University of Texas Press, 2010. Print.

"The Piquetes." *The Dominion* 27 Sept. 2003. Web. 16 Mar. 2011.

Plato. *Plato's Cosmology, the Timaeus of Plato.* Trans. Frances MacDonald Cornford. New York: Humanities Press, 1971. Print.

Poniatowska, Elena. *La noche de Tlatelolco.* México, D.F.: Biblioteca Era, 1971. Print.

Rabasa, José. "Of Zapatismo: Reflections on the Folkloric and the Impossible in a Subaltern Insurrection." *The Latin American Cultural Studies Reader.* Ed. Ana Del Sarto, Alicia Ríos, and Abril Trigo. Durham: Duke University Press, 2004. 562–83. Print.

Radio Insurgente: La voz de los sin voz. Web. 8 Dec. 2012.

Ramos Minor, Gerardo. "Derriban altares de la Santa Muerte en la autopista de Nuevo Laredo." *Hora Cero* 24 Mar. 2009. Web. 8 Feb. 2012.

Rau, Alia Beard. "Arizona immigration law: Supreme Court upholds key portion of Senate
Bill 1070." Azcentral.com. 25 Jun. 2012. Web. 9 Mar. 2013.

Rebolledo, Tey Diana. "Foreword to *Puppet*." *Puppet: A Chicano Novella*. By Margarita Cota-
Cárdenas. Trans. Barbara D. Reiss and Trino Sandoval. Albuquerque: University of New
Mexico Press, 2000. Print.

Reed, John. *Insurgent Mexico*. 1914. New York: International Publishers, 1969. Print.

Relatos de Ultratumba: La Santa Muerte. YouTube channel "bungolio." YouTube. Uploaded
Sept. 27, 2008. Web. Accessed 18 Jan. 2011.

Rivera, Tomás. *. . . y no se lo tragó la tierra / . . . And the Earth Did Not Devour Him*. Trans. Evangelina Vigil-Piñón. Houston: Arte Público Press, 1987. Print.

Roach, Joseph. "The Doubting-Thomas Effect." *PMLA* 126.4 (Oct. 2011): 1127–30. Print.

———. *It*. Ann Arbor: University of Michigan Press, 2007. Print.

Rocha, Gregorio. Review of "*And Starring Pancho Villa as Himself*, directed by Bruce Beres-
ford, DVD from Warner Home Video, 2003." *The Moving Image* 6.1 (2006): 142–45.
Print.

———. *Los rollos perdidos de Pancho Villa/The Lost Reels of Pancho Villa*. 2003. DVD.

———. "La Venganza de Pancho Villa: A Lost and Found Border Film." *F Is for Phony: Fake
Documentary and Truth's Undoing*. Ed. Alexandra Juhasz and Jesse Lerner. Minneapolis:
University of Minnesota Press, 2006. 50–58. Print.

Rodríguez, Richard. *Days of Obligation: An Argument with My Mexican Father*. New York:
Viking, 1992. Print.

Rodríguez-Martín, Manuel. "En la lengua maternal: Las escritoras chicanas y la novela en
español." *Latin American Literary Review* 45 (1995): 64–84. Print.

Rojek, Chris. *Celebrity*. London: Reaktion Books, 2001. Print.

Romano-V., Octavio, ed. *El Espejo/The Mirror*. Berkeley: Quinto Sol Publications, 1969. Print.

Rubio Goldsmith, Raquel, Daniel Nugent, and Eva Tessler. "Trece Días/Thirteen Days: A
Performance by Borderlands Theater and the San Francisco Mime Troupe." *Critique of
Anthropology* 19.4 (1999): 327–71. Print.

Rutherford, John. "The Novel of the Mexican Revolution." *The Cambridge History of Latin
American Literature*. Vol. 2. *The Twentieth Century*. Ed. Roberto González Echeverría and
Enrique Pupo-Walker. Cambridge: Cambridge University Press, 1996. 213–25. Print.

Saborit, Antonio. *Los doblados de Tomóchic*. Mexico City: Cal y Arena, 1994. Print.

Saldaña-Portillo, María Josefina. *The Revolutionary Imagination in the Americas and the Age of
Development*. Durham: Duke University Press, 2003. Print.

"Santa Muerte, 'narcoaltares' de Tamaulipas." *El Siglo de Torreón* [Torreón, Coah, México] 27
Oct. 2007. Web. 8 Feb. 2012.

"Santitos y santones." *Canal Once TV Mexico*. 2005. Web. 15 Jan. 2013.

Schechner, Richard. *Performance Studies: An Introduction*. London and New York: Routledge,
2002. Print.

Scherer García, Julio, and Carlos Monsiváis. *Los patriotas: De Tlatelolco a la guerra sucia*.
México: Aguilar, 2004. Print.

Schmidt Camacho, Alicia. *Migrant Imaginaries: Latino Cultural Politics in the U.S.-Mexico Borderlands*. New York: NYU Press, 2008. Print.

Slivka, Andrey. "Leftist Noir." *New York Times* 19 Nov. 2006. Web. 11 May 2011.

Sommer, Doris. *Bilingual Aesthetics: A New Sentimental Education*. Durham: Duke University
Press, 2004. Print.

Sommers, Joseph. "Literatura e historia: Las contradicciones ideológicas de la ficción indigenista." *Revista de Crítica Literaria Latinoamericana* 5.10 (1979): 9–39. Print.

Taibo, Paco Ignacio II. *No habrá final feliz.* New York: HarperCollins, 2009. Print.

———. *Pancho Villa: Una biografía narrativa.* México, DF: Editorial Planeta, 2006. Print.

Taussig, Michael. *Defacement.* Stanford: Stanford University Press, 1999. Print.

———. *The Magic of the State.* New York: Routledge, 1997. Print.

Taylor, Diana. *The Archive and the Repertoire.* Durham: Duke University Press, 2003. Print.

Tejada-Flores, Rick. "César Chávez." *The Oxford Encyclopedia of Latinos and Latinas in the United States.* Vol. 1. Ed. Suzanne Oboler and Deena J. González. Oxford: Oxford University Press, 2005. Print.

Templo Santa Muerte. Web. 15 Aug. 2011.

Thompson, Ginger. "Mexico City Journal; On Mexico's Mean Streets, the Sinners Have a Saint." *New York Times* 26 Mar. 2004. Web. 10 Feb. 2012.

Toriz, Rafael. "Entre lo kitsch y lo naco: Aproximaciones a una estética masificada." Destiempos .com. Año 1, número 3, 2006. Web. 5 June 2012.

Tuckman, Jo. "Mexican 'Saint Death' Cult Members Protest at Destruction of Shrines." *The Guardian* 10 Apr. 2009. Web. 9 Feb. 2012.

Ulloa Bornemann, Alberto. *Surviving Mexico's Dirty War: A Political Prisoner's Memoir.* Ed. and trans. Arthur Schmidt and Aurora Camacho de Schmidt. Philadelphia: Temple University Press, 2007. Print.

Urquizo, Francisco. *Tropa vieja.* México: Talleres Gráficos, 1943. Print.

Urrea, Luis Alberto. *By the Lake of Sleeping Children: The Secret Life of the Mexican Border.* New York: Anchor Books, 1996. Print.

———. *The Hummingbird's Daughter.* New York: Little, Brown, 2005. Print.

———. *Luis Alberto Urrea.* Web. 16 Mar. 2012.

———. *Queen of America.* New York: Little, Brown, 2011. Print.

Valdez, Luis. *The Shrunken Head of Pancho Villa. Necessary Theater.* Ed. Jorge Huerta. Houston: Arte Público Press, 1989. 142–207. Print.

Vanden Berghe, Kristine, and Bart Maddens. "Ethnocentrism, Nationalism, and Post-Nationalism in the Tales of Subcomandante Marcos." *Mexican Studies/Estudios Mexicanos* 20.1 (Winter 2004): 123–44. Print.

Vanderwood, Paul. *Juan Soldado: Rapist, Murderer, Martyr, Saint.* Durham: Duke University Press, 2004. Print.

———. *The Power of God against the Guns of Government: Religious Upheaval in Mexico at the Turn of the Nineteenth Century.* Stanford: Stanford University Press, 1998. Print.

———. "Los Tomoches en camino hacía el milenio." *Tomóchic: La revolución adelantada.* Vol. 2. Ed. Jesús Vargas Valdez. Ciudad Juárez: Universidad Autónoma de Ciudad Juárez, 1994. Print.

Vargas González, Alfredo. "¡Oh, Muerte Sagrada, reliquia de Dios! La Santa Muerte: Religiosidad popular en la ribera de Pátzcuaro." Dirección General de Bibliotecas de la Universidad Veracruzana. 25 Sept. 2009. Print.

Vargas Valdez, Jesús, ed. *Tomóchic: La revolución adelantada.* 2 vols. Ciudad Juárez: Universidad Autónoma de Ciudad Juárez, 1994. Print.

Vázquez Montalbán, Manuel. *Marcos: El señor de los espejos.* México, DF: Aguilar, 1999. Print.

Wald, Elijah. *Narcocorrido.* New York: Rayo/HarperCollins, 2001. Print.

Wicke, Jennifer. "Epilogue: Celebrity's Face Book." *PMLA* 126.4 (Oct. 2011): 1131–38. Print.

Wilkinson, Tracy. "Mexico Has Arrested a Leader of Santa Muerte 'Church.'" *Los Angeles Times* 5 Jan. 2011. Web.

Wood, Silviana. "And Where Was Pancho Villa When You Really Needed Him?" *Puro Teatro: A Latina Anthology*. Ed. Alberto Sandoval-Sánchez and Nancy Saporta Sternbach. Tucson: University of Arizona Press, 2000. 176–93. Print.

Woodward, Kenneth. *The Making of Saints*. New York: Simon and Schuster, 1990. Print.

Yúdice, George. *The Expediency of Culture: Uses of Culture in the Global Era*. Durham: Duke University Press, 2004. Print.

INDEX

ABOUT THE AUTHOR

DESIRÉE A. MARTÍN is an associate professor of English at the University of California, Davis.

CPSIA information can be obtained at www.ICGtesting.com
Printed in the USA
BVOW08s1942071113

335571BV00002B/8/P

9 780813 562339